ABOUT THE AUTHORS

DANA FACAROS and MICHAEL PAULS are professional travel writers. Over the past ten years they have lived in several countries concentrating mainly on the Mediterranean area. In addition to this guide, their travel books include highly successful guides to the Greek Islands, Spanish Islands and Turkey. They are married with two children and are at present based in Spain, researching their next guide.

CADOGAN GUIDES

CADOGAN GUIDES

ITALIAN ISLANDS

DANA FACAROS & MICHAEL PAULS

Illustrations by Pauline Pears
Series Editors: Janey Morris and Rachel Fielding

CADOGAN BOOKS
LONDON

To Jackson, who was a good boy

ACKNOWLEDGEMENTS

We gratefully acknowledge the assistance of the Ente Nazionale di Turismo in London; the staff of the provincial tourist offices and AASTs on the Italian islands, especially Maria Luisa Manca of Oristano, Giovanni Pais of Alghero, Dr Massimo Manca of Elba, Tommaso Mesolella of Ponza and Dr Solar of Nuoro, Sardinia.

Copyright © Dana Facaros 1981, 1986
Illustrations © Pauline Pears 1986
First published 1981
This revised edition published in 1986
by Cadogan Books Ltd
16a Lower Marsh, London SE1
(Holding Company Metal Bulletin PLC)
ISBN 0–946–313–39 3

Phototypeset in Ehrhardt on a Linotron 202
Printed and bound in Great Britain by Redwood Burn Ltd,
Trowbridge, Wiltshire

CONTENTS

v

Part IV

Islands off the Coast of Sicily *Page 215*

Part V

Sardinia *Page 277*

Conversion Charts *Page 338*

Further Reading *Page 339*

Index *Page 342*

LIST OF MAPS

LIVORNO
TUSCAN
ISLANDS
Piombino
CORSICA
Porto S. Stefano
Civitavecchia
● ROME
Anzio

YUGOSLAVIA

ADRIATIC
SEA
Ortona
Vieste
TREMITI
ISLANDS

ISCHIA
PONTINE
ISLANDS
CAPRI
NAPLES

SARDINIA

TYRRHENIAN
SEA

USTICA
AEOLIAN
ISLANDS

EGADI
ISLANDS
PALERMO
SICILY
Agrigento
CATANIA

PANTELLERIA

PELAGIE
ISLANDS

MEDITERRANEAN
SEA

N

miles   100   200
km   100   200   300

THE ITALIAN ISLANDS

INTRODUCTION

There are 32 islands off the coasts of Italy, ranging in size from Sicily and Sardinia—the largest in the Mediterranean—to little specks in the sea, where convicts get government-paid holidays for life. Some islands, Capri-fashion, have blossomed (or withered, depending on your point of view) into full-blown resorts, where you can count more signs in English and German than in Italian. Others, such as Ponza, Pantelleria and the Egadi Islands, are among Italy's best-kept secrets.

We who aren't Italian rarely think of the islands as a separate geographical entity the way we regard, say, the Greek islands. The Italians, however, look upon them as very distinct characters and treasure them as their last refuges from the polluted sea that has sullied even some of the choicest Riviera resorts on the mainland. The islands—especially Sardinia and Sicily—have preserved many traditional customs long lost on the wealthier, industrialised mainland; their own dialects are alive and well. They are Italian but different, in many ways self-contained, each 'an epitome of the whole earth', as Bishop Berkeley described his own favourite island, Ischia.

Generally speaking, Italy's islands had their Golden Age in the centuries before Christ, when the Mediterranean was a busy highway instead of a deep blue barrier. The beautiful cave incisions on the island of Levanzo, stylistically similar to the prehistoric cave art of the Rhône, have been carbon-dated to 10 000 BC. Lipari, in the Aeolian archipelago, was an important Neolithic trading centre with samples of its prized obsidian (volcanic glass) found as far afield as Malta. On Sardinia, the fascinating Nuraghic civilisation lasted from 1500 BC to Roman times, producing Europe's first castles and literally thousands of the sturdy stone towers known as *nuraghes*. A similar culture developed on distant Pantelleria, leaving the monumental *sesis* behind to confound us. And then of course there is the Sicily of the Ancient Greeks, where great cities rivalled, and then surpassed, Athens itself in wealth and power. For most islands, their importance has been steadily declining ever since those heady days when Phoenician ships and triremes brought trade and prosperity to their shores.

Nowadays it's their very isolation from the world that is so alluring, and their often startling physical beauty: these islands have been sculpted by volcanoes and split by cataclysmic, prehistoric earthquakes into 'sheer, towering cliffs and mighty monolith's, but they also display a lush beauty, strewn as they are with wild flowers, and cultivated with orchards and vines, almonds and capers, chestnuts and orange groves, olives and pine nuts. Add the charm and artistry of their Italian heritage and culture, and you have a mixture that's almost irresistible.

Every effort has been made to ensure the accuracy of the information in this book at the time of going to press. However, practical details such as opening hours, travel information, standards in hotels and restaurants and, in particular, prices are liable to change.

We intend to keep this book as up-to-date as possible in the coming years. Please write to us if there is anything you feel should be included in future editions.

Part I

GENERAL INFORMATION

A Town Market

Getting to the Italian Islands

By air to Italy

British Airways schedules

From	*To*	*Frequency*
London	Milan	9 a day
London	Naples (via Milan)	2 a day
London	Rome	5 a day
London	Pisa	2 a day
London	Bologna	3 a week
London	Genoa	2 a day
London	Turin	1 a day
London	Venice	2 a day
Manchester	Milan	2 a day
Manchester	Rome	1 a week

Alitalia schedules

From	To	Frequency
London	Alghero (via Milan)	1 a day
London	Bari (via Rome)	1 a day
London	Brindisi (via Rome)	1 a day
London	Cagliari (via Rome)	1 a day
London	Catania (non-stop, summer)	2 a week
	(via Rome)	1 a day
London	Genoa	2 a day
London	Milan	7 a day
London	Naples	2 a week
	(via Rome)	2 a day
London	Palermo (non-stop, summer)	2 a week
London	Pisa	2 a day
London	Rome	3 a day
London	Turin	6 a week
London	Venice	2 a day
Manchester	Milan	6 a week
Manchester	Rome (via Milan)	6 a week

Air Lingus

From	To	Frequency
Dublin	Rome (via London)	Sundays

Be sure to check the pages of *Time Out* and *The Times* for bargain flights, as well as your local bucket shop.

BY AIR FROM THE USA AND CANADA

Alitalia offers non-stop flights to Rome and Milan from New York and Boston, and from Toronto and Montreal (for possible connections, see 'Domestic flights' below). TWA has a daily non-stop service between New York and Rome and Milan, and between Boston and Rome. Pan Am also flies from New York to Rome non-stop.

Note: If you fly to Italy on Alitalia you are eligible for their Jetdrive car rental scheme at economical rates. Be sure to inquire when booking.

BY AIR: DOMESTIC FLIGHTS

These are all on Alitalia, the national airline, or its subsidiaries ATI Aligiulia and Alisarda. Information on all of these lines can be had from Alitalia offices.

From Rome to	*Frequency*	*Duration*
Alghero	3 a day	50 min
Bari (for Tremiti Islands)	3 a day	50 min
Cagliari	8 a day	55 min
Catania	6 a day	70 min
Naples (Bay of Naples islands)	4 a day	45 min
Palermo	7 a day	60 min
Pisa (Tuscan Islands)	2 a day	45 min
Reggio Calabria (for Messina)	2 a day	60 min
Trapani/Marsala	1 a day	90 min
From Milan to		
Alghero	3 a day	60 min
Bari	1 a day	80 min
Cagliari	5 a day	75 min
Catania	5 a day	105 min
Naples	4 a day	75 min
Olbia	4 a day	60 min
Palermo	2 a day	90 min
Pisa	3 a day	45 min
Reggio Calabria	1 a day	90 min
From Naples to		
Palermo	2 a day	45 min
Catania (via Reggio Calabria)	2 a day	65 min
From Pisa to		
Alghero	1 a day	55 min
Cagliari	1 a day	60 min
Olbia	1 a day	50 min

Inter-island flights

From Palermo to		
Cagliari	1 a day	50 min
Lampedusa	1 a day	65 min
Pantelleria	2 a day	45 min
Trapani	2 a day	25 min
From Trapani to		
Pantelleria	2 a day	35 min
From Cagliari to		
Alghero	4 a day	35 min
Olbia	Saturdays	60 min

On domestic flights, children under 2 fly at a 90% discount; between the ages of 2 and 12 they receive a 50% discount, and between the ages of 12 and 21 they receive a 30% discount. There are also a number of weekend discounts on domestic flights. Addresses of Alitalia's offices on the islands are:

In Sicily

Agrigento: Akratur, Viaggi e Turismo, Via Cicerone 11 (tel. (0922) 25949).
Augusta: G. Bozzanca & Figlio, Via C. Colombo 50 (tel. (0931) 974106).
Caltanissetta: Kaltour, Viaggi e Turismo, Corso Umberto 1 (tel. (0934) 21004).
Catania: Corso Sicilia 111/113 (tel. (095) 317311).
Marsala: Agenzia Ruggieri, Via Mazzini 111 (tel. (0923) 951426).
Messina: A. Meo & Figli, Via del Vespro 56 (tel. (090) 719192).
Palermo: Via Mazzini 59 (tel. (091) 588931).
Ragusa: Ufficio Turistico Ibleo, Viale del Fante 4 (tel. (0932) 22063).
Syracuse: Bozzanca & Figlio, Corso Matteotti 80/90 (tel. (0931) 67122); Corso Gelone 92 (tel. (0931) 60978).
Termini Imerese: F. Paolo Manzo, Viale Vittorio Amedeo 18 (tel. (091) 942080).
Trapani: Agenzia Nattale Salvo, Corso Italia 52/56 (tel. (0923) 23819).

In Sardinia

Cagliari: Via Caprera 12/14 (tel. (070) 669221); Alisarda only Via Barone Rossi 27 (tel. (070) 651381).
Nuoro: Agenzia Ancor, Via Manzoni (tel. (0784) 30463); Alisarda, Via Lamarmora 117 (tel. (0784) 37446).
Olbia: Alisarda, Corso Umberto 195/C (tel. (0789) 69400).
Sassari: Sarda Viaggi, Via Vagliari 30 (tel. (079) 234498).

In Lampedusa

Scalo Ati, at the airport (tel. (0922) 970299).

In Pantelleria

La Cossira, Via Borgo (tel. (0923) 911078).

By train

Most trains to Italy from London go via Paris; the easiest route is to take an early train to Paris and catch the 8pm train from Paris which arrives at noon or so in Rome (via Genoa, Livorno, Civitavecchia for island connections).

From Rome there are frequent trains south for Gaeta (Pontine Islands), Naples (Bay of Naples islands and Aeolian Islands), and Palermo, Catania and Syracuse in Sicily.

Italian trains, known as the FS (*Ferrovie del Stato*), are not expensive and run quite frequently up and down the 'boot' of Italy. Sicily's trains pass through all the important centres (see the general map of Sicily for routes) and are almost invariably slow, whether you take the *rapido* (the fastest), the *direto* (which makes a few stops), or the *locale* (which stops at every village on the map). Sardinia, besides the FS, has its own narrow-gauge railway, the *Strada Ferrate Sarde*—scenic but slow. Anyone who travels the FS regularly may encounter the word *sciopero* which means 'strike'. The average *sciopero* lasts only an hour or two and comes without warning, but one train's stoppage causes delays in a domino effect throughout the system.

In the larger towns of Italy, the stations have a *Prenotazione* counter, where you may, for a small fee, reserve a seat on a train of any class. This often proves to be a good exercise in the summer months, especially on long, tourist-crowded routes. If you don't make a reservation to Sicily, particularly in season and on Friday evenings (when all the workers go home from their jobs in Rome and Naples), make sure you arrive at the station a good hour before your train departs or you'll never get a seat. You can also buy tickets and make reservations at authorised travel agencies. If you wait to buy your ticket on the train, there's a 20% surcharge. Also note that domestic rail tickets are valid only for the day they're issued.

A good bargain for those planning extensive rail travel is the BTLC ticket, which can be purchased for periods of 8, 15, 21 or 30 days of unlimited travel on Italy's trains, with the special advantage of free seat reservations. Another ticket, the Italian Kilometric Ticket, is valid for 20 trips or 3000 km, whichever comes first. One advantage of this ticket is that it can be used by up to five people, and is calculated by multiplying the distance travelled by the number of travellers. Thus five people going 10 km would count as 50 km on the ticket. For both of these, children under 12 pay half (or count half the distance travelled) and tots under 4 go free. There are also reductions for family groups of more than four people. These tickets may be purchased at CIT offices (which are good sources for precise schedules, etc.), whose foreign addresses are listed below.

In the USA
666 Fifth Avenue, New York, NY 10103 (tel. (212) 397 2666).
In Canada
2055 Peel Street, Suite 102 Montreal, Quebec H3A 1VA (tel. (514) 845 9101).

In the UK
50 Conduit Street, London W1 (tel. (01) 434 3844).

By sea

There are several shipping lines serving all of Italy, apart from Tirrenia, the largest, which is government-subsidised. Their names are a typical continental alphabet soup—SNAV, SAS, NAV.AR.MA, TO.RE.MAR and the like. Their ticket offices are usually right on the quayside. Long-distance Tirrenia tickets, however, can and should be reserved at one of their many agencies (head offices of all the lines are listed below, if you want to obtain the most up-to-date schedules). Fares are moderate—it is almost always cheaper to go by sea than land.

Note that, in case of *mare brutto* (rough seas), the ship will remain in port until its next scheduled voyage.

Many islands are served by hydrofoils (*aliscafi*) as well as by ferryboats. Hydrofoils tend to be twice as fast and twice as expensive as the ships, and are even more choosy about the state of the sea.

For some of the most popular routes (especially to Sardinia) you must reserve car space in advance for the peak season (mid July–mid September).

On long, overnight trips (to Sardinia, Palermo–Naples, to Lampedusa, etc.) it is definitely worth your while to spend a few extra lire on a cabin. There are few things more excruciating than spending a night trying to sleep in an armchair, and, if you're a woman, being pestered by frisky Italian youths.

Addresses of shipping lines
Alilauro Aliscafi, Via Caracciolo 11, 80122 Naples (tel. (081) 323013).
Aliscafi SNAV, Cortina del Porto, 98100 Messina (tel. (090) 364044).
CAREMAR, Molo Beverello, 90133 Naples (tel. (081) 315384).
Caronte, Viale della Liberta 515, 98100 Messina (tel. (090) 45183).
Grandi Traghetti, Via Fieshi 17, 16128 Genoa (tel. (010) 567832).
    Via Mariano Stabile 179, 90139 Palermo (tel. (091) 587832).
    Associated Oceanic Agencies, Eagle House, 109–110 Jermyn Street, London SW1 6E6 (tel. (01) 930 5683).
Libera Navigazione Lauro, Molo Beverello, 80133 Naples (tel. (081) 322838).
    Via Iasolino 21, Porto d'Ischia 80077 (tel. (081) 991963).
NAVARMA, Viale Elba 4, 57037 Portoferraio (tel. (0565) 916743).

AMAR, Corso V. Emanuele 19, Porto Torres, Sardinia (tel. (079) 516154).

Serena Holidays, 40/42 Kenway Road, London SW5 0RA (tel. (01) 373 6548).

Navigazione Libera del Golfo, Molo Beverello, 80133 Naples (tel. (081) 320763).

SIREMAR, Via Francesco Crispi 120, Palermo (tel. (091) 582688).

Carlo Genovese, Via Depretis 78, 80133 Naples (tel. (081) 312109).

Societa di Navigazione ARL Maregiglio, Giglio Porto, Isola di Giglio (tel. (0564) 809309).

Tirrenia, Stazione Marittima, Molo Angionino, Naples (tel. (081) 720 1111).

TOREMAR, Scali del Corso 5, 57100 Livorno (tel. (0586) 22772).

By yacht

Almost all the islands have some sort of facilities for yachts, though they may not be equipped for a long stay. The harbourmaster (*capitaniera di porto)* at your first Italian port of call will give you a document called a *costituto*, which you will have to produce for subsequent harbourmasters; this permits the purchase of tax-free fuel. For further information write to either of these organisations:

Federazione Italiana Vela, Porticciolo Duca degli Abruzzi, Genoa.

Federazione Italiana Motonautica, Via Cappuccio 19, Milan.

Main yacht harbours

Gulf of Naples—Capri: Procida. Ischia: Porto, Casamicciola, Lacco Ameno, Forio d'Ischia.

Tuscan Islands—Elba: Cavo, Rio Marina, Porto Azzurro, Marciana Marina, Portoferraio. Also: Giglio.

Sardinia—Santa Teresa di Gallura, La Maddalena, Porto Torres, Castelsardo, Porto Teulada, Ponteromano, Calasella, Portoscuso, Portovesme, Alghero, Basa Marina, Porto Conte, Palau, Porto Cervo, Porto Rotondo, Olbia, La Caletta, Arbatax, Poetto, Capo Carbonara, Cagliari.

Sicily—Palermo, Cefalu, Castellammare del Golfo, Capo d'Orlando, Milazzo, Messina, Termini Imerese, Augusta, Catania, Stazzo, Riposto, Syracuse, Marina di Ragusa, Marzameni, Gela, Scogliotto, Licata, Porto Empedocle, Sciacca, Mazara del Vallo, Marsala, Trapani, Giardini.

The islands off Sicily—Lipari, Vulcano, Panarea, Salina, Ustica, Favignana, Pantelleria, Lampedusa.

9

Port taxes—paid by the tonnage of your yacht—are reduced by two-thirds if you take out a subscription between June and September, by half for the four months June to September or for an entire 12-month period.

Helpful guides include *The Tyrrhenian Sea* by H. A. Denham and *Round the Italian Coast* by P. Bristow.

Getting Around the Islands

By car

The reasons for bringing your own car to Italy (or renting one) are obvious, convenience being foremost, although putting up with Italian motorists may be something of a trial. On the small islands, however, a car can be a bit cumbersome and unparkable. Also, it defeats one of the main reasons for getting away from it all—'it all' surely including the noise and pollution of motor cars. Of the larger islands, Sicily has an extensive public transport system, which is cheap and goes to all places of interest, although sometimes in a roundabout way. Unfortunately, the same cannot be said for Sardinia, where public transport to the provincial capitals is good, but difficult when you want to go anywhere else. The best 'sights'—the *nuraghes*, the Pisan churches and the beauties of nature—can only be reached by private transport. On Sardinia you'll wish you had a car.

To encourage tourism, the Italian government offers visitors and Italians living abroad (with a vehicle registered outside Italy) a discount on petrol through Gasoline Coupons. These, which are available through the ENIT, CIT offices, Italian banks and travel offices abroad, and at automobile club offices at the border, must be purchased with foreign currency. The coupons come in books: 10 coupons for 150 litres of petrol for the *pacchetto Italia*, good for all the country, or the *pacchetto Italia-Mezzogiorno* which have additional coupons good for 200 litres of petrol south of Rome and in Sicily and Sardinia. Along with the coupons you will receive a *Carta Carburente e Turistica* (CCT) which includes two coupons entitling you to free road service, should you experience any difficulty. For a tow, dial 116 and your car will be taken to the nearest ACI office (there is one in every provincial capital).

If driving your own car, your ordinary licence is valid in Italy if it is accompanied by a translation, although an International Driving Licence is more convenient to carry (and necessary for those who hire cars). Insurance is mandatory in Italy. A 'Green Card' will be sufficient for 40 to 45 days (you

10

can also purchase 'Frontier Insurance' when you enter), but for longer stays an Italian insurance policy is required. You also need a *triangolo*, a triangular-shaped placard for warning passing motorists when you are stalled; these can be obtained from ACI offices. If you are caught breaking the Italian highway code (note that the size of your car determines your speed limit), it is advisable to pay the fine for your *infrazione* to the policeman writing your ticket.

Like their Roman forefathers, the Italians have built many good roads. The biggest of these are the *autostrade*—super highways. In Sicily these *autoducts* are built on piers for miles on end. Tolls are charged on the *autostrade* (a foreign licence plate entitles you to a discount) but the Sicilian Catania–Palermo–Mazara del Vallo *autostrade* (A19 or A29) are free. Other main roads are the *strade statali* (SS), which are always free. Motorists going to Sicily or Sardinia should purchase the excellent maps issued by the Italian Touring Club (obtainable from Stanfords, 12 Long Acre, London WC2; or from Rizzoli International Bookstore, 712 Fifth Avenue, New York).

For any motoring question or difficulty, ring the English-speaking operators at the 24-hour ACI assistance number 116.

Hiring a car is simple if not particularly cheap. Italian car rental firms are called *Autonoleggi*. There are both large international firms through which you can reserve a car in advance, and local agencies, which often have lower prices. Air or train travellers should check out possible discount packages.

Most companies will require a deposit amounting to the estimated cost of the hire, and there's an 18% VAT added to the final cost. At time of writing, a 5-seat Fiat Panda costs around 32 000 lire a day. Petrol is around 1300 lire for a litre.

By coach

Euroways Express Coaches offer an economical service to Italy from London. An adult single to Rome is £63 (£45 for students). In the summer the service continues down to Naples. For information, contact Wallace Arnold, 52 Grosvenor Gardens, London W1 (tel. (01) 730 3433), or 73 Russell Square, London WC2 (tel. (01) 837 6543).

On all the islands except for Sicily and Sardinia, which have a rail service, coaches provide the main means of public transport. Vehicles range from luxurious landyachts to minibuses, and all are run by private companies. Prices have gone up in recent years, and on routes where they compete with trains there isn't that much difference in fares. Often, however, the buses are faster, and the drivers will drop you off at destinations where trains don't stop.

New visitors to Sicily who want to take in the principal sights may want to consider the long-established Golden Ribbon, or *Nastro d'Oro* tour, which run for between 5 and 8 days all year-round. Tours include a guide, admission fees, hotel discounts and transport. Schedules, bookings and the latest fares are available at CIT Offices (see 'By train').

For city buses you may have to purchase tickets from tobacconist shops or news-stands and validate them on the bus. Vendors of the tickets will know how many you need to reach your destination.

By taxi

Unfortunately the taxi drivers, especially in Sicily, see visitors as fair game and will invariably overcharge. Even when they have meters, as in Palermo, it's a fight to get them to turn them on. Always negotiate the price before you get in to avoid unpleasantness when you arrive. The average fixed charge is 1500 lire, plus 400 lire per kilometre. There's an extra charge for luggage and night and holiday trips.

Hitch hiking

It's legal to thumb a ride anywhere in Italy except on the autostrade. The problem is that in most places on the islands there isn't that much traffic, and you may have a long wait. Increase your chances by looking respectable and carrying a small suitcase instead of a huge backpack.

Where to Stay

Like everywhere else in Europe, the **hotels** and **pensions** in Italy are classified and their prices accordingly regulated by the Provincial Tourist Boards. Price lists are posted on the door of every room, along with the prices of extras like continental breakfast or full or half board, and air conditioning if it is considered an 'extra'. Heating, if called for, is free of charge, although in modest establishments you may have to pay extra for a bath.

In Italy the hotel rates are annually adjusted (always upward) in March, although some places retain the right to boost prices during the tourist season and lower them after September. Reservations are indispensable in summer. The Italian Tourist Office publishes lists of hotels annually and pensions with their most recent rates and amenities, which are very helpful (although note that the Tourist Boards do *not* make reservations). For a general guide, expect to pay on average (in lire) in 1986:

Category	Single	With bath	Double	With bath
Luxury (*****)	—	130 000	—	200 000
Class I (****)	—	70 000	—	90 000
Class II (***)	30 000	42 000	38 000	55 000
Class III (**)	22 000	30 000	30 000	42 000
Class IV (*)	17 000	21 000	26 000	30 000
Pension 1 (P1)	25 000	30 000	32 000	42 000
Pension 2 (P2)	18 000	24 000	24 000	35 000
Pension 3 (P3)	11 000	14 000	22 000	25 000

Even cheaper than third-class pensions are the inns known as *locande* and rooms in private houses, which can be had almost everywhere, although you have to pound the pavements to find them. Single travellers should be aware that, if a hotel has only double rooms left, the charge is legally only supposed to be the same as a single room. Many hoteliers will nevertheless try to charge you double.

Note that a first-class pension (P1) is generally equivalent to a Class II hotel, a second-class pension (P2) to a Class III hotel, and a third-class pension (P3) to a Class IV hotel—with certain differences. In pensions they expect you to eat at least half your meals there (when they have restaurants, that is; some do not) and to stay a minimum of three days, especially in summer. Italian pensions are usually family-run establishments, so they are more relaxed (and noisier) than their hotel equivalents. In the south of Italy, especially in Sicily, a stay in a P3 may be an unforgettable adventure—do make the owners show you the room and WC before you commit yourself. For some reason, toilet seats are a luxury in this part of the world, but even if you end up in a dive, the sheets at least will be spotless. Beware, also, of assuming anything at all about a hotel by its classification, although 'Luxury' *is* luxury. The owners of the hotels are given enough discretion in rating their hotels to make guidelines useless. Some hotels are purposely classed lower to attract the bargain-minded traveller, although they may charge as much as a Class I hotel.

The equivalent of Holiday Inns in Italy are the **Jolly Hotels,** if you prefer the reliable establishment; these can generally be found near the centre of larger towns. **Motels** are operated by the ACI (the Italian Automobile Club) or by AGIP (the big oil company; usually located along major routes outside cities). These cater for motorists and are adequate, if nothing special. For

AGIP motel reservations contact (in London) Quo Vadis Ltd, 243 Euston Road, London NW1 (tel. (01) 388 7512).

It is hard to make generalisations about the new crop of **Tourist Villages** (*Villagio Turistica*) sprouting up along the coasts of Italy. Almost all of them consist of separate units (white Mediterranean tourist-style bungalows or Polynesian-style grass huts) near a beach, and offer a number of recreational facilities in Club Méditerranée style, which chiefly attract a youthful sun-and-fun crowd. Lists of these can be obtained from EPT offices.

Youth Hostels, unfortunately, are few and far between, especially on the islands. Students with valid student cards may, however, find inexpensive accommodation in university towns in summer by making inquiries to the person in charge of the *Casa dello Studente*. On the islands there are student houses at Casa del Goliardo in Palermo, and at the universities of Messina and Sassari. Further information can be had from the Ufficio Centrale Studenti Esteri in Italia, Via Monti Parioli 59, 00197 Rome (tel. (06) 561 019). The Italian Youth Hostel Association maintains hostels in the following island locations:

Bolai, Porto Torres, near Sassari in Sardinia.

Dei Giuliani, in Fertilia, near Alghero (15 April–30 September).

Delle Aquile, in Castoreale, Messina (1 June–30 September).

Eleonara d'Arborea, Torregrande-Oristano.

Lipari, Lipari Island.

In Sicily, the Italian Alpine Club operates **refuges** on the main mountain trails. These offer simple accommodation, often with restaurants (listed along with the hotels in the sections on individual provinces). For up-to-date information on the refuges, write to the Club Alpino Italiano, Via Ugo Foscolo 3, Milano (tel. (02) 802554). Charges average 5000 lire a night, with a 20% increase from December to April.

Note that for all overnight accommodation you will be asked for your passport for registration purposes. Contact the local Provincial Tourist Board (EPT) if you feel you have any genuine grievance about your hotel.

Renting accommodation

An agency known as Agriturist can arrange holiday rentals at farmhouses and country villas. For information, write to Corso Vittorio Emanuele 101, Rome (tel. (06) 651 2342). To rent a flat or villa, write to the local tourist office (AAST) for information a few months before you go. The ENT offices have lists of agencies in the UK and the USA which specialise in rentals. The one with the widest selection on the islands is Interhome Ltd, 383 Richmond Road, Twickenham (tel. (01) 891 1294; telex 928539).

14

Camping

There are two forms of this increasingly popular way to spend a holiday. You can either pitch your tent where you please, which requires permission from the local authorities or landowner, or you can stay on an organised campsite—but don't expect any kind of 'communing with nature' here, as most Europeans regard camping only as a cheap alternative to resort hotels. Most campsites have beaches nearby, and their facilities can include anything from basic toilets and showers to tennis courts and swimming pools. It is possible to book a place at any of these by writing to the Centro Internazionale Prenotazioni Campeggio, Casella Postale 23, 50041, Calenzano, Firenze, Italy—you can request a list of camp sites with the booking form. At sites belonging to the Federcampeggio, expect to pay around 3000–4000 lire per person, per day (children under 3 are free) and an additional charge for your car, tent or caravan.

Eating Out

There are people who return to different regions of Italy year after year just to eat and drink. It's no wonder: the average snack in a Sicilian railway station bar is better than the best of some entire national cuisines (and that's only a slight exaggeration). If this is your first trip to Italy, know that the lasagne at your local neighbourhood café or restaurant is but a pale shade of the beast in its native land. Even the smallest islands have their own culinary specialities.

Italian eating establishments open from noon to 3 or 4pm and from 7 or 8 until 11pm. They come in many forms—the *ristorante, trattoria, rosticceria, tavola calda* and *pizzeria*. Although traditionally a *trattoria* is a cheaper, simpler place than a *ristorante*, in reality they are often exactly the same, both in quality and price, the only difference being that a *ristorante* has more pretensions. Every restaurant displays a menu outside so that you know what to expect, at least as regards the price.

The *rosticceria* and *tavola calda* are quite similar, the latter now the more popular name for the counters of prepared hot and cold food, where you choose what looks good, eat, pay and go. Some of these are quite elaborate, while the modest ones don't even have chairs or stools.

You can tell a good *pizzeria* by the traditional Neapolitan pizza oven in the back. *Pizzerie* are often combined with *trattorie*, as many Italians like to eat pizza for the first course (the *primero*) of a large meal. In these places, the service charge may be 20% if you order just a pizza and beer. Service in *ristoranti* and *trattorie* is generally 12%, and there is also a *coperto e pane* (cover and bread) charge of 1500 lire or so. Tipping is discretionary, but customary. A new law in Italy orders restaurants to give patrons receipts for the sales tax they've paid, which you are supposed to take out of the restaurant with you. This is to keep the restaurateurs honest, so don't be upset if they insist you take the ticket along.

Many places offer *prezzo fisso* (set price) or *menu turistico* meals—often a real bargain—or of course you can always order *alla carta* from the menu, which is divided into the following categories (a fuller list of items on the menu can be found at the end of this book).

Antipasti (hors d'oeuvres). These are often sumptuously displayed to tempt you the minute you walk in, and consist of seafoods, vegetables, salami, ham, olives, etc. Depending on the restaurant, you can choose these yourself or order them from the menu.

Minestre. Broth or ministrone soups, or pasta dishes. The latter come under the sub-heading of *Pasta Asciutta.* Many Italians skip the *antipasti,* which are often as dear as they are good, and go straight for the spaghetti.

Pesce. Fish, often according to availability, since it is always fresh.

Carne. Meat, which includes chicken, beef, lamb, veal and pork. With meat or fish, you eat a *contorno* (side dish) of your choice—often salad, vegetables or potatoes.

Dolce o Frutta. Sweet or fruit, the latter being more popular after a big meal. Common sweets are the famous Italian icecream, exotic cakes or pastries.

Wine of course is the most popular accompaniment to dinner. *Vino locale* (house wine) is the cheapest and usually quite good, and this is what you'll get unless you order a specific label. Mineral water (*acqua minerale*) comes under as many labels as the wine, with or without added or natural carbonisation (*con* or *sin gaz*). Italian beer, always served cold, is average, and of course you can always order the ubiquitous Coca-cola or Fanta.

A small, black espresso coffee puts the final touch to an Italian meal.

First-timers to Italy will be pleasantly surprised by the depth and mastery of Italian cuisine—it certainly isn't all pasta, tomatoes and olive oil. Italian chefs do particularly good things to fish, the thick *zuppa di pesce* (fish soup) being a speciality on the coasts. The big secret of Italian cooking is the freshness of the ingredients, which will surely convert those who feel indifferent about the mass-market Italian-style food and restaurants that they experience at home.

Bars have little in common with American bars or English pubs, and can be anything from luxurious open-air cafés to dingy back-alley meeting places for the boys. All serve primarily coffee in the form of *espresso* (small, stormy and black), *cappuccino* (with milk and a sprinkling of chocolate), or simply *café con latte* (coffee with milk), often served in a glass. Many people have breakfast at a bar, where you can help yourself to *cornetti* (croissants) or whatever other pastries are available. Here the problems begin when you have to pay and haven't the slightest idea of what your pastry was called.

Of course you can also get alcohol, soft drinks, mineral water, juices, etc. at a bar, at any time of the day from 7am to midnight. Alcohol is cheap, as long as it's not imported. Standing at the bar is about a third cheaper than sitting at a table to be served. The *scontino* is the receipt, and you may be asked to collect one from the *cassa* (cashier) before being served, especially in the big cities.

Note: The prices quoted for restaurants in this book are averages for a meal of three courses and wine, per person. In many you can eat for less, depending on what you order, but beware of the extra charges—service, *coperto*, and tax—that can add up to 20% to the bill.

Grocery shopping

Italian groceries (*alimentari*) are open in the morning and after the siesta. They sell mainly canned and dried goods, milk, biscuits, wine and cheese, salami and olives. For fresh vegetables and fruit you will have to go to the market (*mercado*); for meat, to the butcher (*carneceria*); for bread, to the bakery (*panificio*); and for fish, to the fish market (*pesceria*). Besides normal metric weights, you may also purchase by the *etto* (100 grams, or a little less than a quarter pound). Prices are comparable to home except of course that wine is much cheaper. If you are doing your own cooking you'll have to do it from scratch; Italians disdain prepared foods, and the *alimentari* generally lack refrigeration for frozen foods, especially on the islands.

Other Practical Concerns

Frontier formalities

To enter Italy you need a passport, or if you're from a Common Market country, an identification card valid for foreign travel. Unless you have a special visa, you are allowed to stay in Italy for up to three months. Drivers must be able to produce a green insurance card (or purchase one at the border) as well as their civil liability accident insurance policy. If you're bringing along a cat or dog you'll need a veterinarian's certificate from home—the Italians are sticklers for forms, so get the proper international one (available from the ENIT). It must show that your pet is in good health and has been vaccinated for rabies in the past 11 months.

Italy restricts exportation of antiques and works of art, for which permission must be granted by the Ufficio Esportazione di Oggetti d'Arte e d'Antichita, Ministero Pubblica Instruzione, Via Cernaia 1, Rome.

Currency

If you're carrying a lot of cash (more than the equivalent of 1 million lire) that you'll want to take with you when you leave Italy, you should declare the amount on form V2 when you arrive. You may take up to 400 000 lire in Italian currency in or out of the country (though really they hardly ever check). The best exchange rates for currency or traveller's cheques are given by the major banks and exchange bureaux licensed by the Bank of Italy. Hotels and FS-run exchanges at railway stations are usually not as good, but operate on Sundays. Currency exchanges usually stay open until 7 or 8pm.

Banking hours in Italy are Monday to Friday 8.30–1 and 2.30–3.30, though these vary slightly from place to place. Most banks, shops and museums are closed on the following national holidays:

1 January (New Year's Day)
6 January (Epiphany)
Easter Monday
25 April (Liberation Day)
1 May (Labour Day)
15 August (Assumption, also known as *Ferragosto*, the official start of the Italian holiday season)
1 November (All Saints' Day)
8 December (Immaculate Conception)
25 December (Christmas Day)
26 December (*Santo Stefano*, St Stephen's Day)

Time

Italy is one hour ahead of Greenwich Mean Time. From the last weekend of March to the end of September, Italian Summer Time (daylight savings time) puts the country ahead another hour.

Tourist information

There are two types of organisation in Italy equipped to deal with any

18

question a traveller may have: *Ente Provinciale per il Turismo* (EPT), which has offices in every provincial capital and most main tourist resorts, and *Azienda Autonoma di Soggiorno e Turismo* (AAST), which can also be found in major centres but with more frequency. The EPTs are funded by the Italian government and sponsor annual summer events such as sports and theatres; the AASTs are supported by civic funds, and often have exchange facilities (open at odd hours), along with brochures about the rest of Italy. On small islands and in hopeful resorts, there are the *Pro Loco* tourist offices—generally one-room, one-employee seasonal operations, with a few brochures about the area. Although these information offices can provide up-to-the-minute lists of hotels and prices, they cannot make reservations for you. For hotel reservations, see a travel agent.

You can get information, before you go, from ENIT offices (Italian State Tourist Offices) whose addresses are listed below.

In the UK:
1 Princes Street, London W1R 8AY (tel. (01) 408 1254; telex 22402).
In Ireland:
47 Merrion Square, Dublin 2 (tel. (01) 766397; telex 31682).
In the USA:
630 Fifth Avenue, Suite 1565, New York, NY 10111 (tel. (212) 245 4961; telex 236024).
500 N. Michigan Avenue, Chicago, Illinois 60611 (tel. (312) 644 0990/1; telex 0255160).
360 Post Street, Suite 801, San Francisco, California 94108 (tel. (415) 392 6206; telex 67623).
In Canada:
Store 56, Plaza 3, Place Ville Marie, Montreal, Quebec (tel. (514) 866 7667; telex 525607).

Another important source of information in Italy is the ACI, the Italian Automobile Club. It has established a 24-hour multilingual information service that can be reached by dialling 116 anywhere in the country. It also has offices on the islands at the following addresses:
In Sicily: Acireale (Via Romeo 69), Agrigento (Via San Vito 25), Caltanissetta (Via N. Colajanni 11), Catania (Via Etnea 28), Enna (Via Roma 729), Messina (Via L. Manara 129), Palermo (Viale delle Alpi 2), Ragusa (Via Ercolano 22), Syracuse (Via Foro Siracusano 27), Trapani (Via Virgilio 71).
In Sardinia: Cagliari (Via E. Carboni Boi 2), Nuoro (Via Sicilia 39), Oristano (Via Tirso, Palazzo Sisini), Sassari (Viale Adua 32/b).

In the Tuscan Islands: Livorno (Via Verdi 32).
In the Bay of Naples: Naples (Piazzale Tecchio 49/d).
In the Tremiti Islands: Foggia (Via Monte Grappa 95).
In the Pontine Islands: Latina (Via A: Saffi 8).

Consulates in Italy

British: Via XX Settembre 80a, Rome (tel. 475 5441).
          Consulate in Cagliari: Via San Lucifero 87 (tel. 662 755).
Irish: Via del Pozzetto 105, Rome (tel. 678 2541).
American: Via Veneto 121, Rome (tel. 4674).
Canadian: Via Zara 30, Rome (tel. 854 825).

Health

Citizens of Common Market countries should bring the E111 form with them to Italy, entitling them to free health care in Italy's National Health Service. Citizens of other countries would do well to take out a traveller's insurance policy, which is not expensive.

If there's an emergency, dial 113 for ambulance, police or fire services. Less serious problems can be treated at a *Pronto Soccorso* (casualty department) at any hospital, or at a local health unit (*Unità Sanitaria Locale*).

Pharmacies are generally open 8.30–1 and 4–8. Any large town has a pharmacy that stays open 24 hours; its address will be in the windows of the other pharmacies.

Post Offices

These are usually open from 9am–6pm, with or without a break at midday, according to local custom. To have your mail sent general delivery (*Poste Restante*), have it addressed to the post office (*Fermo Posta*). To pick up your mail you must present your passport. Stamps may be purchased in post offices or at tobacconists (*tabbachi*, identified by their black signs with a white T). The rates for letters and postcards (depending how much of the card you write on) are remarkably inconsistent—every tobacconist and postal clerk has his own idea on how many stamps you need.

You can also have money telegraphed to you through the post office which is one of the speedier ways of doing it. Italian banks, especially when

20

money has to be transferred from a central branch in Rome, take their time, even if the money is sent by telex.

Telephones

Public telephones for international calls may be found in the offices of two of Italy's phone companies, SIP or ASST. They tend to be non-existent on the smaller islands, however, and you may have to call from your hotel. SIP offices are open 7am–10pm; rates are lower on Sundays and holidays, on Saturdays after 1pm and 10pm–8am on weekdays. It is possible to make reverse-charge calls (collect calls) from a telephone office, but be prepared for a wait, as all these calls go through the operator in Rome. Direct calls may be made by dialling the international prefix, but even these may take a while if the international line is busy.

Local or long-distance calls can be made with *gettones*, 200-lire tokens available in bars, from tobacconists or news-stands, or *gettone* machines (though these never function). Other telephones will take 100- or 200-lire coins. Others, run by the SIP company, take magnetic cards (for 6000 or 9000 lire) which may be purchased at their offices and come in handy for international calls; or you can do the same with *gettones*—unused ones are returned at the end of the call.

Museums

National museums in Italy are generally open 9am–1pm and closed on Mondays and holidays. Most outdoor sites (archaeological excavations, castles, etc.) are open from 9am until sunset. Admission prices have gone up rapidly in recent years; in general the more visited and well known the site, the more you'll pay—usually between 1000 and 2500 lire. Children under 12 are free. Privately-run museums and sites, of which there are few, have different hours and are more expensive on the whole (these will be referred to in the text).

Weather

The Italian islands enjoy a typically Mediterranean climate, though Sicily can get particularly hot in the summer when the sirocco wind blows up from North Africa. In the spring, as the winter rains diminish, the weather is at its

21

most pleasant, and hills which are dried out by late summer are a glorious green and covered with wild flowers. In the autumn it stays warm enough to swim in Sicily, usually until the end of October; the snow starts falling in the mountains of Sardinia in November.

Temperature chart:

Average monthly temperatures in °Fahrenheit   *Sea temperatures*

	J	F	M	A	M	J	J	A	S	O	N	D	A	M	J	J	A	S	O
Cagliari	49	50	55	59	65	73	79	79	73	68	61	53	59	62	68	73	75	73	70
Capri	52	52	53	55	62	71	75	78	70	62	57	53	57	64	68	77	80	75	57
Palermo	50	51	55	61	65	73	78	76	73	68	62	55	62	68	73	82	80	77	73
Sassari	47	47	51	53	62	72	75	78	71	64	57	50	64	66	73	77	75	75	73
Taormina	52	51	55	61	68	75	80	80	75	68	61	55	64	66	73	75	77	75	66

Shopping

Italian shops are generally open 9am–1pm and 4pm–8pm. Measurements and sizes are the same as for the rest of Europe, but do try clothing and shoes on before making a purchase. Italians tend to have narrower feet for the length of the shoe, and their waists tend to be smaller than those of British and American women, so beware, especially since there are no refunds (although you may get an exchange). Men's shirts are sold by collar-size alone, so you may have trouble with the sleeves. Nevertheless, clothing and shoes are the most attractive buys in Italy these days, as Italian designers muscle in on territory the French once thought exclusively theirs.

Apart from the fashionable shops, you may find some good buys in the open-air markets, especially in Palermo. Popular items include lace and embroideries in Sicily, baskets in Sardinia, pottery and ceramics—and little plastic robots, if you know someone under the age of 10.

Entertainments

The islands have maintained—or are in the process of reviving—old festivals and entertainments. In Sicily many places have traditional puppet shows in the summer; in Sardinia the festivals are occasions for Sard music and choral songs. Palermo and Catania have regular opera seasons, and performances of all sorts are often staged in Sicily's ancient theatres in the summer. Easter is especially impressive in Sicily.

On a more contemporary note, there are nightclubs, discothèques, piano bars, cinemas and so on, in the popular centres.

Water sports

It's no secret that Italy's coasts are no longer as inviting as they used to be—the dubious corollary of industrialisation. However, the islands, with few exceptions, have at least one shore free of pollution, which is one reason why they're so popular among the Italians themselves. The only bad areas are around the major ports like Palermo, Catania and Cagliari; also watch the east coasts of the islands along the mainland, especially those in the Bay of Naples.

The islands are especially popular among scuba enthusiasts (although note that it's illegal to fish in Italian waters with an aqualung). Every province has information on fishing from boats and from the shore or with a snorkel, available from the local branch of the Federazione Italiana della Pesca Sportiva.

Calendar of major annual events

These are the major celebrations on the Italian islands; for detailed descriptions of the activities, see the individual towns or islands. Besides these, there are numerous small local *festas*, usually dedicated to a village's patron saint (we've included many of these in the text as well). If you're in the vicinity of one, especially in Sardinia's mountains, don't miss the chance to attend—you may very well become the guest of honour.

6 January: Byzantine-Orthodox Epiphany celebrations, Piano degli Albanesi (Sicily).
3–5 February: Sant' Agata, Catania (Sicily).
February: Almond Blossom Festival, Agrigento (Sicily); carnival celebrations throughout Sardinia and Acireale (Sicily); also the Sa Sartiglia, Oristano (Sardinia).
Maundy Thursday: Procession of the *Misteri*, Caltanisetta (Sicily).
Good Friday: Processions in Acireale and Enna (Sicily) and Procida.
Easter (Orthodox): Traditional celebrations at Piano degli Albanesi (Sicily).
1 May: Sant'Efisio, Cagliari (Sardinia).
End May: Sicilian Folklore Festival, Taormina.
June: La Mattanza (tuna fish slaughters), Favignana, Trapani (Sicily).
20 June: San Silverio, Ponza
July: International Film Festival, Messina and Taormina (Sicily).

13–16 July: Festa di Santa Rosalia, Palermo (Sicily).

13–14 August: Norman Joust, Piazza Armerina (Sicily).

14 August: Li Candlieri, Sassari (Sardinia); Giganti Procession, Messina (Sicily).

15 August: Cavalcata Sarda, Sassari (Sardinia).

29 August: Festa del Redentore, Nuoro (Sardinia).

27 September: San Cosimo, Mamoiada (Sardinia).

Part II

ISLANDS ALONG THE COAST OF ITALY

Madonna di Monserrato, Elba

Elba and the Tuscan Archipelago

Thanks to Napoleon, everyone has heard of Elba. What is not so well known, however, is that Elba is only the largest of a group of islands, ranged in a semi-circle off the coast of Tuscany. These smaller islands—there are six of them—have truly earned their obscurity. Three are penal colonies, and two others have no permanent residents. Here is a brief introduction to them, from north to south.

Gorgona, the tiniest, is a prison. **Capraia** is too, but only one-quarter of it. The rest has a small population and is beginning to attract tourists. **Pianosa,** the flat island, like Gorgona has only crooks and guards. **Montecristo** no longer has a Count, only a custodian; it is now a nature reserve. **Giglio,** the largest and most populated, is full of tourists. Finally there is **Giannutri,** a summer paradise for a select few.

25

Geographically the islands have much in common with nearby Corsica. There's lots of pink granite and Laricio pines. All of the group except Pianosa are mountainous—the archipelago is really only the summits of a submerged mountain range. Historically, they have moved in the orbit of Italy since the days of the Etruscans. While perhaps lacking in 'sights' and tourist attractions, the six smaller islands each have their share of natural beauty. Elba itself, surprisingly, is one of the more popular vacation spots in the western Mediterranean, and by no means lacking in diversions.

Elba

HISTORY.

The island of Elba is close enough to the mainland of Italy (about 8 miles) to have been inhabited since earliest times. Indeed, it is so near—both for invasions and for dissemination of cultures and ideas—that no distinctive civilisation was ever founded there. When Neanderthal Man was tramping through the neighbourhood, about 50,000 years ago, Elba may still have been connected to the mainland. Later peoples, a seemingly unending parade of them, colonised the island after 3000 BC, drawn by Elba's great economic attraction—metals. In the Copper Age they mined its copper; in the Bronze Age they alloyed the copper into bronze. The copper gave out just in time for the Iron Age, when Mediterranean peoples learned to make sharper and longer-lasting tools by smelting iron ore. Elba, conveniently, had vast deposits of this also. Competition for it was fierce: Etruscans and Greeks fought over the island, and both established settlements to exploit the mineral resources, but neither left sizeable permanent colonies. The Greeks gave the island its early name of *Aethalia* (sparks) for its many forges, whose fire and smoke were visible far out at sea. In spite of Greek victories elsewhere, the Etruscans gained control of the island, fighting off incursions first by the eastern Greeks and later, after the Peloponnesian Wars, by powerful Syracuse.

For Rome, establishing its hold on the Italian peninsula in the 4th century BC, Elba was an important prize. After its conquest of the island at the end of the century, towns were founded to consolidate Roman rule at modern Pomonte, Capoliveri, Marciana, and a capital at Fabricia, the site of Portoferraio. For the Romans, the island's ore was invaluable; when Roman legions ran their swords through Teutons, Persians, Gauls, Carthaginians or each other, throughout the history of the Republic and Empire, they usually did it with Elban iron. The mines and forges, then as now, were concentrated in the eastern third of the island; the remainder, being sparsely populated, pretty, and relatively close to Rome, became a vacation spot for the wealthy. The only significant Roman remains on the island are large villas, of which the best preserved is near Portoferraio.

The Fall of Rome, and the advent of what we call the Dark Ages, brought the usual invasions, disorder, depopulation and pirates to Elba. Besides the iron ore, the Romans also used Elba as a source of building stone (the Pantheon in Rome is built of Elban granite). In the 6th century the Lombards—under one of the bloodiest chieftains of all that murderous crew, Gummarith—subjugated the island, after burning and sacking it. When the Lombards receded into senility, Saracen pirates and adventurous barons from Italy fought over Elba, as they did in nearby Corsica. The Republic of Pisa became involved in the 9th century, as the island lay across its most important trade route to the south and west, and by the 11th century the Pisans had complete control.

By this time the island had acquired its modern name of Elba, first recorded in a document of Pope Gregory the Great. Before then, back into Roman times, it was called *Ilva*, the name of the indigenous Ligurian tribesmen who formed the bulk of the population. The Pisans held the island for almost 500 years, constructing fortresses at Luceri and Volterraio and exploiting the mineral resources, but surprisingly building none of their beautiful Romanesque churches, such a prominent feature in Corsica, another medieval Pisan possession. At this time the capital of Elba was a town called *Feraia*, of which the city built on the site of modern Portoferraio was only the port. Not a trace remains of this city, and Elban archaeologists are still trying to discover its site.

For 300 years, from the 13th century, Genoa contested Pisa's possession of the island. In the 16th century, when Pisa was too weak to hold it and Genoa still not strong enough to take it, the resourceful Duke Cosimo di Medici of Florence saw his opportunity and seized it. He built Portoferraio, and the wall around it. (The plaque he erected to take the credit can still be seen over the city's main gate.) Cosimo, however, was soon forced to contend with the growing power of Spain in the western Mediterranean; after inconclusive skirmishes the island was partitioned between the two states. Spain built the town and fortress of Porto Azzurro as a counter to Portoferraio. This arrangement lasted peacefully throughout the 18th century, in spite of French efforts to grab the island. Then Cosimo's place was taken by the Austrians, 'happy Austria' having acquired the Duchy of Tuscany through marriage.

During the Napoleonic Wars, Elba was occupied for a time by the English, and Portoferraio was unsuccessfully besieged for over a year by Napoleon's troops in 1799. Napoleon finally annexed it in 1802, probably with no premonition that this island was one day to constitute the whole of his empire. In 1814, the Treaty of Fontainebleau put a temporary end to the First Empire and sent him to Elba, as if the once-ruler of all Europe would be content as sovereign—prince, duke, emperor, first consul, or whatever he desired to call himself—of the little island. Elba, after all these centuries, suddenly found itself on the centre stage of world history.

Napoleon himself chose Elba, from the variety of small Mediterranean outposts offered him, for 'the gentleness of its climate and its inhabitants'. Also, perhaps, because on clear days he could see his own island of Corsica, just a short distance to the west. No one, however, seems to have consulted the Elbans themselves on this point, and they can be excused for the cold indifference with which they received their new ruler. On 4 May 1814, he arrived at Portoferraio with some 500 of his most loyal officers and soldiers and a British Commissioner charged with keeping an eye on him. But Napoleon soon won over the hearts of the Elbans by being the best governor they ever had. New systems of law and education were established, the last vestiges of feudalism abolished, and what we would today call economic planning was begun; he reorganised the iron mines and started Elba's

28

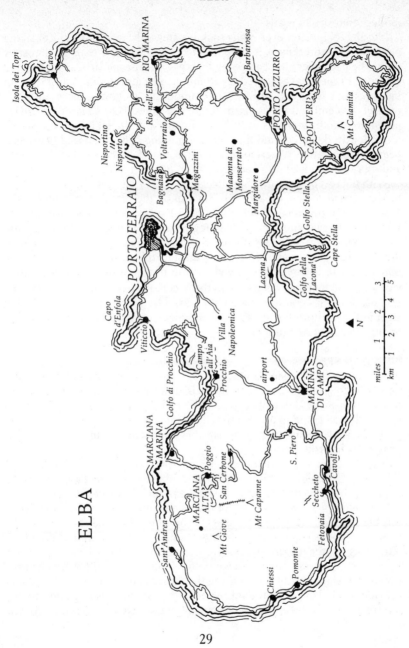

ELBA

Isola dei Topi
Cavo
RIO MARINA
Barbarossa
PORTO AZZURRO
Nisportino
Nisporto
Rio nell'Elba
Volterraio
CAPOLIVERI
Mt Calamita
Bagnaia
Magazzini
Madonna di
Monserrato
Margidore
Golfo Stella
PORTOFERRAIO
Cape Stella
Lacona
Golfo della
Lacona
Capo
d'Enfola
Viticcio
Campo
all'Aia
Villa
Napoleonica
airport
MARCIANA
MARINA
Golfo di Procchio
Procchio
MARINA
DI CAMPO
MARCIANA
ALTA
Poggio
San Cerbone
S. Piero
Cavoli
Sant'Andrea
Mt Giove
Mt Capanne
Fetovaia
Secheto
Pomonte
Chiessi

miles
km

N

1 2 3
1 2 3 4 5

29

modern network of roads.

Not that Napoleon ever really took his stewardship seriously. Remaking nations and institutions was a job his energetic character took on almost by reflex; he had, after all, been doing it across Europe for 20 years. It was the return to France that occupied his attention. The atmosphere was thick with intrigues and rumours, and secret communications flowed incessantly between Napoleon and his partisans on the Continent. On 20 February 1815, just nine months after his arrival, the Elbans and the embarrassed British watchdog awakened to find the emperor missing. The 'Hundred Days' had begun. Later, after Waterloo, the Powers would find a smaller, gloomier and more distant island to keep Napoleon out of trouble.

With the rest of Tuscany, Elba became a part of the new Kingdom of Italy in 1860. History then took an 80-year nap on the island, awakening to the disasters of World War II, which hit Elba harder than almost anywhere in Italy. Portoferraio and the surrounding area was bombed in 1943–44, first by the Allies, then by the Germans, causing the inhabitants to take refuge in the hills. In 1944, in one of the more disgraceful episodes of the war, Elba was 'liberated' by Free French and African troops, with more murder, pillage and rape than had been seen in the Mediterranean since the days of the pirates. Troubles continued after the war. The government closed the big steel mill near Portoferraio as 'uneconomical', thus depriving the island of its only major source of income.

WHAT TO SEE

To make up for the steel mills, the national and local governments have done a lot to encourage tourism on the island. An institution called Ente per la Valorizzazzione dell'Isola d'Elba (EVE), charged with the task, has been extremely successful in turning the island into one of Europe's holiday playgrounds. With the number of tourists now approaching 2 million every year, prosperity has returned.

Tourist Elba is no glamorous resort spot on the lines of the Costa Smeralda or Mallorca. It is a comfortable, homely place that attracts mostly families. Germans in particular favour the island; they have bought up most of the southern coast, and many of them come back every year. There is no one big crowded tourist ghetto, as is true on some other islands in the Mediterranean, but a large number of quiet, small resorts all around the coast. The lives of the Elbans themselves have been adjusted to the cyclical rhythm of tourist migrations. In winter the island seems empty; much of the population stays only to work during the season. Other activities do exist to provide a supplement to the tourist economy, such as fishing and mining, but the old iron mines, after thousands of years, have finally given out. The last of them closed in 1984.

In an unspectacular way, Elba is beautiful. Like Corsica, the predominant colours are pink and green—pink for the granite outcrops and Tuscan houses, green because the island is heavily forested. Also like Corsica, Elba is a chain of mountains rising out of the sea. The tallest mountains are at the western end of the island, grouped around 3300-ft Monte Capanne. Even more than Corsica, Elba is the mineralogist's dream place for a vacation. Besides the iron ore, dozens of common and rare minerals are found here, from andalusite to zircon. There is a mineralogical museum in Rio Marina to introduce you to them. For most people, though, Elba's greatest attraction is its wealth of beaches. The coastline, all bays and peninsulas, is over 100 miles in length, and there are beaches everywhere, large and small, sand and pebbles. Even in the crush of August, sun-and-sand addicts won't be packed like sardines. If you look carefully, you just might find a beach all to yourself.

There are few culinary specialities that Elba can truly call its own; the cooking is similar to that of Tuscany, but because Elba is an island there is a great emphasis on fish. Similarly, there is very little native folklore or folk traditions. The island is just too close to the mainland for an independent way of life to have developed. Where Elba really excels is in its wine. Viticulture is the biggest agricultural endeavour on the island, and for good reason. Elban wine, besides being cheap and plentiful, is of a very high quality even by Italian standards. White (*Procanico*), rosé and red (*Sangioveto*) wines are produced, as well as distinctive dessert wines such as the *Aleatico*, and even a sparkling wine, *Elba Spumante*.

Portoferraio

Portoferraio (pop. 11 000) is the capital and only city of Elba. The site has always been the island's port, but the modern city was built in the 16th century by Duke Cosimo di Medici of Florence and extensively fortified. The massive walls remain, though Portoferraio has spilled out towards the west along the bay. Here the ferries dock on the Calata Italia, where the visitor's introduction to Elba is the **Gratticielo** ('skyscraper'), a ten-storey pile of peeling paint built in the 1950s that is one of the most endearingly hideous buildings in the Mediterranean. It is also the most important building for the tourist, since it contains the offices of the AAST tourist information office, most of the ferryboat offices, and the Portoferraio bus terminal, at the back, with connections to all Elba's town and resorts.

Towards the old town, Calata Italia becomes the Via Vittorio Emanuele II, and then the Calata Mazzini under the walls, next to the old U-shaped harbour. On the far side is the **Torre del Martello**, from which in the old

31

days a chain was stretched across the harbour at night and in times of danger. The main gate of the city is the **Porta a Mare,** at the base of the U, over which can be seen the inscription of Duke Cosimo reminding us how he built the whole town 'from the foundations upwards'. Florentines, let alone Medicis, never lacked vanity; the new town had originally been dubbed Cosmopolis.

Directly inside the gate is the **Piazza Cavour.** Portoferraio is a big natural amphitheatre; from the piazza the town slopes upwards in all directions towards the walls on the high cliffs. North of the piazza, Via Garibaldi leads up to the big attraction, Napoleon's house, the **Palazzo dei Mulini.** Napoleon had the house built according to his own simple tastes; inside can be seen his furnishings, books and other paraphernalia, including the flag with three golden bees that he bestowed on the Elbans. It's worth the trip just to see the contemporary political cartoons mocking the emperor. The gardens around the house give fine views over the city walls. Along the walls on either side are the two Medici fortresses occupying the highest points in the city: *Forte Falcone* to the west and **Forte Stella** to the east, the former still used by the Italian Navy and the latter converted to housing.

On the way up to the Palazzo, along Via Garibaldi are the Town Hall and main post office and the two parish churches, the **Misericordia** and the **Holy Sacrament.** Both have copies of Napoleon's death mask, and both are home to one of Portoferraio's two religious fraternities, the 'Blacks' and the 'Whites'. The **Town Hall,** originally a bakery for Cosimo's troops, was the boyhood home of Victor Hugo, whose father was the French military governor in Elba. There is a Roman altar on display in the courtyard and inside is the **Biblioteca Foresiana,** a collection of books about Elba and a small picture collection.

Two blocks west is the **Teatro dei Vigilanti,** built by Napoleon around an old abandoned church (presently being restored). East of Via Garibaldi is the **Piazza della Republica,** the centre of Portoferraio, with several cafés. On its eastern side is the 18th-century **Cathedral,** not really a cathedral at all these days, and nearby is the big covered **market.**

In the modern extension outside the city walls are most of the hotels of Portoferraio, and many of the restaurants. There is a pebble beach, **Le Ghiaie,** on the northern side, and another called **Le Viste** under the walls near Forte Falcone. Two roads lead from the capital, one along the northern coast to the small resorts of **Acquaviva** and **Viticcio,** and to **Capo d'Enfola,** a lovely hill rising sheer out of the sea, barely connected to the rest of the island. The other road runs south to the junction at **Bivio Boni,** where it branches to the east and west. Nearby there is a thermal spa at **San Giovanni,** and the extensive ruins of a Roman villa at **Le Grotte,** on the southern shore of the Gulf of Portoferraio. Also on the gulf are beaches at Bagnaia, Ottone and Magazzini. Near Bagnaia is the simple, beautiful 12th-century Pisan **Church of Santo Stefano,** recently restored. It is the best Pisan monument in the archipelago. At **Acquabona** is Elba's sole golf course, operated by a hotel. Westwards from Bivio Boni are the resort at **Biodola Bay** and the **Villa Napoleonica** at San Martino. The emperor soon grew tired of life in Portoferraio and built this house as his country retreat. In later years an admirer bought the place and added a pretentious neo-Classical facade with big Ns pasted everywhere; it is now another Napoleonic museum.

FESTIVALS.
San Cristino (29 April). Misericordia procession (29 August). On Ascension Day there is a pilgrimage to the Shrine of Santa Lucia. On 5 May the Misericordia church commemorates the death of Napoleon with a procession (including a replica of his coffin). At the end of July there is a wine-tasting festival, the *Rassegna dei Vini Elbani* at Le Ghiaie.

Eastern Elba
Rio nell'Elba is the old centre of the mining industry. It is not at all what one would expect a mining town to look like. Like all Elban towns, it is quite pleasant, set in the hills overlooking the eastern coast. The neighbourhood is dotted with archaeological sites, the scanty remains of the mines and mining camps of the Etruscans and later peoples. There are many undeveloped beaches on the western side of Rio's peninsula, including those at Nisporto, Nisportino and Bagnaia. The road from Rio to Portoferraio passes the steep hill of **Volterraio,** where you can make the long climb to the 11th-century Pisan castle on the summit.

    Rio Marina, as its name implies, is the port for Rio nell'Elba. Here, the **Mineralogical Museum** (open 9–12 and 3–6, closed holidays; admission fee) can be visited. It's on the third floor of the Town Hall, and has displays of all the island's unusual rocks and minerals. Rio Marina has a busy harbour; besides the ore boats, many small fishing boats operate from here, under the vigilant eye of an octagonal Pisan watchtower.

    The eastern side of this peninsula, like the western side, has a number of fine beaches where you can sometimes escape the tourist crowds—Ortano, Porticciolo, Barbarossa and many others. On the northern tip of the peninsula is **Cavo,** an older resort town, while off the coast to the west there are two small uninhabited islands—**Palmaiola** and the **Isola dei Topi,** named after the rats that once formed its sole population.

FESTIVALS
SS Giacomo and Quirico (15 July), at Rio nell'Elba. San Rocco (16 August), at Rio Marina.

South of Rio, the wood passes through some difficult terrain towards **Porto Azzurro,** a large holiday town. In the 17th century, in the days when Elba was partitioned, the Spaniards built Porto Azzurro as a stronghold to counter Austrian Portoferraio. Until 1947 it was called *Porto Longone*. The fortress, built in 1603, withstood sieges from both the Austrians and the French. Since then it has been a famous Italian calaboose, often in the past entertaining political prisoners and criminal celebrities. Besides the town beach, there are several others nearby, including one at a bizarre spot called **Terrenere,** where a yellow-green sulphurous pond festers near the blue sea in a landscape of pebble beach and ancient mine debris—for those who like something different on their vacation. During the season, day excursions are operated from Porto Azzurro to the island of Montecristo.

Just north of Porto Azzurro is the **Sanctuary of Monserrato,** a famous shrine with an icon known as the 'Black Madonna'. The Spanish governor built this here in 1606 because the mountain (Monte Castello) reminded him of the site of the shrine at Monserrat in Spain. (What is the significance of the Black Madonna, revered from Portugal to Poland? It's simply a matter of the oxidation of yellow paint over the centuries—Van Gogh's famous sunflowers could eventually suffer the same fate.) South of Porto Azzurro is another old Spanish fortress at **Capo Focardo,** on a large oval-shaped peninsula consisting of Monte Calamita and the rough hilly country around it.

On this peninsula is **Capoliveri,** one of the oldest inhabited sites on the island. The town takes its name from the Roman *Caput Liberi*, which may refer either to the worship of Liber, an Italian equivalent of Dionysus (this has always been a wine-growing area), or to the free men (*liberi*) who lived there. Capoliveri was in Roman times an 'Alsatia', a refuge for any man who could escape to it. It has had a reputation for independence ever since, giving a bad time to the Pisans, the Spanish (who pulled down its walls) and even Napoleon. Today it is a peaceful place, with views from its hilltop over the surrounding countryside and the sea. Capoliveri's peninsula is very scenic, and surrounded by many beaches, but much of the land is privately owned. South of Capoliveri, near the coast, is the **Sanctuary of the Madonna delle Grazie,** with a painting of the Madonna and Child, from the school of Raphael, miraculously saved from a shipwreck.

The coast west of Capoliveri is marked by two lovely broad gulfs, **Golfo Stella** and **Golfo della Lacona,** separated by a steep, narrow tongue of land. Both are developed resort areas, with centres at Lacona and Lido Margidore.

FESTIVALS
8–15 September—the 8th is celebrated as the Nativity of Mary in Porto Azzurro, followed by a week of pilgrimages to the Sanctuary of Monserrato. Immaculate Conception, in Capoliveri (8 December).

Western Elba
Beyond Biodola, the scenic corniche road west from Portoferraio passes through **Procchio** and **Campo all'Aia,** adjacent resort towns. Procchio is much the larger, and one of the more expensive places on the island. Four miles to the west is **Marciana Marina,** another popular resort, with a 15th-century Pisan watchtower, the **Torre Saracena.** This is the port for Marciana, the oldest continuously inhabited town on Elba.

In the 14th and 15th centuries, when life close to the coast wasn't especially safe, Marciana was the 'capital' of the feudal Appiani barons, the most powerful family on the island. Today, high in the mountain forests on the slopes of Monte Capanne, it is a surprisingly beautiful town of narrow streets, stone stairs, archways and belvederes. Parts of the old city wall and gateway are still present, and the old Pisan **fortress** hangs over the town (not open to visitors). The palace of the Appiani can also be seen on a narrow *vicolo* in the oldest part of town. Marciana has an **Archaeological Museum** (open 10–12.30 and 4–7.30; closed Wednesdays; also closed October–March) with a small collection of prehistoric and Roman objects found in the area.

From Marciana a cable-lift travels to the summit of **Monte Capanne,** the highest point in Elba, with a view over Corsica, Italy and all the Tuscan archipelago. Three religious sites outside the town may be of interest: the ruined Pisan **Church of San Lorenzo,** the **Sanctuary of San Cerbone,** who escaped here from the troublesome Lombards (later his body was buried in a miraculous rainstorm, provided so that the Lombards wouldn't see), and the **Sanctuary of the Madonna del Monte,** dating from the 11th century. This is one of the most important shrines on the island and was probably the site of pre-Christian worship. The pious Napoleon spent two weeks here, dallying with his Polish mistress, Maria Walewska. Another mountain village, almost a twin of Marciana, is just east of the town: **Poggio.** Poggio has a natural spring where the Elbans bottle their own local *acqua minerale*—called 'Napoleone', of course. It's very good, but the Elbans keep it all to themselves.

FESTIVALS

On 1–3 May, Easter Monday and the Assumption, there are pilgrimages to the Sanctuary of the Madonna del Monte. Santa Chiara (12 August) is celebrated in Marciana Marina, and Santa Caterina (25 November) in Marciana.

On the rugged coast to the west and south of Marciana, there are more beaches and resorts: Sant'Andrea, Patresi, Chiessi, Pomonte, Fetovaia, Seccheto and Cavoli. Seccheto has ancient granite quarries, from which the stone was cut for the Pantheon in Rome.

Four miles east of Marciana is Elba's plain, the **Campo nell'Elba,** extending across the island from Procchio to Marina di Campo, separating the western mountains from the central range. Elba's small airport is here—the only place they could put it. Two old, pretty towns lie on the edge of the plain; **Sant'Ilario in Campo** and **San Piero in Campo.** San Piero's parish church of San Nicolo has interesting frescoes; it was built on the ruins of an ancient temple to Glaucus. Halfway between the two towns are the ruins of the Pisan **Church of San Giovanni,** along with a Pisan watchtower.

On the coast is **Marina di Campo,** perhaps the largest resort area. It was the first to become popular, and it has the largest beach on Elba. The watchtower in the harbour was built by the Medicis.

GETTING TO AND AROUND ELBA

You'll never have to wait long for a ferry to Elba, especially during the summer. Gritty Piombino is the major point of departure, an industrial town on the Tuscan coast. Any train going up Italy's western coast can take you as far as the station called Campiglia Marittima; from there the FS operates a regular shuttle train to Piombino (don't get off at the Central Station; the train has a short stop there before it goes on to the port). Two companies run services to Elba. Toremar and Navarma (a single passage on either is about 6000 lire). The most frequent passage is the 1-hour Piombino–Cavo–Portoferraio trip, and there are also Toremar boats that go from Piombino to Rio Marina and then to Porto Azzura (2 hours). Services to Elba can be as frequent as every half-hour in July, down to two or three a day in the winter. Toremar also has a daily Livorno–Portoferraio run (5 hours) by way of the islands of Gorgona and Capraia. Note that the Navarma service is really a part of the ferry trip from Piombino to Bastia, in Corsica. To keep up with demand in the summer, Toremar also runs hydrofoils on the Piombino–Portoferraio run; these are faster (30–40 minutes) but more expensive.

Shipping company addresses:
Toremar: in Livorno, 5 Scali del Corso (tel. (0586) 22772).
Navarma: in Piombino, 13 Piazzale Premuda (tel. (0565) 33032).

Elba has an efficient bus service to all corners of the island, and buses depart with some frequency. The hub of the system is Portoferraio, with buses leaving and returning to the terminal by the *Gratticielo*, facing the harbour.

From Portoferraio to
Lido Biodola
Bagnaia and Lacona
Capoliveri, Porto Azzurro, Rio nell'Elba, Rio Marina and Cavo
Procchio, Marciana Marina, Marciana, Marina di Campo
Procchio, Marina di Campo, Fetovaia, Pomonte
Procchio, Sant'Ilario, San Piero, Marina di Campo
Marciana Marina, Marciana, Pomonte
Capoliveri and Porto Azzurro
Procchio, Marciana Marina and Marina di Campo

TOURIST INFORMATION
The AAST for the whole of Elba is in the Gratticielo, 26 Calata Italia in Portoferraio, just across from the ferry dock (tel. (0569) 92671). During the summer the Livorno EPT runs a booth in Piombino, just across from the ferry dock (tel. (0565) 36432).

WHERE TO STAY
With more than 150 hotels around the island, Elba has something for everyone. The emphasis is on the not-too-expensive resort, attractive to family holidaymakers. Many hotels stay open all the year round, with substantial off-season discounts.

It you want to stay in Portoferraio, an interesting possibility is the **Ape Elbana**** (2 Via de Medici; tel. (0565) 92245; 17–31 000 lire single, 22–44 000 double). The 'Elban Bee' is the oldest hotel on the island; it entertained Napoleon's guests. Some of the city's hotels are near the beach of Le Ghaiae and the city park; one that is quite pleasant is the **Villa Ombrosa**** (on Via de Gasperi; tel. (0565) 92363; 24–32 000 lire single, 32–48 000 double). The resorts begin where Portoferraio's suburbs end. Some areas within a few miles offer good value in lovely settings, such as the **Mare**** (tel. (0565) 66069; 22–30 000 lire single, 35–47 000 double) and **Tirrene**** (tel. (0565) 966002; 18–23 000 lire single, 27–36 000 double), which are both on the beach at Magazzini, or the **Clare**** (tel. (0565) 961077; 18–22 000 lire single, 30–37 000 double) a little further out in peaceful Bagnaia. South of the city at Acquabona is the **Aquabona Golf Hotel***** (tel. (0565) 940064; 30–42 000 lire single, 46–75 000 double) with Elba's only golf course—sorry, there's only room for nine holes.

At Cavo, on the east coast, prices tend to be slightly higher, and Porto

37

Azzurro is often very crowded, there are plenty of campsites and holiday apartments there. The same is true of most of the beaches on the south eastern peninsula around Capoliveri, although many pleasant hotels are right on the beach, like the **Voce del Mare**** at Naregno beach (tel. (0565) 968 455; 16–24 000 lire single, 26–37 000 double). The best beach in Elba may be at Cavoli, west of Campo nell'Elba; there you'll find the **Lorenza**** (tel. (0565) 987054; 18–23 000 lire single, 30–36 500 double) with a good restaurant. Of the resorts at the west end of the island, there are some smart establishments around Procchio, more modest hotels at Santa Andre and Pomonte, and some which are blissfully out-of-the-way, like the **Andreina**** (tel. (0565) 908150; 23 500 lire single, 26–36 000 double) on the beach at La Cala, west of Marciana Marina.

EATING OUT

To start with, while you're waiting for the ferry at Piombino you might try the **Ristorante Terrazza**, above the bar in the port area, with truly fine *spaghetti alla vongole*, and a big picture window with a panoramic view of Piombino's steel mills. In Portoferraio the **Arsa** is a good, honest, inexpensive trattoria by the port (Via Manzoni 8, 12–16 000 lire). Pizzerias and seafood places abound: the **Garden** (Via Vit. Emanuele 14) specialises in both (20 000 lire for fish). In Porto Azzurro, among the many seafood restaurants on the beach, is the **Delfino Verde**, built over the sea for a fine view (25 000 lire and up); at Marina di Campo, the **Kon-tiki**, on Via Molo Nuovo, justifies the expense with some very innovative seafood dishes (30–40 000 lire for a full meal). Finally, when in Marciana up in the mountains, seek out the little unnamed restaurant near the bus stop that looks like grandma's dining room (that's just what it is, in fact). Almost anywhere you go you can try the island's wines—*Elba Bianco* and *Elba Rosso*—which can hold their own with any grown in Tuscany.

Other islands in the Tuscan archipelago

Of the remainder of the Tuscan archipelago, none of the islands has much historical or present importance. All of them taken together are only a quarter of the size of Elba, and the total population is about 2000, almost all of them on Giglio. That's not counting the involuntary residents, for Capraia, Gorgona and Pianosa are penal colonies, the latter two inaccessible without special permission.

Torre di San Giovanni, Elba

Capraia

Capraia is the third largest of the islands, after Elba and Giglio. It measures about 6 miles by 3, and has about 300 inhabitants. Like Elba, it is mountainous, but has fewer trees; most of the island is covered with scrubby *macchia*.

HISTORY

In Roman times Capraia seems to have been a private estate, and the ruins of an extensive villa can be seen. In the late days of the Empire, the island was occupied by a colony of Christian monks. Such an island was perfect for the Christian ideal of withdrawal and contemplation, but it also prevented the Church authorities from keeping a close watch on the colony, and the monks slipped into unorthodoxy and loose behaviour; an armed mission from Pope Gregory the Great was needed to force them back in line in the late 6th century.

When Saracen pirates began to infest the Tyrrhenian Sea, Capraia, like most of the group, became deserted. The Pisans thought it important enough to repopulate and fortify in the 11th century. Genoa eventually gained control, as she did in Corsica only about 20 miles away. The proximity to Corsica gave Capraia its one big moment in history: in 1767 the revolutionary forces of the Corsican nationalist leader, Pasquale Paoli, and the weakness of the Genoese, resulted in, of all things, an independent Capraia, which soon learned to support itself by piracy. French occupation put an end to that four years later.

CAPRAIA

Scoglio della Capra

penal colony

port lighthouse

CAPRAIA

beach

Mt Castello

ISOLA
DEI
GABBIANI

Mt
Pontica

Santo Stefano

CALA
DEL CEPPO

Grotta di
Parino

N

Grotta
della Foca

miles 1 2

km 1 2 3

Torre dello
Zenobito

WHAT TO SEE

Five years ago tourist accommodation on Capraia consisted of one hotel and two tiny pensions. Today, by a miracle of 20th-century Eurotourism, these have all grown into three-star hotels, with three more sprouting up to join them. It helps that Capraia is an island, and a pretty one, but its real attraction is its natural setting, its deep-sea diving and marine grottoes. In the last century the northern quarter of the island was put to use as an agricultural penal colony, which is what it still is today. The civilian population of the island is almost entirely concentrated in the port and only town, **Capraia Isola**. The port is actually a quarter of a mile away from the town, connected by the island's only paved road. In the town are the baroque church and convent of **Sant'Antonio**. Used as a barracks in the last century it is now crumbling and abandoned. Next to the convent is the town's lighthouse. On the outskirts are the ruins of the **Roman villa,** apocryphally the abode of Augustus' profligate daughter Julia, and an 11th-century Pisan chapel dedicated to the **Vergine Assunta.** Overlooking it all is the large and impressive fortress of **San Giorgio**, begun by the Pisans and completed by the

40

Genoese. The well-preserved **watchtower** at the port was built by the Genoese Bank of St George, famous exploiters of Corsica.

On the eastern side of town there is a beach under the cliffs with an interesting tower, built by the Pisans, connected to the cliff by a natural bridge. A visiting Californian at the turn of the century was so struck by it that he built a copy of it on a beach near San Diego.

From Capraia Isola a road leads southwest across the island, passing another Pisan church, that of **Santo Stefano**, built on the ruins of a 5th-century church used by the early monks, destroyed by Saracen pirates. Near Monte Pontica is a cave, the **Grotta di Parino**, a sacred spot used as a place of meditation by the monks. The road ends at a lighthouse on the western coast. Just south of here is a sea cave, the **Grotta della Foca**, where some Mediterranean seals are still reported to live. At the southern tip of the island is another Genoese watchtower, the **Torre dello Zenobito**.

Gorgona

This unhappy island was first used as a prison by none other than Pope Gregory. There were monasteries here too, until pirate raids in the 15th century forced the island's abandonment. The Carthusian monks came back in 1705, but in 1869 the new Italian kingdom appropriated the entire island for a 'model' penal colony. A model it was in its early years, with bright modern buildings and extensive farms. Almost all of the island was covered with vineyards. Today all have been abandoned, and Gorgona is just another prison.

There are few inhabitants besides the guards and prisoners, but permission to visit must be obtained from the Ministero di Grazia e Giustizia in Rome. Don't expect to get it without a good reason for going. There isn't much to see; Gorgona is a hilly, rectangular square mile. A 17th-century Medici tower and a Carthusian monastery have disappeared since the island became a prison; you'll have to be content with the view from the boat. The Elba–Livorno ferry stops here and at Capraia.

Pianosa

Pianosa is the black sheep of the family of Tuscan islands—its name, from the Roman *Planasia*, explains why: it's flat, as level as a pool table, broken only by a few tiny conical mounds, and about 7 square miles in area. Its only port is the Cala Giovanna, near the entrance of the prison. The island has had a troubled history in modern times. The Genoese sacked and depopulated it, as did Dragut's pirates in the 1550s. Even so, it managed to support a sizeable population of farmers and fishermen until it was taken over as a penal colony in 1856.

The prison occupies the entire island, and, as with Gorgona, you will need to get special permission, or else punch a *carabiniero*, to gain admittance. Also like Gorgona, the early dreams of a modern progressive prison with rehabilitation through farm labour have been allowed to die, and most of Pianosa is just wasteland. There are substantial **Roman ruins** on the island. It was the property of Augustus' famous general Cornelius Agrippa, who left behind his big villa, complete with theatre, and some remnants of the ancient port of Cala Giovanna.

Montecristo

Montecristo, administratively a part of the commune of Portoferraio, in Elba, has recently been declared a nature reserve. It has a population of three: the guard and his family. The island (5 square miles) is roughly round in shape and very mountainous. Its summit, **Monte della Fortezza** (2,096 ft), is the highest in the archipelago outside western Elba. There is little vegetation on most of Montecristo, and it is generally so rocky and inaccessible—there are no roads and few level places to build them—that it has never been deemed worth settling by anyone except monks.

The island has had religious importance since ancient times. Under the Romans, both the island and its peak were called *Mons Jovis*, and an important temple of Jupiter was built on the summit. Of this not a trace remains; unless the Christian monks themselves destroyed it, its fate is a mystery. These monks, living as hermits, occupied Montecristo in the last stages of Roman decline. The most famous of them was St Mamilian, a 6th-century bishop of Palermo who fled here, via Elba, from the Arian heretic Vandals. He was reputed to have killed a dragon upon arrival. When he died, a divine signal was seen by fishermen from Elba, Giglio and Genoa, who all made haste to the island. Realising that he was a suitable subject for canonisation, they began to fight over the remains. In the true tradition of Christian brotherhood, they struck a deal and cut Mamilian up in three pieces. Giglio got an arm, which proved its worth by repulsing the Turks in an 18th-century pirate raid. Charity might have bade them leave some bones behind for Montecristo, for without any relics to protect them the last colony of monks was carried off by pirates in 1553.

More recently Montecristo became a household word, thanks to

Alexander Dumas' novel, even though none of the action of the book takes place there. The island served as a hunting retreat for the pathetic fool Vittorio Emanuele III, penultimate king of Italy, until his death in 1945.

Montecristo today might as well be a prison, like Pianosa or Gorgona: so seriously does the Portoferraio government take its status as a nature reserve that it won't let anyone see it. Private boats, and day excursions from Giglio Porto and Porto Azzurro in Elba, are allowed to dock at Cala Maestra, one of the many coves around the island's coast, and visitors are allowed on the fine beach in the cove, but no further. The mountains, the ruins of the old monastery and the royal villa (now the custodian's house)—all are out of bounds.

Incidentally, the trees and exotic plants you'll see at Cala Maestra don't really belong there. They are not native to the island, but were planted when Montecristo was a royal playground.

Giglio

Giglio, like, nearby Giannutri, lies a little apart from the rest of the archipelago. Both islands are further to the south and closer to the mainland (about 7 miles for Giglio). Administratively they are a part of the province of Grosseto. By sea, they are reached not from Piombino or Livorno but from Porto Santo Stefano, near Orbetello on the Argentario peninsula.

HISTORY
The word *giglio* means lily, and the lily has become the island's symbol, although it has in fact nothing to do with the island's name. The Romans called it *Aegilium* or *Gilium*. Under the Empire the island was a resort for the very wealthy, like most of the Tuscan archipelago. In the Middle Ages the island had various feudal owners; later it was ruled for a time by both the Aragonese and the Pisans. Cosimo di Medici also seized it, along with Elba, in the 16th century. All of these rulers contributed to the island's fortifications, but none was any more successful in deterring the raids of Turkish pirates than they were on the other islands in the area. As we have seen, the Giglians used St Mamilian's holy right arm to chase the pirates away in 1799, but it didn't do them much good on other occasions. The redoubtable Barbarossa carried off most of the population in 1534, and his understudy, Dragut, came back for the rest in 1550.

WHAT TO SEE
When the pirate threat was ended, Giglio became a happy and prosperous

place, living on agriculture, fishing and wine. Since the last war, however, tourism has become so important to the island that honest ways of making a living have suffered. Wide areas of land have been abandoned, giving Giglio a somewhat barren appearance, although the island was once covered with trees—just another example of the little ecological tragedies that can be seen on most of the small Italian islands. The land is cleared for agriculture, then just ignored when there is more money to be had running hotels. The land reverts to *macchia*, or else the soil blows away, and the island becomes a wasteland (like Lampedusa). Giglio is by no means that far deteriorated; it is still quite green and pretty, but continual poor stewardship of the land does little good for the island's future.

Giglio is the largest of the Tuscan islands after Elba, measuring about 13 by 5 miles. It is also second in population, with about 1100 souls, almost all of them in the island's three small villages: Giglio Porto, Giglio Castello and Campese.

Giglio Porto is the island's metropolis. At first view it looks very much like the town on the island of Ponza (see below), with the houses stacked up the steep hillsides around the little port. It is also the island's major tourist centre, with most of the shops and restaurants on the **Via Umberto I**, the main street. There are two beaches south of the town, at **Cala delle Cannelle** and **Cala delle Caldane**, and one to the north at **Punta Aranella**; all three are more or less developed. From Giglio Porto a difficult mountain road leads up to **Giglio Castello**, in pirate days the only secure refuge, and so the only real town. The fortress itself was begun by the Pisans and completed by the Tuscans, and the picturesque old town inside, much of it dating from the Tuscans' occupation, was until recently the centre of the island's life. Here can be seen the **Church of St Mamilian**, with its famous relic.

From Giglio Castello a road leads southwards past **Poggio della Pagana**, the highest peak (1612 ft), to the lighthouse at Punta del Capel Rosso, at the southern tip, and back along the eastern coast to Giglio Porto. The main road from Giglio Castello continues on through many twists and bends to **Campese**, a growing resort area. Here are a watchtower of the Tuscan era, and a large sandy beach.

Giannutri

Among the Tuscan islands, only Gorgona is smaller than Giannutri. Because the island is small, lacks water and has little level ground for agriculture, it has never been continuously inhabited. With no population to attract the pirates, Giannutri has little history to speak of, although it has been known since ancient times. The Greeks called the island *Artemesia*, after the goddess, and the Romans converted it to *Dianium*. Perhaps the island acquired these associations from its crescent-moon shape. Like Gorgona and Pianosa, Giannutri was a private estate; there are remains of a Roman villa on the northern coast, near Cala Maestra.

Until recently the island's ownership was shared by a few families who had holiday cottages near Cala Maestra. Now, a tourist village has been built on the other side of the island, at Cala Spalmatoio, which is where you'll have to stay if you want a holiday on Giannutri—there are no hotels. There is no permanent population either, only the workers in the tourist village.

The island is about 3 miles around the crescent and never more than 500 yards wide. It is hilly, with many trees, and surrounded by a rocky coast broken only by beaches at Cala Maestra and Cala Spalmatoio. Besides the Roman villa, there are interesting caves near Spalmatoio and near the lighthouse at the southern tip.

GETTING TO AND AROUND THE TUSCAN ARCHIPELAGO

The Toremar ferry from Livorno to Elba (see Elba) stops at Capraia, a

45

3-hour trip, daily except Sundays; sometimes it stops at Gorgona and Pianosa to drop off supplies and fresh convicts. Giannutri can be reached on a regular basis only in July and August, on a daily ferry from Porto San Stefano, along the mainland near the city of Orbetello. For Montecristo, tourist excursions are arranged from Giglio and Porto Azzurro in the summer only.

Porto San Stefano is also the port for Giglio, a 1-hour trip run twice daily, more frequently in the summer by Toremar. The railway station for Porto San Stefano, along the main coastal route north from Rome, is at Orbetello Scalo; buses meet the trains to carry passengers to the port.

TOURIST INFORMATION
In Capraia, the Pro Loco association is at 2 Via Roma (tel. (0586) 905025). For Giglio, there's an AAST with an office in Giglio Porto at 48 Via Umberto I (tel. (0564) 809265).

WHERE TO STAY
Of the three former pensions on Capraia that have recently become three-star hotels, only **Da Beppone** (tel. (0586) 905001; 18–20 000 lire single, 28–32 500 double) has kept down its prices. On Giglio there is a small collection of hotels both at Giglio Porto and Campese; those in Giglio Porto are actually quite reasonable, like the **Castello Monticello***** (tel. (0564) 809252; single room with bath 22 500–36 000 lire, double 32–34 000).

EATING OUT
At Campese, on Giglio, the **Campese** (in the hotel of the same name) offers Giglio's own *Ansonico* wine to go with its *risotto alla marinara*. One of the better restaurants is the **Vecchia Frantoio** on Piazza Gloriosa up in Giglio Castello, with a number of specialities of its own (35 000 lire). Also in the Castello, there's a pizzeria, **La Castellana**, on the Via Panoramica (15,000 lire). Many new places have appeared on Capraia, along with the new hotels, and you may sample the day's catch at **La Cala Bossa** on Via Vitt. Emanuele (30–35 000 lire), or **Lo Scortano** on Via Assunzione.

The Pontine Islands

Scattered across the Gulf of Gaeta, there are five Pontine (or Ponziane) islands: two are inhabited (Ponza and Ventotene) and three are now abandoned (Palmarola, Zanone and Santo Stefano). Although all are volcanic in origin, they belong to two different chains: Ventotene and Santo Stefano are

PONTINE AND BAY OF NAPLES ISLANDS

47

part of the same formation as Ischia and Procida in the Bay of Naples, while Ponza, Palmarola and Zanone belong to the volcanic substructure of the mainland, near Anzio. Accordingly, the islands are quite fertile, producing wine and lentils.

All are dramatically beautiful, and until recently all were almost unknown to the flood of tourists which swept down on the nearby Bay of Naples. This changed noticeably in 1985, when Ponza enjoyed (or endured) a veritable stampede of visitors in the summer months, fleeing the denser crowds on Capri and Ischia. But as yet the island has done little to change its character—here are no designer shops or trendy cafés, and if you can visit outside the high season, you'll find an island as peaceful, charming and unspoiled as Capri was 50 years ago.

Ponza

HISTORY
Inhabited in the Paleolithic era, Ponza later became an exporter of that most valuable Stone Age commodity, obsidian, used to make tools. This hard volcanic glass was mined on the island of Palmarola, worked at Fieno on Ponza and then shipped to Cuma, an important centre on the mainland.

The Volscians, one of the early tribes near Rome, were the first historic inhabitants of Ponza, and they used it as a naval yard. The increasing power of Rome forced the Volscians out in 313 BC; at first favouring the island, the Romans built temples to the Dioscuri and later to Mithras, an aqueduct, and the two Imperial villas owned by Augustus. In the later years of Tiberius, however, Ponza became a place of political exile, hosting such notables as Caligula's brothers, his wife Orestilia, and his sister Agrippina the Younger, who was accused of plotting against him. Liberated after his assassination, she returned to Rome with baby Nero, who might have been born on Ponza—no credit to the island there.

After the Fall of Rome, Ponza was deserted by all but a group of monks at Santa Maria, where the exiled Pope, San Silverio, was lodged in 537. The monks, however, were no match for the pirates, who forced them to flee shortly thereafter. Little of note marked the passing of centuries on Ponza; the island was ignored even by its owners, the Farnese family, who had it for many years, although they occasionally sent expeditions to see what they could exploit. The last of the dynasty, Elisabetta, Queen of Spain, gave the island to her son Charles III of Naples in 1731.

When Charles became King of Spain, he left the islands to his son, Ferdinand IV of Naples. The Bourbons, for all their faults, tried to promote colonies on abandoned islands like Ponza, where the settlers, sponsored by the king, received generous tax incentives to develop the island. They fished, planted the first vineyards, and made a good living from the abundant coral along the coasts. These early Ponzese colonists must have wondered what they had got themselves into when an earthquake knocked a whole peninsula into the sea in 1821, and when a fierce hailstorm in 1835 destroyed all the crops, and even some of the houses.

But they persevered, and by the time of the Unification of Italy (1860) there were enough Ponzese to export. Some migrated to South America, and a large colony settled outside New York city, where they still celebrate the island's festivals. Under the Fascists, Ponza once more became an island of exile, first for anti-Fascists and, after the liberation, for Il Duce himself, for six days. More recently, Fellini filmed the last scenes of his classic *Satyricon* on Ponza, and other directors have since followed, attracted by the unspoilt charm of the island.

WHAT TO SEE
The 3-hour journey by boat from Formia to Ponza has two lovely highlights. The first is the vision of the old walled town of Gaeta on the rocks just off Formia, and the second is the most unusual sight of Ponza in the distance. At first it appears large and mountainous; then you realise that, as in a child's drawing, the mountains are all a single narrow chain, with no other mountains to back them up. After sailing past the uninhabited island of Zanone and the islet of Gavi, the rough-cut nature of the coast, untidy with numerous *scoglios* and *faraglioni* (standing sea rocks and islets), sheer cliffs, grottoes and beaches, adds to the delightful first impression of Ponza.

The port
All boats arrive in the principal town and port, known variously as Ponza or simple **Porto**. For many this is the archetypical Tyrrhenian town, its pretty pastel-and-whitewashed houses arranged artistically around the amphitheatre of the busy fishing port, overlooking the sea and its stately assortment of monolithic *scoglios*. One side of the town is dominated by the **Torre dei Borboni**, now a hotel, and the lighthouse at Punta Madonna. The parish church, dating back to the 17th century, has recently been restored with funds from the Ponzese in America and contains the statue of San Silverio, the island's patron saint. Dominating the town is the **Municipio**, with its yellow arcades surrounded by cafés, restaurants, and a monument known as the **Mamozio**.

Tunnels link the port with its suburbs of **Sant'Antonio** (with a small but not very clean beach) and **Santa Maria**. According to local tradition, Santa

49

GAVI

Punta Incenso

Piano d'Incenso

Punta Beppe Antonio

Spiaggia Schiavone

Punta Forte Papa

S. EVANGELISTA

Cala Fontana

Le Forna

Cala Feola

Cala Inferno

N

PONZA

Spiaggia del Core

Punta Bianca

Spiaggia di Lucia Rosa

miles   ½   1

km   1   2

Spiaggia di Frontone

Santa Maria

Punta Madonna

San Antonio

LE FORMICHE

PONZA

Capo Bianco   Chiaia di Luna

Mt Guardia

CALZONE MUTO

Punta Fieno

Faro della Guardia

Maria was once the residence of Circe, seductress of Odysseus, at a time when Ponza was known as *Eea*. Such traditions are never total fabrications; it is quite possible that a local but similar sorceress–goddess was once worshipped at Santa Maria and her identity was confused with Circe under the Romans. A sea cave known as the **Grotto di Circe** nearby may be visited by boat. In the vicinity of Santa Maria are numerous Roman cisterns and an underground aqueduct known as the **Grotta del Serpente** which once supplied a population of 20 000; the water was stored in a great reservoir, the **Piscinae Limariae**. Unfortunately all these features are hard to find on your own, and you'll have to inquire locally for exact directions. It's rather easier to find the small pension that housed Mussolini during his six-day exile on Ponza.

Besides waterworks, the Romans dug several tunnels on Ponza. One leads from the port area to the loveliest of the island's many small bays (*calas*), the **Chiaia di Luna** ('moonlight bay'), a luminescent crescent of beach beneath a steep, pale, 300-ft pale cliff that amply deserves its romantic name. Although across the island, it's within walking distance—Ponza is a long, thin sickle, following the shape of an ancient crater.

Around the island

The main attractions on the rest of Ponza are most easily seen by boat. Small motor launches are readily available for hire at the port and at Santa Maria, as are the rubber rafts, popular with underwater enthusiasts. Scuba-diving is very popular in the clean waters surrounding Ponza, with their sunken ships, coral, odd rock formations and big eels. Beginners can apply at the Nautilus sub-aqua school at Le Forna. In the summer there are organised sea excursions around the island.

Outside the port area, white houses are scattered along the island's single road, which twists and turns through the vineyard-clad hills with frequent panoramas of cliff and sea. The only real settlement along the way is **Le Forna**, named for the kilns that line the bottom of Capo Bosca hill. From here the houses and farms extend to Punta Forte Papa, many of them built in the North African *domus* style (with low domes), a style more flamboyantly expressed on another Italian island, Pantelleria, close to Tunis. What are particularly impressive at Le Forna, however, are the *case di tartufa*—elaborate cisterns dug in the rock designed to collect the maximum amount of rainwater. The centre of Le Forna is the church Maria Assunta, begun in 1770. A pension and various restaurants open here in the summer.

A narrow lane and steps descend from Le Forna to the **Piscina Naturale**, a volcanically-created pool separated from the sea by a narrow strip of land pierced by a tunnel-grotto that permits small boats to enter. Many

51

The Beach of the Chiaia di Luna, Ponza

people come here to swim. Other beaches near Le Forna are **Cala Feola** and **Cala Fontana**, which derives its name from a natural spring utilized by the Romans. A pretty stairway takes you down to the small beach. From here you can see the jetty of the company that mines the white bentonite of Ponza, reputedly unique to the island. On the promontory of **Forte Papa** to the northwest is a 16th-century watchtower built by the Farnese family, named for Pope Paul III, a member of the clan. In 1944 an English cargo ship carrying German prisoners foundered on the rocks, with few survivors.

Cala Inferno, on the other side of the island (within easy walking distance), derives its name from the 'infernal' whiteness of its cliffs. Here you can see the fragmentary remains of the Roman aqueduct which transported water to Santa Maria.

East of Le Forna, towards the end of the road, is the district known as La Piana, followed by **Calacaparra** with the sole Ponzese football field and a restaurant. The trans-Ponza highway stops at **Piano d'Incenso**, from where some of the best views of the island may be had for the price of a short walk. On a clear day you can make out Gaeta on the mainland.

Many of the island's wonders are accessible only (or at least most easily) by sea. Most interesting from a scholarly viewpoint is the **Grotte di Pilato**, not far from the port. Its name has nothing to do with Pontius Pilate and everything to do with an imaginative Neapolitan compiler centuries ago, who associated Ponza with Pontius.

The Grotte di Pilato is a natural grotto containing a rock-cut pool, with something resembling an apse carved in the back and four corridors leading

52

into the rock. In ancient times this cave was used by augurers who would dissect the entrails not of birds or goats but of sea eels, in order to discern the future. On the right side of the cave a hole bored in the wall opens up towards the constellations of the Great Bear and Draco, thought to have had some magical significance in auguries. Even today the grotto is a mysterious place, especially at night, should you have the good fortune to visit it then.

On the same eastern side of Ponza are two fine beaches, Frontone and Core, with the magnificent cliffs of Punta Bianca in between. From Core you can take a small boat into the **Grotta degli Smeralda**, where the water lives up to its name, 'emerald'. Due east of Cala Inferno many amphorae from ancient shipwrecks have been found. Passing the small islet of Sant'Evangelista, the enormous **Natural Arch** comes into view, and the beach of Schiavone.

Round the islet of Gavi and continuing down the west coast of Ponza you come to **Punta Beppe Antonio**, with another grotto and beach. From there you come to the cliffs and beaches of Le Forna, and from there to the **Spiaggia di Lucia Rosa**. Lucia Rosa was the daughter of one of the early colonists who had an unfortunate infatuation with a man of beautiful moustaches. Father said no, and so the love-lorn Lucia Rosa flung herself over the cliff near the tiny islets or *faraglioni* that still bear her name. South of here stretch two long beaches of white pebbles, a perlite mine and Capo Bianco Grotto. The beautiful Chiaia di Luna follows, and then the major wine-producing district of Ponza, **Punta Fieno**. Here a German father-and-son team, the archaeologists Schneider, found the remains of the Neolithic obsidian works, where the obsidian of Palmarola was worked. A lighthouse commands the southern tip of the island, on a leg of the island's tallest mountain, Monte Guardia. The remainder of the trip to the port, around the Punta Madonna and Le Grotte di Pilato, takes you past a pair of rocks with the odd name **Calzone Muto**—'Silent Pants'.

FESTIVALS
San Silverio di Frosinone is honoured with two festivals, on the last Sunday in February, and on 20 June. Silverio was Pope until Theadora, wife of the Byzantine Emperor Justinian, removed him in favour of her friend Vigilius, sending Silverio into exile, first in the Peloponnese and then in Naples and Ponza. He became the islanders' spiritual leader, and a council of bishops on Ponza inveighed against Theadora's anti-Pope. Realising that a schism was in the making, the Empress sent assassins after Silverio, and he was murdered on 20 June 537 as he was fleeing to Palmarola. He's been the island's patron saint ever since.

The *festa* on 20 June is the island's event of the year. Houses are given a new coat of whitewash, and the port and Santa Maria are brightly decorated with streamers and lights. On the big day itself, San Silverio's statue, adorned with coral and gold, is carried from the church to Santa Maria, the entire population of Ponza following the procession either by land or in small boats. Later in the day the *Gallina* takes place at Punta Bianca: a pole is extended out over the sea with a chicken at one end, and the young gallants of Ponza vie to see who can walk along the pole, pluck a feather from the chicken and return without mishap. The day ends with a concert in front of the Municipio.

SPECIALITIES
Lenticchie alla ponzese (lentil soup), *coniglio alla cacciatora* (rabbit with onions, tomatoes etc.) and lobster dishes. The best wines of Ponza are *Forna Grande, del Fieno* and *delle Grottelle*.

GETTING TO AND AROUND PONZA
The main year-round port for Ponza is Formia, halfway between Rome and Naples. Trains run along that route every half-hour on average, but note that not all stop at Formia, so make sure you board the right one. Caremar sells tickets at the quayside both for its morning ferry and for the hydrofoil; the ferry takes 3 hours and costs 7500 lire (return). In the summer additional services out of Formia for both Ponza and Ventotene are offered by Basso Lazio, whose office in Formia is at Via Vitruvio 60. There is also a daily boat (Mazzella Line) from Terracina (tel. (0773) 74840) which departs at 8.15am and arrives at 10.45, with an additional service in August departing at 7.45am. In the summer Aliscafi SNAV offers a hydrofoil service from Anzio to Ponza (1 hour), continuing to Capri and Ischia; a single to Ponza costs around 18 000 lire. SNAV offices in Anzio are at Via Porto Innocenziano 18, (tel. (06)984 5085). Caremar also operates a summer ferry from Anzio to Ponza and Ventotene; the office is at Via Porto Innocenziano 51 (tel. (06) 983 1231) in Anzio.

On Ponza itself small buses run between Sant'Antonio and Piano d'Incenso every 1½ hours. They tend to be packed, so try to make your cross-island excursions early in the day.

TOURIST INFORMATION
In the summer there's a Pro Loco office open near the Municipio. The very helpful AAST in Formia, just up the road from the port, also has plenty of information about the Pontine islands (tel. (0771) 21490).

WHERE TO STAY
The most picturesque place to stay on Ponza is the **Hotel La Torre dei**

Borboni*** in the port (Via Madonna; tel. (0771) 80109), with a third of its rooms and apartments in the 18th-century castle, affording wonderful views over the town and port. The hotel's restaurant has won many awards, and steps lead down to a small private beach—as similar ones may have done in the days of Augustus, who had a villa on the same commanding site. Prices begin at 38 000 lire for a single room, 48 000 for a double with bath. For something less pricey and right on the sea, try **Gennarino a Mare** (P2) on the Via Dante (tel. (0771) 80071), with balconies overlooking the sea, and a restaurant (single room 18 000 lire, double 22 000). There are also many inexpensive rooms to let in private homes; inquire at the Pro Loco for a list.

EATING OUT

Il Gambero, in the Piazza Pisacane, specialises in fish and lobster dishes and is open all year, with prices for a complete meal around 20 000 lire. **Le Querce** in Santa Maria specialises in local dishes and *zuppa di pesce* (15 000 lire). Outside the port area there's the **Ristorante alle Piscine**, with moderately priced local dishes and a fine view of the sea, and in Le Forna, on the Via Chiesa, is the **Ortensia**, with a similar cuisine and views over Palmarola.

Palmarola

West of Ponza and most easily reached from that island by hired or excursion boat is the small island of Palmarola which is uninhabited but not without charm. The mountains of Palmarola have an Alpine dignity, and like Ponza the island is surrounded by all sorts of picturesque volcanic debris, most spectacularly a rock known as the **Cathedral** on the west side of the island. Also on the coast are the beach, located beneath a rugged cliff of white and gold, and its small port.

Striking and beautiful as it is, Palmarola has been bad luck to many: here in 303 the Romans abandoned a group of 300 Christians to die of thirst and hunger; in 537 the ex-Pope San Silverio was murdered here when he escaped from Ponza to Palmarola; the boilers of the English cargo ship that sank at Forte Papa blew up at Palmarola, initiating that disaster; and even more recently an aeroplane crashed on the island. The deserted fields and terraces of the farmers who once lived here add another touch of melancholy

Zanone

An hour-and-a-half northeast of Ponza lies Zanone. Unlike Ponza and Palmarola, this island has never been cultivated or deforested, and remains splendidly pristine today. The last human inhabitants were the monks of Santo Spirito; today the island is the natural reserve of the shy, curved-horn *mouflons* (rare wild sheep), and over a hundred species of birds and rare plants. The main attraction of the island, though, is its rich fishing grounds, which beckon the scuba-divers from Ponza. Although there are no organised excursions to Zanone, it is easy to hire a motor boat and visit this ecological island paradise on your own.

Ventotene

HISTORY

Called *Pandataria* by the Romans, the little island of Ventotene, less than one square mile in area, saw a disproportionate number of Imperial celebrities come and go—on holiday, in disgrace, or in pieces. The first to come was Julia, only child of Caesar Augustus and the most famous adultress of her day. In 25 BC she had a grand summer villa built at Punta Eolo and brought the cult of Venus–Isis to Ventotene, building a temple near the modern lighthouse. The second of her three husbands, Agrippa, Augustus' admiral, was probably the guiding light behind the artificial port, still in use today.

Julia's villa was her pleasure palace far from the wagging tongues of Rome, and such was the respect she—or her father—commanded that even 200 years later the fishermen of Gaeta wouldn't divulge the names of the men their great-grandfathers had ferried in the night to her villa. Detested by her third husband, Tiberius, whom Augustus had forced to divorce his wife in order to wed her, Julia's escapades eventually caught up with her and she was exiled to Ventotene by her own father. Here she suffered for five years without men or wine, and with only the company of her mother Scribonia (first wife of Augustus) to comfort her. Although the Roman people several times interceded for Julia's return, Augustus was adamant that she should never enter Rome again, although he eventually sent her to more comfortable surroundings at Reggio Calabria.

The presence of Julia's villa on tiny Ventotene, close to yet so far from Rome, made it an ideal place for exiles of noble blood. Julia's daughter Agrippina, one of the few decent characters in the bloody soap opera of the Imperial family, was framed in a conspiracy against Tiberius, her dead husband's uncle, and exiled by him to Ventotene. When she protested, Tiberius had her beaten; realising that her rage was futile, she starved herself to death. Later Tiberius passed a bill in the Senate praising himself for not having had the poor woman strangled! When her son Caligula became emperor, he retrieved her ashes from Ventotene and gave them a proper burial (this was before he went mad).

Agrippina's grandson Nero (son of her no-good daughter Agrippina the Younger) perpetuated the cruelties on the little island when he had his wife Octavia exiled there to pacify his new mistress, the cunning Poppea Sabina. When the people of Rome clamoured for 20-year-old Octavia's return, felling the recently erected statues of Poppea, the latter persuaded Nero to have her rival permanently removed. Nero sent his henchmen to the villa, where they slit the veins of the young Empress, and, when through sheer terror she took too long to die, they scalded her in a hot bath, after which they cut off her head and gave it to Poppea.

The last member of the Imperial family to languish on Ventotene was Flavia Domitilla, who was banished for professing Christianity.

During the Middle Ages Pandataria gradually became known as Ventotene, for the many winds that sweep across the unprotected island. For a while the only inhabitants were Benedictine monks; in 1249 Pope Innocent IV ceded their monastery to that of Santo Spirito on Zanone, then five years later he transferred all the monks to Salerno. Ventotene was then left to the mercy of pirates, who made it a base, and to the Farnese, who owned the island for many years, exploiting the coral and minerals and stealing the ancient statues (a job finished off by an 18th-century Englishman, Sir George Hamilton).

The first colony sent to Ventotene under the Bourbons was an experiment à la Rousseau. In 1768 some 300 thieves, prostitutes and other evildoers from the prisons and gutters of Naples were brought to the island to demonstrate that, once removed from the evils of society, they would become models of virtue. They were left free to build their own shelters and marry whom they pleased; in short, it wasn't long before Ventotene became the Sodom and Gomorrah of the Tyrrhenian Sea. Armed forces had forcibly to evict the wild islanders, and an honest colony from Torre del Greco near Naples replaced them in 1772. In Fascist times 800 political prisoners were incarcerated on the island, and it was in this anti-Fascist climate in the middle of World War II that two of the prisoners, Rossi and Spinelli, wrote the important *Manifesto di Ventotene* (1942) formulating the idea of a united Europe—ideas that were to be the basis of the modern European parliament.

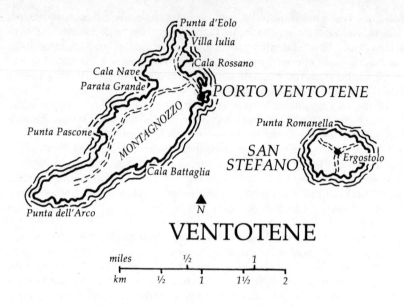

VENTOTENE

WHAT TO SEE

Tiny, rural Ventotene resembles a table from many angles, a flat, green land on a platform of tufa, carved into curious shapes by the wind. The island, along with tiny Santo Stefano, belongs to the cone of the great underwater volcano Campano, and locals say their home will never erode away (an obvious concern on such a small piece of real estate) because San Paolo della Croce anchored it down with basalt. With no hills or forests to shelter it, Ventotene deserves its name, and it has acquired two interesting scientific phenomena: the highest part of the island, Montagnozzo (452 ft), is covered with sand carried there from Africa and elsewhere by the wind; the sand is particularly deep around Cala Nave and Parata Grande, where roots of ancient trees have chemically petrified in the fine, loose layers of sand.

The single town, **Porto Ventotene**, is piled over the old **Roman port**, carved out of the tufa by Julia's husband, Agrippa. It forms a basin (7980 square yards; now used mainly by the island's fishing fleet) and is considered something of an engineering feat, its dark sides neatly cut and contrasting nicely with the white lighthouse and pale yellow town. Equally impressive are the two subterranean aqueducts, or **condotti**, dug out by the

58

Romans, one extending inland to the Piazza Castello. This supplied not only the people of the port, but also the sacred fishpond by the temple of Venus–Isis near the modern lighthouse. Here a small head of the goddess was discovered (now in the museum of Naples).

The centre of activity in the village is La Piazzetta, where the simple, pink baroque **Church of San Candida,** patron saint of Ventotene, has recently been restored inside with bright colours. According to tradition Candida suffered martyrdom with iron combs in North Africa, after which her body was placed in a small boat which miraculously drifted to Ventotene, and lay hidden in the Grotto di San Candida. The statue of the saint by the altar was donated by a father and son who were abducted by Algerian pirates while cutting wood on the island. When ransomed by the king, they thus offered their thanks to San Candida for promoting their safe return. Notice the little figures of woodcarvers beside her.

There's a small **museum** in the Municipio, open in the mornings, displaying items found on Ventotene. You can also see the bleak prison, and can walk along beyond the rocky beach at **Cala Rossano** to the northernmost point of Ventotene, **Punta d'Eolo,** where Julia's villa once stood. Clambering over the rocks you soon discover that it was truly enormous— scattered all over the promontory are ruined walls, sections of mosaic floor, archways and steps leading down to the sea. Unfortunately the Bourbon colony on the island quarried the site thoroughly, and it takes an effort of imagination to conjure up the Imperial villa. A local engineer and architect, Luigi Jacono, made detailed drawings and studies of the site, and if you can find copies they are helpful in sorting out where the odeon, baths, grand entrance, reservoirs, guardhouse and courts once stood.

You can stroll around the rest of the island in less than an hour, past little farms of lentils and barbed-wire gardens of twisted metal. In the autumn, hunters come from the mainland to shoot migratory birds, so if you come then take care. Here and there you'll find little paths winding towards the sea, the cliffs and beaches. With so many cliffs and small grottoes, the island is perhaps best circumnavigated by sea, and in the summer there are several small boats in the Porto Romano offering such an excursion, as well as to the islet of San Stefano nearby, to the east.

FESTIVALS

San Candida (20 September), with a procession, music, and display of small, multicoloured hot-air balloons. In August there is a lentil festival, celebrating the island's main crop, consumed most often in the island's special soup.

GETTING TO VENTOTENE
Caremar runs a daily ferry service year-round to the island from Formia (see Ponza). In the summer the same company runs a service from Anzio and links Ventotene to Ponza. Basso Lazio also offers a daily service linking Formia and Ventotene in the summer. The trip takes 2½ hours and costs 8000 lire return.

TOURIST INFORMATION
Pro Loco, in the Municipio (tel. (0771) 85132).

WHERE TO STAY
Although there are plans to build a large hotel on the island—a subject of hot debate between the island purists and those wanting to encourage tourism—there are only small pensions and rooms to let in private houses. The two pensions—both inexpensive P3s—are **Il Cacciatore** (tel. (0771) 85055) and **Isolabella** (tel. (0771) 85027).

EATING OUT
The few restaurants on Ventotene are stretched to the limit serving the summer visitors. One that stays open all year, specialising in lentil soup and fresh fish, is **Zi Amalia** on the Via Roma (around 15 000 lire for fish). There are a couple of other places down by the port.

Santo Stefano

Just east of Ventotene lies the islet of Santo Stefano, not much more than a cliff in the sea. In 1795 the Bourbons built a penitentiary here, originally used to house political enemies, generally those advocating the Unification of Italy. The most famous in this respect was Luigi Settembrini, founder of the 'Sons of Young Italy' and father of a character in Thomas Mann's *Magic Mountain*. Settembrini gives an account of his uncomfortable stay on Santo Stefano in his memoirs (*Le Ricordanze*).

La Citadella, as the prison is known, was built in the form of a semi-circle, with all the cells facing inwards. It was designed by Francesco Carpi, who himself became one of the first inmates and later died on the island.

During World War II, the prisoners almost caused La Citadella to be blown to smithereens by the Allies when they took over the prison. The chaplain, however, finally persuaded them to lay down their arms and raise the white flag. Since 1965 the prison has been closed; a developer wanted to turn it into a hotel, but nothing has come of it. Today Santo Stefano is used for grazing livestock, and may be visited from Ventotene.

Islands in the Bay of Naples:
Ischia, Procida and Capri

Without a doubt, the islands in the Bay of Naples—Capri, Ischia, and to a far lesser extent Procida—are the holiday queens of the Italian islands. Every schoolchild has heard of Capri, made so notorious by the antics of Emperor Tiberius and Norman Douglas' 'gentlemanly freaks'.

Ischia, fifty years ago, was the favourite island of jet-setters jaded by Capri. Renowned in ancient times for its mud baths, it has become a home-from-home for the German bourgeoisie. If anyone tries to tell you it's still 'unspoiled', take this into consideration: Ischia is Italy's biggest buyer of spaghetti-flavoured icecream. Both Ischia and Capri are connected to Naples' Capodichino Airport by helicopter.

Procida, on the other hand, has hardly been developed at all, though not through any lack of charm. For many Italians, the very name of the island conjures up the same associations that Alcatraz does for Americans, although neither has been a prison for many years.

Despite their location, the three islands are of very different geological origins. Ischia and Procida are a part of the enormous submerged volcano of Campano, which stretches from Ventotene in the Pontine Islands down to Stromboli and the Aeolian Islands. In not too ancient times, the two islands were connected to each other and, if the Greek geographer Strabo is to be believed, also to the Phlegrean Fields on the mainland. *Phlegrean* means 'fiery' in Greek, and Strabo records how, during an eruption of the now dormant volcano Epomeo on Ischia, an earthquake split Ischia–Procida from the mainland, then, in another upheaval, jolted the once united island in twain. In this same geological cataclysm, Capri broke off from the Sorrentine peninsula, a blow that shattered its coasts to form the island's famous cliffs.

Ischia

HISTORY

Inhabited by 2000 BC, Ischia became an important stop along one of the earliest trade routes in the Mediterranean, from Mycenean Greece to the Etruscans of northern Italy and the mineral wealth of Elba. The prevailing currents and winds made it natural for the Greek ships sailing west to circumvent Sicily and land in the Bay of Naples—as did that most famous sailor, Odysseus himself. As an island along the sea lane, Ischia was the perfect place to found an outpost to secure the route and trade, and here in 756 BC Chalcidians and Eretrians from the Greek island of Euboea settled the first Greek colony in western Europe.

They called the island *Pithekoussai*, referring to its abundant pottery clay (*pithos*). However, when Montagnone (a now extinct volcano on Ischia) erupted, the colonists fled to the mainland, establishing themselves at Cumae, where they prospered. Roman writers later refer to the island as *Eneria*, deriving from Aeneas' supposed stop on the island to repair his ships, or *Inarime*, a name of unknown origins. The name Ischia is believed to be a corruption of the word for island—*insula*.

In the year AD 6, Augustus traded the larger, more fertile island of Ischia for Capri, which then belonged to Naples. For most of its history Ischia and its famous castle remained attached to that great city, sheltering many of its nobles from political adversity; but during one period, in the early 16th century, the island outshone Naples as a cultural centre. This was due to one woman, Vittoria Colonna, who lived much of her childhood in the castle of Ischia, when her father's estates were confiscated by the Pope Alexander VI. She was betrothed in the castle at the age of 6 to another leading personage of the era, Francesco Ferrante, nephew of Constanza d'Avolas, the duchess who ruled Ischia for 50 years. On 27 December 1509, Vittoria and Francesco were married at the castle of Ischia in the celebrity wedding of the decade, but two years later Francesco was drawn away by the wars in the north and only once returned to Vittoria and Ischia before he died.

Vittoria was one of the greatest poets of her day, and is particularly known through her friendship with Michelangelo, who wrote sonnets to her. Indeed, few poets of the time were untouched by her graciousness. She was on close terms with the most brilliant men of Rome, her opinions were sought after, and her behaviour was always perfectly proper amidst the intrigues that surrounded her family. The contrast between the elegant court that surrounded her during her years on Ischia and the ravages and slave-taking wrought on the island by the corsairs Barbarossa and Dragut, a few years after her departure for Rome, illustrate the extremities of the period.

Another writer of far-reaching influence to find inspiration on Ischia was Gian Battista Vico. When down-and-out in his native Naples, the Bishop of Ischia offered him an easy tutoring job on the island, which Vico willingly accepted. *The Principles of New Science*, which he wrote at the end of the 17th century, had a profound influence on James Joyce. George Bishop Berkeley, the Irish philosopher, visited the island at the beginning of the 18th century and wrote of it extensively in his Journals; Henrik Ibsen spent the summer of 1867 at Casamicciola and wrote much of the play *Peer Gynt* during his stay. Ischia becomes part of literature itself in one of Boccaccio's tales of *The Decameron* (Fifth Day in the Sixth Novella), which involves a brother of John of Procida, a noble maiden of Ischia, Sicilian bandits, Palermo's palace of La Cuba, and Frederick of Aragon, King of Sicily, as the villain: interesting reading for Italian island travellers.

In the 19th century, Ischia, like so many islands, was a political prison. During the Napoleonic Wars it suffered in the battles between French and English, and for a brief period was Nelson's base.

WHAT TO SEE

Ischia today is a remarkably lovely island, able to hold its own even with Capri. The sea of vineyards encircling the island's highest peak, volcanic Monte Epomeo (2600 ft), produces the excellent wine named after the mountain, and the villages high on its slopes, like Fontana and Buonapane, remain untouched by the international onslaught of tourists at the resorts of Casamicciola, Forio, Lacco Ameno and Ischia town.

Unlike Capri, Ischia has many long, first-class beaches, on one of which, Maronti, the volcanic nature of the island is very evident. The hot mineral springs that gush all year-round have attracted cure-seekers since Roman times, and are still recommended today for people suffering from rheumatism, arthritis, neuralgia and obesity, among other complaints. Because many of the springs are radioactive, a doctor's permission is often required before a cure can be sought (there are physicians on the island who specialise in prescribing such treatments, and they charge a pretty penny). The hottest spring on the island is Terme Rita, which comes out of the earth at around 180°F, at Casamicciola. If bathing in a hot spring is more for fun than for cure, try the Terme Comunali at the port, or the unique baths at Cavascura above Sant'Angelo.

Ischia Porto

The first hint you receive of Ischia's volcanic origins comes when you enter the almost perfectly round harbour of Ischia Porto, formed by a sister crater of Monte Epomeo. Only in 1854 was it connected to the sea, the narrow strip of land carved out by the engineers of Ferdinand II. Full of yachts, lined with restaurants, and a step away from the tourist information office, it is everything a Mediterranean port should be. Note that while ships to Naples and Capri dock at one side, by the neo-Classical **Church of Santa Maria di Portosalvo,** and the hydrofoils near the newly modernised **Terme Comunali** (built in 1845), ships to Procida and Pozzuoli call at the other side of the lighthouse.

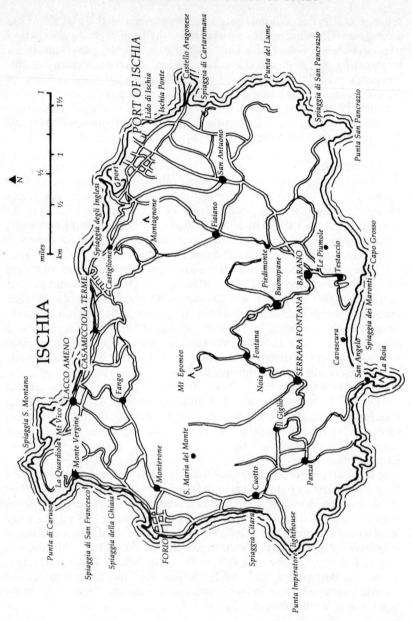

ISCHIA

PORT OF ISCHIA

Via Roma, the main shopping street of Porto, with cafés and boutiques, passes the **Chiesa dell'Assunta,** built in 1300 and since remodelled in the baroque style. Further on, when Via Roma becomes the more fashionable Corso Vittoria Colonna, turn down Via V. F. d'Avalos for the numerous seaside hotels and pensions, or in the other direction, Via V. E. Cortese for the **Pineta** (pinewood), a lovely shady divider between Ischia Porto and Ischia Ponte.

Ischia Ponte, once a separate fishing village, is slowly being gobbled up by tourist sprawl. 'Ponte' refers to the causeway built by Alfonso (*il Magnifico*) of Aragon in 1438 to the **Castello d'Ischia** on its offshore rock. With the large dome of its abandoned church in the centre, the fortress where Vittoria Colonna spent so many years looks like a fairytale illustration from the distance. As King Alfonso also financed most of the walls around the islet, it is sometimes called the Castello Aragonese, and can be visited. Not only are the narrow streets and 500-year-old houses interesting; the views from the walls are superb.

Even better views can be had from the summit of the extinct volcano, **Montagnone** (835 ft); a cablecar goes from Via Baldassarre Cossa at Ischia Porto (only 5 minutes from the station). The panorama of the Phlegrean Fields on the mainland, Ischia's little sister island Procida, and the rest of Ischia as well, make the short trip more than worth while

Popular **beaches** line much of the town's shore. Some are organised, like Ciro, Medusa, Lauro and Starace; others, like the Spiaggia degli Inglesi (named for the English occupation at the beginning of the 18th century) and Dei Pini, are free. The public **tennis courts** are on the Lido C. Colombo (tel. (081) 991013).

Around Ischia (counterclockwise)

Besides the state highway (SS270) there are many scenic secondary roads zigzagging across the island that you will be able to enjoy if you have brought a car. A few miles west of Ischia Porto (bus every half-hour) is the popular resort of **Casamicciola Terme,** the oldest spa on the island and the probable location of a Greek settlement. All remains of this, however, were obliterated in the 1883 earthquake in which 7000 people were killed. Henrik Ibsen spent a summer in a nearby villa (a medallion minted in his honour can be seen in the Piazza). The mineral springs of Casamicciola are particularly potent—*Rita* and *Gurgitello* rate as the hottest—and contain large quantities of iodine.

Casamicciola, spread out under its pines, is more a conglomeration of hotels than a proper town, although there is a centre at the Piazza Marina with shops, car-hire firms, banks and the AVET tourist information office (tel. (081) 994441). Besides the Lido, there are beaches at Suorangela and Castagna. The heliport lies just west of the town.

From the Piazza Marina, an hour's walk will take you to the **Geophysical Observatory,** built in 1891, while a half-hour's walk along the coast leads you to Lacco Ameno, another large resort which is currently very fashionable. Dominating the beach is the famous **Fungho** (mushroom rock). In the centre of town is the bright pink **Sanctuary of Santa Restituta,** patron saint of Ischia. Martyred in the 3rd century, her body was thrown into the sea, then floated ashore at Lacco Ameno. The oldest part of the Sanctuary dates from 1036, and was constructed on the site of an early Christian basilica. Excavations in the church crypt have produced evidence of Roman baths. Greek and Roman tools and vases have also been discovered west of Lacco Ameno at Monte Vico and behind the town on Fundera plain. Some of these may be seen in the **Museum** (open mornings only) near the church and the Pompeian Terme Regina Isabella, connected to the luxury hotel in Piazza Santa Restituta.

For the hardy, there is a charming country path, the **Calata Sant'Antonio,** leading from Lacco Ameno (off Via Roma) to the Chiesa dell'Immacolata in Casamicciola. Peasants once herded their goats home along this path every evening.

Nearby beaches include the Lido, Varuli and San Montano (the prettiest).

Forio

Forio, the wine-producing centre of Ischia and a growing resort, is one of the prettiest towns on the island and supports a small art colony. Forio has three outstanding landmarks, the first of which is the huge tower known as the **Torrione,** built by King Ferrante in 1480 on the site of an even older tower. It did little, however, to defend the island from pirate raids and was later converted to a prison, and nowadays is a gallery of local art. Near it rises the dome of **Santa Maria di Loreto,** a fine baroque church built in the 14th century; the two towers are decorated with majolica tiles. On the point furthest west stands the white **Church of the Soccorso,** to whom the local fishermen pray for help, as can be seen from the numerous votive offerings inside.

Behind Forio there are several paths leading up into the hills, towards Monterone, Sant'Antuono and Santa Maria del Monte, below Monte Epomeo. There are beaches on either side of Forio, along with the very popular Citara and Cava dell'Isola to the south, and at Ghiaia and San Francesco to the north. Near Citara are the **Gardens of Poseidon,** a recently-built complex of swimming pools set in a Mediterranean formal garden.

Sant'Angelo

From Forio, still heading counterclockwise, the SS270 passes through the hill village of Oanza and on to Serrara Fontana, both of which have roads leading down to Sant'Angelo. The buses to this lovely fishing port stop at the top of the hill because there isn't enough room for them to turn around in Sant'Angelo itself. The walk down at the edge of the cliff is quite lovely, with numerous views of the **Punta Sant'Angelo,** a small islet connected to Ischia by a narrow isthmus of sand. Only a stump remains of the Torre Sant'Angelo which once stood on top.

East of the village stretches the lovely beach of Maronti, which you can reach either by taking the path or by hiring a boat. The path runs past numerous fumaroles, hissing and steaming, and the beach itself has patches of scalding hot sand where you can wrap your picnic lunch in foil and cook it, if you so wish. Above the beach are the hot springs of **Cavascura,** at the mouth of an old river canyon; the sheer sides of the canyon, the little wooden bridges and the individual baths carved in the rock—each named for a mythological deity—make it an unusual place indeed.

Monte Epomeo

From Serrara Fontana the road towards Barano is most picturesque, winding its way around the inner valleys of Monte Epomeo (2600 ft). If you're going by bus, stop off at **Fontana,** where you can start your climb up to the old volcano itself—it hasn't erupted since 1302. Mules may be hired if you're not up to the climb yourself, and there's a hermitage where you can spend the night, located in the very crater itself. Watching the sun rise or set from such vantage points is always memorable, but with the entire Bay of Naples spread out below you it is sublime.

The next village along the route is Buonopane (the name means 'good bread'), followed by **Barano.** Barano has many of Ischia's hotels, actually on Maronti beach, some with thermal facilities. The town itself is a relaxed, quiet place compared with the rest of exuberant Ischia. In the Piazza San Rocco, in the centre of town, the church of the same name has a characteristic campanile. The road from here to Ischia Ponte passes scattered homes and summer villas, half-hidden in the lush vegetation and pine trees.

SPECIALITIES

Wines: *Epomeo* (red or white), *Ischia* (red or white) and *Biancolella.* Also: rabbit stew.

FESTIVALS

There is a film festival 'Angelo Rizzoli' in May at the Porto and at Lacco

Amero, and wine festivals in September. During the festival of Sant'Anna (end July), near the castle, you can see the island's traditional dance, the *ndrezzata*, a ritualistic dagger dance dating from the time of Vittoria Colonna, accompanied by clarinets and tambours. Santa Restituta (17 May), patron saint of Ischia, is celebrated on Monte Vico and Lacco Ameno, with fireworks, etc.

GETTING TO AND AROUND ISCHIA

The boats from Naples are all clustered around the Molo Beverello in the centre of the port. You can simply look at the timetables of the various companies and board the next ferry. They go so often, especially in the summer, that the wait is never long. The ferryboats take about 1½ hours to reach Ischia; the numerous hydrofoils take 30 to 40 minutes. Caremar hydrofoils depart from the Molo Beverello, others from the Mergellina (Via Caracciolo) a few miles away. Steamer fares from Naples are around 3000 lire; hydrofoil 6700 lire. Caremar also offers 4 daily connections between Procida and Pozzuoli and Ischia (but not between Capri and Ischia); in the summer Aliscafi SNAV runs a hydrofoil service between Anzio, Ponza, Ischia and Capri.

Buses to the various towns on the island depart from the square next to Santa Maria di Portosalvo, near the beginning of SS270 which encircles Ischia. The service (SEPSA) is very good to all parts, but be prepared to put up with crowded buses from June onwards. Another form of transport, three-wheeled, canopied mini-taxis, queue near the baths.

TOURIST INFORMATION

AAST, at Via Iasolino (tel. (081)991146).

WHERE TO STAY

In Ischia Porto

The finest hotel in the town is the **Excelsior Belvedere****** on Via E. Gianturco 3 (tel. (081) 991020), open from April until October. Not only is it quieter than most, but guests can enjoy the fine pool and garden; rates are 72–82 000 lire for a single room, 110–170 000 for a double. A pleasant, moderately priced small hotel with a thermal bath is the **Felix Hotel Terme***** on Via A. de Luca 60 (tel. (081) 991201); open from May to October, its rates are 25 500–33 000 lire for a single room 37–44 000 for a double. Near the beach and in the same price category, the **Villa Paradiso**** on Via R. Gianturco (tel. (081) 991169) is more intimate.

The least expensive place to stay is near the Castello Aragonese and is open all year: **Il Monasterio** (P3; tel. (081) 992435); here you can get a single room for 13 000 lire and a double for 17 500; the showers are usually hot.

Around Ischia

It would take pages to list all the hotels on Ischia; most of those outside Ischia Porto are in Forio, Lacco Ameno, Casamicciola, Barano and Sant'Angelo, and almost all close in the winter months. Many hotels in Forio are connected to thermal establishments, like the modern **Punta del Sole***, on Via R.G. Maltese (tel. (081) 998208), with a pool and garden (single 32 000 lire, double 45 000). For something less expensive, the **San Francesco****, on Via T. Cigliano in nearby San Francesco, has similar facilities but no thermal baths; 10 000 lire for a single room, 16 000 double, all with shower.

In Lacco Ameno, **San Montano***** on Via Monte Vico, is a hotel that offers—in addition to thermal baths—a pool, tennis courts and many other comforts (tel. (081) 994033; single 81 000 lire, doubles around 150 000. A bargain—by Ischia standards—is the **Bristol****, at Via Fundera 46 in Lacco Ameno (tel. (081) 994566), with a small garden and swimming pool (single room with bath 17 000 lire, double 25 000).

In Casamicciola prices tend to be a little lower. There's the **Ibsen,***** with a pool and thermal bath on the Corso V. Emanuele (tel. (081) 994588; single room 22 000 lire, double 35 000), with special facilities for the handicapped. Less expensive **Delle Rose** (P3), Via Casa Mennella 9 (tel. (081) 994082) has no rooms with private bath but makes up for it with charm and a swimming pool (rates 14 000 lire for a single room, 24 000 for a double).

Most of the hotels in Barano are on Maronti beach, like the moderately priced **Helios**** (tel. (081) 990001; single room with bath 28 000 lire in the summer, double 41 000). In Sant'Angelo, the **Romantica Terme** on Via Ruffano (tel. (081) 999216) is good value, near the sea, with a pool, tennis courts and spa for 14–20 000 lire for a single room, double 20–33 000.

EATING OUT

In Ischia Porto

Prices on Ischia tend to be high, and many people eat in their hotels. For fish the best place to look is along the Via Porto; one that's exceptionally good here is **Portucciullo,** which is fairly expensive (30 000 lire a meal). Less costly, at 66 Via Porto, is **Gennaro,** open from April until October, and **Da Ciccio,** at Via Porto 1, specialising in *risotto alla pescatore*. There are also many snack bars and pizzerias that save the pocket of budget

travellers—but again, you'll pay more at these than elsewhere in Italy. One
is the **Pizzeria Romana** at 6 Via Alfredo da Luca.

Around Ischia

On San Francesco Beach near Forio, **La Meridiana** specialises in various
lobster dishes at around 30 000 lire for an average meal. Less expensive is
La Giara at 40 Via Marina. In Lacco Ameno is the **Padrone d'o Mare,**
open all year round and specialising in various fish dishes for around 27 000
lire; here too is the **Pizzeria da Vito Marie,** on Il Tenne, which is good,
and less expensive. In Casamicciola is the **Trattoria Nizzola** on Via Piccola
Sentinelle, where you can eat well for around 20 000 lire; in Sant'Angelo
the best eating place is **Dal Pescatore** on the Piazza Troia, open from
March to October, with good fish, as its name suggests, for around 25 000
lire.

Procida

HISTORY

Only a few miles from the mainland and Monte Procida itself, Procida the
island was near enough to Naples to have a minor, or at least a spectator's
role in many of the turbulent events that transpired there, but far enough
away to stay out of trouble. Like Ischia, to which it was once connected, Procida (anciently *Prochyta*) was inhabited in the Neolithic period. The Romans
used the island as a hunting reserve, and there was an early agricultural
settlement there—Pope Gregory the Great wrote a letter in the 6th century
praising the wine of Procida. Shortly thereafter the first chapel of San
Michele Arcangelo was erected on Punta Lingua, on the site where a statue
of the saint stood; according to legend, during a pirate attack the people
prayed fervently to the statue for deliverance, and the saint responded and
saved his beloved Procida at least this once.

In the 11th century a Benedictine abbey was founded by the chapel, and
the fortifications of the *Terra Murata* ('the walled land') were begun. These
proved insufficient against the ravages of first Barbarossa (1544), then
Dragut (1562) and Bolla (1572). After Barbarossa burned the church, the
fishermen had to donate a third of their income to reconstruct it—Pope
Julius III generously decreed they could fish on Sundays and holidays as
well for ten years to make ends meet, permission which was extended for fifteen more years after Dragut. By then, however, the Benedictines had long
abandoned Procida.

The Bourbon kings, like the Romans before them, often came to Procida
to hunt; Fernando IV made the island and its town a royal domain, but

turned its fortress into a prison. In 1811–12 the French poet Alphonse Lamartine visited the island; when he went, he left behind him a native girl who loved him, the story of whom can be read in his novel *Graziella*.

Another famous personage connected with the island was so fond of it that he incorporated it in his name, becoming John of Procida. Born in 1210 in Salerno, this nobleman, a good friend of Emperor Frederick 'Stupor Mundi' and his son Manfred, had a castle on the island which he visited often, as it belonged to his domains. When Charles of Anjou, a Guelph, took Naples, he confiscated all of the property of Ghibelines like John of Procida, and the latter was forced to flee to Spain. Here Constance, the last of the Swabians and wife of King Peter of Aragon, received him well and made him Baron of Valencia.

But John of Procida got his revenge on Charles of Anjou. When the proud Sicilians began to chafe under the harsh rule of the French, John acted as a middleman to assure them that should they rise up in arms, Peter of Aragon would support their cause and be their king. The Sicilian Vespers resulted, and some 8000 Frenchmen died in that island's spontaneous combustion.

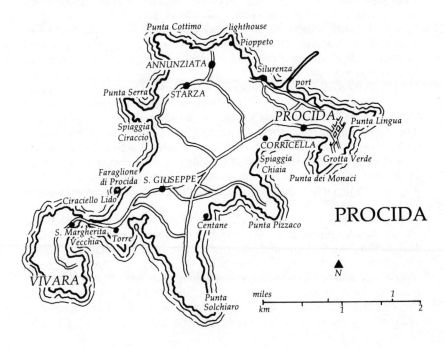

The French were at least symbolically revenged on John of Procida. When they occupied Procida in 1806 during the Napoleonic Wars—about 650 years after the Sicilian Vespers—they destroyed his marble coat-of-arms, the last reminder of his presence on the island.

WHAT TO SEE

Procida today, close as it is to Naples and Ischia, has surprisingly few tourists, perhaps because the islanders have chosen not to court them—which only adds to its charm.

Procida is the island of lemon groves, said to be among the best in Italy, as well as vineyards and artichokes. Connected to it by a modern bridge, the islet of Vivara has been declared a natural park of Naples, and teems with wild rabbits, an important ingredient in Procida's cuisine. Many still make their living from the sea, not only by fishing but also by carving exquisite models of historic ships. Life on Procida thus remains much the same as in the past, outside the tourist mainstream that has engulfed Ischia and Capri.

The port and surroundings

Ships and hydrofoils call at the port, divided into the **Marina Grande** and the **Marina di San Cattolico** (known locally as *Sent'Co*).

Near the port is the Church of Santa Maria della Pieta, built in 1760. This gives you a taste of Procida's architecture—wide arches, moulded lines and fading colours. For the best examples of this, follow the signs up the hill to Corricella.

Corricella is the oldest village on the island, founded by fishermen under the walls of the Abbey of San Michele. Steep stone stairways give it a pleasing slope-effect. The arches are like a hundred watchful eyes, scanning the sea for the fishermen's return. Here is a simple church, San Rocco, restored numerous times throughout the centuries; Via San Rocco leads to the Piazza dei Martiri where twelve Procidanese were executed in 1799 by the Bourbons for political reasons. Near the Piazza is the domed church of Madonna delle Grazie, built in 1700, containing a much-loved statue of the Virgin.

The Via Madonna delle Grazie leads to the **Terra Murata** and the Abbey, passing on the right the very picturesque roofless ruins of Santa Margherita Nuova, built in 1586 at the edge of the Punta dei Monaci. (Below here, the **Grotta Verde**—'green cave'—can be entered by small boats.) The fortifications of the citadel belong to different dates; the oldest walls may be seen near the **Porta Mezz'Olmo,** at the beginning of the Via San Michele. The walls and the ditch dug around them were finished in 1521. Rising above the walls, houses and prison of Terra Murata are the three domes of the **Church of San Michele Arcangelo,** with a rather Saracen look about it from a distance. Close to, though, its yellow facade is very simple, rebuilt after the various pirates' depredations. Of the original pre-16th-century structure, only part of the ceiling in the Sala del Capitolo remains. Many rich works of art in the three-naved church itself attest to the former splendour of the monastery; the paintings on the ceiling date from the 17th century, as do the apse paintings by Nicola Rosso, the most interesting of which shows the Archangel and his *putti* swooping down to save Procida from the Turks.

In the Piazza d'Armi is the **Castello d'Aragona,** so named for the Cardinal of Aragon who had it built in 1563, along with parts of the walls, in which are crammed tortuous alleyways and steep narrow houses. Other old palaces may be seen along the escarpment over Chiaia beach—including the *Palazzo Minichini,* on **Via Marcello** Scotti, adjacent to the fine old church of San Tommaso d'Aquino.

Across Procida

North of Marina Grande is the quarter known as Annunziata, after the old **Chiesa dell'Annunziata,** reconstructed in 1600 and containing a miraculous Madonna, to whom are given the many, varied votive offerings that adorn the interior of the church. There are pretty views from here of Punta Pioppeto and the lighthouse where people often come for a swim. Nearby stands the only remaining **watchtower** of the original three constructed in the 16th century. From Punta Cottimo you can see the island of Ventotene, geologically related to Procida.

The rest of the island has many rural beauty spots, shaded walkways and narrow roads, old farmhouses and crumbling small palazzi, such as that of John of Procida on Via Giovanni da Procida. The areas around Centane and Punta Solchiaro are most typical, and offer many views.

On the other side of the island, the long stretch of sand between Punta Serra and the peninsula of Santa Margherita Vecchia has been divided into three beaches—**Spiaggia Ciraccio,** where two Roman tombs were discovered; **Spiaggia Ciraciello,** on the other side of the pyramid-shaped rock, *Il Faraglione di Procida*; and towards the peninsula, the **Lido.** The hillock on the peninsula is capped by the tower-like ruin of the church of Santa Margherita Vecchia; on the other side of it lies the small fishing port and beach **Chiaiolella,** the bus terminus.

From here you can cross the new bridge to the islet of **Vivara,** where the birds are protected these days but the rabbits are fair game. Here were discovered the Neolithic implements (at Capitello and Punta di Mezzodi) now in Ischia's museum. A narrow road leads towards the summit of Vivara, through the crumbling arch of an old hunting lodge, to the **Belvedere,** with fine panoramas of Procida and Pozzuoli on the mainland.

FESTIVALS
Famous Good Friday processions of the *Misteri* (figures from Christ's Passion), borne along by men in blue and white costumes. San Michele (29 September), patron saint; farmers deliver offerings to the saint at Terra Murata. The island's beauty contest (August) at which the islanders elect the annual 'Graziella'.

GETTING TO PROCIDA
Caremar runs 4 ferries daily from Naples to Procida from the Molo Beverello, taking a little over 1 hour; other connections are between Ischia and Pozzuoli. There are also at least 4 hydrofoils daily from Naples to Procida, a trip that takes 30 minutes.

The public bus system on the island is good; one departs from the port to Chiaiolella to coincide with the arrival of each ferry.

WHERE TO STAY
The only hotel open all year round on Procida is **L'Oasi**** at Ciraccio (tel. (081) 896 7499; single room 26 000 lire, double 37 000), a villa with a restaurant and garden. Others include the **Arcate**** (open April–October) on the beach in Chiaia (tel. (081) 896 7120; single room with bath 32 000 lire, double 44 000) and the **Riviera****, in Chiaiolella, which has fine views (tel. (081) 896 7197; single room 22 000 lire with bath, double 34 000). If these hotels are full, you'll have to find a private house with rooms, or resort to the campsite at Punta Serra.

EATING OUT
There are several fairly inexpensive restaurants along the port, like **La Medusa,** with dinner around 10 000 lire. Other good ones are **Crescenzo** at 28 Via Marina in Chiaiolella and the **Lido Conchigla** on the beach at Chiaia, both specialising in seafood for around 20–25 000 lire.

Capri

There are various schools of thought on the etymology of the island's name. The belief that it came from the Latin word for goat (*capra*) is now in disfavour; those who think it derived from the Greek *kapros* (boar) have fossils to back them up. Yet another group maintains that it comes from an ancient

Tyrrhenian (Etruscan) word meaning 'rocky' (*capr*—) as evidenced by the many other places that begin with this suffix, such as Caprera (an island off Sardinia), Cabrera (off Majorca) and Caprara in the Tremiti Islands, to name just a few. It is the first syllable that is emphasised in the pronunciation of Capri—CAPri, not CapRI, like the car.

HISTORY
Some time in the Quaternary Period Capri broke away from the Sorrentine peninsula, taking with it elephants and tigers, as we have learnt from the remains discovered by Ignazio Cerio at the beginning of this century. Other finds have dated the first inhabitants back to the Paleolithic Era. A strong tradition associates the island with the Sirens of *The Odyssey*, and with the mysterious Teleboeans from the Greek island of Kephalonia, led by their King Telon. Neolithic ceramic-ware decorated with red bands, first found on the island, has since been designated the 'Capri style'.

Little is known of Capri at the time when Augustus arrived, except that it was still very Greek and that a dying ilex (holm oak) suddenly revived and sprouted new leaves. The Emperor thought this was a good portent, and he traded Ischia to Naples for Capri and made the island one of his retreats, reputedly building as many as twelve sumptuous palaces. Life must have been good on Capri; at one point Augustus called it *Apragopolis*, or 'Lubberland', as Robert Graves translates Suetonius' 'land of lay-abouts'.

Augustus was succeeded by his step-son Tiberius, whose exploits reported by the same Suetonius gave Capri much of its early notoriety. The Roman writer turned the island into a dirty old man's dream come true, with Tiberius hurling his victims off the cliffs to add a touch of reality. Although scholars have now discredited Suetonius' fictions, that imaginative writer's images of sexual acrobats dressing up as nymphs and frolicking in Tiberius' gardens, along with the anthropophagous Sirens singing seductive songs on the sea shore, have permeated the Capri legends.

In reality, Tiberius made Capri the capital of the Roman Empire between AD 27 and 37. The sheer cliffs made it into a natural citadel, from where the ageing Emperor could conduct (or neglect) the affairs of state as he pleased. Here he nurtured the future Emperor Caligula.

After the death of Tiberius, Capri is occasionally mentioned as a place of exile. Then the Benedictine friars arrived and built chapels on the island, and of course it suffered the usual ravages of Saracens and pirates. In 1371 a Carthusian monastery (La Certosa) was founded on Capri, on land granted by the Angevins, whom the Capriots favoured over the Aragonese until 1442 when they rather capriciously changed sides. A plague in 1656 left the island all but abandoned; only the Carthusians stayed behind, safe inside the walls of La Certosa, picking up the titles to land that had no owners and becoming quite wealthy (and unpopular) in the process.

In 1806, Hudson Lowe was commander of the English garrison on Capri; he's the man who was quartered in Napoleon's house in Ajaccio when the English were occupying Corsica and who later became Napoleon's jailer on St Helena. He fortified the island, turning it into 'a little Gibraltar', but he still managed to lose it to the French in 1808—a 'discreditable Lowe business' according to Norman Douglas, the English novelist and expatriate. (Incidentally, anyone contemplating an extended stay on Capri should read Norman Douglas' books, for they are part of the Capri legend, and very witty.)

The last chapter of the island's history began with the 'discovery' of the Blue Grotto by a German artist called Kopisch in 1826; he swam into it 'by accident'. Perhaps it was just a coincidence that Kopisch's discovery followed the landslide that had covered the entrance of another lovelier cave. Anyway, the magic of the name, Blue Grotto of Capri, proved irresistible, and the Capriots converted their fishing boats into excursion boats to take tourists to the cave, while farmers sold their land and built hotels.

WHAT TO SEE

Capri today is nevertheless an enchanting place. With more than 800 species of plant, it is very much a garden perched on a rugged chunk of limestone. Unlike Ischia and other, more recent, tourist haunts, Capri has the relaxed air of having seen it all. No room remains for property speculators. Everything has been built and planted; the tourists come and go every day and night, and they seem to be invisible to the Capriots and other residents who have learned to turn a blind eye to them, since the space they occupy will be filled next day by another anonymous camera-clutching tourist. Beware that from June until September the island tends to be so crowded that it's literally standing room only, and you begin to understand why the word 'trash' is inscribed on the bins in 30 different languages. However, if you don't mind all the trendy shops being closed, try going in November or February, when you may be lucky to arrive for a few brilliant days between the rains, and have this Garden of Eden practically to yourself. It's worth the risk of a soaking or two.

But first you have to leave the port, **Marina Grande,** where all the boats from Naples and elsewhere call (most pleasure boats anchor in the Marina Piccola on the other side of the island). Here in the Marina Grande, Capri's economic dependence on tourism is at its most evident; it is little more than a commercialised station platform.

From here you can take the *funivia* (cablecar) up to the town of Capri (it

76

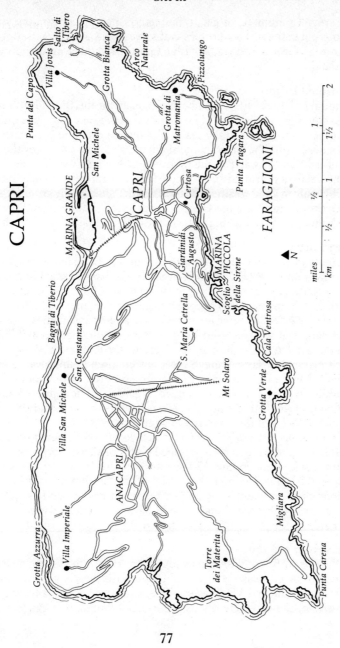

CAPRI

runs every 15 minutes) or catch the bus to Anacapri, or hire one of those glorious old bath-tub convertibles that serve as the island's taxis, or board a boat for the Grotta Azzurra (the Blue Grotto) and other excursions around the island.

The Blue Grotto

In summer (1 June–30 September), the boats for the Blue Grotto leave at 9am—when the sea is calm. The entrance to the Blue Grotto is quite low, and if there's any swell on the sea at all someone is sure to get a nasty knock on the head. Still, the sheer, magical blueness of it all, caused by the reflection of light on the water in the morning, makes it all worth while.

The excursion around the whole island is a rare experience, but again possible only in good weather. Besides visiting other lovely grottoes, such as the **Grotta Bianca** and the **Grotta Verde** (the White Cave and the Green Cave), there are breathtaking views of the cliffs and various rock formations.

Capri town

Gracie Fields may no longer be with us, but the charm of the lovely town of Capri lives on for ever. Megalithic walls at the base of some of the houses prove that the site has been occupied for at least 3000 years. Much of what is typical and 'home made' in Mediterranean architecture can be seen here in the older quarters of town—the moulded arches and domes, the narrow streets and stairways crossed by buttresses supporting the buildings, the ubiquitous whitewash, the play of light and shadow, and sudden beautiful little squares, just large enough for a few children to improvise a game of football. Most of the island's hotels are scattered throughout the town, generally very tasteful and surrounded by gardens. The supreme example is the famous **Quisisana,** a hotel whose register over the years is like a veritable Who's Who of the famous and pampered.

If you go up to Capri by *funivia,* you'll surface right next to the **Piazza Umberto** and the much photographed **Cathedral,** with its joyful campanile and clock. Built in the 17th century in the local baroque style, the Cathedral has a charming buttressed roof. In the church's shadow are the outdoor cafés frequented by such a variety of past eccentrics, dilettantes and celebrities that each chair should have a historical plaque on it. The other side of the piazza is a sheer drop down to Marina Grande.

Walks from the town

For the **post office** and for **buses to Anacapri,** take the Via Roma from the piazza; for the exclusive boutiques, head towards the Via Vittoria Emanuele to Via Camarelle and Via Tragara. The latter street eventually leads to the **Faraglioni,** the three enormous sheer-sided limestone rocks towering in

La Piazetta, Capri

the ever-blue sea. These rocks are home to the rare blue lizard (*Lacerta caerulea Faraglionensis*) and a rare species of seagull that supposedly guffaws. From Via Tragara a stairway descends to the point and the **Porto di Tragara,** where you can take a swim from the platforms beneath the vertical rocks.

Nearby is the Tragara Terrace, with magnificent views, and the tall skinny rock called **Pizzolungo.** Still following the main track along the coast and up the stairway, you will come upon the **Grotta di Matromania** (always open). The Romans worshipped the goddess Cybele in this cave; she was a fertility goddess also known as the *Mater Magna.* Part of Capri's reputation as an island of orgies may derive from this Roman cult's noisy hypnotic rituals, imported from the East. Only vestiges now remain of the once elaborate decor inside the cave.

From the Grotta di Matromania a stepped path leads down to yet another famous eroded rock: the **Arco Naturale,** where dark pines—as everywhere else on Capri—cling to every tiny ledge they can sink their roots into. On the way back to town you'll pass some of the island's vineyards that produce the rare and famous *Lachrimae Tiberii,* and, in the Piazza Cerio, the **Centro Caprense Ignazio Cerio,** with fossils and archaeological finds from Capri (open 10–12, Monday to Friday).

A shorter but equally enjoyable walk starting from the Piazza Umberto (take Via Vittorio Emanuele, which becomes Via F. Serena, then Via Matteotti) leads you to **La Certosa,** the Carthusian charterhouse founded in 1371 by Giacomo Arcucci (a member of a famous Capriot family) and suppressed in 1808. Built over one of Tiberius' villas, the golden-hued church and cloisters are very pleasing, topped by a baroque tower added in the 17th century. La Certosa, with its collection of paintings from the 17th to 19th centuries, is open daily from 9 until 2, closed Mondays (admittance free).

A few minutes away from La Certosa are the **Gardens of Augustus**—they were indeed founded by Caesar. A wide variety of trees and plants grow on the fertile terraces and belvederes overlooking one of the most striking views in the world. A narrow road (Via Krupp, built by the arms manufacturer, who also studied lamprey larvae off the Salto di Tiberio) takes you down the cliffs in a hundred hairpin turns to the **Marina Piccola,** the charming little port with most of Capri's bathing establishments—Da Maria, La Canzione del Mare, Le Sirene and Internazionale (all but the last connected to restaurants). On one side are the ruins of a **Saracen tower;** on the other is the **Scoglio delle Sirene** (Sirens' Rock); if you read the books of Norman Douglas and Edwin Cerio, son of Ignazio Cerio the archaeologist, they will convince you that this really was the home of the Sirens. There is a bus, fortunately, that makes the steep climb back up the cliffs to Capri town.

A much longer but equally rewarding walk or drive is to the Villa Jovis (Via Botteghe to Via Tiberio) passing the **Church of Monte San Michele,** a fine example of local architecture, built in the 14th century. The **Villa Jovis** on Punta Lo Capo (1028 ft) was the most important of the twelve villas on Capri: from here Tiberius governed the Roman Empire for his last ten years. Although much has been sacked through the centuries, the extent of the remaining walls and foundations gives a fair idea of the grandeur of the former Imperial Palace. Near here, the **Faro,** or lighthouse, was believed to have been part of a system of semaphores through which messages were sent to Rome. The great sheer cliff beside the villa, the **Salto di Tiberio,** is always pointed out as the precipice from which the emperor hurled his victims—according to Suetonius. The view of the Bays of Salerno and Naples is as spectacular as any.

Towards Anacapri
On the north coast between Capri and Anacapri, the only other town on the island, are the so-called **Baths of Tiberius** and the meagre remains of Augustus' sea palace, the **Palazzo a Mare.** You can swim here at the establishment Bagni di Tiberio. Above here, on the escarpment of Anacapri, is carved the **Scala Fenicia,** in truth Greco-Roman in origin and for thousands of years the only way to reach the upper part of the island. Originally 800 in number, these steps have crumbled over the years and are impassable today. Near here, on the road from Marina Grande to Anacapri, lies the first

Christian church on the island, dedicated to patron saint **San Costanzo.** According to legend Costanzo was a bishop of Constantinople whose body, packed in a barrel, floated to Capri during the Iconoclasm in Greece. A church, with a reputation for defending the island from Saracens, was built for him over one of the Roman villas. Four ancient columns support the Byzantine dome of this 11th-century church, designed in the form of a Greek cross.

Anacapri

On top of the green plateau spreads the town of Anacapri (980 ft), once a fierce rival to Capri below, but since the building of the roads connecting them in 1874, the two towns have learned to reconcile their differences. Although it has its share of hotels, Anacapri retains a rustic air, with its many olive trees and vineyards surrounding it on all sides, and its simple style of architecture, rather Moorish in style with cubic, flat-roofed houses.

In Anacapri's Piazza San Nicola, the 18th-century **Church of San Michele** (open 10–6 April–October, 10–2 Sundays, admission fee) contains a magnificent mosaic floor of majolica tiles, by the Abrussian artist Leonardo Chiaiese. The design itself, showing Adam and Eve in the Garden of Eden, and their Expulsion, is by D. A. Vaccaro. The **Church of Santa Sofia** very near it, on the Piazza Diaz, was built in the Middle Ages, but remodelled in the baroque style.

From Piazza Vittoria a chairlift travels to the summit of **Monte Solaro,** the highest point on the island at 1920 ft. Also from Piazza Vittoria, take Via Orlandi to Via Capodimonte and the **Villa San Michele of Axel Munthe.** For the benefit of children of the post-war baby boom, the Swedish Axel Munthe (1857–1949) was one of the greatest physicians of his day, and a leader in the field of psychiatry. He was also an extremely generous man, donating his services to the victims of plagues, earthquakes and World War I. On Capri and elsewhere he established bird sanctuaries, and in 1929 he wrote his best-selling autobiography *The Story of San Michele* to which his villa owes most of its fame. The house contains Roman artefacts discovered on Capri (open daily, 9am until sunset; admission fee). Near here is the so-called **Castello di Barbarossa,** after the pirate captain who plagued the Mediterranean for so many years. These ruins date from the 8th and 9th centuries. Via Capodimonte continues through the valley of **Santa Maria a Cetrella,** another white church of local design. From the church the road goes to the top of Monte Solaro.

Another path from Piazza Vittoria (Via Caposcuro to Via Maigliara) skirts Monte Solaro, passing through the vineyards to the **Belvedere della Migliara,** from where you can see the Faraglioni and the entrance of the

Green Grotto. The bus leaves every hour in the summer for **Punta Carena** and its lighthouse at the southernmost tip of the island. The unusual arched doorways on the left belonged to the **Torre di Materita;** further on, over-looking the Cala del Tombosiello, is a ruined watchtower. Punta Carena is the most out-of-the-way place on the island for a quiet swim.

Another bus leaves from the piazza for the Grotta Azzurra and the bathing area adjacent to it, passing by way of the old windmill and the **Villa Imperiale,** another of the summer residences built by Augustus, known also as the 'Damecuta' for the tower next to it. After the Villa Jovis, this villa is the best preserved, and has recently been further excavated (open from 9am until one hour before sunset; closed Mondays).

FESTIVALS
Patron saint San Costanzo (14 May); swimming marathon to Naples (August); lively New Year's celebration.

SPECIALITIES
Capri wine (delicious and rare) and *Certosina* liqueur distilled from herbs.

GETTING TO AND AROUND CAPRI
Jet-setters may fly into Anacapri's heliport from Naples; the rest of us must rely on the ferries and hydrofoils. Minimum year round service: 6 Caremar or NLG ferries daily from Naples (1½ hours); 5 a day from Sorrento (35 minutes); 1 (NLG) from Castellammare (1¾ hours). From Naples, 3000 lire; from Sorrento, 2000 lire. Hydrofoils: 8 a day on the Aliscafi SNAV line from Molo Mergellina in Naples; 4 from Molo Beverello on Aliscafi Caremar (7000 lire); from Sorrento, Aliscafi Alivit has 4 services daily.

In the summer, you can catch a steamer or hydrofoil to Capri nearly every hour, from Naples or Sorrento. There are also daily hydrofoils from Amalfi and from Anzio, via Ponza and Ischia (3½ hours on Aliscafi SNAV).

Arriving in Marina Grande, you can ascend to either Capri or Anacapri by bus; after 10pm they run every half-hour. The funicular ascends to Capri town every 15 minutes from 6.35am until 10pm; the chairlift from Anacapri to Monte Solaro (a 12-minute trip) runs continuously from 9am to sunset. There are also buses from Anacapri to the Blue Grotto, Faro and Marina Piccola; and buses from Capri town to Damecuta and Marina Piccola. From June until September, there are daily tours of Capri by motor launch starting at 9am from Marina Grande.

TOURIST INFORMATION
AAST: Main office: Piazza I. Cerio 11, Capri (tel. (081) 837 0424).

Information offices: on the quay, Marina Grande (tel. (081) 837 0634).
Piazza Umberto L, Capri town (tel. (081) 837 0686).
Via G. Orlandi 19/A, Anacapri (tel. (081) 837 1524).

WHERE TO STAY

If you have the money, the smart place to stay on Capri is the sumptuous
Quisisana (L) in the middle of town on Via Camarelle (tel. (081) 837 0788);
open April–1 January, where a single room in the high season will set you
back some 180 000 lire, a double 250 000. For something less pricey and
boasting a wonderful view, there's **La Scalinatella****, on Via Tragara
(tel. (081) 837 0633; single room 60–79 000 lire, double 100–190 000).
Open all year, **La Floridana*****, Via Campo di Teste (tel. (081) 837 0101)
also has fine panoramas of the sea and single rooms 38 000–53 000 lire,
doubles 72 000–100 000. Less expensive, the **Villa Krupp**** (Via Matteoti; tel. (081) 837 0362) is also open all year round (single room without
bath 14 500 lire, double with bath 37–43 000 lire). For the record, the
Faraglioni (P3; Via Camerelle; tel. (081) 837 0320), opens from April to
October, and is the cheapest place to stay on Capri, with single rooms for
8500 lire, doubles for 14 000, without bath.

In Anacapri, **San Michele***** (Via G. Orlandi; tel. (081) 837 1427) is in
an elegant villa with wonderful views. Open all year round, rates are 25–
34 000 lire for a single room without bath, 34–48 000 with bath; double
room without bath 46–63 000, with bath 52–71 000. The **Bellavista**** (Via
G. Orlandi; tel. (081) 837 1463) has a fine view as well, and many facilities
for 21–33 000 lire single, 37–44 000 for a double room; open all year.

EATING OUT

In Capri prices are high, and if you want to eat reasonably you'll have to go
down to Marina Grande, where there are a number of pizzerias and trattorias. If money is no object, there's **La Pigna,** Via Roma 8 (closed Tuesdays),
with its huge pine trees, crowd of 'Beautiful People', splendid views and elegant cuisine for around 50 000 lire a meal. Also in the 'chic' zone, with
even higher prices, is **Faraglioni** on pretty Via Camerella 75, with delec-
table house specialities like *filetto alla Voronof*. **La Capannina,** Via delle
Botteghe 14, has long been a popular spot among visiting celebrities, with
seafood specialities. **Bagni Tiberio,** in Marina Grande, is more moderately
priced but very good, with dinners for around 35 000 lire. If you have your
heart set on tasting Capri's famous wine, try **Da Paolino** on Via Palazzo a
Mare 11 (35–40 000 lire).

In Anacapri, **Da Gelsomina la Migliera,** on Via Migliera 6, offers not
only homemade wine, but true homecooked island spcialities, including

mushrooms collected on Monte Solaro, for around 40 000 lire a person (closed Tuesdays). For something less costly, **Materita,** on Via G. Orlandi 140, has pizza and other trattoria specialities for 10–15 000 lire.

The Tremiti Islands

The four main Tremiti Islands—San Domino, San Nicola, Caprara and Pianosa—20 miles off the Gargano coast, are the extent of Italian territory in the Adriatic Sea; the uninhabited Pelagose Islands to the northeast now belong to Yugoslavia. Originally the name Tremiti referred only to San Nicola, and probably derives from *Tre Monti,* 'three mountains'—the three central islands of San Nicola and San Domino, both inhabited, and Caprara. The Tremiti Islands are also known as the *Isole Diomedes'* (Diomedes' islands) after the Achaean hero who fought so bravely at Troy while Achilles sulked in his tent. After the war, Diomedes discovered that Venus, who hated him and had sided with the Trojans, had made his wife Aegialea fall in love with another man and conspire against his life. Diomedes and his followers escaped just in time; they sailed to the Gargano coast, where he founded a new kingdom, *Daunia,* and marked its frontiers by hurling limestone boulders out into the sea—which, of course, are the Tremiti Islands today.

Venus, however, would not let Diomedes off so easily, and abruptly put all of his followers to death. Their spirits were transformed into birds, who still lament the cruelty of the goddess of love. The most common species of these still on the islands are the greater and lesser Berta (*Procellaria diomedea*), or puffins, whose cry is indeed very much like an infant's wail.

HISTORY
The Tremiti Islands were inhabited in the Neolithic era, around 4000 BC, leaving us clay pots and tools and evidence of a cemetery at Cala Tramontana, on San Domino. In Roman times, when that island was called *Teutria,* Caesar Augustus exiled his granddaughter Julia there for her adultery and promiscuity, just as he had had her mother Julia banished to Ventotene (Pontine Islands). Julia bore a child on San Domino, which the Emperor ordered to be exposed to the elements until it died, and 20 years later she herself died without ever seeing the mainland again. Popular legend has it, however, that she took advantage of her Nubian guard's infatuation for her, convincing him to build a raft and sail with her to a love-nest on the Italian shore. Mother Nature intervened and sank the boat, drowning the two of them off the coast at Vieste.

TREMITI ISLANDS

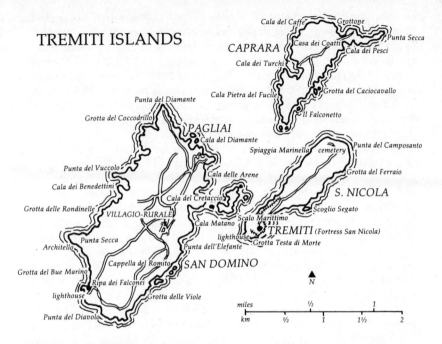

Another, stronger tradition tells of a hermit, perhaps named Nicola, who lived on San Nicola in the 4th century, when the island was deserted. In a vision, the Madonna showed Nicola where a great treasure lay and advised him to build a church with the money. He dilly-dallied so long that the Mother of God had to reappear and admonish him, but eventually he found the treasure and built the first chapel of Santa Maria a Mare.

In 786, Charlemagne's father-in-law Paolo Vinifrido was accused of conspiracy and exiled to the Tremiti Islands, minus his hands and eyes. He somehow managed to escape to Montecassino, the monastery founded by St Benedict. Perhaps he told them tales of his short stay, for in 1010 monks of this order founded a monastery on San Domino. When this larger island proved indefensible, they moved to nearby San Nicola (1045) and built their abbey near Nicola's humble church, which they rebuilt.

When the Normans invaded southern Italy and Sicily shortly afterwards, the feudal lords of the mainland stored their treasures in the monastery of San Nicola, increasing its already growing reputation of power and wealth. The monks owned vast tracts of land in Italy, not to mention rivers, castles, ports, salt mines and so on, with numerous rights and jurisdictions. They

85

became quite independent of Montecassino, and acquired notoriety for their licentious living. The Popes and Benedictine headquarters attempted to assert their authority over the monks (who were in league with the pirates) but failed; in the end it was the monks themselves who caused their own demise: when the debts from their high living came due, they were forced to sell their property and smuggle just to make ends meet. In 1194 leaders of the Fourth Crusade sacked the monastery, supposedly to punish the monks for their wickedness, and finally, after several Inquisitions into the monks' depravity, the monastery was dissolved in 1236.

The following year they were replaced by the Cistercians, a reformed order founded by Bernardo di Chiaravalle in 1112. The Benedictines had left enough behind for the Cistercians to prosper, and the 400 monks were self-sufficient. Among their works are many of the monastery's fortifications, as its fabulous reputation attracted pirates with some regularity. Eventually, in the mid 14th century, these corsairs forced the abandonment of San Nicola, either because the monks had had enough and left for the mainland, or, in another version, because they were all massacred when a pirate captain tricked them into believing he was dead and desired a Christian burial. The Cistercians dutifully complied, and during the night the captain rose from the grave and let in his men through the gate.

In 1412 another monastic order, little known outside Italy—the Lateranesi (or Lateran Canons), founded by San Frediano di Lucca and obeying the Mystic Rules of St Augustine—was sent by Pope Gregory XII to restore the monastery of San Nicola Tremiti. The few monks were not enthusiastic about their task, fearful of the pirates, but they obeyed and repaired the church and monastery. Although the Lateranesi started on a pious and humble path, like the monks before them they were soon cursed with riches donated by pilgrims and nobles attracted by their very saintliness. By 1465, however, the Abbot had requested and received the title of prince of Tremiti; in 1535 Pope Paul III allowed them to administer justice and use torture if necessary to promote it. Nevertheless the monks did well by the lay population, building a school and a hospital, as well as more fortifications, new cloisters, cisterns, and a watchtower on the then uninhabited San Domino.

The requirements of defending San Nicola put the monks into perpetual debt, although it must have seemed worth while when in 1567 the Sultan's fleet besieged the island for three days without success. The Lateranesi emerged victorious, but their fortunes rapidly declined. The monks took to smuggling, and their affairs were in such disorder that they lost many privileges. Things became so bad that they tried to sell their islands to Spain in 1574 and 1610 to pay back their debts. When they did succeed in selling them to a Florentine cardinal, the Spanish viceroys of Naples quickly stepped in with soldiers and imprisoned the Abbot. This, in turn, displeased the Republic of Venice, which didn't want the Spanish in the Adriatic, and the Spaniards were diplomatically persuaded to go home, leaving the monks back where they started—in deep debt.

In 1737 Charles III of Naples claimed the Tremiti Islands as his inheritance and garrisoned them. King Fernando IV went a step further in 1781, claiming for the crown all of the islands' property, thus ending the rule of the monastic orders on the islands. Instead Fernando initiated—what else?—a penal colony in the fortress, used to confine mainly political prisoners until the 1860 unification of Italy. In 1912, during the war in Libya, prisoners of war were brought to the islands, along with an epidemic of smallpox. The Fascists also sent their undesirables to San Nicola and San Domino.

Tremiti Islands today

People are no longer condemned for life on the little islands—they pay good money to go there, at least in the months of July and August. In the past decade over 100 000 people annually have visited San Domino and San Nicola, mostly on day trips. During the summer the native population of the islands is around 400; in winter 40 people hold the fort, and ships from Manfredonia are infrequent. Almost everyone makes a living from tourism. Still, the islands are practically unknown to most foreign visitors (which means you may have trouble communicating in English). The picture-postcard beauty of this tiny Adriatic archipelago is its main attraction—its incredibly blue sea, shady pine trees and unusual calcareous cliffs. The only beach on the islands, Cala delle Arene (on San Domino), becomes as crowded as a Japanese subway at rush hour in the summer, although many people do their sun-worshipping on the rocks.

San Nicola

Unlike the verdant paradise of its sister island, the third of a square mile that comprises San Nicola is covered with *macchia*, and green as it may be in the spring, without trees it seems desolate, like part of the Irish coast. The famous **fortress-monastery** of the three successive orders dominates it from all sides, from its most impressive angle, below the Torrione del Cavaliere it looks like a gaping-mouthed cyclops with antennae. Ships call at the port directly beneath it.

WHAT TO SEE

To visit the monastery—and the town—enter the **Porta Marina,** the gate in the outer series of walls, where the statue of Santa Maria a Mare once stood, and climb to the **Torre del Cavaliere del Crocefisso.** From the window over the gate here the monks and their defenders would pour boiling oil on the heads of their enemies. An inscription on the gate reads *Conteret et Confringet,* which translates roughly as 'Crush and Kill', hardly a Christian sentiment, referring to the rights granted to the Abbot of Tremiti by Pope Paul III to torture and kill heretics and other trouble-makers in the area.

A ramp from this tower leads up to another, the square **Torre del Pennello,** and to the main streets of San Nicola town, Via Diomede and Via Roma. Within the walls here you can see the small houses once inhabited by prisoners. Via Diomede ends in front of the 14th-century Cistercian fortifications; to the right is the **Torrione Angioino,** near the restaurant of the same name. Charles II of Anjou, married to the Queen of Naples, ordered it to be built in 1294 to defend the Kingdom's east coast from pirates.

The stairway continues up from here to another portico and the lovely octagonal **Cisterna della Meridiana,** which got its name from its orientation towards the four cardinal points. It is still used today to collct precious rainwater. The date on the stairs from here recalls the Bourbon reconstruction of the castle.

Still ascending, you arrive at the **Church of Santa Maria a Mare,** built by the Benedictines in 1045 on the site of the 4th-century chapel of the hermit Nicola, restored by the Lateranesi. Four statues, two of them headless, adorn the rather severe facade, and between them is an interesting relief of the Crowning of the Virgin. Note the walls of the church, pockmarked by cannon fire. Inside, the floor of the church still retains its original mosaics of birds and a griffon, along with a wooden ceiling. The centrepiece is the wooden statue of Santa Maria a Mare brought to the island by the Benedictines, but more interesting is the large Byzantine crucifix, *Il Cristo Grande,* in the right-hand chapel. This, according to legend, floated ashore in the 9th century from Greece. When the faithful attempted to carry it inside the church, they found that the door was too small and left it outside. When they returned the next day, they found that the crucifix had miraculously entered the church of its own accord, without enlarging the door. Whenever the monks tried to move it from the right-hand chapel, it always returned to its chosen place in the night, so they left it where it stands today.

On the right as you leave the church are the old cloisters, a finely made cistern restored by the Bourbons, and the rather grand **Dormitorio Nuovo,** built by the then wealthy Lateranesi monks. The huge tower near here, the **Torrione del Cavaliere di San Nicola,** is the highest, overlooking the rest of the island, its flat plain and one road. Directly below it is **La Tagliata,** a ditch dug by the monks, initiated by the Benedictines as a defensive fosse dividing the island in two. Near the Torrione the **Prigione** with its partially blocked windows, is where prisoners were held in solitary confinement. Some of their graffiti can still be seen on the walls.

From a gate in the Torrione the island's road passes across the **Prato Asinaro** (asses' meadow) to the decrepit cemetery at the far end of San Nicola. There is little of note along this lonely highway: a few pieces of an ancient sepulchre that once belonged to Diomedes, cisterns, and a modern, rather powerful iron crucifix with a little roof.

FESTIVAL
Religious celebrations for Assumption (15 August).

SPECIALITIES
Troccoli (homemade pasta dish), eggs with sea urchins, fish dishes, and *spaghetti alla pirata* (with lobster).

GETTING TO SAN NICOLA
To reach the numerous small ports that serve the Tremiti Islands is no mean task. The quickest way is to catch one of the infrequent flights to Pescara, then take the bus or train to Ortona, Vasto or Termoli for the hydrofoil. Or you can catch a more regular flight to Bari (from Milan or Rome), then take the bus or train to Manfredonia for the ferry. Trains to the Adriatic coast leave Venice, Milan and Rome several times a day.

Adriatica Lines run most of the steamers and hydrofoils to the Tremiti Islands; the islands themselves are linked by sea taxis. In the winter Manfredonia is the main port (5 hours), the steamer departing several times a week; there are also connections from Rodi Garganico which take only $1\frac{1}{2}$ hours. In the summer these departures are daily, and there are additional ones from the ports of Vieste (3 hours), Pugnochiuso (4 hours) and Peschici (2 hours). In the summer you can take a hydrofoil from Ortona (2 hours), Vasto (1 hour) and Termoli (45 minutes).

TOURIST INFORMATION
Information can be found at the Municipio (tel. (0882) 663002). While there are a post office, telephones (in Belvedere Bar), church and tourist office on San Nicola, the Tremiti Islands' only bank branch (open in summer) is on San Domino, in the Villagio Rurale.

WHERE TO STAY
There are no hotels on San Nicola; the Municipio has a list of rooms to let in private houses.

EATING OUT

San Nicola's restaurants cater mainly for the influx of trippers from San Domino; there are good moderately priced meals at **La Conchiglia** on Via Roma, **Al Torrione** at 74 Via Marconi, and **Bella Ida** on Via Roma. Average prices are 15–20 000 lire.

San Domino

San Domino's name is believed to derive from a misspelling of San Doimo, a saint from Spalato (modern Split). Although it is the largest, most luxuriant island in the group, its indefensible position condemned it to be uninhabited throughout most of history. In 1935 the government built the little rose-coloured **Villagio Rurale** to encourage agriculture on the island, and these houses are the oldest buildings on San Domino apart from the dilapidated ruins of Cappella del Romito, built by a 13th-century hermit called Pietro Polono.

WHAT TO SEE

The tourist brochures are right to call San Domino 'the pearl of the Adriatic'. With its marvellous coastline of cliffs and jutting rocks, penetrated by grottoes, the island is covered with lush greenery and pine bosques, a far cry from the rugged, sparsely vegetated isles surrounding it, such as the Isola Cretaccio stuck between San Domino and San Nicola.

Perhaps unfortunately for San Domino, its small size and compact beauties make it ideal for day-trippers to explore, either by boat or on foot (there are also little 'buses' that go up and down the one-mile-long stretch of road). Punta del Diamante, the northernmost tip, may perhaps have acquired its name from the hard shiny rocks. A rather unhappily sited electricity plant sits at the end of the point, overlooking a group of pyramid-shaped rocks in the sea, **I Pagliai** (*pagliai* is the Italian word for the traditional hayricks).

To the southeast, many of the island's tourist facilities and restaurants are concentrated around its one beach, **Cala delle Arene,** although many prefer to swim off the shady rocks at **Cala Matano,** just to the south by the Eden Hotel and the Villagio Rurale. From here you can take the Strada Comunale past the lighthouse, then find your own way up to the **Cappella del Romito,** the highest point of the island (280 ft).

Continuing generally south along the coast are the **Punta dell' Elefante** that looks like an elephant drinking the sea; the violet-coloured **Grotta delle Viole;** and the **Grotto delle Murene** where sea eels are said to breed. The often devilish sea off the **Punta del Diavolo** earned it its name.

The most spectacular feature on the island, the 250-ft crag known as the **Ripa dei Falconei,** and the deep **Grotta del Bue Marino** beneath it, may seem vaguely familiar to many—the film, *The Guns of Navarone,* used it as a backdrop. In the Middle Ages San Domino was famous for its peregrine and Elanora falcons, which brave souls would steal from the nests on top of the crag to train for the genteel sport of falconry. Although the falcons are now protected, they are rare, but still nest on top of the Ripa.

The Grotta del Bue Marino, named for the almost extinct Mediterranean seals that once lived there, is the largest cave on San Domino, more than 150 ft long. If you go in by boat, be sure to take a torch to see all the rock formations and the entrance to a narrow passageway, said to lead to the Cappella del Romito, perhaps used by pirates when the monks occupied the island.

North along the coast is the unusually barren **Punta Secca** and the natural arch, the **Architello.** Above the Cala die Benedettini is a cistern built by the monks during their brief stay on San Domino in the 11th century. You have to look hard at the **Grotto del Coccodrillo** to see the crocodile.

GETTING AROUND
See San Nicola.

WHERE TO STAY
The plushest place to stay on San Domino is the **Kyrie***,** at Vuccolo (tel. (0882) 663055), with showers in every room for 50–95 000 lire single, 80–155 000 lire for a double; facilities include a pool, tennis courts and sailing. Far more reasonable and with shower in every room is **Gabbiano*,** at Belvedere (tel. (0882) 663044), with pleasant single rooms for 10–20 000, double 18–44 000, open all year. In between, there's the comfortable **San Domino***,** at Cameroni (tel. (0882)663027; 25 rooms, single 30–37 000, double 42–54 000). The last two hotels are open all year round, but for all accommodation reserve early for the summer months.

There is one campsite, near Punta del Diamante, with room for 800 tents (tel. (0883) 663034). It is connected to the Tourist Village Internazionale, and rents out tents if you don't bring your own.

EATING OUT
La Livornese in the Cala delle Arene, and **Trattoria del Pesce** on Via

Diomede (the former more expensive at 20–30 000 lire per person) are very good, specialising in local fish dishes. Less expensive is the **Rosticceria Martella,** with good pizzas for 8 000 lire.

Pianosa and Caprara

Of the other two Tremiti Islands, Pianosa is a low, very flat island 11 miles northeast of San Nicola. Uninhabited, the few shelters on its coast are used by Italian and Yugoslav fishermen on overnight trips. Caprara, north of San Nicola and the same area as that island, is inhabited mainly by wild rabbits, who live in the brush. Near the lighthouse is an enormous natural arch, **L'Architiello,** grander than the one on San Domino, and the lovely **Grottone,** almost 100 ft high at its mouth. Small boats can anchor in the **Cala dei Turchi,** as the Sultan's fleet did during its unsuccessful siege of San Nicola. From here a path leads up to the pretty lighthouse and the long abandoned Casa dei Coatti, a building used when Caprara was cultivated. Caprara's name comes from the capers (*capperaia*) which still grow wild there.

Part III

SICILY

Archaeological Ruins at Tindari, Sicily

On the map, Sicily, the largest island in the Mediterranean, lies southwest of the Italian 'toe' which seems ready to give the island a smart kick up to Sardinia. The narrow Strait of Messina separates it from the mainland, and since the monsters Scylla and Charybdis no longer inhabit its waters, having been subdued by a great earthquake, a strong swimmer can easily swim to Sicily. Why, it hardly qualifies as an island, you might say, but you'll be wrong. For thousands of years, Sicily has had its own history, civilisations, kings and language. The Sicilians and their customs are so distinct that mainland Italians speak of them as another race—as indeed the Sicilians consider themselves to be.

One of the names given to Sicily by the Greeks was *Trinacria* (the word means 'three-cornered', referring to the three headlands). Its modern name derives from one of the island's earliest peoples, the Sikels. Mount Etna, the highest volcano in Europe, is the outstanding geographical feature of the island, and its lava has made the soil of Sicily rich—inexhaustibly rich,

93

thought the Arabs, who called it Paradise. Along with Etna, most of Sicily's other mountains are in the eastern half—Nebrodi, Peloritani and Iblean, the main ranges—with the highest, the Madonie, in the north central part of the island. Sicily's main rivers, some navigable in ancient times, have since filled with silt from careless farming and irrigation practices. Forests that once covered the island fell prey to ancient shipbuilders, and now cover less than 0.75% of the total land area.

Sicily is still incredibly fertile; any building over 100 years old is likely to have plants sprouting out of it. The best months to visit the island are March and April, when the spring goddess Persephone, who was abducted into the underworld near Lake Pergusa, returns to Sicily, strewing it with wild flowers of every imaginable hue. Summers tend to be long and hot, leaving the wheatfields on the plains as brown as the tourists on the beaches. In September the grapes are harvested and crushed into wine. The olives come later, at the beginning of the mild but wet winter. In February many parts of Sicily are adorned with the frilly lace of almond blossoms.

Tourism is only a sideline on this rich and colourful island; few people outside hotels speak English, although they are always ready to interpret your sign language and pidgin Italian, to help you out. If you go to a small, seldom-frequented village, you will be the event of the day. Resorts and sights that attract an international crowd have very distinct boundaries— easy to find and easy to escape, whatever your preference.

There are a few things that the first-timer to Sicily won't want to miss— such as smouldering Mount Etna, with views of the entire island and of Malta from its summit; history-rich Syracuse, once the greatest city in the western world; Palermo, with its Norman churches full of magnificent mosaics; the Valley of the Temples in Agrigento, with some of the best Greek temples in existence; and Piazza Armerina, the medieval hill town, where an Imperial Roman villa with an incredible mosaic floor is still being excavated.

History

PREHISTORY

Old as the Mediterranean is in human history, in geological terms it is a newcomer and still undergoing change, with volcanic eruptions, earthquakes and the like. The island of Sicily was once connected to North Africa on the mainland, but it became separated in the Tertiary Period, long before the coming of the first peoples, who are believed to have crossed the Strait of Messina in the Upper (or Advanced) Palaeolithic Period, around 20 000 BC. Inhabiting mostly the coastal areas, these Stone Age peoples

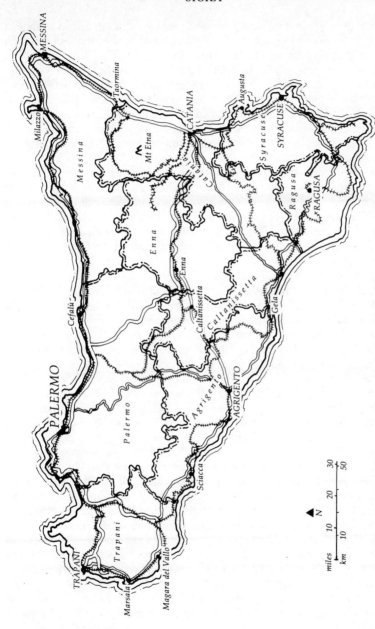

SICILY: PROVINCES, MAIN TOWNS AND RAILWAYS

have left us not only their simple tools but also beautiful incised drawings in the caves of Monte Pellegrino near Palermo and on the island of Levanzo which was connected with Sicily at the time.

Sometime around 4000–3000 BC, influences from the eastern Mediterranean introduced the first Neolithic culture on Sicily, known as the 'Stentinello' after the village in Syracuse Province where Sicily's great archaeologist Paolo Orsi first identified the new culture. These people lived in settlements instead of caves, made weapons of obsidian, and decorated their pottery with incisions or sea-shell impressions. They were farmers, sailors and merchants.

After 3000 BC copper and rock-cut oven tombs were the new fashion, brought over to Sicily from the Aegean, although metal as a material for weapons and tools didn't become important until the Bronze Age (1400 BC). This was a period of turmoil and immigration in the Mediterranean, and Sicily received people and ideas not only from the east but also from the Iberians in the west, who worked in metal and made the bell beakers found on the island.

THE ARRIVAL OF THE GREEKS AND CARTHAGINIANS

In 1200 BC, Troy fell. Some survivors of the Bronze Age holocausts in Asia Minor migrated to the safer shores of Sicily; these were the Elymnians of Segesta and Erice. Various references to Sicily in *The Odyssey* confirmed this early connection between Sicily and the Mycenean world of Greece. The other ancient pre-Greek peoples of Sicily called themselves the Sikans and the Sikels, and they divided the island east/west between them.

Sometime during the 8th century BC, Greeks from Chalcis and Eretria began to colonise Italy—first the island of Ischia off Naples, and then the eastern coast of Sicily, at Naxos, Leontini and Catania. The reasons behind this western expansion are unclear. The Greeks may have simply felt the pressures of a growing population and exhausted soil, or perhaps wanted to protect their growing trade routes in the west. Whatever the cause, the colonies prospered and expanded, much to the alarm of the Phoenicians who felt their own sea-trading livelihood threatened by the colonists. From their centre at Carthage the Phoenicians established outposts in western Sicily at Palermo and Motya, and were generally allied with the Elymnians.

The rivalry between Carthage and the Greeks in Sicily came to a head in 480 BC at Himera (near modern Termini Imerese), when the combined Greek forces of Syracuse, Gela and Akragas (Agrigento) defeated the Punic armies in a great battle. Some sources claim the Battle of Himera took place on the very day that the Athenians defeated the Persians in the Battle of Salamis. Whether or not this is true, these two important Greek victories over the Barbarians initiated a long period of relative peace, which saw many of the most magnificent achievements of the Ancient Greeks. The city of Syracuse grew to be the New York City of its day, extremely rich and powerful. Athens became jealous, and on various pretexts launched a mighty expedition to capture Syracuse, which failed miserably (for details, see the section on the history of Syracuse). But the Greek colonies were in no position to benefit from the Athenian humiliation; petty tyrants, inter-city rivalries and democracy eroded their power and ability to unify.

THE ROMANS

In the First Punic War (mid 3rd century BC) most of Sicily fell under Roman rule, but in the Second Punic War Hannibal's victories encouraged the Sicilians to change sides—a fatal mistake, since the Romans defeated Carthage then came south to exact revenge for what they considered treason. One of the Praetors later sent to govern the island, Verres, systematically stole all its treasures and works of art. Sicily was to remain a grain-producing backwater for more than 1000 years, and like many islands its history was reduced to a list of subsequent invaders—Vandals, Ostrogoths, Byzantines and Saracens.

THE SARACEN–NORMAN CIVILISATION

The Saracens founded a great civilisation in Sicily which was later to influence their successors, the Normans. They made Palermo a glorious, splendid city in the 10th century. They grew the first orange and lemon trees, date palms and sugar cane in Sicily. They tolerated the Christian religions of the native population, founded by St Paul himself (mainly because non-Muslims had to pay more taxes!). By 1060, however, Arab Sicily was divided against itself and square in the path of Norman ambitions in southern Italy. Several factions invited the Normans to Sicily to put down their rivals, only to realise too late that the Normans had come to stay.

The adventurous Normans were led by Robert and Roger Guiscard, sons of an obscure noble of northern France, Tancred de Hauteville. After serving as mercenaries for and against the Pope in northern Italy, Pope Nicholas II authorised them to rule whatever pieces of southern Italy they could take, probably in the hope that they would self-destruct. Robert occupied Apulia and left the conquest of Sicily to his younger brother Roger, whose remarkable success, through a combination of fighting skill and diplomacy, won him all of Sicily by 1091, and the title Count of Sicily.

Because Roger wasn't followed by a wave of Norman immigrants, necessity dictated reconciliation with the native Byzantine and Arab population.

Their religions were tolerated, and their languages. Indeed, Arabic, Greek and Latin were the official languages of Sicily, while the Count spoke Norman French. Both Arabs and Greeks served in the government and armies of Roger, and built—especially under Roger's son, King Roger II— the magnificent churches and palaces that are still one of the wonders of Sicily today.

King Roger's rule was a glorious time for Sicily, and although his son and grandson (William I, 'the Bad', and William II, 'the Good') were not the intelligent, powerful kings he was, the island thrived, perfecting its unique mixture of culture that brought a second Golden Age to Sicily, which lasted 100 years.

Dissensions followed the early death of William II, who left no heirs. Many Sicilian barons preferred Tancred, Count of Lecce, William II's bastard nephew, but the crown was claimed by the Swabian Henry of Hohenstaufen, son of Emperor Frederick Barbarossa and husband of Constance, a posthumous daughter of King Roger. Henry only succeeded in his claim after Tancred's death—by which time he was Emperor and had only three years to live (he died of dysentery in Messina in 1197).

FREDERICK 'STUPOR MUNDI'

At the age of 44, Henry's wife Constance became regent for their 3-year-old son Frederick. Crowned in 1198, he was left totally orphaned six months later. Although Pope Innocent III was his appointed guardian, the Swabian barons took control of Frederick, and it was their grasping influences Frederick had to shake off to establish himself as King and later as Emperor. 'Stupor Mundi', 'a baptised Sultan', 'the first modern man' are just some of the epithets that rationalist Frederick acquired during and after his lifetime. His court was one of the most brilliant in Europe. The seeds of modern Italian literature and poetry were nurtured in Palermo, Greek and Arabic classics were translated, new scientific theories propounded and mathematicians congregated under Frederick's patronage. Frederick himself spent 30 years writing a Latin treatise on falcons, still regarded as a definitive work today. Politically, Sicily felt the power of his awe-inspiring personality and benefited from his good works while he lived, although the island was constantly called upon to assist him in his numerous quarrels with the Pope. In his later years Frederick all but abandoned Palermo and Sicily for the mainland. Now that the island was firmly in the sphere of Europe with few connections to Africa or the East, it began its long decline.

FRENCH AND SPANISH RULE

Following Frederick's death in 1250, the powerful central administration crumbled. Frederick's heirs were unable to assert their authority in the face of both baronial and Papal opposition. One of his sons, Manfred, was crowned in Palermo in 1258 and generally accepted by the Sicilians, but the Pope, the enemy of the Hohenstaufens, appointed Charles of Anjou as King of Sicily. Charles sent his plundering mercenaries to defeat Manfred and secure the island, and introduced religious intolerance, heavy taxes and unpopular French customs. He himself only visited Sicily once, preferring to stay in Naples, which was an unforgivable insult to the proud Sicilians. In 1282 they revolted and massacred all the French in Sicily, initiating the War of the Vespers, named after the incident at a Palermitan church that triggered the rebellion. The Sicilian barons quickly convened a parliament and invited Peter of Aragon to wear the crown of Sicily; he duly accepted, but he and his Spaniards had to defend their new holding against the French for 21 years.

Under Peter and his son James, Sicily was treated as a mere appendage, a supplier to Aragon. James eventually tried to return the island to the Pope and the Angevins for political reasons. The Sicilian barons and James' younger brother, the Viceroy Frederick, reacted to this by holding a parliament in Enna and crowning Frederick 'King of Trinacria'.

The manoeuvrings of Frederick III kept Sicily independent and very feudal. He died in 1337, and the Black Death arrived ten years later—two factors contributing to the disintegration of Sicilian society. Power existed primarily in the hands of two wealthy families, the Ventimiglia who sided with the Spaniards, and the Chiaramonte who tried to bring the Angevins back. Civil war and anarchy were the order of the day.

Aragonese and later Castilian princes ruled Sicily through Viceroys until 1713. In the 15th century Sicily became a joint Spanish possession with Naples, and the island suffered by comparison. The Spanish Inquisition arrived in 1487, and Sicily remained an intolerant backwater throughout the Renaissance. Barbary pirates attacked the coasts, and the Viceroys had great difficulty recruiting Sicilians to defend themselves. At the end of the War of the Spanish Succession, the Treaty of the Hague (1720) gave Sicily to Savoy, then to Austria.

THE BOURBONS

The Sicilians liked neither the Piedmontese nor the Austrians and were relieved when in 1734 the Spanish Infante, Charles of Bourbon, came and took this southern headache away from Austria, meeting little resistance. Charles stayed a week before moving to Naples. When he became King of Spain, he left Sicily and Naples to his son Ferdinand, then 8 years old. With his Austrian wife, Maria Caroline, Ferdinand IV lived a merry life in Naples and only made two trips to Sicily—once to avoid Napoleon and again when his brother Joseph was proclaimed King of Naples in 1805.

Ferdinand managed to regain Naples in 1815, and crowned himself 'Ferdinand I of the Two Sicilies'. He was succeeded by Francis I, and in turn by Ferdinand II, who earned himself the nickname *Re Bomba* ('King Bomb') for the ferocity with which he put down a Sicilian revolt in 1848.

UNION WITH ITALY

In 1860 Garibaldi and his 'Thousand' landed in Sicily at Marsala and, after meeting initial indifference, was soon joined by the Sicilians in his efforts to unify Italy under the Piedmontese Vittorio Emanuele. Within the year he had succeeded, and the island's political history has been the same as the rest of Italy ever since.

During World War II, Sicily was the first territory in Europe to be successfully retaken by the Allies (Operation Husky, July 1943). The Americans under Patton stormed the beach at Gela, and the British under Montgomery took the beaches at Pozzallo, then advanced on the German garrisons around Mount Etna. The Nazis were finally forced to abandon Sicily on 18 August.

During and after the war, Sicilian separatists, disillusioned with 80 years of Italian rule, were clamouring for independence. The peasants, intellectuals and landowners who supported the separatist cause (which was also promoted by Turiddu Giuliano, the modern Sicilian version of Robin Hood) hoped to achieve independence at the end of the war, with a little help from the Allies. However, in 1943 the Italian army, the Communists and the Mafia, each for their own reasons fearing an independent Sicily, joined forces against the separatists. When the United Nations was founded in 1945, the Sicilians could not obtain recognition, and the United States wasn't interested when Giuliano proposed Sicily as the 49th State. But such was the power of the separatist movement that Italy had to grant Sicily regional autonomy, although the Sicilians will be the first to tell you that it is superficial and ineffective against their many problems. When the popular Giuliano was assassinated in 1950, at the age of 27, the spirit of Free Sicily died with him.

Sicily today

The hills of western Sicily which had been Giuliano's domain have today become the last stronghold of the Mafia on the island. These gangsters make their living from protection and extortion rackets, as well as the drug trade, based in Palermo, where their activities still make headline news, usually at the expense of the public prosecution. For many years reformers, notably Danilo Dolci, the Turinese architect who took up the cause of Sicily's poor, were courageous but lonely voices in the battle against the Mafia's hold; the general populace was far too intimidated by the organisation's brutal tactics to protest.

However, in the past few years, especially in Palermo, there's been a wonderful change of attitude, like a breath of fresh air. Posters opposing the Mafia have appeared throughout the city, people are willing to talk about it and oppose it openly, and a kind of mass sense of revulsion has set in towards it and all it represents. The Sicilians will tell you it's because they're simply fed up with all the murders, but one can't help but feel it's only a part of the grand revival of Sicilian dignity and pride. Bookshops in Sicily these days are packed with books about Sicilian history, culture and literature; puppet shows and other traditional arts are on the increase, often promoted by young people intent on preserving their heritage.

Perhaps the main reason behind this great surge of interest in things Sicilian is the island's own economic prosperity. A number of economic reforms initiated in the post-war years—the *Cassa per il Mezzogiorno* (Fund for the South), supported by the World Bank and Common Market, agricultural reforms (50% of the arable land had been owned by 1% of the population), and industrial programmes—are now bearing fruit. Baroque shop fronts are now crammed with smart new video recorders and electric toasters, and the narrow medieval streets in some towns have become permanent traffic jams of new shiny cars.

Sicily's population has now stabilised at about 5 million. Smaller families are beginning to alleviate the need to emigrate, although many Sicilians still hold jobs, generally administrative, in the north of Italy, returning home to their families whenever possible. Tourism is an important but certainly not overriding element in the island's economy, and almost invisible once you leave the coast.

Religion

Sicilians, of course, belong to the Roman Catholic faith, although descendants of Greek immigrants of the 18th and 19th centuries still practise the Orthodox rite. Whether or not the Church exerts much control over the lives of the people any more is debatable; older women, as usual, are the only ones to attend mass regularly, and they keep the roadside shrines supplied with flowers and candles or lightbulbs. The sacraments of the Church,

101

however, are practised with enthusiasm by all. Parents buy elaborate gowns for their baby's baptism and throw great parties. Little white suits and lace dresses or miniature nun's habits, palm branches, flowers, and corny photographs are called for at confirmations. Weddings are sumptuous occasions, often after long engagements, and funerals, with long lines of mourners solemnly walking behind the hearse through the streets on their way to the hilltop cemetery, are moving scenes that make passersby cross themselves and sigh. Horseshoe-shaped wreaths as big as a man are bought in remembrance of 'Uncle' or 'Colleague', and black-bordered obituaries are posted all over town; houses and businesses often have signs on the doors saying 'Per mia Mama' (or whoever), advising visitors that the occupant is in mourning. Cemeteries, by the way, are quite palatial and often the main tourist attraction in a small town.

Festivals

Feast days may be marked with a simple extra mass, or with exuberant fireworks as at the *Festa di Santa Rosalia* in Palermo. During the *festa* of a town's patron saint, the streets around the church are decorated with coloured lights and bunting, and stalls offer toys, candy and local delicacies. After mass, the saint's statue or relics are carried in a procession and there may be dances and fireworks in the evening. Pilgrimages to mountain sanctuaries are common, and many towns have lavish carnival celebrations (the most traditional, with masks and parades, is at Acireale). Holy Week is the climax of the Sicilians' religious calendar, when the influence of centuries of Spanish occupation can be observed. In many towns, beautiful (or sometimes maudlin) scenes from Christ's Passion—known as the *Misteri*—are borne in solemn procession through the streets by men dressed in hooded robes or Spanish costumes of the various medieval guilds. The most authentic of these processions are in the interior of the island (Caltanissetta and Enna Provinces) where the Middle Ages seem like yesterday. Another all-Sicilian holiday is All Souls' Day (1 November). On All Souls' Eve, presents are given to children, supposedly from the dead, and cemeteries are adorned and illuminated for the many visitors who come to commune with the bones of their ancestors.

Unfortunately, unless you go to a special folk festival you are unlikely to find any traditional Sicilian music, dances or costumes. Sicilian music is played on instruments like the *guartara* (a terracotta wind instrument), the *ciaramedda* (the shepherd's goatskin bagpipe), the *friscalettu* (reed flute) and the *tambureddu* (skin drum). The women's costumes favour red and black with wide skirts, though they vary widely from town to town. Traditional male costumes feature baggy black caps, white shirts, vests and dark breeches. Their Spanish-period attire which you can see at some *festas* is more colourful with its doublets and wide hats.

Something every visitor to Sicily notices, however, are the carved and painted carts—or their modern counterparts, the three-wheelers. The carts, with scenes from Orlando Furioso, Garibaldi's battles, the Norman Conquest, etc., dazzle the eyes with their bright primary colours. Traditionally these are pulled by horses embellished with feathers, bands and ribbons (you can see them at most carnivals). Realising that the days of the cart were numbered, cart-painters have adapted their art to the farmers' new vehicles, and some of these buzzing three-wheeled Vespa scooters are almost as beautiful as the carts.

The *Teatro dei Pupi* or Sicilian puppet theatres are currently enjoying a small revival as people have suddenly become aware that the art is in danger of dying out. Although souvenir shops everywhere peddle cheap versions of the marionettes, regular performances are to be found only in Palermo, Acireale, Catania and Messina. Many festivals often feature puppet shows as well.

There is only one play performed by the puppeteers, but it has thousands of chapters. It is the story of Orlando (Roland) and his Christian Paladins fighting the Saracens—a story that the Normans brought to Sicily in their *Chansons de Geste* and the Sicilians took as their own, adapting it to their dialect. Some of the puppets stand 4 or 5 feet high and wear real metal armour and swords, which are banged around for a good part of the show. Like a soap opera, a performance always ends in the air, tempting audiences back for the next evening's entertainment.

Cuisine

Generally Sicilian food is hotter, spicier or sweeter than the rest of Italy. *Pasta con le sarde*, perhaps the most typical dish on the island, includes sardines, fennel, peppers, olive oil, capers and pine nuts. Tuna and swordfish can be had along the coasts of the island; these and fried seafood are Sicilian specialities. *Involtini* (rolled meat filled with ham, cheese and salami, on a spit) can be found on most menus and should be tried when you're tired of fish.

When it comes to sweets, the Sicilians are artists. The most prominent displays in any pastry shop window are of candied fruit and *frutta alla Martorana*, which is marzipan shaped and coloured to look like figs, tomatoes, bananas or even spaghetti or fried eggs, and was once the secret of the monks at La Martorana in Palermo. For festivals little manikins of pure sugar are made with exquisite skill. Sicilian icecream (*gelati*) is renowned for the fresh fruit it often contains. *Cassata* is a fancy cake made of icecream and almonds. Most famous are the *cannoli*, tubes of pastry filled with cream, ricotta cheese or chocolate.

Besides the delicious blood oranges and big lemons grown in Sicily, medlar fruits, peaches, apricots, strawberries and grapes are the main fruits of the island. Almond trees, breathtaking in February when in blossom, are mainly grown in the south. Sicilian wines are rightly renowned, and wine connoisseurs will want to try the *Corvo* (*bianco* or *rosso*) *di Casteldaccia*, *Etna bianco* (or *rosso*), *Faro*, the various *Marsalas*, the wines of Linguaglossa, *Moscato di Siracusa*, sweet and white, and *Mamertino* from Messina, a favourite of the ancient Romans. Sicily also has its own brewery, which produces Messina beer.

Art and architecture

This is an immense subject which, owing to limitations of space, will get but short shrift here. Great Sicilian painters are not numerous. Apart from the ubiquitous 'Anonymous', the only one is Antonello da Messina, the Sicilian who learned from the Flemish in the latter part of the 15th century how to paint in oils. Four of his paintings may be seen in Sicily, two damaged by earthquakes at Messina and Syracuse, a third at Cefalù, and the fourth, his masterpiece, at Palermo. Da Messina's exquisite subtlety and understatement, his quiet colours and simple compositions, lift him to the highest ranks of Renaissance art.

The other famous painting in Palermo, *The Triumph of Death*, is by 'Anonymous'—a 15th-century artist. One can only guess at a Sicilian artist here, and the same goes for the anonymous Master of the Polittico of Trapani, another fine medieval artist. Both the museums at Palermo and Syracuse contain a fine array of local 13th–16th century paintings by unknown or unheralded artists.

In sculpture Sicily fares somewhat better. Besides the treasures left by the Ancient Greeks, every other church in Sicily seems to have a work by the prolific Gagini family, who originally came from the north and then found their fortune embellishing altars and choirs in the 14th and 15th centuries. Artistically the head of the clan was Antonello, whose many Madonnas and Annunciations are quite moving. Other family members specialised in architectural details, and still others worked in silver. Another fine Renaissance sculptor, Francesco Laurana, left some beautiful samples of his art on the island, the best being a Madonna in Palermo Cathedral. A native Palermitan, Serpotta, decorated a number of chapels around the capital with gorgeous baroque stuccoes. Fra Umile of Petralia, high in the mountains, is renowned for his rare wood-carved crucifixes.

Somewhere between art and architecture are the Norman cathedrals of Sicily, perfect examples of the creative spark lit by the combination of very different cultures. When the rather severe architectural concepts of the northern French of the 12th century were combined with the imaginative intricate masonry of the Arabs and embellished by Byzantine mosaicists, the results left us with one of the best medieval churches in the world—Monreale. Other examples of the lovely hybrid style may be seen at Cefalù and Palermo. The so-called Chiaramonte style in Sicily, often seen in 14th-century palaces, was also a hybrid of sorts, put together by the powerful family of the same name when they commissioned yet another *palazzo*. It is an exuberant but delicate style, best seen in the arched mullioned windows.

The ancients bequeathed many fine buildings to Sicily—among them the beautiful lone temple of Segesta and the Doric temples of ancient Akragas (Agrigento), including one that is the largest Greek temple in the world, and another that is one of the best preserved. One huge theatre in Syracuse was carved in the living rock. The stage of the theatre at Taormina is well preserved, and it enjoys the magnificent backdrop of Mount Etna. In the middle of Sicily, the Roman Villa of Casale has floor after floor of wondrous lifelike mosaics, a few surely done by Michelangelo during an earlier incarnation.

While the Spanish Inquisition seemingly nipped the flower of the Sicilian Renaissance in the bud, the baroque blossomed, even more fantastical in Sicily than elsewhere. Rosario Gagliardi, who lived in the southern corner of the island, designed churches that express the ideal best in Noto, Ragusa and Modica—places few foreigners visit, so that Gagliardi remains undeservedly unknown. At the opposite extreme are the extravagances in Bagheria, once a fashionable suburb of Palermo, where the Villa Palagonia, built in 1713 by Tomaso Napoli, takes the prize for folly.

Post-baroque architecture in Sicily is rather nondescript. Mussolini meant well when he constructed a large number of public buildings on the island, but unfortunately they won't go away. Invariably made of cheap stone, with ambiguous slogans about mystic power engraved on their facades, these Fascist monuments stick out like sore thumbs in every large town.

Quite a few Sicilians have made names for themselves in the other arts. Alessandro Scarlatti and Vincenzo Bellini (composer of *Norma*) are the island's most notable musicians. Luigi Pirandello, the 1934 Nobel Prize-winning playwright who revolutionised modern drama, was born in Sicily. In literature, Guiseppe di Lampedusa, author of *The Leopard*, and Giovanni Verga, who wrote *Maestro Don Gesualdo*, were also sons of Sicily. Both books offer rare visions of Sicilian life in the past. Another book, *Report from Palermo* by Danilo Dolci, the man who fought so many of Sicily's wrongs after the war, offers a more modern view, as does his recent compilation of interviews with Sicilians from every walk of life, *Sicilian Lives*.

Getting to and around Sicily

By air
There are frequent domestic flights to the airports of Palermo, Catania, and Trapani-Marsala from domestic airports, and occasional non-stop scheduled flights from London. Many charters go directly from London to Palermo all year round, and if they have any extra seats you may find this the most economical route.

By train
Numerous trains travel southwards along the mainland, timed to coincide with the frequent ferry services across the Straits from Villa S. Giovanni to Messina, and from there trains continue to either Palermo or Catania. If Palermo is your goal, you may want to consider taking the overnight ferry there from Naples, which runs daily, and is inexpensive and far more pleasant than the lengthy train journey (see below).

Trains within Sicily (see map) are either frequent and fast or poky and irregular. Some routes that look possible on the map, for example from Syracuse to Agrigento, actually take a whole day to complete (if you're lucky). Between Palermo and Messina and Messina and Syracuse the FS runs comfortable, regular trains; elsewhere expect *locales* that may make half-hour stops in the middle of nowhere.

By sea
Tirrenia links Sicily with the rest of the Mediterranean. Its ferries depart from Naples daily at 8.30pm for Palermo, arriving at 6.30 the next morning. Fares in the high season (June–September) are around 37 000 lire per passenger in a second-class cabin; the charge for a small car will be around 45 000 lire. There are 4 services a week between Genoa and Palermo, departing at 3pm and arriving at 2pm the following day, and a weekly service between Cagliari and Palermo, departing from Cagliari at 7pm and arriving

in Palermo at 7.30am the next day. Once a week there's a ferry from Tunis, leaving at 8pm and arriving the next day at 6am in Palermo. Three times a week there is also a ferry from Reggio Calabria to Catania, Syracuse and Malta.

There is a regular hydrofoil run by Aliscafi SNAV from Reggio Calabria to Messina 19 times a day (15 minutes). Caronte Lines ferries vehicles over the strait every 30 minutes or so. Siremar (Sicilia Regionale Marittima) operates nearly all the services to the outlying Sicilian islands (see the individual islands for more details).

By coach
A number of private companies run services from the mainland to Sicily, while others serve the island itself. For many trips into the interior they are far superior to the trains and cost about the same.

By car
Sicily has its share of autostrade: one almost encircles the island (except between Gela and Campobelle del Mazara), and several criss-cross the interior. Unlike those on the mainland, Sicilian autostrade are free of tolls and are rarely crowded. The state roads are almost invariably in an excellent state of repair. However, driving in the large cities and in nearly every provincial capital can be highly exasperating, and in many cases you'd get to your destination faster by walking—especially when you include the headache of finding a place to park; you're better off leaving the car in a hotel garage.

Messina and the Ionian Coast

Messina

HISTORY
Messina, third city of Sicily, has been bandied about by the fates more than most. With its harbour and strategic situation on the Straits, Messina has had naval and military importance since ancient times. Initially colonised by the Cumaeans and Chalcidians in the 8th century BC, Messina was then known as 'Zancle' (sickle) after the shape of its harbour. In 493 BC, Zancle was captured by Anaxilas, tyrant of Rhegium across the Straits, who renamed it Messana after his native Messenia in Greece. The Carthaginian Himilco destroyed the town in 397, then Syracuse rebuilt it, only to see it occupied by the belligerent mercenaries of the tyrant Agathocles, the Marmertines (sons of Mars). The Marmertines controlled large areas of Sicily

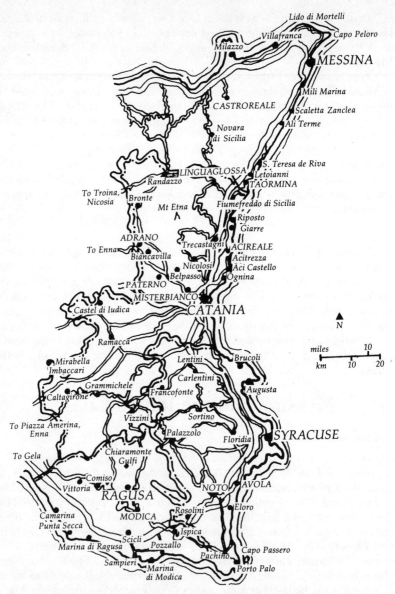

SICILY – THE IONIAN COAST

and Calabria until conquered by Hieron II. From then on the city, described by Cicero as 'great and wealthy', was an ally of Rome.

The Normans, who arrived in 1061, brought a new prosperity. During the Crusades, Messina became an important port, famous for its monastery of St Salvador of the Greeks. Richard the Lionheart spent a winter here in 1190–91, sacked the town and rebuilt the Castle of Matefriffon. Messina stubbornly resisted the grasping Charles of Anjou in 1282, but had less luck against the Spaniards, under whom the population was decimated in the 17th century. This began a series of hard knocks for Messina. In 1743, the plague killed 40 000, then in 1783 an earthquake demolished the city, and in 1848, the Bourbons, under 'Re Bomba' (Ferdinand II), bombarded the city fiercely from the sea to quell Sicilian cries for independence. There was a cholera epidemic in 1854, another earthquake in 1894, and then, on 28 December 1908, the most devastating tremor of all, which killed 84 000 inhabitants in the small hours of the morning, caused the coast to sink 2 feet into the sea, and altered the dreaded whirlpool Charybdis so that it no longer posed a threat to sailors. Organisations all over the world contributed to the rebuilding of Messina, but before the great work was complete the Americans bombed it, destroying much that had been built and causing some 45 000 more casualties.

WHAT TO SEE

In consequence, Messina today is the most modern city in Sicily, but not oppressively so, despite its tragic history. Today's architects could learn a lesson here (but beware the somewhat Byzantine street plan). Messina's pleasant position at the foot of the Peloritani Mountains, on an unindustrialised coast, adds to its charm, and its importance as 'the Gateway to Sicily' remains undiminished.

The Cathedral

The centre of the city is the Piazza del Duomo, with Messina's most important building, the Cathedral. Built by Roger II in 1160, it was shattered by the 1908 earthquake, rebuilt, and destroyed again by World War II bombs, after which it burned for three days. Again the Messinians rebuilt their *duomo* on the old Norman model, incorporating pieces of the original that had survived the destruction—including the charming reliefs of farming peasants and part of the Norman portal. In the campanile, a fascinating **astronomical clock,** built in Strasbourg in 1933 and reputedly the largest in the world, tells the year, the date, the phase of the moon and the location of the planets. As if that weren't enough, the clock also provides a display of bronze mechanical figures. Every day at noon, a crowd gathers to watch: the lion waves his banner and roars three times, the cock flaps his wings and crows, Jesus pops out of the tomb, the dove circles around as a model of the church of Montalto rises from the ground (the real one can be seen on the hill to the left), and Mary is saluted by various dignitaries to the tune of Schubert's 'Ave Maria' on the loudspeaker. Inside the cathedral are its restored treasures, including Antonello Gagini's John the Baptist and part of the tomb of the English Archbishop of Messina, Palmer, who died in 1195. Also on the Piazza del Duomo is the beautifully restored 16th-century *Orion Fountain* by Angelo Montorsoli, a pupil of Michelangelo.

Nearby, on the broad Via Garibaldi, is another reconstruction, the pretty Arab–Norman church of **Annunziata dei Catalani.** From the Via Garibaldi you can see why the Greeks named Messina 'The Sickle', the very tip of which is marked by one of the Italians' beloved Madonnas on a Pillar at the Spanish **Fort of San Salvatore,** built in 1546. Across from it, still on the Via Garibaldi, is the hydrofoil dock. At the crossroads of Vias Garibaldi and della Libertà is a public garden, the Villa Mazzini, with a charming little **Aquarium** of Mediterranean sea creatures (open Tuesdays, Thursdays, Saturdays and Sundays, 9–1). Across the street stands the **Church of San Giovanni di Malta;** and in the Piazza Unità d'Italia is another fountain by Montorsoli, the **Fonte Netune.**

On down the Via della Libertà (bus 8 from the railway station) are the buildings where the big *Fiera di Messina* is held each August, the dock for car ferries to the mainland, and at the end the **Museo Nazionale** (open 9–2, festivals 9–1; closed Mondays). This contains objects removed from the earthquake-shattered churches, two large paintings by Caravaggio, and a damaged but still lovely triptych by native son Antonello da Messina, one of the masters of the Italian Renaissance and the first to paint in oils instead of the then popular tempera—an influence thought to be Flemish, as one can detect in his work.

Seven miles north of Messina is the very popular beach, the **Lido Mortelle** (frequent bus from Messina), right by the Capo Peloro or Punto del Faro, the northeasternmost corner of Sicily. From here a huge power cable stretches over the Straits, supported by two monster pylons to permit ships to pass beneath.

The Straits of Messina
The Straits of Messina, known to the Romans as 'Fretum Siculum', have been famous since the dawn of Western civilisation. Odysseus' ships were almost wrecked by the two monsters, Scylla (the rock) and Charybdis (the whirlpool). Although the Straits are narrow enough for a hardy swimmer to cross, they are wide enough to keep Sicily distinct from the rest of Italy. In

summer they sometimes produce the mirage called 'Fata Morgana' which distorts the coast of Calabria, supposedly caused by the spells of Morgan the Faye. (When the Normans brought the Tales of Roland with them to Sicily, they also brought the legends of King Arthur and transplanted them in the fertile Sicilian imagination. Mt Etna became the fairy kingdom of Mongibel, where Morgan lived and where her sprites entrapped Arthur.) Nowadays the Straits swarm with swordfish, the quarry of fishermen from the small villages that dot the headland.

FESTIVALS
Patron saint Madonna della Lettera (3 June and 13–15 August). *Giganti* processions (14 August); the giants, some 20 ft high, represent the legendary procreators of Messina, Mata and Grifone. Good Friday processions. The *Fiera di Messina* in August with folklore, sports and exhibitions.

SPECIALITIES
Swordfish dishes, *cassata* made from almond paste, candied fruit and *ricotta*.

GETTING TO AND AROUND MESSINA PROVINCE
By ferry: crossings every half-hour from the mainland at either Reggio di Calabria or Villa San Giovanni (the easiest way of getting to either place is to drive down the Autostrada del Sole from Milan).
By train: all trains going to Sicily stop at Messina via the FS ferries, which also take cars and passengers.
By hydrofoil (SNAV): these depart every half-hour or so from Reggio di Calabria (15-minute trip) and Villa San Giovanni (8-minute trip).
By air: the nearest airport is at Reggio di Calabria.
   In the summer (June to September) hydrofoils leave Messina for the Aeolian Islands on the SNAV line. Tickets and information from SNAV Aliscafi, Cortina del Porto, Messina (tel. (090) 64044).
   The buses that leave Messina for the rest of the province and Sicily all depart from the vicinity of the railway station, from Via Primo Settembre. The SAIS line takes the popular Taormina–Catania route from here. For Milazzo, take the Giunta bus from Via Teranova.

TOURIST INFORMATION
EPT, Via Calabria Isolato 301 bis (tel. (090) 775356).
EPT (information office), across from the railway station (tel. (090) 777 0731).
AAST, Viale San Martino 227 (tel. (090) 33541).
AAST (information office), Via G. Bruno 121 (tel. (090) 36494).

111

WHERE TO STAY

The **Riviera Grand Hotel******, Viale della Liberta 516 (tel. (090) 57101); single 34–48 000 lire, double 65–80 000 lire with bath) is air-conditioned and large, and is not far from the centre; it has a good restaurant with a view. For some fine *art nouveau* furnishings, check in at the less expensive **Monza****, Viale San Martino 63 (tel. (090) 773775), where a single room with a bath is 17–24 000 lire, a double 28–42 000. For something clean, cheap, and within hearing distance of the clock, there's the **Roma**, Piazza Duomo 3 (tel. (090) 775566; singles 7000 lire, double 13 000). From May to September you can camp at 'S. Margherita' (tel. (090) 831033), or all year round at Dello Stretto (tel. (090) 321624) at Torre Faro.

EATING OUT

For a first-rate introduction to the island's cuisine, try **Pippo Nunnari** on Via Ugo Bassi 157, but expect to pay around 35 000 lire for a full meal. Among the various restaurants on Via Risorgimento is **Donna Giovanna** at no. 16, with good basic Italian fare for around 20 000 lire. For something inexpensive, a good place to look is around the University (Piazza Maurolico).

South to Taormina

The Ionian coast south of Messina is fringed with small towns and beaches wedged between the Peloritani Mountains, the handmaidens of Queen Etna. The closer you get to Taormina, the more spectacular the scenery, whether you go by car or train; the latter, even the *rapidos*, seems to stop at every little town along the way, though few offer much to detain the traveller.

Mili Marina, directly across the Straits from Reggio di Calabria, has a lovely old Basilian monastery church, **Santa Maria,** founded in 1082 by Count Roger, whose son Jordanus was buried there ten years later. **Giampilieri Marina** is an old resort nearby. In the mountains above **Scaletta Zanclea** (another beach) are the melancholy ruins of a 13th-century castle. Medicinal treatments may be had at the spa of **Ali Terme** with its mineral springs and mud baths, located on a wide stretch of beach. In **Sàvoca,** above Santa Teresa di Riva where the Pentetur *banditti* once lived in the ruined castle, is a small series of **catacombs** with mummified bodies, a tidier miniature of the macabre galleries in Palermo. The **Church of San Michele** has some good Gothic porches. A little way inland, at 1400 ft, **Forza d'Agro** is a pretty, medieval village, dominated by a 16th-century

The Theatre at Taormina

castle; its main church, the 16th-century **Sant'Agostino,** contains a beautiful painting by Antonio Giuffrè of *Three Angels visiting Abraham,* and a medieval gonfalon. From here you can visit the exquisite Norman **Santi Pietro e Paolo,** built by a certain Master Gerard the Frank in 1172 for the Orthodox Basilian monks. Situated on the banks of the Fiumara d'Agro, the building reflects the lavish Norman–Byzantine decorative ideal, with local lava added for multicoloured effect. **Capo Sant' Alessio,** with its castle perched on the 400-ft cliffs, offers a striking view from the window of your train or car. Below it lie the budding resorts of **Letoianni** and **Sant' Alessio Siculo,** both with wide beaches.

Taormina

Enchanting and unique, Taormina is Sicily's resort *extraordinaire,* discovered by Europe's leisure classes who began to winter there at the turn of the century—D. H. Lawrence lived in a villa in Taormina during 1920–23. Since then, this fantastic medieval town—on a 700-ft high terrace, overlooking the sea and under the shadow of blue, snow-capped Mt Etna—has become a year-round attraction.

HISTORY
Taormina was founded in 358 BC, after Dionysius of Syracuse destroyed the ancient colony of Naxos below. Andromachus, father of Timaeus the

historian, took the refugees of Naxos to Tauromenium, as it was then known; later Andromachus was the only tyrant to join Timoleon, the new ruler of Syracuse, in his efforts to restore democracy in Sicily. During this time the town prospered (the Romans made it a privileged 'civitas foedecata') but later it erred in supporting Pompey against Octavian, who as Augustus turned it into a strategic military colony. The Saracens destroyed Taormina in 902 but then had a change of heart and rebuilt it. In 1410 the Sicilian parliament deliberated here in electing a new king for the island when the Aragonese line died out with Martin II. During World War II Marshal Kesselring made Taormina his headquarters, and the town consequently suffered bomb damage.

WHAT TO SEE

Two roads lead up to Taormina, both branching off Strada Statale 114. **Via Luigi Pirandello,** the most picturesque, is also the route of the buses from the railway station Taormina–Giardini. After a long, winding climb past villas, hotels, the Anglican Church of St George and the **funivia station,** Via Pirandello finally gives onto the main street, **Corso Umberto.** To the right is the **Church of San Pancrazio,** built on the site of a temple to Serapidean Zeus, where you can make out the *cella* foundations. Through the **Porta Messina,** the main entrance of the town, the Corso leads to the central Piazza Vittorio Emanuele, where the outstanding building is the **Palazzo Corvaia,** once the seat of the Sicilian parliament and today an art gallery. Built in the 14th century, the palace (recently restored) is typically decorated with black lava and white pumice stone. Behind the Church of Santa Caterina on the same square are a few vestiges of the ancient **Odeon.** Some imperial **Roman baths** have been excavated towards the beginning of Via Teatro Greco. This is the street from which to gain access to the Greek theatre. The Ancient Greeks, modern scholars argue, had little thought for views, but dug their theatres out of the hills and mountains wherever it was most convenient. Yet here in Taormina it's hard to imagine that they didn't give the backdrop at least a thought—indeed, one wonders how the drama could ever compete against such a spectacular panorama of sea, jutting coastline, rolling hills and a smouldering volcano. The theatre itself (open daily 9am to sunset; admission fee) was originally constructed in the 3rd century BC and rebuilt in their characteristic brick by the Romans in the 2nd century AD; it was used exclusively for gladiatorial bouts. Some 358 ft in diameter, it is the second largest in Sicily, after the theatre in Syracuse, and although the *cavea* has fallen somewhat into disrepair, the *skene* is very well preserved. The columns above the theatre belonged to a portico which once encircled the *cavea*. By the entrance to the theatre, the small **anti-**

quarium contains a few tablets from ancient Tauromenium.

Back on the Corso, in the main shopping area of town, steps descend to the so-called **Naumachia** (perhaps the ancient cistern) with a barrel-vaulted roof. At the top of the steps in the lively Piazza Nove Aprile is the 17th-century **Church of San Guiseppe.** In the square itself, the **Church of Sant' Agostino,** built in 1488, has been converted into a library. It is the **Belvedere,** however, that attracts most attention. Passing beneath the **Torre dell' Orologio** (12th century, restored in the 17th) you enter the **Borgo Medioevale,** the oldest and most charming quarter of Taormina, still retaining an Arabic touch or two.

The **Cathedral,** on the Piazza del Duomo, is a simple structure from the 13th century, with a later rose window and some fine paintings inside, including a 15th-century triptych by Giuffrè. In front of the cathedral is a small **fountain** (1635) by the Montorsoli school. Below this square, the 16th-century **San Domenico Convent,** the Nazi headquarters during the war, has been turned into a luxury hotel. At the very end of the Corso Umberto is the **Porto del Tocco** (1440). Down the steps, just off Piazza Sant' Antonio, is the **Palazzo del Duca di Santo Stefano,** one of the last palaces built by the Normans in Sicily, and recently restored; note the elegant windows.

Above the Corso, on Via Dionisio Primo, stands the battlemented tower of the **Badia Vecchia** (the old convent), with its wide, pointed window. Belonging to the 15th century, this is the loveliest medieval monument in Taormina. Below the town, on Via Bagnoli Croce, are the beautiful public gardens, with unusual wooden toy palaces scattered throughout. For a superb view of the surrounding region, you can go on foot (Via Circonvallazione to the Mulattiera Castel Taormina) or by car (Via Castelmola) to the **Sanctuario Madonna della Rocca** and the **Castle of Taormina**—of little interest in themselves, but commanding unforgettable panoramas. For an even better view, drive or take the bus to the village of **Castelmola** and its medieval castle. The village is also famous for its almond wine.

The main beach of Taormina, **Mazzarò,** can be reached by the cablecar, or *funivia* (frequent departures from Via Pirandello all year round). A tourist card may be purchased to make a number of trips at a discount. Mazzarò has every facility, including restaurants—as have other beaches in the area, such as **Lido Spisone** and **Lido Mazzeo** and the coves around pretty **Isola Bella** and **Capo Taormina** (connected to Taormina, as is Letoianni, by bus). There are also daily coach excursions to Mt Etna (see travel agent).

FESTIVALS

One of the main displays of Sicilian folklore takes place annually on the last three days of May in Taormina—*Il Raduno del Costume e del Carretto Siciliano*. Traditional puppet shows are performed, as well as folksongs and dances, and painted carts trundle around in a spectacularly colourful parade. Also, towards the end of July, there is an International Film Festival, and from June to August there are various dances, and dramatic and musical performances in the Greek theatre (see the tourist offices for details). Every Friday there's a puppet show in the Teatro S. Nicola.

TOURIST INFORMATION

EPT, Corso Umberto (tel. (0942) 3751).
AAST (information), Stazione Taormina–Giardini; summer only (tel. (0942) 3410).

WHERE TO STAY

Taormina is packed with luxurious accommodation of every description, most elegantly the **San Domenico Palace******* on the Piazza San Domenico (tel. (0942) 980013), many of its rooms occupying a 15th-century monastery; its pool is the loveliest in Taormina and its rates by far the steepest at 120–150 000 lire for a single room, 200–250 000 for a double (open all year). The **Excelsior Palace******, Via Toselli 8 (tel. (0942) 23975), about 54 000 lire single, 86 000 double, is one of many with a spectacular location (and pool). Smaller and quieter, but also affording great views, are the **Bel Soggiorno***** (open all year), Via Luigi Pirandello 60 (tel. (0942) 23342), with a single room as low as 20 500 lire (without bath) and a double as high as 50 000 lire with bath; the **Villa Belvedere*****, Via Bagnoli Croce 79 tel. (0942) 23791), with a garden terrace and pool (single room with bath, 35 500 lire, double 62 000); and, perhaps most famous of all, the **Timeo******, on Via Teatro Greco 59 (tel. (0942) 23801), with panoramic views and a lovely garden (single rooms range from 48 000 to 55 000 lire, double rooms from 86 000 to 111 000 lire).

Less expensive is the castle-like **Villa Carlotta****, below town on Via Luigi Pirandello 81 (tel. (0942) 98039; single room 22 000 lire, double 42 000, with bath). Further up the same street, at no. 26, the **Pensione Svizzera** (tel. (0942) 23790) also has fine views (single room with bath 19 000 lire, double 30–32 000). For something very cheap, try **Diane** at Via Giovanni 6 (tel. (0942) 23898), where one of four rooms costs 10 000 lire (double).

There are many other places by the sea, like the elegant old **Lido Mediterranee***** at Spisone (tel. (0942) 24422), where a double room with bath is 82 000 lire and the more cosy, bright pink **Villino Gallodoro, Via**

Nazionale 151 (tel. (0942) 23860), where a single room is 16–20 000, double 33 000 lire.

EATING OUT

Nor surprisingly there are many places to choose from, although many are spoilt by having to cater for too many tourists. An elegant exception is **Le Terrazze,** where you can dine in a 16th-century Spanish hall or eat out with a view of Etna (closed Mondays) on Corso Umberto 172 (dinners for around 60 000 lire). Less expensive is **Ciclope,** with meals for 35–45 000 lire, and **Taormina,** serving good pizzas and local wines for around 40 000 lire. Both are on Corso Umberto. For good deals, check out the 'menu turistico' posted on many of the little places along the side streets, like **Mama Rosa** (around 15 000 lire) and the **Nuova Grotta di Ulisse** (around 20 000 lire.

Giardini–Naxos

South of Taormina, Giardini is growing into a resort in its own right, with its beach of golden sand. From here in 1860 Garibaldi and his Redcaps set sail to defeat the Bourbon armies in Calabria. Signposted from Giardini, on Capo Schiso, are the ruins of ancient Naxos, the first Greek colony in Sicily, founded about 750 BC. The name derives from the Cycladian island of Naxos, but most of the original colonists are thought to have been refugees from Euboea and Ionia while powerful Syracuse was inhabited by Dorians. With few defences, Naxos was captured in turn by Hippocrates of Gela and Hieron of Syracuse, only to be destroyed by the Syracusan tyrant Dionysius the Elder in 403 BC in retaliation for Naxos' alliance with Athens during the Great Expedition; he gave the territory to the Sikels, and the Naxians eventually settled Taormina. The excavations at Naxos (open 9am to sunset, Sundays 9–12) have uncovered the city walls, remains of the temple of Aphrodite and the street plan (a new one superimposed on the more ancient one), along with some Hellenistic tombs, which suggests that at one time settlers returned to Naxos. Also at Giardini you can visit the long **Alcantara Gorge,** 65 ft deep and a mere 10 ft wide.

Along the scenic valley of the Alcantara river, which serves as the border between the provinces of Messina and Catania, lies **Francavilla di Sicilia,** with a medieval castle and bridge spanning the Alcantara; the ruins near the bridge belong to a domed Byzantine church.

Around Mt Etna

Awesome smouldering Mt Etna (in Arabic 'Gibel Utlamat'—hence the Sicilian name 'Mongibello') at 10 725 ft has little to do with the rest of Sicily's geology. Vulcanologists believe its career began under the sea from where it pushed its way up to become part of Sicily. More than 135 eruptions have been recorded, beginning in 475 BC, when both Pindar and Aeschylus wrote about a great volcanic explosion. Some 30 or 40 years later the pre-Socratic philosopher Empedocles, from Agrigento, committed a strange suicide by leaping into Etna's 25-mile-diameter crater, either to prove his divinity or that hot air rises. Several eruptions in the Middle Ages reached the sea. The worst eruption on record was in 1669, when a wide gap opened up from the summit to the town of Nicolosi, and lava overwhelmed most of Catania. The volcano has continued to be quite active since then, if not as ruinously, and tourist excursions to the summit may occasionally be cancelled owing to uncertain volcanic conditions. An observatory at the summit monitors Etna's activity.

For many, the ascent up the mountain is the highlight of a visit to Sicily. The main route up on wheels is from the south. If you do not have a car, there is a daily bus (*Etna Trasporti*) from the Stazione Centrale in Catania at 7am, and various tour excursions from Catania and Taormina, which have the advantage of supplying the necessary outer wear for the top of the volcano (it's very cold, even in August). The trip takes an entire day.

The Strada dell' Etna from Catania passes through **Gravina,** where the craters Pomiciari di Santa Maria were formed in 1381; **Mascalucia,** a wine centre; and, above it, **Massa Annunziata** where pistachio trees flourish on the cooled lava of 1669. **Nicolosi,** at 2 290 ft, lies east of the smoking **Monti Rossi** craters, also formed in 1669, and one can walk up it in an hour. Nicolosi has become a popular ski resort with two ski lifts and a chair lift. From here, you cross fields of more recent lava to the **Serra la Nave** ski slopes, overlooked by the fine old Grand Hotel dell' Etna and to the **Casa Cantoniera,** which has wonderful views. The Strada dell' Etna ends at the **Rifugio G. Sapienza,** a hostel operated by the Italian Alpine Club at 6260 ft. Here you can sleep and eat, but to ascend to the crater you need to find a guide or take the cablecar to the site of the **Observatory** (9653 ft), and a jeep or coach to the crater from there. Forests grow up to 6900 ft; above that height the only plant is the Spino Santo (*Astigalus aetnensis*) amid the barren lunar landscape of volcanic matter, smoking and reeking of sulphur. Peering into the multiple depths of the crater is an experience that defies words—as is the view of Sicily, Calabria, the Aeolian Islands and, on a clear day, Malta far in the distance. While on top it is well worth your time to visit the **Torre**

del Filosofo, which actually dates from Hadrian's ascent of the volcano, and the chasm known as the **Valle del Bove,** whose sides are sheer 3000-ft cliffs.

The crater of Mt Etna

The **Ascent of Etna North** (Highway 114) rises to the pretty ski resort of Linguaglossa and its tall pine trees. Turn off at Mangano for **Zafferana Etnea,** which has many hotels, and **Fornazzo** with views of the Valle del Bove. Here the road branches off to the refuges **Citelli** and **Sucai,** while the main road goes to **Linguaglossa,** a newer ski resort with a National Ski School on the Piano della Provenzana, which has three ski lifts. There's a tourist information office in Linguaglossa (tel. (95) 643094).

Villages around Mt Etna

The very beautiful small towns and villages at the foot of Etna can easily be visited on the Circumetnea railway, departing from Catania; to see everything take the 8.45am train. In **Paternò,** the first important stop, the 13th-century **Norman castle** at the top of the town has been restored. Here Frederick II of Aragon died on his way to his beloved Enna, and there are some good frescoes in the chapel of Santa Barbara. **Biancavilla** glistens with its orange groves; **Adrano,** the next town along the track, was founded in 400 BC by Dionysius I of Syracuse as 'Adranon', named for the god whose temple was near the site. The **castle,** founded by Count Roger in the 11th century, has been turned into a prehistory museum and art gallery

119

(open 9–1 and 3–6; in winter 9–4; festivals 9–1; closed Mondays). Near here are a few vestiges of the Greek Wall, and the **Chiesa Madre,** also Norman, incorporating columns from an ancient Greek temple. At Easter, Adrano presents a passion play, one of the most famous in Sicily. Near Adrano is the recently excavated Sikel town of **Mendolito** (8th–6th centuries BC), where a long, as yet untranslatable, inscription in Sikel was discovered, along with a treasure-trove of bronze artefacts.

Bronte, also on the Circumetnea route, is a small town named for the castle and dukedom that Ferdinand IV (King of Naples) bestowed on Nelson in 1799. The castle now belongs to the Bridport family. The **Castello Maniace,** the seat of the Dukes of Bronte, was founded by Margaret of Navarre in 1173 as a convent, on the site where the Byzantine George Maniakes defeated the Saracens in 1040. In 1905, the Scottish poet 'Fiona Macleod' (a pseudonym adopted by the writer William Sharp) died here, and he is buried under an Ionic cross. For permission to visit the castle, you have to have applied in advance, in writing.

Randazzo is the most interesting village of Mt Etna. Although built out of lava, it has never succumbed to an eruption, and has preserved its medieval atmosphere, although it suffered Allied bombardment when the Nazis made it one of their last strongholds in Sicily. A private museum, **Museo Vagliasindi** (on the Corso no. 265), houses a good collection of finds from a nearby Greek necropolis (ask the owner to see it). The town's **Cathedral of Santa Maria** dates from the 13th century. The church of **San Martino** has a lovely campanile, although the church itself was damaged in the war. There is also a fine medieval castle.

Down the coast to Catania

Acireale

The coast of Catania province is lined with campsites, castles and beaches. Starting from the north, **Calatabiano** has a lofty medieval castle, north of which are steps descending into the Alcantara Gorge. **Giarre,** further south, is a major wine-producing centre; beyond that, **Acireale** is built on streams of lava, and has become an attractive tourist centre for its sandy beach and the sulphur baths at Santa Venera. The town itself, 500 feet above the sea, was rebuilt after the 1693 earthquake and has a pleasant baroque character. In the **Biblioteca Zelantea** (open 10–1 and 4–6) on Via Marchese di Siciliano, there is a library, museum and art gallery, including some beautiful drawings and a painting attributed to Rubens. The **Puppet**

Theatre on Via Alessi gives performances in the summer; there are lovely views of Etna from the park Villa Belvedere. The **Palazzo Comunale** (1659) is a good example of bizarre Spanish–Sicilian baroque, as is the genuinely baroque **Basilica San Sebastiano** on Piazza Vigo, finished in 1705.

FESTIVALS
'The most beautiful carnival in Sicily' takes place in February. Good Friday processions in traditional costumes. Santa Venera (week-long celebration beginning first Sunday in July). Acireale also has a display of Christmas cribs that are known as the finest in Sicily.

TOURIST INFORMATION
Corso Umberto 177 (tel. (095) 604521).

WHERE TO STAY AND EAT
The **Aloha d'Oro***, Strada Panoramica (tel. (095) 604344) is the best bet, with a pool, proximity to the sea and the best restaurant in the area (single room 35–44 000 lire, double 52–70 000).

Aci Castello

Many other towns on the coast have names prefixed with 'Aci'—after the River Aci, which according to the Ancient Greeks sprang out of the earth where the shepherd Acis died, murdered by Polythemus, the Cyclops, for jealousy of the maiden Galatea. Some rocks off the coast are known as 'Il Ciclopi', the rocks thrown by Polythemus after Odysseus' ships when the Greeks made their escape from his cave. The fiery cauldron of Etna, of course, was the Forge of Hesphestus (Vulcan), or the monster Typhon, conceived by Mother Earth to do battle with the Olympian gods.

Aci Castello, facing the islets of the Cyclops, derives its name both from Acis, and from the **castle** built by Roger di Lauria in 1297, who rebelled against Frederick II of Aragon. So impregnable was this fortress that only by building a wooden castle the same height right next to it could Frederick reduce it. The castle is still well preserved today, overlooking the sea, the strange rocks of the Cyclops, and the holidaymakers from Catania who have made the 'Riviera dei Ciclopi' the most popular resort in the province.

Just inland from here is **Trecastagni** ('the three chestnut trees') with the most beautiful Renaissance church in Sicily, the **Chiesa Madre,** built by Sicily's greatest sculptor, Antonello Gagini. Here also, on 9 May, thousands

121

of pilgrims pay tribute to the Three Saintly Brothers (see Catania's festivals). On the coast south of Catania is the beach of Lido de Plaia, the airport at Fontanarossa and, near the mouth of the River Simeto, the **necropolis** of ancient Symaethus.

Catania

HISTORY
Chalcidians from Naxos founded Catania in 729 BC, on its fertile plain (known as the Laestrygonian Fields in ancient times, for the cannibalistic Laestrygones in Book 10 of *The Odyssey*), and it prospered from the first. Catania's tyrant drew up a code of laws in the 7th century BC which were adopted by all the Ionian colonies of Magna Grecia. The Syracusans under Hieron I took the city in 476 BC and exiled its inhabitants, but in 461 the Catanians triumphantly returned and sent Hieron's Doric colonists packing. An ally of Athens, Catania was the Athenians' base in the ill-starred Great Expedition and suffered the consequences when Dionysius of Syracuse sold the inhabitants into slavery in 403 BC. Himilco the Carthaginian, Timoleon and Pyrrhus, followed by the inevitable Romans, trace the domination of the city up until Christian times. Augustus rewarded Catania for having supported him in the civil war against Pompey. In AD 253, one of Italy's most famous saints, St Agatha, was martyred in Catania.

In the early Middle Ages, Catania suffered a series of disasters. A major earthquake devastated the city in 1169, and it was sacked twice, first by Henry IV, then by Frederick II. In 1669, the worst eruption in Etna's history buried it in lava, and before it could recover, the 1693 earthquake destroyed almost everything else. However, with their usual resilience the Catanians rebuilt the city, better than ever. Modern Catania is a showcase of Sicilian baroque.

Famous sons include the great operatic composer Vincenzo Bellini, the novelist Giovanni Verga and the poet Mario Rapisardi.

WHAT TO SEE
Catania today is Sicily's second largest city, the island's industrial and business centre. Its very prosperity has caused great neglect in the old baroque quarter of the city, as people desert it for the anonymous apartment buildings on the outskirts of the town, leaving the piles of crumbling terracotta to fend for themselves. The oldest areas are in bad shape even by Sicilian standards, and a modern 'urban redevelopment' area east of the Giardino Bellini adds nothing to the city's prestige. And yet, at least in one respect,

change is evident. Five years ago it was impossible to find any kind of restaurant in baroque Catania. Today there's one on every block.

Il Piazza del Duomo
In the centre of the Piazza del Duomo, the baroque showcase at the heart of the city, stands an ancient fountain, with an elephant—Catania's symbol—made of lava supporting an obelisk on its back, thought to have been a turning-post in the Roman circus. Vaccarini turned the statue into a fountain, and Napoleon was so struck with it that he incorporated the elephant-obelisk emblem into several buildings in Paris. The elephant smiles benignly towards the **Cathedral of St Agatha,** patroness of Catania. Count Rosa founded the church in 1094, but following the eruption and the earthquake it had to be rebuilt, only the two apses of lava having survived from the original Norman structure. The facade was designed by Vaccarini, and the columns he placed in the lower front of this came from the Roman amphitheatre. Inside are the tombs of Bellini and the Aragonese Viceroy Fernandez d'Acuna (1494), which is in the chapel of Sant' Agata. The saint's relics are only displayed on high feast days—Agatha's veil is accredited with halting the lava flow in 1669, when the inhabitants tossed it to the molten matter. A fresco in the sacristy, painted in 1675, portrays Etna's attack on Catania. Also in the Piazza del Duomo are the 1741 **Municipio** with fine windows, another work of Vaccarini; the **Church of Sant' Agata;** the 18th-century **Palazzo** by Di Benedetto on the south side; and next to it the **Porta Uzeda,** an 18th-century archway through which you will find a small park where old men sun themselves and suspiciously eye all foreigners.

Around Piazza Mazzini
Two main streets, Via Garibaldi and Via Vittorio Emanuele run west from the piazza. On Via Garibaldi is the elegant Piazza Mazzini with its arcades of Roman columns from a nearby basilica. The effect of this little piazza, as with all of old Catania's numerous squares, is somewhat tarnished by its use as a parking lot. Just beyond, to the left, the Via Castello Ursino leads directly up to the **Castello Ursino** in the Piazza Federico di Svevia (Swabia). Built by Frederick II to intimidate local hotheads, the castle was restored in the 19th century after being damaged by the 1669 eruption. Only the keep remains, but it is still impressive and contains the **Museo Civico** (open 10–2, Sundays 10–1), which houses Prince Biscari's archaeological collection, objects from San Nicolo Monastery, and an example of the Sicilian carved and painted carts.

On the other side of the Piazza Mazzini, at the intersection of Via Vittorio Emanuele, is the Piazza San Francesco where you will find **Bellini's house**

and museum (open 9–1.30; Tuesday and Thursdays also 4–7; Sundays and holidays 8.30–1; admission free) with mementoes of the composer's life, some of his original scores, and models of scenes from his operas. Next to it, passing beneath an archway, is the famous **Via Crociferi,** one of the prettiest streets in Sicily, with its baroque palazzi and small churches—the best of these being **San Benedetto,** with an elegant facade.

The Greek Theatre and San Nicolo d'Arena
Continuing down Via Vittorio Emanuele, the **Greek Theatre** can be seen on the right; to enter, walk up Via Tineo to the Via Teatro Greco (no. 47). The theatre is open daily from 9–1 and 4pm to dusk. The present structure actually belongs to the Roman era, built in the 2nd century AD, on the site of the Greek theatre where Alcibiades spoke to gain support for the Athenian cause. Next to it are the ruins of the **Odeon.** Both are made of lava, which was originally covered with marble.

A few blocks west on Via Teatro stands the **Piazza Dante,** a beautifully laid-out square that has deteriorated through lack of care. Facing it is the gigantic church and monastery of **San Nicolo d'Arena**—surely one of the oddest, spookiest monuments in Sicily. The Italians say it has a 'mastodonic aspect'. The largest church on the island and the second largest convent in Europe (after the Mafra in Portugal), it was begun in the 16th century but never finished, then restored in 1735 after an earthquake destroyed it. Still unfinished, its facade is dominated by stumps of columns. The vast interior is presently undergoing badly needed renovation, but if the door is open you can peep in and see the huge organ, of 2916 pipes—its builder, Donato del Piano, was buried underneath it—and the meridian line on the transept floor. To visit the dome for its view, apply to the sacristan. The **Convent of San Nicolo** now houses the library—and a few bulldozers and asphalt spreaders; it's a maintenance yard for the city road crews. There is also an astrophysical observatory in the San Nicolo complex, but it too has suffered from Catanese indifference.

Via Etnea
Back at the Piazza del Duomo, Via Etnea, the main street of Catania, cuts straight across the city, with a view of Mt Etna at its very end. Every evening the most enthusiastic *passegiata* in Sicily takes place on this long street, the pavements crammed with icecream-eating Catanese peering in the windows of the many shoe, silver, jewellery and baby-clothes shops. At the end of the street, near the Piazza del Duomo, is the **Università,** with the pretty **Collegiata** church, a royal chapel built by the Bourbons in 1768. The University itself, Sicily's first, was founded by Alfonso V in 1434 and rebuilt

after the earthquake (Vaccarini worked on the courtyard in 1752).

Further up, Via Etnea gives on to the **Piazza Stesicoro,** a main city bus stop and location of the Bellini monument, and the remains of the 2nd-century **Roman amphitheatre.** This was once the world's second largest amphitheatre, after the Colosseum in Rome—a painting on the site shows the amphitheatre in its glory, before the Ostrogoths started using it as a quarry. Here, according to tradition, St Agatha suffered martyrdom. All the marble facing has worn away to expose the lava foundation. From here, Via dei Cappuccini leads past the **Church of Santo Carcere,** built on the supposed site of the prison of St Agatha. It has a beautiful 13th-century door and the old **Church of Sant' Agata la Vetere,** the ancient cathedral. Beneath the ruined Church of St Euplio, in Piazza Stesicoro, was the Roman Hypogeum.

The Via Etnea continues north to the elaborate main post office and the **Giardino Bellini**—the prettiest public park in Sicily, meticulously cared for (unlike most of Catania's public places). The flower clock and calendar on the hillside are unique in Italy.

At the east end of the park runs the main street of many names—Viale Regina Margherita here, Viale Venti Settembre and Corso Italia further east. The **Church of Santa Maria di Gesù** stands to the northwest of the park; Antonello Gagini designed the chapel doorway and sculpted the 'Madonna with the Angels' inside. At Corso Italia 21 is the **Palazzo delle Scienze** (by the modern Piazza Giovanni Verga). There are three museums nearby (all open 10–12, closed on holidays): the **Geology Museum,** and the **Mineralogy** and **Vulcanology Museums** (Corso Italia 55). Not surprisingly Catania has one of the best schools of vulcanology anywhere. In the untidy quarter east of the Piazza del Duomo, in the Piazza Bellini, is the beautiful **Teatro Massimo,** where operas are performed in winter and spring. The **Stazione Centrale,** by the sea, is the terminus for most provincial buses and the 7am bus to Mt Etna. The nearby fountain of the Rape of Persephone is floodlit at night to suggest the underworld.

The nearest **beaches** to the city are Lido de Plaia in the south (bus D in the summer from Piazza Giovanni Verga and Via Etnea) and Ognina, a pretty place with lava cliffs, to the north of town.

FESTIVALS

Sant' Agata (3–5 February), climaxing with the *Cannelore,* a procession of large wooden floats, some 18 ft high, carried on the men's shoulders. On the floats are tableaux representing scenes from the life of Sant' Agata, elaborately decorated. The procession stops at various places in the city associated with the saint. Another important *festa*, of the Three Sainted Brothers

(Cirino, Alfio and Filadelfo), takes place on the night of 9 May. Here barefoot pilgrims dressed all in red run from Catania to the Sanctuary of Trecastagni, at the base of Mt Etna, where they light candles to the three saints. Traditional carts pulled by bedecked horses and mules, and Catanians on bicycles, accompany the valiant runners.

SPECIALITIES

Scacciata, made at Christmas, with anchovies, fresh cheese, pepper and sauces, stuffed in a pastry envelope; *cannelloni alla Catanese*. Favourite wines are *Trecastagni* and *Il Sparviero dell' Etna* (reds), *Castelriccio* (rosé) and *Ciclope-Mazzullo* (white).

GETTING TO AND AROUND CATANIA

By air: to Palermo, Venice, Bologna, Rome, Milan and Naples. The airport is at Fontanarossa, 4½ miles from the town. The terminal is at Corso Sicilia 105; buses leave from here and Piazza Stesicoro for the airport. A Giunta bus links the airport to Milazzo (for the Aeolian Islands).

By train: to Messina and the south; also to Enna, Caltanissetta, Palermo and all major tourist centres. Ditto for buses. Catania is the hub of all transport in eastern Sicily and you may have to back-track to Catania from Syracuse, for example, to get to your destination. Buses depart from the Stazione Centrale. The narrow-gauge Circumetnea, which calls at all the major villages around Mt Etna, leaves from the Corso Italia Station.

TOURIST INFORMATION

Fontana Rossa Airport (tel. (095) 311711); Stazione Centrale (tel. (095) 328440); main EPT office at Largo Paisiello 5 (tel. (095) 317720). For information on Mt Etna call in at the 'Italian Alpine Club', Via Napoli 116 (guides available for climbers).

WHERE TO STAY

Excelsior****, on the Piazza G. Verga (tel. (095) 325733) is the most comfortable hotel in Catania; open all year round, single rooms are available for 40–75 000 lire, double 61–120 000 lire. On the main street, Via Etnea 310, **Italia**** has a selection of comfortable rooms: 24 000 lire for a single room without a bath, 31 000 with; double 37 000 lire without, 50 000 with; also open all year round (tel. (095) 317833). The **Savona***, on Vittorio Emanuele 210 (tel. (095) 326982), has good clean rooms for 22 000 lire single with bath, 35 000 double (less without bath).

EATING OUT

La Siciliana, Viale Marco Polo 52 (closed Mondays) is considered by many to be one of Sicily's finest restaurants, serving true local cuisine (outside dining in the summer). Meals here are in the 50–60 000 lire range. For seafood, **Pagano al Mare** on Via Acque Casse 18 is another of Catania's best (40 000 lire and up). Less expensive fish may be found at the **Trattoria Enzo** on Via Malta 26. **Don Saro,** Viale della Liberta 129, serves good Sicilian dishes for around 15 000 lire.

Caltagirone

The **Plain of Catania,** drained by the rivers Simeto and Pittano, like the rest of the province of Catania has little to interest the traveller, though two towns in the south do merit a visit. Caltagirone, on the main highway south of Piazza Armerina (Enna), has the sobriquet 'Queen of the Hills'. It spreads out in a charming array over three hills, some 2000 ft above sea level. Originally inhabited in 2000 BC by the Sikels, the Syracusans Hellenised it. The name 'Caltagirone' dates from the Arabic occupation (*kalat* = castle and *gerum* = caves). The Genoese briefly conquered the town in 1030, the earthquake of 1693 destroyed it, and the bombs in 1943 caused much damage and some 700 deaths.

As you can see as you stroll through Caltagirone, ceramics are a local speciality. In the **Museo della Ceramica** (Via Roma; open 9–2, Sundays 9–1, closed Mondays) are examples of the town's ceramic art from prehistoric times to the 19th century. Here also is the **Villa,** the public garden, the **Teatrino** (1792) and the **Chiesa del Gesù** (16th century) with a painting by Caravaggio. Near here, at the centre of town, is the Piazza Umberto Primo, a survival of the earthquake, dominated by the **Corte Capitaniale,** decorated by members of the Gagini family (Antonello is thought to have lived part of his life in Caltagirone).

What impresses vistors most in Caltagirone is the **Stair of Santa Maria del Monte,** each of its 142 steps adorned with colourful ceramic designs. On 23 July it is brilliantly illuminated for the *festa* of San Giacomo.

Grammichele and Vizzini

To the east, Grammichele often receives special mention in books on urban design. The modern town is built on the site of Occialà, which was destroyed in the earthquake of 1693. The new town was designed in a strict hexagonal form by Nicola Branci Forte, after a book by Tommaso Camporpornella (*Civitas Solis*), reviving the 8th-century BC Babylonian idea of radioconcentric city planning. From the air it is a perfect geometric symbol. Grammichele is also renowned for its dried figs.

Further along the SS124 lies Vizzini, 2030 ft high in the Iblean Mountains on the site of ancient Bidis, mentioned by Cicero. Vizzini and Francofonte in Syracuse Province both claim to be the setting for Mascagni's beloved opera, *Cavalleria Rusticana* and Sicilian novelist Giovanni Verga's *Mastro Don Gesualdo*. In the **Church of Santa Maria di Gesù** the altarpiece of the Madonna and Child (1527) is by Antonello Gagini.

Catania to Syracuse

Augusta

In between the two capitals, below the honey-producing Iblean Hills that inspired Theocritus' bucolic poetry, lies Augusta, Italy's main oil port and a naval base. Like Syracuse, Augusta is built on an islet connected by bridge to the mainland. Frederick II founded Augusta on the site of the ancient Xiphonia in 1232 for refugees from Centuripe and Montalbano. Most of the original buildings were destroyed in the 1693 earthquake and again in the 1943 air raids, although the cathedral still stands (dating from the 17th century) and two 16th-century towers along the Porto Megarese. The Municipio still sports Stupor Mundi's imperial eagle over the door. Augusta's main interest for the tourist, however, is its proximity to the excavations of Megara Hyblaea and the beach resorts at **Brucoli** and **Agnone**.

Megara Hyblaea

Across the bay from Augusta (signposted on SS114 on the Augusta–Syracuse bus route) is Megara Hyblaea, founded in 730 BC by the Megarians. This site, at the mouth of the River Cantera, was originally inhabited in the Neolithic period. Pantalica, the Sikel king of Hybla, offered it to the Greek colonists, who made it prosper through the manufacture of ceramics. Gelon of Syracuse destroyed the city in 483 BC, Timoleon had the site resettled, but the Consul Marcellus delivered the *coup de grâce* in 214 when the new town defied the Romans. A part of the ruins has been covered by the sea; those visible on land include a Doric temple, possibly dedicated to Aphrodite; the monumental *agora*; Archaic tombs; and some Hellenistic houses on a regular plan. In the Antiquarium on the site are a few of the finds. Both the digs and the Antiquarium are open from 9am till dusk (closed Mondays).

Carlentini

Inland from Augusta is Carlentini, founded in 1551 by Charles V as a summer town for the inhabitants of Lentini. From here one can visit **Lentini** itself (ancient Leontinoi), the second oldest Greek colony in Sicily after Naxos. Founded by the Chalcidians on the site of an early Sikel town, it soon became important as an agricultural centre. Syracuse ruled over the city for most of its existence, though in the mid 5th century BC, in a brief interlude of independence, it became allied with Athens and sent the renowned orator Gorgias to the Athenian assembly to plead for protection from its old master. When Syracuse attacked Leontinoi in 427 BC, the Athenians jumped at the chance to send aid. Although the Syracusans eventually made a treaty with them, the Athenians used the Leontinoi conflict as one of their major reasons for the disastrous Great Expedition a few years later. Leontinoi, like Syracuse, sided with Carthage in the Second Punic War, and was also attacked by the vengeance-seeking Romans; however, unlike Syracuse, Leontinoi was granted no mercy, and the Romans beheaded 2000 citizens for desertion, in accordance with Roman law.

The medieval town of Lentini fell in the 1693 earthquake although you can still see the ruins of **Frederick II's castle**. The **Chiesa Madre's** right-hand nave was a 3rd-century Christian hypogeum; also note the beloved 9th-century Byzantine icon of the Madonna Odigistria. At the **Museum** in Piazza del Liceo (open 9.30–1; closed Mondays) are items from various stages of the town's history. The **ancient city** itself lies between Lentini and Carlentini, spread over two hills, Metapiccola and San Mauro. Traces of the early Sikel town may be seen on Metapiccola, while around San Mauro are remains of Leontinoi's defences, a Hellenistic necropolis and part of the south gate to the city.

Melilli, at the crossroads to the southwest, is famous for the festival of St Sebastian which takes place every 4 May. Here, in return for a favour from the saint, parents promise that their children will take part in the procession of St Sebastian—stark naked. The discarded clothing is later given to the poor children of the town. At **Cava Secchiera,** near Melilli, are some prehistoric rock-cut tombs.

Pantalica

West of Melilli the road leads through the Anapo valley to **Sortino,** which has an impressive church. A new road (from highway 124, turn off at Ferla) takes you to the vast Bronze Age **necropolis of Pantalica,** in the deep valleys of the Anapo and Calcinara rivers. The settlement of Pantalica, dating from 1200 BC when invaders forced the coastal residents to move inland, is now believed to be the legendary Sikel town of Hybla. Few traces remain of this: one building, perhaps the *anactoron* or palace, along with signs of a wall. In the surrounding cliffs, however, are some 5000 family tombs carved in the rock like a honeycomb, attesting to the large size of ancient Hybla. In the 8th century BC, Pantalica was abandoned for reasons unknown. Later, threatened like the Sikels by invaders on the coast, the Byzantines sought shelter at Pantalica and expanded the tombs for dwellings. Two small chapels remain from this period.

Syracuse

HISTORY

According to Thucydides, ancient Syracuse (from 'Suraka', the Phoenician name of a nearby marsh) was founded in 733 BC by colonists from Corinth, who usurped the native Sikels and soon established a thriving town. The location was ideal; the small offshore island of Ortygia could easily be defended, the plains facing it were fertile, and the natural harbour offered immense possibilities for maritime activities. It wasn't long before the oligarchs of Syracuse were founding colonies of their own on Sicily, at Akrae and Camarina, increasing the city's sphere of influence to the borders of powerful Gela and Megara Hyblaea.

In 485 BC political turmoil within Syracuse caused the oligarchs to invite Gelon, the tyrant of Gela, to take control of the city. Gelon realised the potential of the Grand Harbour and made Syracuse a sea power; on land he annexed Megara Hyblaea and moved much of the population of his native Gela and that of Camarina to Syracuse. It was Gelon, in alliance with Theron of Akragas, who defeated the massive Carthaginian attack on Himera in 480.

Two years later Gelon was succeeded by his brother Hieron, a cruel tyrant, yet at the same time enamoured of poetry, inviting to his court such leading lights as Simonides, Pindar and the magnificent Aeschylus. Pindar praised Hieron's victories in the chariot race, and Aeschylus is thought to have written *Prometheus Bound* and *Prometheus Unbound* in Syracuse, where they had their debut. Militarily, Hieron aided the Greek navy in defeating the Etruscans at Cumae (474 BC), ending another Barbarian threat to Greek holdings.

Shortly after Hieron's death in 466, Syracuse turned democratic, but remained nonetheless powerful. Athens grew jealous of this new rival, and feared for its own allies and interests in western Greece. As Syracuse was allied with Sparta, Athens' arch-enemy, in the Peloponnesian War, Athens had all the rationale it needed for an attack on Syracuse—with the eventual goal of adding all of Sicily to its mighty empire. For the details of this haughty, grandiose expedition of the Athenians, one must turn to Thucydides. Briefly, however, the 134 Athenian triremes, led by the indecisive Nicias, set sail in 415 BC and almost succeeded in taking Syracuse, blockading it by land from Eurayalus. The Spartans sent reinforcements to Syracuse, under Gylippos, who in turn blockaded the Athenian fleet in the Grand Harbour. When the Athenians attempted to escape, Syracuse attacked and sank half their ships, and completely routed the soldiers who tried to flee south. 'This was the greatest Hellenic achievement of any war ... at once most glorious to the victors and most calamitous to the conquered', wrote Thucydides. Indeed, this surprise victory over the most powerful city of its day was a shot in the arm for the prestige of Syracuse; within the next few years it overtook Athens as the premier city of the Western world. On the other side of the coin, the miserable Athenians captured at Syracuse were kept in the quarries (*latomiae*) under inhuman conditions. Few ever returned to Athens; the story goes that only those who were able to recite passages of Aeschylus or Euripides, the two favourite poets of the Syracusans, were set free.

The next tyrant of Syracuse, the ambitious Dionysius, was also a poet, and wrote numerous tragedies which he entered year after year in the festivals of his namesake, only to be begrudged a prize by the Athenians (still no doubt miffed by their humiliation at Syracuse). However, in 368, when Athens sought an alliance with Syracuse, the festival judges declared Dionysius' entry that year quite prizeworthy, whereupon Dionysius celebrated his long-sought victory so lavishly that it killed him.

Unfortunately—or perhaps fortunately—none of Dionysius' poetry has come down to us, and history remembers him instead for his military genius. He built the fortress and walls on the strategic Epipolae Ridge west of Syracuse which proved so crucial to the city's defence during his campaign to rid Sicily of the Carthaginians. In this, however, he never quite succeeded, despite his gathering of engineers from all over Greece and Italy to design new weapons. Most spectacular of these was the catapult, which was instrumental in the Greeks' victory over the Carthaginians at Motya in western Sicily (see the section on the Stagnone Islands).

Dionysius made Syracuse a powerful empire, but his son and successor Dionysius II was rather ineffectual, despite Plato's efforts to teach him the ideals of *The Republic*. When Dion, the uncle of Dionysius II and friend of Plato, grew tired of his nephew's tyranny, he rose to overthrow him, and was in turn assassinated for acting the tyrant. The year 343 BC found Syracuse in a bad way through the neglect of its despots. Fearing a new Carthaginian offensive, the citizens appealed to mother Corinth for aid and were sent Timoleon, a man of justice and peace who, after overthrowing all the petty tyrants of Sicily, established democracy and made a peace treaty with Carthage.

Timoleon's good works lasted through his lifetime, but when he died in 336 BC the internecine bickering among the Greeks began again, eventually bringing the bellicose adventurer Agathocles to power in 317 BC. Throughout his rule, Syracuse was at war, conquering most of Greek Sicily except for Akragas. When Agathocles died in 289 without an heir, his fragile empire crumbled. In the confusion that followed, the Carthaginians saw their chance and sailed into the Grand Harbour—this time deterred by Pyrrhus of Epirus, who came to the rescue at the request of Syracuse and Akragas. Once again, the Barbarian threat temporarily served to unite the Greek factions.

The Syracusans elected Hieron II (ruled 275–216 BC), one of Pyrrhus' officers, as their new ruler. As wise as he was long-lived, Hieron II was a blessing to the city. Besides making a treaty with the Romans and supporting them in the First Punic War, he improved the laws and life of Syracuse, re-designing the Neopolis quarter and building the mammoth altar to Zeus the Giver of Freedom (or 'Zeus Eleftherios'). Theocritus, the first writer of idyllic poetry, frequented the court of Hieron II, along with the great scientist Archimedes who was a cousin of the king.

Hieron II was succeeded by his grandson Hieronymus, who made the mistake of pledging allegiance to Hannibal in 215, when that Carthaginian was at the height of his power. This brought the wrath of Rome down upon Syracuse in the form of the Consul Marcellus, who laid siege to Syracuse. Here the Romans faced not so much the defending army of a city as the genius of one man—Archimedes. In his role as General of Ordnance in Syracuse, Archimedes had for some time been busy designing ingenious war machinery to defend the city. His contraptions dropped 600-lb lead weights onto the Roman scaling engines and his grapnels were lowered to snatch the Roman ships in the harbour, lift them up by their hulls and spill their crews into the sea. According to legend, Archimedes even reflected the sun's rays with mirrors to ignite the more distant Roman ships.

Despite all these devices, however, the Romans prevailed, surprising the Syracusans during a festival. Archimedes was slain by accident. From then on, Syracuse dwindled in importance, although admired by the Romans for its beauty. Christianity found Syracuse a fertile field in its early days, especially after St Paul stopped there for three days en route from Malta to Rome.

Late in the 3rd century AD, the first of the tribes of ransacking Barbarians passed through, and in 535 Belisarius captured Syracuse from the Ostrogoths in the name of Byzantium. One of the Eastern emperors, Constans, moved his capital from Constantinople to Syracuse in 663, but he died five years later when a disgruntled servant hit him with a soap dish. The court then returned to Constantinople. A key Byzantine port, Syracuse was besieged and destroyed by the Arabs in 878. Liberated again by the Byzantines in 1040, this time under George Maniakes, Syracuse regained some of its former prosperity under the Normans. From 1361 to 1536 the Camera Regionale sat at Syracuse, though many of the fine palaces of that period were felled in the 1693 earthquake. The city also suffered from both Allied and Luftwaffe bombings 250 years later.

WHAT TO SEE

Although the spiritual heart of the city still rests in the narrow lanes of Ortygia island, the inexorable urge towards modernisation has pushed the commercial centre deep into the adjacent mainland. Yet the city (pop. 120 000) is small compared to the size of ancient Syracuse; you can easily walk to all the main points of interest. Syracuse is renowned for its excellent climate, and the visitor can readily combine the exploration of the city's past with a swim on one of many fine beaches to the south—Pantanelli being the closest, with the more organised Lido Arenella, Fontane Bianche and Lido Sayonara further on. Unfortunately an oilrig has recently been installed in the centre of the bay, like some ungainly robot from outer space.

Ortygia Island

Ortygia (Greek for 'quail'), a name associated with the goddess Artemis, originally referred to the whole of Syracuse, but later (though still in ancient times) it became sole property of the island. Two bridges connect it to the mainland; the main one, Ponte Nuovo, leads on to the large **Piazza della Poste** (main post office, stops for provincial buses) and the adjacent Piazza Pancali, which boasts the ruins of the Doric **Temple of Apollo,** excavated in 1943. Dating back to the mid 6th century BC, this temple was the first large structure built by the Greek colonists in Sicily. Two of its columns and part of the *cella* walls have been reconstructed, though it is still hard to imagine what the temple originally looked like. Painted terracotta fragments from the cornice are in the Archaeology Museum.

From here the narrow Via Cavour leads up to the **Piazza Archimede,** the old heart of Ortygia. The 19th-century fountain in its centre has been confusingly dubbed 'the Fountain of Arethusa', but this isn't the real one. Note the **Palazzo Lanza** (15th century) and the **Banco d'Italia,** housed in a medieval Catalan building. Just off the piazza, on Via Montalto, the 1397 **Palazzo Montalto** offers an inspired example of the Chiaramonte style, with its delicate mullioned triple windows.

Piazza del Duomo
Continuing up the Via Cavour you come to the Piazza del Duomo, one of Sicily's most elegant squares. The site was sacred even in Sikel times; here the 5th-century Greeks dedicated a temple to Athena in thanksgiving for their victory at Himera. This temple was adapted by the Christians and became the Syracuse **Cathedral** in 640, under Bishop Zosimus. Further remodelling took place under the Normans, and when the facade toppled in the earthquake, Andrea Palma designed the lovely baroque front (finished 1754) that one sees today. Inside, the ancient Doric columns trace the plan of Athena's temple, the excellent proportions of which are felt throughout the building. To the immediate left is the baptistry, containing an ancient Greek marble font resting on Norman bronze lions. This is followed by the Chapel of Santa Lucia, patroness of Syracuse, and at the far end of the same aisle is the Cappella del Crocifisso with a painting of St Zosimus by Antonello da Messina, and one of St Marcian attributed to the school of Antonello, which also painted the thirteen panels in the sacristy (door in the chapel).

Other buildings on the Piazza del Duomo include the **Palazzo Arcivescovile,** housing the Biblioteca Alagoniana with its 13th-century manuscripts; the church of **Santa Lucia alla Badia,** begun in 1695 after the earthquake; and the **Municipio,** a 17th-century palace built over the ruins of an 8th-century BC settlement, which houses the small Ionic **Temple Antiquarium** (usually open in office hours).

The Fountain of Arethusa
To the west of the piazza is the Fountain of Arethusa, the freshwater spring so close to the sea's edge, which fascinated the Ancient Greeks. According to their legends, the nymph Arethusa was being pursued by the river god Alpheus (of the Peloponnese), and she begged the goddess Artemis to help her. Artemis obliged by turning her into a fountain, in which form she fled

across the sea to Sicily, with Alpheus in hot pursuit, rising up in Ortygia where their waters were mixed. Strabo records in this connection that a cup thrown in the River Alpheus in the Peloponnese would turn up in Arethusa's fountain in Syracuse. Before the Battle of the Nile, Nelson's fleet replenished its water supplies here. Nowadays, rumour has it that the fountain has turned to salt water, although the luxuriant papyrus growing out of it would seem to refute this. Recently the fountain has been lovingly restored. A small **Tropical Aquarium** (open 9–1; closed Fridays and Sundays) can be found close by, along with the tree-lined promenade, the **Foro Italico,** whence the steamers depart for Malta. At the far end of the street is the 15th-century **Porta Marina,** with Gothic inscriptions.

On the southernmost tip of Ortygia rises the **Castello Maniace,** named for George Maniakes the Byzantine liberator of the city. Built by Frederick II in 1239, the keep is 170 ft square but only two-thirds of its original height. Now a barracks, it can be visited only with permission from the military authority on the Longomare Ortygia. Beneath the castle one can also visit the imaginatively named Bagno della Regina (the Queen's Bath), actually an ancient underground reservoir.

The only other example of Swabian architecture on Ortygia is the **Palazzo Bellomo** (Via Capodieci), although later additions almost overwhelm the original building. The Palazzo now contains the **Museum of Medieval and Modern Art** (open 9–2; closed Mondays), an interesting collection with some fine medieval paintings, including the partly damaged *Annunciation* of Antonello da Messina. On the other side of the street is the 14th-century **Church of San Martino,** with a fine interior and a 15th-century triptych of the Madonna and Child. Two other churches of interest lie at the opposite end of Ortygia: **San Filippo,** on the Via Vittorio Veneto, a fine street of 17th-century Spanish mansions, is also from the 17th century; **San Pietro** around the corner of Via San Pietro was founded in the 4th century by St Germanus. Its original form as a Roman basilica can still be discerned despite later alterations.

The Mainland

In the ancient quarter of Achradina, facing Ortygia, is the large square called **Foro Siracusano,** the site of the Greek *agora*, now dominated by the Fascist-built Pantheon to the Fallen. Towards the railway station (Via Elorina) are the ruins known as the **Ginnasio Romano,** although they actually encompass a small 1st-century theatre, its *cavea* picturesquely flooded. Archaeologists believe it was constructed for the minority who still appreciated drama after gladiatorial contests became the fare at the far larger Greek Theatre.

Borgo Santa Lucia

The quarter of Borgo Santa Lucia to the east is named for the saint who suffered martyrdom in 304 on the site where the **Santa Lucia Church** now stands, built in 1629. A few elements remain of the original Norman church, including the doorway and rose window. Hanging in the apse is one of Caravaggio's masterpieces, *The Burial of St Lucia*, and two very old crucifixes. Until the Byzantines transported her body to Constantinople in 1038, St Lucia lay in the octagonal **Sepolcro Chapel,** built by Giovanni 'The Lizard' Vermexio. Beneath the church is a vast series of **catacombs,** the oldest in Sicily—used by the Christians since the 2nd century—and the second largest in Italy, after those in Rome. A small underground chapel has traces of Byzantine paintings.

Also in Borgo Santa Lucia, on Via Dell'Arsenale, are the rather scanty remains of the ancient **Arsenal,** and next to it, a Byzantine bath-house. In the summer a boat leaves from St Lucia for **Capo Santa Panagia,** the Athenian base in the Great Expedition. Fossils have been found in the caves there, along with signs of Neolithic habitation. Inquire at the quay for departure times.

Latomia and the Catacombs

To the north and west of St Lucia is the ancient quarter of **Tyche.** Where the Riviera Dionisio il Grande and the Via Bassa meet is the entrance to the Latomia dei Cappuccini, the quarries begun in the 6th century BC. Once the horrible prison of the captured Athenian soldiers, the quarries are now the lovely peaceful gardens of the Capuchin friars (open 9–1). To the west, on Via August von Platen, are the Catacombs of Vigna Cassia (open 9–12.30 and 4–6) from the 3rd century BC, with a few traces of paintings, and the Protestant Cemetery of **Villa Landolina** in a small *latomia* where the German Romantic poet August von Platen is buried.

In the same vicinity (Via San Giovanni) is the beautiful ruined church of **San Giovanni,** built on the site of the first cathedral of Syracuse, rebuilt by the Normans, then destroyed by the 1693 earthquake—though the rose window somehow managed to escape intact. The main point of interest here is the crypt (open 9–12.30 and 3.30–6.30) where the first Bishop of Syracuse, San Marcian, was martyred in the 3rd century. The symbols of the four Evangelists are carved on the columns of the small chapel, which also contains an altar on the site where St Paul is said to have preached to the Syracusans, the pillar where St Marcian was martyred, and what is believed to be the first painting of St Lucia on the wall, dating back to the 4th century—a fine work of art. The friar on duty will conduct you through the catacombs used in the 6th century, which still retain traces of early Christian paintings. Back outside, numerous yellow signs show the way to the as yet unfinished **Sanctuary of the Madonnina delle Lacrime,** built to house a small factory-made statue of the Madonna which wept for five days in 1953. When finished, the sanctuary will resemble a grotesque, giant Christmas tree.

Across Viale Teocrito from the sanctuary is the equally new **Archaeology Museum.** Syracuse observers have long wondered which would be finished first. At the time of writing the last few items of an excellent collection, perhaps the greatest hoard of Greek art between Athens and London, are being moved from their old quarters in the Piazza del Duomo; the collection's star exhibit is the notorious, voluptuous Landolina Venus (Landolina was the name of the archaeologist who found her); equally striking are the statue of an unknown fertility goddess suckling twins, and the sarcophagus of Valerius and Adelphia with its quaint biblical scenes.

The Landolina Venus, Museum of Archaeology, Syracuse

Archaeological Zone

The Archaeological Zone (open from 9am until one hour before sunset, closed Mondays and major holidays; admission fee) is in the quarter of Neopolis, that part of Syracuse built by Hieron II. The Spaniards in the 16th century rifled Neopolis for stone to build their walls, but the ruins are still very impressive, even the much-pilfered **Altar of Hieron II** (241–215 BC), over 200 yards long, dedicated to Zeus Eleftherios. Hieron II built this altar in honour of Timoleon's expulsion of tyrants, which the ancient Syra-

137

cusans commemorated annually with a great sacrifice. Although only the base of the altar remains, it does give one some idea of the magnitude of the public monuments built by the western Greeks. This grandeur is also evident in the **Greek Theatre,** carved out of the living rock. One of the largest in the world, it measures 453 ft in diameter and seats 15 000. The original theatre, built by Timoleon, which saw performances of *The Persians* of Aeschylus, was enlarged by Hieron II and later partially reconstructed by the Romans, who staged gladiatorial matches there and, by flooding the orchestra, mock naval engagements (*naumachiae*). Along the top of the seats are inscriptions dedicating various parts of the theatre to Zeus and the family of Hieron II. As in ancient times, Greek dramas are still performed here in even-numbered years (apply to the Tourist Board for details).

Above the theatre runs a long terrace called **the Street of the Tombs,** mostly Byzantine graves. The largest niche is a *nymphaeum* built by Hieron II, where the waters of an ancient aqueduct still cascade. West of the theatre, the very ancient **Sanctuary of Apollo Temenites,** sacred since the 7th century BC, may be visited, along with the early **Linear Theatre** where the seats consist of 17 steps on the hillside.

East of the Greek Theatre is the luxurious **Latomia del Paradiso,** where the main attraction lies in the odd **Ear of Dionysius,** an artificial cavern 213 ft long and 70 ft high, of uncertain purpose, but known for its excellent acoustics. Caravaggio christened it for its ear-shaped entrance, although some have speculated that the tyrant Dionysius incarcerated political prisoners in here so that he could secretly listen to their conversations. Next to the cavern is the **Grotta dei Cordari,** the Ropemakers' Cave, where for centuries the Syracusans made their ropes.

One enters through another gate (but with the same ticket) to the **Roman Amphitheatre,** built in the 3rd century AD. Like the Greek Theatre, it is one of the largest of its kind, measuring 459 ft across. From the corridor below the front seats, the wild beasts and gladiators, would enter the arena, in the centre of which is a mysterious pit. The names of their wealthy owners can be seen inscribed on some of the seats.

Euryalus Castle and the Olympieion

One interesting short excursion from Syracuse (city bus 8 or 10) is to the Euryalus Castle; get off the bus in front of the Albergo della Gioventù (the youth hostel). The castle (open from 9am until dusk; closed Mondays), built on the Epipolae Ridge, was begun by Dionysius the Elder in the early 4th century BC, and later modified by Archimedes. *Euryalus* means 'broad nail' in Greek, and the castle defended the crucial inland supply route to Syracuse in times of siege. Three great trenches, connected by underground passages, were constructed to repulse the rapidly evolving machines of war. The castle and its five huge towers was only part of the vast 17-mile-long system of defence designed by Dionysius; mysteriously, however, the defenders surrendered without a fight to the Roman Marcellus in 212 BC. The castle is the best preserved and most intriguing example of Greek defensive works in the world; it also affords an excellent view of the Syracusan plain below.

The Olympieion, the scant but picturesque ruins of a Doric temple of Olympian Zeus, can also be reached by buses 8 or 10. Still standing on the right bank of the River Cyane are two columns and part of the stylobate. From here one can walk to the **Source of the Cyane** (*cyane* means 'blue' in Greek), the river named after Persephone's nymph who wept so much at the goddess's abduction that she turned into a spring. Along the banks of the Cyane grows the exotic papyrus, reputedly a gift to Syracuse from the Hellenistic ruler Ptolemy Philadelphus of Egypt. It grows wild nowhere else outside North Africa. If one has the time, a more leisurely way to visit the Olympieion and the Cyane is by boat (inquire at the Tourist Office or at the Marina for availability and price).

FESTIVALS
St Lucia (13 December); St Sebastian (20 January); Madonnina delle Lacrime (29 August–3 September); International Ballet Festival (June–July); Greek theatre (every other year); Palio del Mare (last Sunday in July).

SPECIALITIES
Pasta fritta (sweet balls of pasta covered with honey), *tonno alla marinara* (tuna fish with onions and spices), stuffed artichokes.

GETTING TO AND AROUND SYRACUSE
By rail: frequent service to and from Messina and Catania, less frequent to Ragusa and Licata and stops in between.
By bus: hourly coach service to and from Catania (nearest airport), less often to Palermo, Agrigento, Gela, Caltanissetta, Piazza Armerina, Ragusa, Palazzolo Acreide, Noto and all other towns in the province, departing from the Piazza della Posta. To get to the Archaeology Zone, take the city bus from the Corso Gelone.
By sea: there are ferries 3 times a week from the Foro Italico to Reggio Calabria, Catania and Malta via Tirrenia Lines whose office is at Viale Mazzini 4 (tel. (0931) 66956/65684).

TOURIST INFORMATION
EPT: Via S. Sebastiano 43/45 (tel. (0931) 67710).

EPT: information office in the Archaeological Zone (tel. (0931) 60510).
AAST: Via Maestranza 33; also in the railway station (tel. (0931) 66932, summer only).
Information office of the city of Syracuse: Corso Umberto.

WHERE TO STAY

Despite its role as one of the leading tourist centres in Sicily, Syracuse is not well endowed with good hotels. In Ortygia, the **Grand Hotel*****, Viale Mazzini 12 (tel. (0931) 65101), is the most comfortable, a fine old establishment with single rooms for 26 000 lire, double for 42 500 with bath, less expensive without. Also pleasant, in a quiet garden setting, is the **Villa Politi*****, Via M. Politi 2 (tel. (0931) 32100; single room 38 000 lire, double 58 000). Best among the less expensive choices is the **Gran Bretagne***, near the Tirrenia dock at Via Savoia 21 (tel. (0931) 68765), where single rooms are 11 000 lire, double 20 000 without bath. There's a pleasant **youth hostel** by the Euryalus Castle on Via Epipoli 45 (tel. (0931) 711118), open all year, and a campsite (open April–October) at Fontance Bianche (tel. (0931) 790356).

EATING OUT

There are many good restaurants in Syracuse: on Ortygia there is **Minerva,** 20 Piazza del Ducco, with local and fish dishes (closed Mondays), around 25 000 lire; and **Fratelli Bandiera,** with good seafood, on Via Trieste 42 (30–40 000 lire). On the mainland, two good, old and inexpensive trattorias are **Da Luigi** on the Corso Luigi near the rail tracks, and **Fiasco d'Oro** on Via Malta 37. According to many the best place in town is by the sea: **Ionico-Rutta e Ciauli** at Riv. Dionysio il Grande, featuring many local and house specialities, with fine views from the terrace in the summer (50–60 000 lire).

Thapsos

North of Syracuse, on the Magnisi peninsula, are the ruins of Thapsos, the largest Bronze Age town in Sicily (nearest town is Priolo, and the excavations are 1½ miles away, by the lighthouse). Dating from the 14th century BC, the settlement consists of circular and multi-roomed huts, only recently discovered. Most interesting are the tombs carved out of the rock with little cupolas, where vases imported from Mycenae and Malta have been found. Thapsos gave its name to the Bronze Age culture on Sicily, and is known for its vases on pedestals. Sometime around the beginning of the first millennium BC the inhabitants of Thapsos were forced inland, perhaps to Pantalica.

Inland from Syracuse: Palazzolo Acreide

Further west, on the scenic highway 124 (bus from Syracuse) is the Palazzolo Acreide, modern successor of ancient Akrai, the first Syracusan colony, founded in 664 BC on a high hill. Its ruins are the most extensive in the province after Syracuse itself: a 15-minute walk from town will take you there. The **Archaeology Zone** is open daily from 9am to one hour before sunset. It includes a small (600-seat) but well preserved Hellenistic theatre with pleasant views; Roman silos and mills; the *bouleuterion* (council chamber); and the foundation of the *agora*. Behind the theatre are two quarries, or *latomiae*, the Intagliata and the Intagliatella, one containing Byzantine tombs, the other niches of the Hero cult, with a carved relief. Another *latomia*, more mysterious and 1 mile from the Archaeology Zone (note signposts), contains the **Templi Ferali** (temples of the dead), two great chambers with niches and inscriptions in honour of the deceased. Below, in an enclosure, are the **Santoni**—twelve rough-hewn statues representing various aspects of the goddess Cybele, a Phrygian deity. Her eastern origin may account for the very un-Greek repetition of the same figure in one place.

Palazzolo is a baroque charmer with a complete lack of tourist facilities, but there is a museum, the **Casa Museo** on Via Machiavelli (open 10–1; closed Mondays and Fridays), with a fine ethnographic collection in a turn-of-the-century peasant home.

Among the churches, note the asymmetrical **Chiesa dell' Annunziata** and *The Madonna with Child* by Laurano in the church of the **Convento dei Minori Osservanti,** and the exuberant baroque interior of **San Paulo** in the Piazza Umberto. His festival is celebrated on 29 June.

Another colony of Syracuse, **Casmene** (founded 644 BC), is located on top of Mt Casale, northwest of Palazzolo Acreide. The scenic river valleys around Casmene offer more than the excavations themselves, and the difficult access to the site makes it a destination for the adventuresome. **Buccheri,** the closest village to Mt Casale, is a modest summer resort, surrounded by forests and pretty views. Between Palazzolo and Syracuse lies another hill town, **Canicattini,** from where speleologists can visit the **Grotta del Monello** with stalactites. The cemetery of Canicattini, set apart on a hill, is a true baroque city of the dead.

South of Syracuse: Noto

South of Syracuse the coast offers beach after beach—Lido Arenella, Ognina, Fontane Bianche, Lido di Avola—while inland the blue of the sea is matched by the glistening green of the citrus groves. The main centre here is Noto, a few miles from the coast. The destruction of the town in the 1693 earthquake was so thorough that the inhabitants rebuilt the new town a few miles away from the bleak ruins of the old one (Noto Antica), and the result is pure Sicilian 18th-century baroque. Giovanni Battista Landolina, who laid it out, and the masterful Rosario Gagliardi, a local architect who designed the cathedral and other buildings, are chiefly responsible for this unusually homogeneous town of golden stone. Noto should be entered for fullest effect through the **Porta Reale** (1838) in the Corso Vittorio Emanuele. One passes first the churches of San Francesco (1745) and elliptical Santa Chiara, then the **Museo Civico** at no. 134 (open 9–1; closed Mondays) in a former convent, housing an interesting collection of finds from Eloro and Noto Antica. The Corso opens up here into the Piazza Municipio, with the fine **Cathedral of San Nicola,** the Bishop's Palace and the excellently arcaded Municipio, or Palazzo Ducezio, built around 1750. This is followed by another piazza, Sedici Maggio, where a small fountain contains a statue of Hercules taken from Noto Antica. Facing this is the **Teatro Vittorio Emanuele** (finished in 1842), and the **Church of San Domenico** (1736), with a library. In this square is a bus stop for Syracuse and Ragusa. Off the Corso, the streets are somewhat austere, although the **Villa Dorata Palace** (Via Nicolaci) and the church **Crocifisso** are rather good.

FESTIVALS
San Corrado (last Sunday in August). At nearby Avola: Santa Venera (last Sunday in July).

BEACHES
Easily reached from Noto: Noto Marina, Calabernardo, Marina di Avola, Lido di Avola. Further south and more isolated: Vendicari.

Around Noto

Noto Antica, ancient Netum, is 5½ miles from Noto, off the road to Palazzolo. Founded according to tradition by the Sikel king Ducetius in the 5th century BC, Netum later came under the rule of Syracuse, then of Rome. It was the only town to successfully resist the despoilations of the praetor Verres, and was also the last retreat of the Saracens before their surrender to the Normans in 1091. Never rebuilt after the earthquake, Noto Antica remains a wild, picturesque ruin, which includes a Norman castle, the gateway, tombs and churches.

West of Noto Antica, **Castelluccio** was a prehistoric settlement, inhabited between the 18th and 14th centuries BC. The great archaeologist Paolo Orsi excavated the site and gave its name to the early Bronze Age culture of eastern and central Sicily. You can see the remains of the village and necropolis of Castelluccio, though items found there are in the Syracuse Museum. A more extensive site is **Eloro,** a few miles south of Noto. Founded by the Syracusans in the 7th century BC at the mouth of the River Tellaro, Eloro (ancient Helorus) is still being excavated. At the entrance to the site stands the **Pizzota Column,** a Hellenistic funeral monument, and the Sanctuary of Demeter and Kore, outside the well-preserved city walls. Inside the walls a small theatre and the grandiose *stoa* of the 2nd century BC have been uncovered.

Continuing to the extreme southeast corner of Sicily, where the Ionian and Mediterranean Seas meet, are the lovely remote beaches of Porto Palo and Marzamemi. Just north of Pachino, at the farm San Lorenzo Lo Vecchio, the skeleton of a Hellenistic temple transformed into a Byzantine church may be seen incorporated into the farm buildings. **Rosolini,** further west, has to be one of the ugliest, dustiest little nowheres in Italy, but even it has an interesting site. Beneath the Castello del Principe are large catacombs and an early Christian basilica carved out of the rock.

Ragusa

HISTORY
The town of Ragusa, perched atop a hilly ridge, is divided into two parts, the lower of which—Ragusa Ibla—was the site of the original Sikel town of Hybla Heraea, one of their major settlements. Conquered by the Greeks and Romans in 258 BC, Hybla Heraea declined, only regaining some of its former importance when Count Roger created the County of Ragusa for his son in 1091, although in 1296 Manfred Chiaramonte incorporated it into the powerful County of Modica. After the 1693 earthquake, work was begun on Upper Ragusa, which remained a separate town from Ibla—and its main rival—until they were united in 1926 when Ragusa became the provincial capital.

WHAT TO SEE

Ragusa today is one of the most picturesque and typical of Sicilian towns on the island with its decaying, flamboyant baroque buildings hugging the hillsides, its slow pace of life and lack of tourists. The best way to get a feel of Ragusa is to take the city bus from Upper Ragusa to Ibla, a hair-raising expedition down the narrow winding streets, the busdriver cursing in the front and the conductor acting as navigator in the rear. However, when you reach Santa Maria delle Scale, a marvellous panorama unfolds before you of old Ibla piled on its hill, crowned by the dome of San Giorgio.

Upper Ragusa

Along with most of the city's businesses, the **Archaeology Museum** (open 9–2, holidays 9–1; closed Mondays) is in the new town of Upper Ragusa, located in the Palazzo Mediterraneo, on Via Natelelli. The museum contains a small collection of finds from the province, mainly from the important Syracusan colony of Camarina. The large baroque **Cathedral of San Giovanni Battista** is nearby. At the edge of the new town the **Church of Santa Maria delle Scale** ('of the stairs') dates back to the 14th century, one of the few buildings to survive the earthquake, though reworked in the 17th century. The doorways and chapels are good, as is the 16th-century *bas relief* inside, a work of the prolific Gagini. From the church terrace one has a grand view of Ibla, which may be reached by the long stairway below the church or by the Corso Mazzini.

Ibla

In Ibla (buses 1 and 3 go there from the Piazza del Popolo) the churches attract the most attention, notably the 18th-century **San Giorgio,** designed by the excellent Rosario Gagliardi of Noto. Considered by many to be the finest example of the local baroque, the church is perfectly sited on a curving stairway above the tree-lined Piazza del Duomo: the cathedral treasure, which includes Byzantine religious items dating back to the 7th century, may be seen on request.

The portal of the original Gothic–Catalan San Giorgio, which collapsed in the earthquake, can be seen near the **Giardino Ibleo**. A few blocks from San Giorgio, another fine church in a less monumental position, **San Giuseppe's,** may also be by Gagliardi. The rest of Ibla is an attractive place to explore, with its pretty little churches and piazzas and its baroque-spawned monsters lurking under the balconies and roofs of the houses. In Via 25 Aprile, the **Palazzo Donnafugata** contains a number of works of art, including paintings attributed to Antonella da Messina and Ribera.

FESTIVALS
Good Friday processions; 'The Iblean August' (folklore and sport festivities throughout the month, culminating in a celebration in honour of St John the Baptist on 29 August). San Giorgio (25 April).

SPECIALITIES
Caciocavallo cheese and *pecorino* (goats' cheese with pepper). Local wines include *Ambrato* and *Cervasuolo*.

GETTING TO RAGUSA
By rail: to and from Syracuse and Licata daily (Stazione at Piazza del Popolo).
By bus: from Piazza del Popolo to Syracuse, Agrigento, Palermo, Gela and all other towns in the province.

TOURIST INFORMATION
EPT: Via Natalelli, Palazza Camera di Commercio (tel. (0932) 21421).
AAST: Viale del Fante (tel. (0932) 45185).

WHERE TO STAY
In town, the **Montreal***** on Via San Giuseppe 10 (tel. (0932) 21133), is the most comfortable place to stay, with single rooms for 26 000 lire, doubles for 40–44 000 lire, air conditioning available; always open. If it's full, try the **Mediterraneo*****, Via Roma 189 (tel. (0932) 21944; single room for around 20 000 lire, double 35 000, depending on the room). The only place cheaper is the **Tivoli****, Via G. D'Annuzio 60 (tel. (0932) 24885; single room without bath 10 000 lire, double 20 000; rooms with bath extra).

EATING OUT
Ragusa does better with its restaurants than its hotels. **Fumia,** at 23 Cappuchini, is the best in town, with Italian fare for around 30 000 lire. In Ibla, **U Satacinu** on Via Convento specialises in Sicilian dishes for slightly less. **Orfeo** in Upper Ragusa, at Via Sant'Anna 117, is a popular lunch spot, with meals around 15 000 lire and free TV entertainment. Least expensive is **Biffi,** on Via Lupis, with typical trattoria fare. If you have a car, you may want to go to the **Osteria del Braciere,** a local favourite in the village of San Giacomo northeast of Ragusa, where the good food is plentiful and inexpensive (around 25 000 lire).

Ragusa Province

The Province of Ragusa, the former County of Modica, was the most powerful fiefdom in Sicily. Created in 1091 by Count Roger, later kings rued its semi-independence under the counts of Chiaramonte, Cabrera and Henriquez–Cabrera, who only begrudgingly tipped their hats to Palermo and paid their tribute only when the king's army came to collect it. This state of affairs lasted into the 18th century, and was rather more benevolent to the local population than might at first be thought, with its unique set of laws uniting townsmen and farmers in a common cause, such as the reconstruction of towns after the earthquake.

Ragusa Province has few tourists; Italians come mainly for its beaches which line the southern coast from Scoglitti to the Marina di Modica. The main site, besides Ragusa and its sister city Modica, is the Cava d'Ispica in the rugged eastern part of the province. This narrow gorge was inhabited continuously for centuries.

Modica

Modica, some 5 miles south of Ragusa, was the old capital of the county. However, rather than being built on the surrounding hills, the town is situated in a deep valley: the town's defence depended not on fortifications but on the potential for guerrilla warfare once an invader arrived. The torrents that pass through Modica flooded the town in 1902, following which the rivers have been all but covered over. Modica may no longer be 'the Venice of Sicily' but it is still a lovely town where the houses on the hills peer discreetly over the shoulders of their neighbours, and many of the streets are stairways.

Like Ragusa, Modica consists of two towns, the upper and the lower. In the lower town are the main shopping streets, the bus stop, etc., and the **Church of Santa Maria di Betlem,** where the highest point of the great flood is marked by a plaque. All buses and trains to Ragusa also stop in Modica.

Modica Alta, the upper town, boasts the **Church of San Giorgio,** reminiscent of San Giorgio's in Ragusa, and perhaps also designed by Gagliardi. Dominated by its central tower, the church has a beautiful 18th-century facade, and it is worth-while making the trip up the grandiose baroque stairway to see it. The old conventual church on top of Modica Alta, **Santa Maria di Gesù,** now houses a prison, of all things. The Cathedral of San

Pietro and the 15th-century Church of the Carmine, also in the upper town, offer other examples of the local style of architecture.

Short excursions from Modica or Ragusa are to the **Trabacche Cave** (7 miles from Ragusa) with its large 4th-century catacombs, and to the south (take the train from Ragusa) the **Villa of Donnafugata,** where a fine park and a collection of paintings, some by great masters, can be visited on request of the owners. If the name Donnafugata rings a bell, remember that Giuseppe di Lampedusa borrowed it as the major setting for his novel, *The Leopard.* The closest beaches are Punta Secca, Randello, and the Ragusa and Modica Marinas (the last two equipped with hotels, restaurants and campsites).

Camarina

On the coast to the west Camarina was a Syracusan colony, founded in 598 BC. One of the Greeks' most important outposts, it was alternately destroyed and rebuilt by Gela, Syracuse and Carthage, and finally put out of its misery by the Romans in 258 BC. Little remains of Camarina, though the 5th-century Temple of Athena can be made out, and the grid-pattern street plan and part of the wall. The necropolis, dating back to the 6th century, yielded many interesting objects, some of which are in Ragusa and others in the small museum on the acropolis (open 9–1; closed Mondays). There are three campsites and a large hotel on the beaches near Camarina.

Comiso and Vittoria

West of Ragusa, after a truly stunning descent from the Iblean Hills, one arrives at Comiso, another of the province's pretty but unheralded towns. The Naselli family ruled here for many years, and the 14th-century **Castello Feudale** has recently been restored. Near the town centre, the Piazza delle Erbe, the **Church of San Francesco** (finished 1478) contains the Naselli Chapel with the sepulchre of Count Gaspare Naselli by Antonello Gagini. Just off the piazza is an interesting 19th-century market (Comiso is an agricultural centre). The nearby **Fonte Diana** once supplied water for the Roman baths, now under the Municipio. Comiso's high vines produce excellent table grapes and *l'ambrato* wine.

Neighbouring Vittoria, another farming centre, was named for its 1607 foundress, the daughter of a viceroy. Although the rest of the town isn't much, Vittoria has two very elegant piazze, surrounded by baroque and neo-classical buildings. Scoglitti, some 10 miles away on the coast, is the beginning of the 'Gela Riviera'.

FESTIVAL
Important Good Friday processions in Vittoria.

SPECIALITIES
Vittoria grows numerous vegetables for the south of Sicily and makes its own wine—*il Cervasuolo.*

Cava d'Ispica

Despite its name, **Chiaramonte Gulfi** is an inland village north of Ragusa, famous in Sicily for its food. Specialities include goats' cheese with peppers (*pecorino*), pork galantine, stuffed pork chops, roast lamb, salami and olive oil. From Modica, the road leads to **Scicli,** small and baroque, where the road forks for the beaches at Donnalucata, Cava d'Aliga and Sampieri. **Pozzallo,** to the east, was the port for Ragusa and has a 14th-century tower and a beach.

Ispica, known as 'Spacca' in the Middle Ages, is the last resting place of the painter Sozzi (died 1765), buried in the **Church of Santa Maria Maggiore,** which is decorated with his frescoes. Between Ispica and Modica is the famous Cava d'Ispica (signposted and always open), a narrow 9-mile-long gorge fascinating for its signs of continuous habitation from the Bronze Age right up to the 18th century. Throughout the length of the gorge are catacombs and cave dwellings carved in the rock face, silent testimonies of hardship and courage, dating mostly from between the 5th and 13th centuries.

Northern Coast: Trapani to Messina

Trapani

HISTORY
Trapani is built on the site of ancient Drepanon, on an odd hook of land beckoning to the Egadi Islands. Drepanon was the harbour of Eryx (Erice) and, like that city, populated by Elymnians, a rather mysterious people who claimed Greek descent but who were allies of the Phoenicians.

Samuel Butler and Robert Graves have produced some clever arguments

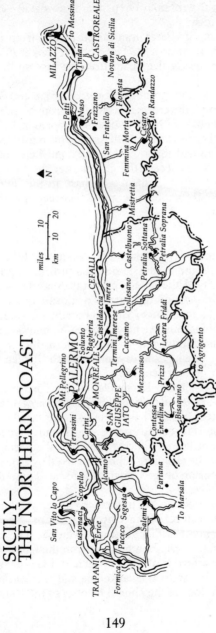

SICILY—
THE NORTHERN COAST

that *The Odyssey* was written in Drepanon by a woman—read them before you shrug off the idea.

In 260 BC Hamilcar Barca transferred people from Eryx to the port, making it a city in its own right. The Romans took it in 241 BC, Lutatio Catullus defeating the Carthaginians from his base on the islet of Colombaia.

Trapani, because of its position between Europe and Tunis, prospered from the 13th century; the crowned heads of Europe were always popping in and out. King Theobald of Navarre died in Trapani in 1270 from a Tunisian fever; Edward I of England landed here on his return from the Crusades and learned that he had inherited his kingdom; Peter of Aragon disembarked here in 1282 to accept the crown after the Sicilian Vespers, and Emperor Charles V used Trapani as a base in the Tunisian campaign. During World War II, bombing seriously damaged the city, especially the San Pietro quarter.

WHAT TO SEE

The port of Trapani today still does a fair amount of business; the saltpans with their windmills and tuna fisheries also provide important income for the bustling little city. Although the post-war expansion inland is as ugly as any in Italy, the old town on the narrow peninsula has a well-kept charm, especially the main street, Corso Vittorio Emanuele, where traffic is prohibited. Here Trapani is only five blocks long—on one side lies the port with views of the Egadi Islands, and on the northern side, the powerful lighthouse and nearest beach, Lido di San Giuliano. It seems as if there is a horsemeat butcher on every corner.

Facing the Corso Vittorio Emanuele on Via Torrearsa is the beautiful **Municipio** (1696), the focal point of the shopping area. On the Corso itself, the **Church of the Collegio** has a fine baroque facade and contains the wooden *Misteri*, the 18th-century processional figures representing Passion scenes carried about the city during the Holy Week celebrations. In the sacristy you can see the elaborate cupboard carved by a local sculptor, Pietro Orlando. And extension of the Corso leads to the **Torre di Ligny**, named after a Spanish prince.

Behind the Municipio, in the triangular Piazzetta Saturno (named after the fountain in the centre) is the **Church of Sant' Agostina,** the 14th-century Templar church with a good rose window. The EPT information office is in the same square. South of here, on the Corso Italia, in the San Pietro quarter, the **Church of Santa Maria del Gesù** contains the lovely *Virgin of the Angels* by Andrea della Robbia and a *baldacchino* by Antonello Gagini. The south door of the church belongs to the Renaissance. On the other side of the Corso, off Via 30 Gennaio, is the **Palazzo della Guidecca**, in the old Jewish ghetto. Strange faces peer from the 16th-century Plateresque windows of this interesting towered palace. To the north, the **Church of San Domenico** (17th century) has a rose window and contains the sarcophagus of Manfred, son of Frederick III of Aragon.

At the end of Via Garibaldi on Piazza Vittorio Veneto is the early Mussolini **post office**, elaborately art nouveau–art deco. Few *fascisti* buildings have such pleasant facades. The **Villa Margherita** near here has a small zoo; operettas and plays are often performed here in summer. Just outside the park is a public trampoline, where you can bounce with the local children for a small fee.

Bus 1 will take you from the Piazza Umberto I to the **Museo Nazionale Pepoli** (open 9.30–4; Sundays 9.30–1; closed Mondays), founded by Agostino Pepoli in 1908 and located in an old convent. It contains a wide variety of paintings, church art, glass and archaeological finds and a pompously amusing painting of Jupiter and Napoleon. The church attached to the museum, the **Santuario dell' Annunziata,** was founded in 1315 and badly restored in 1760, so that only the door and the rose window remain of the original structure. Inside the sacred 14th-century church, the Pisan Madonna can be seen behind the altar, the object of an annual pilgrimage.

FESTIVALS
La Mattanza, the tuna fish massacre (June). The *Misteri* (Good Friday). Carnival (February). *Musicale Trapanese* at Villa Margherita (July). Feast of the Assumption (12–15 August) with puppet shows. Festival of the Madonna of the Church of the Annunziata (25 March).

Erice

High above Trapani, connected by an hour-long bus ride (enjoyable for its lingering views of Trapani and the sea below, as well as the lovely wild flowers that blanket the hillsides) or a shorter cable railway ride, is Erice (known to the ancients as *Eryx*), on top of the 2454-ft mountain of the same name. Eryx was famous all over the ancient world for its temple of the fertility goddess Venus Erycina, mentioned as a landmark in *The Aeneid.* Indeed the mountain seems to rise straight out of the sea, a natural home to magic and myth. That *eryx* means 'heather' and that the symbol of the goddess was the bee attest to the extreme antiquity of this most sacred Elymnian cult. The Elymnians claimed descent not only from the Greeks but also from the Trojans, whose leader, Aeneas, was the son of Aphrodite

151

(Venus). Daedalus offered a golden honeycomb to the goddess when he visited Eryx; and in a later legend, Eryx, another son of Aphrodite, hosted Hercules when he came to Sicily.

Erice has always had an obvious reputation as being impregnable, but in 260 BC Hamilcar Barca seized and destroyed it, moving its population down to the port of Drepanon. The Romans captured it and Tiberius and Claudius rebuilt the temple, paying homage to the mountain. When the Arabs captured the town, they too felt the holiness of the place and named it *Gebel Hamed* (Mahomet's mountain). Count Roger named it Monte San Giuliano after a dream he had there of St Julian. In 1934 Mussolini re-dubbed it Erice.

WHAT TO SEE

The town today is more medieval than any in Sicily—perhaps even in all of Italy. Silence reigns in the narrow, roughly cobbled streets (don't wear high-heels!) that wind up and down the hills, making Erice seem much larger than it actually is. The houses have secretive stone facades, each hiding a delightful courtyard full of plants and cats, and sometimes a pretty girl. Whether or not the goddess of love has a hand in the matter, the women of Erice are reputed to be the most beautiful in Sicily. Nowadays, in addition to the day-trippers, scholars from many lands descend on Erice for conferences on a wide range of topics, some as evocative as the town itself.

You enter the town through the **Porta Trapani,** of Norman construction, as are all the gates. By some of these, particularly on the north side of town, the ancient **walls** are well preserved, having been repaired by the Romans; their foundations date back to the Elymnians. Off the Via Vittorio Emanuele is the **Cathedral** founded by Frederick of Aragon in 1312 with a facade dating from 1426, which for once hasn't been touched since then. The dimly lit interior has an almost Arabic ceiling and contains a statue of the Madonna and Child by Francesco Laurana. Via Vittorio Emanuele leads into the central Piazza Umberto I, where in the Municipio you may visit the small **Museo Comunale** (open 10–12 and 2–4; holidays 10–1), with a lovely Annunciation by Antonello Gagini, a 4th-century BC head of Aphrodite and a wax nativity scene, among other items; the **Library** in the next room contains various *incunabula*.

At the other corner of town, above the communal gardens, stand three towers, the **Torri Mediovali,** the **Torretta Pepoli** and the **Castello Normanno,** the last with stupendous views in all directions; on a clear day it is said you can see to Cape Bon, Tunisia. Only the base remains of the **Temple of Venus Erycina,** on the northeast side, thought to have been destroyed during the construction of the medieval castle. Unlike most Greek temples, which are oriented east–west, the base of this temple is aligned to the northeast and southwest. The Roman-built **Pozzo di Venere** (Well of Venus) can be seen here, as well as a mosaic floor. Fragments of the temple are incorporated in the castle walls.

FESTIVALS
Estate Ericina, the Erice summer festival with dances, exhibitions and competitions. Also Good Friday procession of the *Misteri*. First week in July: annual car race up Monte Erice. August cartoon festival.

Northeast along the coast

North of Trapani the more or less coastal highway passes through the small resort of **Pizzolungo**, and the so-called 'Marble Riviera' of **Custonaci**, up to the tip of the mountainous cape and **San Vito lo Capo** (frequent bus from Trapani), a growing resort with a fine beach, with Monte Monaco providing the backdrop. From 10 July to 10 September, the Pro Loca provides numerous distractions and a feast of the patron saint San Vito to keep sun-seekers amused, including a photography contest. On the other side of the peninsula, facing the Golfo di Castellammare, is picturesque **Scopello**, with its little harbour and sea rocks a completely unspoiled fishing village; while **Castellammare del Golfo**, near the mouth of the River Freddo, is more popular, with hotels and a campsite. The Festival of Sicilian Songs takes place here each year on 2 August.

Alcamo

There is another popular beach just east of here at Alcamo Marina, the old port of Alcamo, a town of pretty churches, 4 miles inland. Frederick II founded Alcamo in 1233 and named it after the Saracen castle of *Alkamuk* on Mount Bonifato (2710 ft). Ciullo, one of Italy's finest poets, was born here in the 13th century, and in the piazza named after him is the **Church of Sant' Oliva**, containing lovely works by the Gagini family. The Flemish painter Borremans painted the frescoes in the **Assunta**, with its 14th-century campanile. On the Corso Sei Aprile there are three other fine churches: the **Madonna del Soccorso, San Tomaso**, with a beautiful 14th-century doorway, and **San Francesco**, containing sculpture by the Gagini. Works by the Sicilian Novelli may be seen in the abbeys of **Badia Grande** and **Badia Nuova**, north of the town. **Santa Chiara** contains stuccoes by Serpotta; while in the ruins of the Saracen castle the **Church of the Madonna dell' Alto** is worth visiting for the panoramic view.

FESTIVALS
Alcamo's patron saint, *Maria SS dei Miracoli* (19–21 June), with a pilgrimage to Monte Bonifato; also various events throughout the summer.

Segesta

West of Alcamo are **Calatafimi** (with an obelisk commemorating Garibaldi's victory here in 1860) and Segesta, a 20-minute walk from the station at Segesta Tempio, open every day. Segesta (Greek *Egesta*) was one of the main Elymnian centres, along with Erice, but whereas Erice came under Carthaginian influence, Segesta became Hellenised, and was famous in Greek Sicily for its sulphurous springs.

Segesta, Trapani

HISTORY
The Elymnians may have settled Monte Barbaro and Segesta as early as the 12th century BC, but little is known about the city until the 6th century BC, when Segesta and Selinunte started squabbling over their borders. In the grand political arena of Greeks, Carthaginians and Romans, Segesta always sided with whoever was the strongest at any given moment. At one point, writes Thucydides, the Segestians were trying to curry favour with Athens

154

to counteract Selinunte's allegiance to Syracuse. To impress the envoys sent by Athens, they collected all the gold and silver drinking cups from their territory and sent them to each house the Athenians were entertained in, successfully tricking them into believing Segesta was an exorbitantly wealthy city; perhaps even the beautiful Doric temple was begun then to impress the foreigners. However, when the Athenians sent their Great Expedition to Sicily to conquer Syracuse, Segesta went back on its promise to pay for the expedition and the Athenians realised they had been fooled. It was only the first of their disappointments.

Afterwards, Segesta became an ally of Carthage, which destroyed Selinunte. Carthage protected Segesta from Dionysius of Syracuse, but couldn't do a thing when Agathocles of Syracuse captured the city in 307 BC, slaying 10 000 people and selling the rest as slaves. He repopulated it with Greeks and named it *Dikaeopolis*, but it drifted back to Carthage. However, when Rome took the upper hand in the First Punic War, the treacherous Segestans massacred the Punic garrison and pledged allegiance to Rome. In the 10th century the Saracens destroyed the city.

The Temple

When travellers first began to trickle into Sicily, the Temple of Segesta was one of the most famous sights, now marred somewhat by the road-building mania of the Italians in the form of the Autostrada 29. Although the temple was never finished (the 36 columns are unfluted, and the *cella* and roof were never built), this temple to an unknown deity is one of the most majestic monuments of the ancient world. An Athenian architect is believed to have designed it, and had the temple ever been completed, it would have certainly been among the loveliest. Views of the surrounding countryside are also ravishing and you can get a drink at the nearby café.

On the other side of the unexcavated Hellenistic town, the road leads up Monte Barbaro to the **theatre,** built in the 3rd century BC. Excellently preserved, it measures 207 ft in diameter and has 20 rows of seats. Beneath the orchestra runs an underground passage from which actors could pop out from the 'underworld'. The theatre, which commands an extraordinary view over the Golfo di Castellammare, still sees occasional summer performances of Greek drama. A rough path below it leads to the **Sanctuary of the Elymnians,** towards the village of Mango. Although built in the 6th century BC, this walled enclosure already shows the Greek influence.

Salemi

South along the SS188A from Segesta (or take the bus from Trapani) is

Salemi, where the Sikan town of *Halicyae* once stood, today dominated by a 13th-century castle. An earthquake in 1968 made the centre of the town unsafe and it has been abandoned. The church of the Collegio is the new Cathedral, as the old one was destroyed. Here in 1860 Garibaldi declared himself ruler of Sicily in the name of Vittorio Emanuele.

Beneath the town you can see the ruins of the **Paleo–Christian Basilica,** which dates, according to the tourist brochure, from the 5th century BC! Most interesting here are the African-influenced mosaics.

East of Salemi, near **Poggioreale,** excavations have begun on Monte Castellazzo of a town believed to be the ancient *Entella*. What has been discovered so far dates back to the 4th century BC.

FESTIVALS

San Biagio (3 February) is marked by tiny figures made out of wheat pasta being given to the children and by people trying to climb a slippery pole for the sausages and roast chickens hung on top. San Giuseppe (19 March) is marked by poetry recitals and women making sculptures of Mary, Joseph and baby Jesus out of 20-lb loaves of bread. Christmas Eve: procession of characters from the Nativity. In early May: a music festival in honour of Alberto Favara, who notated the popular songs of the area in the 19th century.

GETTING TO AND AROUND TRAPANI

By air: to Palermo, Rome and Pantelleria (airport at Birgi, 14 miles away— bus from Corso Italia).

By sea: to Egadi Islands, Pantelleria (5 trips a week); Cagliari and Tunis (by *Tirrenia*).

By train: to Palermo (usually very slow), Segesta, Marsala and Agrigento (also slow) from Stazione Centrale in Piazza Umberto I.

By bus: from behind the station to Palermo, Sciacca and all towns in the province, including Erice.

By *funivia* (cable railway): to Erice—take bus 2 to the station; cars go up every hour.

TOURIST INFORMATION

EPT: Trapani; Corso Italialo (tel. (0923) 27273); information office in the Piazzetta Saturno.

Erice: AAST, Viale Conte Pepole 56, by the Porta Trapani (tel. (0923) 869173).

Alcamo: Corse Sei Aprile 31 (tel. (0924) 21343).

WHERE TO STAY

If you're just passing through on the train, you can't do better than the reliable **Hotel Sole***, at the station of Piazza Umberto I (tel. (0923) 22035; 12 000 lire single, 19 500 double). For something classier, just outside the town there is the **Cavallino Bianco****, by the sea on the Lungomare Dante Alighieri (tel. (0923) 21549), a single room with bath and WC is 23 000 lire, double 37 500. However, there are few things more atmospheric than staying up at Erice and strolling through the town at night when the tourists have all gone: smartest here is the **Ermione*****, with a garden, on Via Pineta Comunale (tel. (0923) 869138; single room 34 000 lire, double 54 000). Cosy and less expensive, the **Edelweiss**, Cortile P. Vincenzo (tel. (0923) 869158), has centrally located rooms, single 20 000 lire, double 38 000 (with bath).

Seaside resort hotels include the **Astoria Park Hotel*****, north of Trapani at Cusumano on the Lungomare D. Alighieri (tel. (0923) 62400), with a pool, garden, beach, tennis courts and more for 42 000 lire single, 65 000 double. The same facilities are available up at San Vito Lo Capo at the **Cala' Mpiso** (tel. (0923) 572666; open May–October; single room 21– 28 500 lire, double 35–46 000). There are many others, simple and cheap, and also one of Italy's 4-star campsites, **El Bahira**, on the beach at Macari (tel. (0923) 972577). In Castallammare del Golfo there are also many inexpensive hotels and *locandas*, mainly catering for Sicilian families on holiday; best here is the **Punta Nord Est****, Via Leonardo da Vinci 67 (tel. (0924) 33633; single room as little as 14 000 lire, double 25 000 lire).

EATING OUT

Couscous with fish is the delicious speciality of Trapani (usually eaten as a first course), and you can get it in several forms at the **Trattoria I Trabinis**, Largo Porto Galli 6, for 15–20 000 lire; **La Carbonella**, Via G.B. Fardella 25 (closed Sundays) also has many other Sicilian specialities, and is in the 20–25 000 lire range. Marsala wines and innovative cuisine are to be found at **Il Salotto**, Via N. Burgio 10 (closed Sundays; 40–45 000 lire). Least expensive, and often serving couscous, is **Safina**, across from the station (10– 12 000 lire).

In Erice prices tend to be higher. The **Re Aceste**, Via C. Ag. Pepoli, has good couscous and other specialities for 20–30 000 lire. In San Vito Lo Capo, fish is served nearly everywhere; look in the Via Savoia. Especially good is **Costa Gaia** at no. 125, with couscous, seafood, *involtini*, etc. In Castellammare the **Pizzeria Il Gambero** on the beach has many other specialities besides pizza (15 000 lire).

Palermo

'Once you've seen all this, you can never forget it'—Goethe, after visiting Palermo.

HISTORY

Palermo was colonised by the Carthaginians in the 5th century BC, in an effort to control the spread of Greek influence in Sicily. Its original name is unknown; the Greeks called it 'Panhormos' (many harbours) for the many safe anchorages that existed in ancient times, but these have since been filled in with silt from the two streams that once traversed the city near the present-day cathedral. Rome fought hard for Palermo in the First Punic War, finally capturing it in 254 BC. The father of Hannibal, Hamilcar Barca, tried for some years to recapture the city, basing himself on Monte Pellegrino, but did not succeed.

The Byzantines, who called it 'Balarma', took it from the Barbarians in 535, holding it until the Saracens defeated them in 831. Under the Arabs, Palermo became the splendid capital of an Emirate. The Arabs built a new quarter, separately walled, for their officials (*el-Halisah*, 'the elect', from whence comes the name 'Kalsa' still used today).

In 1072 Roger de Hauteville retook the city for Christiandom, and under his son, King Roger, Palermo became the most splendid capital in all Europe with its beautiful Norman churches and pleasure palaces.

The city continued as a famous cultural centre under Frederick 'Stupor Mundi' who was raised in Palermo's Palazzo dei Normanni. When Swabian rule gave way to Angevin, the rebellion of the Sicilian Vespers broke out in 1282 at a church in Palermo over a Frenchman's insulting advances to a bride at her wedding.

Under the distant tyranny of the Spanish and Bourbons, the city declined in splendour although it gained in population. By the 18th century it was the second largest city in Italy after Naples, and Ferdinand IV ruled from Palermo when the French occupied that city. Placed under British protection in the 19th century, Palermo rebelled on three occasions, the last of which in 1860 saw the entry of Garibaldi and the Thousand. During World War II, Palermo suffered badly from the American bombardment; even today, bombed ruins in some quarters of the city remind one of that evil time.

Two Palermitans in particular have made their mark on the world: Alessandro Scarlatti, the composer (1660–1725), and Alexandre, Comte de Cagliostro (1743–95), a doctor who dabbled in the occult and was deeply embroiled in French politics at the time of Louis XVI, playing a major role in the 'diamond necklace affair' involving Marie Antoinette. His reputation as the greatest charlatan of his day spread across the Continent from the islands of Rhodes and Malta to London. Finally in Rome he was sentenced for heresy and died serving a life sentence in prison.

WHAT TO SEE
Today, nearly 1 million people inhabit the hurly-burly of Palermo, the capital of Sicily and its largest city. With the odd-shaped Monte Pellegrino on one side, the plain of Conca d'Oro (Golden Shell) surrounding it and the Madonie Mountains in the distance, Palermo is splendidly situated, but what attracts most visitors are its magnificent Norman and baroque monuments. Almost all of these are packed into a small section of the sprawling city. The division between new and old in Palermo is abrupt; around Piazza Ruggero Settimo and to the north of it are the chic shops, the modern apartment buildings and white-collar enterprises, whereas the south side has all the superb churches and palaces—and all the squalor. Here once-elegant residences rot in the exhaust fumes that have turned them black, and the narrow streets of the ghettoes are lined with every variety of rubbish God's children can create. Sporadic hole-in-the-wall *trattorie*, the children growing up in the streets, the shifty men who want to make a deal with you—it is all fascinating, colourful, and probably won't last much longer. The spirit of change and progress that has swept across this great island is most noticeable here in its capital, which like all capitals tends to reflect the best and the worst of the land. Crime (do watch your car, and keep your purse out of the reach of the infamous scooter-mounted *banditti*), drugs (the Mafia don't consign them all to the export trade) and poverty are still problems, but there is a growing public demand for something to be done about them. If it's been a while since you last visited Palermo, you may well be amazed at its bright new face. The only real setback in the growth of the economy is that everyone buys a car as soon as he can afford it, and there are times when this grand old city resembles a baroque parking lot.

The old city: the Norman Cathedral
The centre of the old city is known as the **Quattro Canti**, the 'four corners', where the main streets Via Vittorio Emanuele and Via Maqueda intersect. In 1611 the Viceroy Vigliena built the four buildings at this crossroads and adorned their corners with fountains, allegories of the four seasons, the four kings of Sicily, and the patronesses of the four quarters which the Quattro Canti defines. For hundreds of years these four quarters—the Kalsa (southeast), the Amalfitani (northeast), the Sincaldi (northwest), and the Albergheria (southwest)—had little to do with one another; indeed, they were so clannish that marriages between the quarters were very unusual.

Turning west from the Quattro Canti along the **Via Vittorio Emanuele**, you pass a few blocks of small shops and then the Cathedral makes a sudden appearance on the right. Founded in 1185 by the Archbishop Gualtiero Offamiglio (perhaps the English 'Walter of the Mill'), this masterpiece of Sicilian–Norman architecture was only completed in the 19th century. In the meantime various alterations—most notably the dome, built in the 18th century by the Florentine Ferdinando Fuga—have spoiled the integrity of the building, but its beauty and fine proportions still hold true. The eastern end of the cathedral retains its fine 12th-century structure and embellishments. In the Gothic porch on the south side one of the columns bears an inscription from the Koran—it belonged to the mosque that once stood on the same site.

The spacious interior is stale fare after the lavish feast of the exterior (open daily 7–12 noon and 4–7pm). At the back of the church are the tombs of the Holy Roman Emperor Frederick II (died 1250) and in the same sarcophagus Peter II of Aragon (died 1342), Henry VI (died 1197), Roger II (died 1154) and his daughter Constance (died 1198), wife of Henry VI. Also, set in the wall there, are the tombs of Duke William of Aragon (died 1338), son of Frederick II of Aragon, and Constance of Aragon (died 1222), first wife of 'Stupor Mundi', whom he wed when he turned 14.

In a choir chapel are the relics of Palermo's favourite saint, St Rosalia, who lived and died on Mt Pellegrino (see below for her story). There are many fine statues by Antonello Gagini, as well as a Madonna by Francesco Laurana. The treasury contains some interesting items from the tomb of Constance of Aragon (wife of Emperor Frederick), including her crown—a cap with jewels stuck on it, reminiscent of nothing so much as a child's party hat with pieces of bright paper pasted on it. The crypt contains the sarcophagus of Gualtiero Offamiglio, among those of other archbishops of Palermo.

In the court of the neighbouring Archbishop's Palace (Via Matteo Bonello) is the **Museo Diocesano** (open Mondays, Wednesdays and Fridays, 9–1; admission fee), containing works of art salvaged from the churches bombed in the war, many quite lovely. The door of the **Archbishop's Palace** dates from the 15th century.

The Cappella Palatina
Via Vittorio Emanuele ends in shady Giardino Bonanno (the **Porta Nova** was built in 1535 for Charles V's victory in Tunisia), and the large, strange **Palazzo dei Normanni** (open 9–4, closed Thursdays; November–March, open Mondays, Fridays and Saturdays 9–12.30). Originally a Saracen fort of the 9th century, Roger II and the Normans adapted it for their own uses,

and alterations continued throughout the centuries, so that only the Torre di Santa Ninfa recalls the men of northern France. (From the observatory on its roof, Giuseppe Piazzi discovered the first known asteroid, Ceres, in 1801.) In the Palazzo is the royal chapel of Roger II, the **Cappella Palatina,** one of the jewels of Norman–Eastern art (open 9–1; donations; Sunday Mass 10.20). Like the more grandiose church of Monreale, the walls of the chapel glow with wonderful mosaics on a golden background, but here the scenes are more intimate and easier to study, and the rest of the chapel is spared the minor imperfections of Monreale. With its wooden ceiling— exquisitely carved by Roger's craftsmen—the mosaic floors and marble-covered walls, as a work of art the Cappella Palatina is flawless. The dais at the rear of the chapel supported the thrones of the Sicilian kings. The Palazzo also contains the **Royal Apartments** (second floor). After various sumptuous but unmemorable rooms you enter the Sala di Re Ruggero— where the Norman influence is most obvious—retaining a fine, though formal, mosaic of a hunting scene.

San Giovanni degli Eremiti
Off the main Corso Ruggero to the left of the Palazzo rise the four pink domes of San Giovanni degli Eremiti, Palermo's most photogenic church (entrance on Via dei Benedettini; open 9–2, holidays 9–1). This Arab–Norman–Sicilian piece of confectionery, originally part of a mosque, was built by Roger II in 1132. The charming gardens and old cloisters nearby complete this little oasis. The **Villa d'Orleans,** in the gardens on the other side of Corso Ruggero, is the palace where future French King Louis Philippe lived in exile in 1809, now the residence of the President of Sicily.

Kalsa Quarter
Turning eastwards down the Via Vittorio Emanuele one enters the Kalsa Quarter. A few blocks down from the Quattro Canti, by the Via Roma, is the **Church of Sant' Antonio,** destroyed in the 1823 earthquake, but restored to its original Chiaramonte style. A right turn down curving Via Paternostro takes you to the fine **Church of San Francesco d'Assisi,** built in the 13th century, with a rose window. The interior is particularly lovely, despite bomb damage, and its **Cappella Mastrantonio,** carved in 1468 by Francesco Laurana and Pietro da Bonitate, must be Palermo's best example of Renaissance art. Eight statues by Serpotta adorn the nave, and the two Madonnas are by Domenico Gagini. Next to it, on Via Immacolatella 5, the **Oratorio della Compagnia di San Lorenzo** is the masterpiece of Palermo's baroque sculptor Procopio Serpotta (1679–1755). This extravaganza is open from 9am until dusk on request.

Church of San Giovanni Degli Eremiti, Palermo

Near the Giardino Garibaldi, further east on Via V. Emanuele, the 15th-century **Santa Maria della Catena** derives its name from the restored 17th-century gate, **Porta Felice,** which leads from here to the sea; the chain (*catena*) once closed the Cala Harbour every evening. Beneath the huge banyan trees shading the **Giardino Garibaldi,** you can wander across to the **Piazza Marina,** which as its name implies was once part of the sea until reclaimed by the Arabs in the 10th century as part of their Kalsa quarter. Here the Aragonese held their jousts, and the Inquisitors their *autos-da-fè*. In one corner note the pretty Renaissance **Santa Maria dei Miracoli,** built in 1347.

In the southeast corner of the Giardino Garibaldi is the **Palazzo Chiaramonte,** where in the early 14th century Sicily's most flamboyant noble family resided; like all Sicilian palazzi associated with the Chiaramontes, it is magnificent. Sicily's viceroys lived here, as did the heads of the local Inquisition. Until 1922 it held Palermo's Law Courts; now restored, it belongs to the University.

The National Gallery of Sicily
From here, Via 4 Aprile gives on to **Via Alloro,** the finest street in the quarter, lined with palazzi in various stages of decrepitude. At no. 4 stands the grand **Palazzo Abatelli,** built by Matteo Carnelivari in 1488 and since restored to house the **National Gallery of Sicily** (open 9–2; also Tuesday and Thursday afternoons 4.30–7.30; holidays 9–1; closed Mondays), the richest collection of paintings and sculpture on the island. The master work

of the excellent medieval and Renaissance painting is Antonello da Messina's *Annunciation*, which perhaps should be subtitled *Of the Right Hand*, for along with the Virgin's expression, her right hand makes this one of the greatest yet simplest paintings in the world. The other highlight in the gallery is the large fresco entitled *The Triumph of Death* by a 15th-century (perhaps Flemish) artist who did not sign his work. This macabre scene of the Deadly Archer dealing it out to the wealthy, who tumble beneath the hoofs of Death's dying horse, originally hung in the Palazzo Sclafani—at that time a hospital! Next to the gallery, the **Church of La Gancia** on Santa Maria degli Angeli was built in the 15th century, and contains works by Antonello Gagini, Serpotta and Vincenzo da Pavia.

South of here, across busy Via Lincoln, is the **Botanical Garden** (open mornings, closed Sundays), and the geometrical neo-Classical garden, the **Villa Giulia,** with four pavilions adorning its centre. Not so very long ago the Villa Giulia was a wasteland of rubbish, dying shrubs, alcoholics and assorted human nuisances, its pompous pavilions crumbling to bits—a perfect Italian neo-Realist film set. Over the past couple of years, however, it's been spruced up, and you can take the children there without fear of bacterial or social contamination. Also interesting for children—and adults of course— are the exhibits at the **Marionette Museum** on Via Butera 1 (currently being moved to Via di Allestimento).

Via Lincoln leads to the central Station; halfway there, Via Garibaldi on the right leads to the **Piazza della Rivoluzione,** where the 1848 rebellion began. The fountain here supposedly represents the spirit of Palermo. Just off the Via Garibaldi, the **Palazzo Aiutamicristo,** designed by Matteo Carnelivari, was the residence of Charles V after his triumph in Tunis. Its facade, in the usual happy Sicilian *mélange*, is Catalan–Gothic. Behind this, the large Norman **Church of La Magione** in the piazza of the same name was originally built in the 12th century for the Cistercians, but in 1193 Henry VI donated it to the Teutonic Knights of Jerusalem. Like the rest of the rather scruffy Kalsa quarter, La Magione suffered frightfully in the wartime bombardments, but has been restored to its old stern Norman form.

La Martorana

Returning to the Quattro Canti, just off the southeast corner of Vias Maqueda and Vittorio Emanuele is the large Piazza Pretoria, a baroque square with a grandiose, overpopulated fountain of nymphs, satyrs and other mythical whimsies, designed in the 16th century by Michelangelo Naccherino and Francesco Camilliani. This has to be the greatest abuse of decoration in Sicily; it looks like your grandmother's knick-knack shelf.

163

Surrounding it are the Municipio, **San Guiseppe dei Teatini,** built in 1612 by Giacamo Besio with a lavish interior (entrance in Via V. Emanuele), and facing it, **Santa Caterina** (entrance in Piazza Bellini), built in 1566 and sumptuously baroque, containing a statue of Santa Caterina by Antonello Gagini. Adjacent to Piazza Pretoria lies the **Piazza Bellini,** with the loveliest Church of Santa Maria dell' Ammiraglio, familiarly known as **La Martorana.** Founded in 1173 by Roger II's 'Admiral of Admirals', George of Antioch, this Orthodox church was the meeting place of the nobles following the Sicilian Vespers, where they elected to give the Sicilian Crown to Peter of Aragon (1282). In 1233 King Alfonso transferred the church to the convent founded by Eloisa Martorana (a part of the cloisters remains to the south). In the 19th century La Martorana was used as a post office, but in 1935 Mussolini returned it to the Greeks, who have made it an Orthodox cathedral.

The beautiful campanile by the door dates from the church's foundation, surviving later adaptations. Inside are the earliest mosaics in Palermo, by Greek artists, quite Byzantine, best lit in the morning. On the west walls are two Norman mosaics—One of Christ crowning King Roger II and the other of the founding Admiral at the feet of his beloved Virgin. The 1717 frescoes by Borremans in the newer part of the church seem trivial beside the mosaics.

Immediately next to La Martorana, the small, distinctive **San Cataldo,** built in 1161, has been restored to its original Arab–Norman form, its three pink domes, stone latticework and palm trees adding up to an Arabian Night effect. The plain interior may be seen on request (ask in La Martorana). In the University, on the other side of Via Maqueda, there is a **Geological Museum** (open 9–1). Via Ponticello, beyond the University, leads to the Jesuit Church, the **Casa Professa** (1564–1636), restored after the war and containing two paintings by Pietro Novelli. The **Biblioteca Comunale,** on the west side of the church, houses early manuscripts and *incunabula.* The rest of Via Maqueda south to the **Porta Sant' Antonio** and the station consists of palazzi of the 17th and 18th centuries. The best of these are the **Palazzo Santa Croce** and the **Prefetura,** cornering each other at the intersection of Via Maqueda and Via Bosco, both built in the 18th century.

National Archaeology Museum

Via Maqueda North has been turned into a shopping street, with more to interest the purchaser of shoes than the tourist. From here, to the west, Via Sant' Agostino leads to the 14th-century **Church of Sant' Agostino** with a pretty rose window and lava mosaics on the door. On the opposite side of the Via Maqueda, near the **Teatro Massimo** with the second largest stage in Europe (after the Paris Opera) and two curious kiosks, Via Giacalone gives directly on to the Piazza Olivella with the **National Archaeological Musuem** (open 9–4; holidays and winter 9–1.30). The outstanding exhibits here are in the Sala di Selinunte, with two Archaic metopes from Temple E, unique in Italy; numerous Etruscan finds from Chuisi; Greek vases; the bronze ram from Syracuse's Castello Maniace; the thousands of votive offerings from the Sanctuary of Demeter in Selinunte; and the 'Stone of Palermo'. New exhibits are the casts of the beautiful Paleolithic incisions from the cave of the Addaura on Monte Pellegrino, which are normally difficult to gain access to. Connected to the museum (which was once a convent) is **Sant' Ignazio,** a 17th-century church with a highly decorated interior. Nearby, on Via Monteleone, is the **Oratorio della Compagnia di Santa Caterina,** decorated by Serpotta (ring to enter).

Via Roma

The Via Roma runs east of the museum; here the *fascisti* **main post office** stretches across the block like a dull white elephant on this elegant 19th-century street. The long, oppressive flight of steps leading up to it, and the heavy doors, impress the power of the State on the humble stamp-purchaser.

A few blocks south of the Palazzo della Poste, on Via Roma, the tall **Colonna dell' Immacolata** stands before the large **Church of San Domenico,** built in 1670, although the facade dates from 1726. In its elaborate interior many of Sicily's favourite sons are buried, including Francesco Crispi. This is where Ruggero Settimo called together the rebel parliament of 1848. Behind the church, on Via Bambinai, is another of Palermo's fine oratories: the 17th-century **Oratorio della Compagnia del Rosario di San Domenico,** with a beautiful altar-piece by Van Dyck depicting the four patronesses of Palermo, among other fine works. (The chapel is open from 11–12 noon and 3–4; it may be necessary to ring for the custodian at Via Bambinai 10).

A block south of San Domenico, a little stairway leads down to what seems at first to be a mysterious underground city: it is really one of Palermo's street markets, covering a dozen old narrow streets, busy until late in the evening beneath festive lights. Here you can buy fresh boiled potatoes and live eels and sample popular delicacies in the many restaurants and stands. Also behind San Domenico, on Via Squarcialupo, the 16th-century **Church of Santa Zita** has preserved various works of Antonello Gagini, despite heavy bomb damage. More interesting, though, is the **Oratory** next door, a masterpiece by the native Serpotta, containing a scene from the Battle of Lepanto, along with more typical illustrations of the Old

Testament. At the end of Via Squarcialupo, by the Piazza XIII Vittime, is the fine renaissance **Church of San Giorgio dei Genovesi,** designed by Giorgio di Faccio for the sailors of Genoa.

From this piazza (named for the thirteen leaders of the 1860 rebellion, executed by the Bourbons) the Via Cavour leads to the centre of Palermo, the **Piazza Ruggero Settimo,** which most of the city buses pass through. The theatre here, the **Politeama Garibaldi,** contains a Gallery of Modern Art (open 9–1; closed Mondays). Towering over this is the skyscraper in **Piazzale Ungheria,** an ugly Fascist building. Unfortunately most of the new public buildings in Palermo were put up by Mussolini and company with unmitigated pretentiousness and shoddy workmanship, each building stamped with a vague symbolic relief and a senseless inscription. In these respects, the Palazzo del Proveditorato stands out, along with the post office. The municipal fire station, however, has a certain charm.

Outskirts of Palermo

On the outskirts of Palermo (all within reach of the municipal bus service) are enough sites to occupy a couple of days' serious exploration. In the cemetery of Sant' Orsola, south of Palermo (Via del Vespro) is the Church of Santo Spirito, better known as the **Church of the Vespers,** built in 1173 by the founder of Palermo's Cathedral, Archbishop Offamiglio. At this severe Norman church, a pair of Sicilian newly-weds attended Vespers on 31 March 1282, Easter Tuesday. As they left, an idle Angevin soldier rudely insulted the bride—this, from a hated oppressor, was too much for the Sicilians to bear and the Frenchman was the first to die in the Massacre of the Sicilian Vespers.

A walk south on the broad Corso dei Mille (from the station) takes you to the **Ponte dell' Ammiraglio,** the bridge built by 'the Admiral of Admirals', George of Antioch, in 1113 over the River Oreto, although the river has since been diverted. On this fine piece of Norman engineering Garibaldi skirmished with the Bourbon defenders of Palermo in 1860. Further south on Corso dei Mille (no. 384) is the domed **Church of San Giovanni dei Lebbrosi,** founded by Count Roger in 1072 and considered the best example of early Norman architecture in Sicily. Its name derives from its initial use as a leper hospital. Restored to its original state, it may now be visited by asking the guardian for the key. The Corso dei Mille continues to Brancaccio, where Frederick 'Stupor Mundi' spent his precocious childhood in the **Palazzo di Favara.** Once surrounded by an artificial lake, this 10th-century ruined estate of the Emir Giafar is also known as 'di Mare

166

Dolce'. Although now surrounded by buildings it is still worth a visit.

La Zisa (from Porta Nuova take the Via Colonna Rotta to Piazza Ingastone and Via Zisa; bus 27) means 'magnificent' in Arabic, and indeed the adjective suits this Norman pleasure palace, built by William I in 1160. Bulky but elegant with an Arabic air, La Zisa has recently been restored. Inside, mosaics, fountains, stalactite ceilings and a central court are reminiscent of the Alhambra (inquire at the tourist information office about opening times).

Catacombs of the Cappuccini

From Piazza Ingastone, the Via Cipressi leads west to the catacombs of the Convent of the Cappuccini (open 9–1 and 3–6; leave a donation), surely the most fascinating, macabre site in Sicily. The catacombs had a natural mummifying effect on those entombed, and today, like Palermitans of the 19th century, you can make a pleasant excursion through the corridors of grinning lawyers, friars, virgins and entire families pinned up on the walls, all dressed in their Sunday best. The last to be entombed, in 1920, was a little girl nicknamed 'The Sleeping Beauty'; she and the other small mummies in the catacombs are a sad reminder of how children used to drop like flies before the advent of modern medicine. As you leave, the plump friars will want to sell you wonderful colour postcards, useful for sending obligatory greetings to relatives you don't really like.

From here it is a short walk down Via Pindemonte to Corso Calatafimi, the main thoroughfare west from the Porta Nuova. At no. 94, a barracks, a soldier will guide you to **La Cuba,** another of the Norman pleasure palaces built in what was then a great park outside Palermo by William II. In form it resembles La Zisa, although it is relieved by shallow columns and arches carved in the walls. Boccaccio used La Cuba as a setting for one of his tales.

Monreale

Bus 8/9 from Piazza XIII Vittimi passes down Corso Calatafimi to Monreale and to its glorious **Cathedral,** which should not be missed by any visitor to Palermo. It was built by William II in 1174, supposedly after a dream in which the Virgin revealed to him a great treasure, which he found and used to fund the cathedral. Without doubt it is one of the greatest medieval monuments in the world (open daily, but closed 12.30–2.30).

Monreale Cathedral (Triple Apse)

From the outside, with only one of its towers completed, the Cathedral seems stern, but go around the back to see the celebrated neo-Arabic decoration of the apse. The doors on the west by Bonanno da Pisa (1186) and on the north by Barisano da Trani (1179) are quite beautiful. Inside, however, the impact of golden walls of mosaics overwhelms you; it's as if you had just walked into an illuminated manuscript (especially when someone puts 100 lire into the lighting machines!). The dominant figure in the central apse of Christ Benedicens presides over the stories of the Old and New Testament, and over the angels, apostles, saints and martyrs—among them, surprisingly enough, Thomas à Becket, who suffered martyrdom only a few years before his depiction in the mosaics by William II's own father-in-law, Henry II. A mosaic above the throne portrays William II offering his cathedral to the Virgin. He and his father William 'the Bad' are buried in a chapel by the choir; in another chapel lie the rest of the 'Bad' family, and a plaque marks the spot where the body of St Louis lay (before it was removed to Paris) after the defeat of Tunis. From here you can climb to the roof for a splendid view of the Conca d'Oro, or visit the rich treasury, or the 12th-century **Benedictine cloisters** (enter south of the cathedral; open 9–2.30, holidays 9–1). The columns all have elaborately-detailed individual designs in relief and mosaic. In one corner a pretty Arabic fountain adds a final touch. The 18th-century convent by the cloisters, now the **Instituto Statale d'Arte per il Mosaico** (open 8.30–12), contains an excellent painting of St Benedict by Pietro Novelli, who was born in Monreale in the 17th century.

In the **Municipio** (Piazza V. Emanuele) of Monreale you can visit a small art gallery. There are three good churches on Via Umberto Primo—the **Madonna delle Croce** affords a panoramic view. North of Monreale a road leads to the **Castellaccio,** once a monastery and now a refuge of the Sicilian Alpine Club.

Baida

Baida (Arabic for 'white'), a small village west of Monreale, by Boccadifalco, may be reached by bus 23 from Palermo. In 1377 Benedictine monks founded a convent here, after Manfred Chiaramonte chased them from the Castellaccio above Monreale. The church, 15th-century Gothic, houses one of Antonello Gagini's best pieces, of John the Baptist. Beyond Baida, in the pine-forested Valle del Paradiso, is **San Martino delle Scale,** site of the vast **Abbey of San Martino,** also Benedictine and believed to have originally been founded by Pope Gregory the Great in the 6th century, rebuilt in the 14th. Today it is an orphanage and college; you can visit the convent with its grand stair and fountain, and the later church with many works of art. San Martino itself is a hill resort, popular with picnickers in the summer months.

Monte Pellegrino

West of Palermo, Monte Pellegrino, 1969 ft high, is the city's main landmark, known to the ancients as Heirkte. On the north side of the mountain, in the **Grotta di Addaura** rock incisions dating back to 7000 BC were discovered in three chambers, one depicting human figures, beautifully and sensuously drawn. Permission to visit these lovely Palaeolithic carvings must be obtained from the Soprintendente alle Antichita at the National Archaeological Museum in Palermo.

You do not need permission, however, to visit the **Sanctuary of Santa Rosalia** (bus 12). Rosalia, a niece of King William II, renounced the ways of the world in 1159, and retreated to a hermitage on Monte Pellegrino, where she died. In 1624 when Palermo was suffering a disastrous plague, a holy man had a vision regarding Rosalia's bones; these were found, taken in a procession round the city, and the plague receded. So goes the legend, which is the reason for the great, festive pilgrimage on 15 July. In 1625, the small cave that held Rosalia's bones was converted into a chapel, where water of miraculous properties drips down the wall. From here you can walk to the cliff's edge to see the gigantic statue of the saint; another road from the sanctuary leads to the **Semaforo** near the summit of Monte Pellegrino. Below the sanctuary, the **Scala Vecchia** zigzags down to Le Falde, where the Fiera del Mediteraneo takes place and the long-abandoned Hotel Castello Utreggio presides over marvellous views of Palermo.

Mondello Lido

Below Monte Pellegrino lies Sicily's most popular beach resort, Mondello Lido (bus 14). The route from Palermo passes the wooded part of **La Favorita,** entered through the Piazza Niscemi. Here Queen Maria Carolina built the **Villa La Favorita** during her husband Ferdinand II's exile from Naples, in the deluxe 'Chinese restaurant' style popular around 1797—very elaborate, pretty and silly. On the ballroom wall are prints given to the royal couple by Nelson, who lived next door with the Hamiltons. The villa is open 8.30–1 and 3–5, Sundays 9–1, closed Fridays, and the same hours prevail for the **Museo Etnografico Pitre** next to the villa, in what was once the stables. Founded in 1909, this is Sicily's best collection of ethnographic items, and includes puppets, carts, customes, carriages and utensils from everyday life decades ago. In October and November there is an international folklore competition here for the Guiseppe Pitre Prize.

West of Palermo to Terrasini

The suburban sprawl stretches out along the coast to the airport of Punta Raisi. **Isola delle Femmine** refers both to an offshore islet and to the fishing village facing it. This and **Sferracavallo** next to it have become small resorts with campsites, although the sea here is none too clean. In **Carini,** further inland, there are caves with stalactites, and a 12th-century castle. **Terrasini,** by Monte Pecoraro, a pleasant little fishing tourist resort, also has many caves, the most famous being the Grotta delle Colombe and the Grotta Perciata. The town's **Antiquarium** houses mainly marine finds from the rocky coast (Via Calalossa 4; open 9–1 and 3–6, Sundays 9–12). A private collection of painted Sicilian carts may be seen at the **Palazzo d'Aumale,** which once belonged to the Duke d'Aumale, son of Louis Philippe of France; ask at the local library to see the 'Mostra dei Carretto Siciliano'.

SPECIALITIES
The almond-paste sweets you see in every pastry-shop window in Sicily

were first made at the Convent of La Martorana in Palermo, and are called *Frutti alla Martorana*. These 'fruits' come in a delightful variety of forms— tomatoes, cactus fruits, oranges, and even little dishes of marzipan spaghetti. Also *pasta con le sarde* (pasta with sardines), *involtini alla Siciliana* (rolled meat on a skewer), *caponata* (fried aubergine in sweet and sour sauce) and *pupi di zucchero* (special-occasion statues of people made out of sugar).

FESTIVALS

Epiphany (6 January). The Feast of Santa Rosalia (13–16 July) is one of the most spectacular in the Mediterranean: parades, fireworks and other delights culminate in a torch-lit pilgrimage to the sanctuary of Santa Rosalia on Monte Pellegrino. In August there are operas and concerts. Typical puppet shows are performed all year at many theatres in the old town, generally beginning at 9pm. Palermo's tourist offices can give you a list of current showings. In April, a week of sacred music at Monreale. *Festa di li Schetti* in Terrasini at Easter, when young men lift and swing huge tree trunks, along with traditional music and dancing.

GETTING TO AND AROUND PALERMO

By air: Palermo's airport is at Punta Raisi, 16 miles west of the city; there's a regular bus to the airport and back from Piazza Ruggero Settimo, in front of the Politeama Theatre. The airport connects the city with Naples, Rome and Milan, and also with Italian provincial centres such as Bergama, Bologna and Venice. There is a shuttle service to Catania, and some overseas flights from London in the summer, as well as charter flights available all year round.

By sea: regular ferry services to Naples, Cagliari, Tunis (on Tirrenia; offices at Via Roma 385, tel. (091) 333300 for bookings and information). There are also ferry and hydrofoil connections to Ustica Island (Siremar: Via F. Crispi 124, tel. (091) 582403), as well as occasional summer hydrofoils to the Aeolian Islands and Cefalu.

By rail: besides the central railway station on Piazza Giulio Cesare, at the foot of the Via Roma, there's another station in the new part of town, called Notorbartalo. (On arriving in the city, don't be alarmed when your train stops here first, then reverses out of Palermo; it has to circumnavigate the city to get to the Stazione Centrale.) There are connections to all points, most frequently those along the north coast route to Trapani and Messina, and the cross-island route to Enna and Catania.

By coach: most of the coaches for places around Sicily and Palermo Province also stop in the Piazza Cesare near the station. Some exceptions are: to Agrigento, from the Botanical Gardens on Via Lincoln; to Trapani and Ragusa, from the Giardino Garibaldi; to Santa Flavia, Bagheria, Altavilla, and to the coastal area to the east, from the Piazza Florio (AST line). Several different companies run services around Palermo, which can be confusing.

Within the city, these municipal buses may help: buses 14 and 15 to Mondello Beach, 16 to the Sferracavallo campsite (catch them at the Piazza Cesare); 12 to Monte Pellegrino and 8/9 or 9 to Monreale (from the Piazza XIII Vittime near the port). Buy tickets at a tobacconist and validate them on entering the bus. Driving a car around Palermo is folly. Cab drivers are predatory—as they tend to be elsewhere in Sicily—and don't be shy about reminding them to use the meter. If there isn't one, you've found a gypsy cab, which is all right as long as you negotiate the fare in advance. This is also true for the picturesque horse-drawn carriages that wait in the Piazza Cesare (though they're likely to be cheaper than the taxis). If you're walking in the old town, you won't get lost if you stick to the main streets, like the Via Roma, which were cut through the labyrinthine medieval city a century or two ago. If you stray too far from them you could end up in the Twilight Zone.

TOURIST INFORMATION
Palermo's very able and active EPT has its main office at Piazza Castelnuovo 34 (an extension to the west of the Piazza Ruggiero Settimo; tel. (091) 583847). It also operates these branches:

Stazione Centrale (tel. (091) 235500).
96 Via Notarbartolo, Notarbartolo Station (tel. (091) 266474).
Punta Raisi airport (tel. (091) 591405 or 591698).
Piazza Cavalieri del S. Sepolcro (tel. (091) 230361).
The AAST is at Salita Belmonte 43 (tel. (091) 540122).

WHERE TO STAY
Palermo has some renowned old establishments that truly deserve the appellation 'Grand Hotel'. In a garden overlooking the sea north of the port is the **Villa Igiea*****, famous for its 'Liberty' style (art nouveau) murals and decor by Ernest Basile and Ettore de Maria Bergler (Via Belmonte 43; tel. (0191) 910092; 94–144 000 lire single, 160–222 000 double; tennis, swimming pool). In the centre of town, the **Grande Albergho Delle Palme**** seems a perfectly-preserved time-capsule of early 1900s elegance (Via Roma 395; tel. (091) 583933; 66–72 000 lire single, 85–92 500 double). For the rest, like any of Italy's great cities, Palermo is crowded, and

modest hotels usually take up one or more floors of a larger building—so you can guess little about an establishment from the street. Don't let this discourage you; most are quite decent. On Via Roma, the **Moderno*** has exceptionally nice rooms and an English-speaking owner (no. 276; tel. (091) 588683; 22–30 000 lire single, 38–44 000 double). Even many of the cheapest hotels—Palermo has dozens of them—are comfortable if not always quiet: the **Odeon*** (Via Amari 140; tel. (091) 332778; 11–15 500 lire single, 20–24 000 double) or the **Cavour*** (Via Manzioni 11, near the Stazione Centrale; tel. (091) 231759; 15 500 lire single, 27 000 double without bath). Also, the main EPT office has a list of inexpensive, decent accommodation.

In Monreale, the only hotel is the **Carrubella Park**** (Via Umberto; tel. (091) 90046; 32–35 000 lire single, 48–51 500 double). West of Palermo, along the beaches past Monte Pellegrino, the area is heavily built up and crowded. Most of the more expensive hotels have their own beaches, but a few more modest ones do too, like the **Piccolo Hotel Villa Esperia**** (at Mondello Lido close to the city, Viale Margherita di Savoia; tel. (091) 450004; 28–30 000 lire single, 41–44 000 double).

EATING OUT

The best-known restaurant in Palermo, and possibly in all Sicily, is the **Charleston,** Piazza Ungheria, near the old skyscraper, with serious cuisine in art nouveau surroundings. In summer, like many of Palermo's finer establishments, the Charleston moves itself to Mondello Lido, in an old palace with a terrace on the Viale Regina Elena (35–40 000 lire). **Gourmaund's**, which is decorated in an unusual ultra-modern style, on Via Liberta, is its closest competitor. There are plenty more modest places with typical Sicilian food, but they are easier to find in the newer district around Via Liberta or in the suburbs than in the old town, such as the **Trattoria Fusillo,** Via Carella 38, or **Fontanini,** 49 Via Sella, or **U Strascinu,** Viale Regione Sicilia 2286, all with Sicilian specialities in the 15–25 000 lire range. For a good, simple meal, that's easy on the purse, you can't beat the **Trattoria Trapani,** Via Gregorio (next to the Stazione Centrale). Note also that Palermo contains some fine examples of that vanishing Sicilian amenity, the true *osteria*, with enormous, dusty wine barrels stacked up to the ceiling, meant for serious drinking; food is provided mostly to keep you sober enough to drink more. There are some on and around Via Americo Amari, near the port.

From Palermo to Cefalù

The Province of Palermo, the largest province in Sicily, in antiquity was mainly the territory of the Carthaginians, but they left few souvenirs of their passing between the Madonie Mountains and the Tyrrhenian Sea. These mountains, especially at the eastern end of the province, are high enough (many over 6000 ft) to have winter sports facilities. Of the seaside resorts that have popped up along the coast, Cefalù, the loveliest, is increasingly popular as an international holiday spot, with its Club Méditerranée and the occasional English paper in the kiosks. The villages of the province have some of the prettiest folk costumes in Sicily, which are on show at the summer festivals, particularly in the mountains in August.

Solunto

A frequent train service takes you from Palermo some 10 miles east to Santa Flavia, its station called Solunto for the ruins of ancient Soluntum which may be visited here (open daily from 9am until 2 hours before sunset). Situated in a spectacular position on the heel of Monte Catalfano, Soluntum is the child of Solus, one of the three main Phoenician settlements mentioned by Thucydides, which has recently been located some 3 miles to the southwest at Cozzo Cannita. Very little remains of the earlier town, destroyed by Dionysius of Syracuse in 398 BC in his campaign to rid Sicily of non-Greeks. Later Soluntum was built by Timoleon in a classic grid plan and was very Hellenised. During the First Punic War the Romans annexed it as a *civitas decumana*, and many of the ruins date from that period. At the entrance of the excavations a small **Antiquarium** contains a plan of Soluntum and some finds. Inside are the ruins of the *agora*, the theatre and Odeon, and Roman houses with mosaics (most famously, those of Leda and the swan) and traces of wall paintings. Most striking, however, is the view of the castle of Solanto, the Casteldaccia vineyards and Cefalù along the coast. Santa Flavia itself is a small fishing village turned resort.

Bagheria

Bagheria, the next railway station to the east, was the summer retreat of the Palermitan nobility in the 17th and 18th centuries, although today the word most often used to describe it is 'dusty'. However, among the crumbling villas, on Piazza Garibaldi you can see the most fantastical of Sicily's baroque palaces, the **Villa Palagonia,** built in 1715 by the Prince of Palagonia, Francesco Gravina. Around it leer, writhe, snarl, grin and mock 62 of the most bizarre creatures ever carved in stone, while inside (ring for the custodian at the gate) thousands of mirrors once tricked the eyes. Now owned by the government, the villa has been restored (open daily 9–12.30 and 4–6, admission fee). Also on the square is the lovely **Villa Valguarnera,** built in 1712 by the same architect, Tomaso Napoli. The Corso Umberto leads to the 1685 Villa Butera, better known as **La Certosa** for the waxwork figures it contains of the famous, all dressed in Carthusian robes. On the road towards Palermo, the **Villa dei Principi di Cattolica** houses the collected works of the local artist Renato Guttuso (open 9–1). In **Altavilla Milicia** just to the southeast there is the ruined church **Chiesazza,** built by Robert Guiscard in 1077, at the site where he defeated the Saracens. On 8 September there is a large pilgrimage of Sicilians to the town's Mother Church, followed by a sausage picnic.

Termini Imerese

Further east along the coast are the two castles of **San Nicola d'Arena** (now a nightclub) and **Trabia,** dating back to the Arabs. Termini Imerese, east of Trabia and on the gulf of the same name, was a colony of nearby Himera, captured by Hannibal. The town thrived under the Romans, partly due to its mineral springs, a treatment for arthritis, which may still be drunk at the spa; the good water is also the reason why Termini Imerese produces some of Italy's best spaghetti. The town is divided into two levels; in Città Bassa (the 'lower city') by the station are the remains of the **Roman baths** and the **Amphitheatre,** while in the more attractive Città Alta (the 'upper city') is the 17th-century **Cathedral** with four early 16th-century statues on its front. The **Church of Santa Maria della Misericordia** houses a magnificent triptych of the Madonna, St John and St Michael, painted in 1453 and attributed to Gaspone da Pésaro. Also worth visiting is the **Museo Civico** (open 8–12) with its collection of medieval art and archaeological finds, some from the cave by the citadel where an Upper Palaeolithic family once lived.

The castle at **Cáccamo,** a mountain town 8 miles south, was built in the 12th century and used as the seat of the local dukes into the 20th century. This is one of the largest castles in Italy, spread along the edge of the sheer rock. The **Cathedral,** in the Piazza del Duomo, dates from 1090 but has been altered numerous times since then, and another church near here, **Santa Maria degli Angeli,** retains its original 1797 ceiling and a Madonna by Antonello Gagini.

Imera

Imera, up on the coast near Buonfornello, was founded by Zancle (Messina) in 678 BC and was the home of the lyric poet Stesichorus. In 480 BC, the Greeks of Syracuse and Akragas defeated Hamilcar and an enormous force of Carthaginians in a decisive battle at Imera, winning great spoils and a measure of security; in honour of their victory, they erected a temple on the bank of the Fiume Grande. However, some 70 years later, Hamilcar's nephew Hannibal (not the one who worried Rome, but an ancestor) took revenge on the Greeks by demolishing Imera, slaying many of its inhabitants and sending the survivors to the Carthaginian town of Therma Himeraia (Termini Imerese). Imera was never rebuilt. The **Doric Temple,** perhaps dedicated to Zeus Eleftherios, stands outside the ancient walls, between the modern road and the railway. A clue to the elaborate decoration that once embellished this temple may be the lion head spouts in the Palermo museum. In a sacred area in the city walls, excavations have lately uncovered temples of the 7th, 6th and 5th centuries BC, and some tombs.

Cefalù and its Cathedral

Cefalù, the dramatic site of the ancient Sikel town of Cephaloedium, was settled in the 9th century BC, and later became a fortified outpost of Imera. The name comes from the craggy rock resembling a head (*cephalus*) that overlooks the town. Never large, Cefalù had been continuously inhabited before the arrival of the Normans, who used some of the stone from the walls to build the Cathedral—one of the most magnificent in Sicily. It was founded by Roger II in 1131, in thanksgiving for his safe landing after a storm at sea, but took 100 years to finish; it was consecrated by Monsignor Chat, whose arms of a cat rampant can still be seen. The facade designed in 1240 by Giovanni Panettera is very fine, but better are the Norman decorations on the east end and the three apses which are earlier. Inside, the long nave, with 16 Roman columns leading up to the altar and presbytery, the oldest part of the church, is decorated with the oldest Norman mosaics in Sicily (1148). By Byzantine artists, these seem quite oriental in comparison with the later ones in Palermo and Monreale; the depictions of Christ Pantocrator and the Virgin are excellent, and the former is considered one of the greatest portrayals of Christ in the world. The Madonna in a chapel by the choir is by Antonello Gagini.

On the rock above the cathedral (path above Piazza Garibaldi) the nimble

Cefalu Cathedral, Palermo Province

visitor can explore the **Arabian and feudal fortifications** and the odd megalithic structure of trapezoidal blocks known as the **Temple of Diana,** of prehistoric origins with modifications from the 5th century BC. Its purpose is a mystery, although with its splendid views some scholars believe it might have been a simple watchtower.

Museo Mandralisca

On Via Mandralisca is the private Museo Mandralisca (open 10.30–12.30 and 4.30–6.30 on weekdays; admission fee). Besides many local finds, the museum houses the *Portrait of an Unknown Man* by Antonello da Messina; if you've spent any time at all on the island, you may agree with the critics that it portrays the archetypal Sicilian, sensuous and cunning. Also of interest are the vases from the island of Lipari (one depicting a scene in the fish market), a fine coin collection, and Chinese boxes and other items collected by Enrico Piraino di Mandralisca. Towards the sea on Via Mandralisca are the medieval or **Arabic washrooms** at the foot of a curving stair, where the women of Cefalù did their wash in a picturesque arcade. The **Osterio Magno,** a Norman palace at the corner of Via Amendola and Corso Ruggero, has beautiful arched windows with weeds growing out of them—as they do everywhere else in Sicily.

Although Cefalù is a growing resort, with beaches, a Club Méditerranée and various hotels or restaurants at **Santa Lucia** and **Caldusa** on either side of the Rock, it is still very much a fishing village. The arms of the town depict three fish holding a loaf on their noses. Fish is of course a

177

speciality and the day's catch may be sampled in the many restaurants facing the sea on the Grand Promenade, or Lungomare.

TOURIST INFORMATION
AAST, Corso Ruggero 77 (tel. (0291) 21093).

WHERE TO STAY
There are a number of hotels in town and spread out along the beaches to Santa Lucia in the west and Caldura in the east. One with a beach, **Baia del Capitano*****, at Mazzaforno (tel. (0921) 20005; single room 32 000 lire, double 60 000 with bath) is in an olive grove. In Santa Lucia, the **Santa Lucia**** (tel. (0921) 21340) is a less expensive alternative (single room 25 000 lire, double 42 000, less without bath). In Cefalù itself there's the inexpensive **Santa Dominga*** on Via Gibilmanna (tel. (0921) 22124; single room 16 000 lire, double 19–22 000 without bath), which has the beach just outside its door.

EATING OUT
On Via Vit. Emanuele 77 there's **Al Girasole,** with good basic fare and friendly service, and on the Lungomare **Dan Nino** offers the same, and good fish too (both around 15–20 000 lire). **Il Gabbiano,** also on the Lungomare, serves good pizza and seafood for a little more.

In the Interior of Palermo Province

South of Palermo
South of Palermo, connected by a frequent bus service, lies one of the unique towns of Sicily, **Piana degli Albanesi,** a 15th-century Albanian colony (actually northern Greeks) where the people still speak Greek at home, attend Orthodox (Uniate) services, and wear their old costumes at weddings and feasts, especially at Epiphany and Easter. On the main road south to Agrigento, the town of **Misilmeri** (from the Arabic *Menzil el Emir*—the village of the Emir) saw Roger de Hauteville's victory over the Saracens in 1068, beginning the Norman rule of Sicily. Misilmeri produces the white wine *passito*—good strong stuff. At **Bagni di Cefalù** the ruins of an old Arab town lie near the **Castle of Diana.** A small village further south on SS121, Mezzoiuso, produces an imaginative pantomime every Carnival Sunday (Il Mastro di Campo).

Near **Prizzi** (3323 ft) further south is a lake of the same name and some unusual 'drunken' rocks to the west. Passing Bisacquino you can reach quaint **Contessa Entellina,** where traditional sacred plays are performed during Holy Week. A long hike from Contessa (or drive from Bisacquino) takes you to the **Abbey of Santa Maria del Bosco** of the Olivetan Order, with a 17th-century church and 16th-century cloister.

The big town north of here, **Corleone,** will sound familiar to those who have seen *The Godfather.* Founded by the Saracens, it has a large population of Lombards brought there by Frederick II in the 13th century. On the main Palermo–Sciacca highway, **San Giuseppe Iato** is near the site known as Monte Jato, recently excavated to reveal a Hellenistic settlement, with a theatre and stage, an arcaded *agora*, a temple dedicated to Aphrodite and a well-to-do residential quarter.

South of Cefalù

Just south of Cefalù is the **Sanctuary of Gibilmanna** on a hill called 'Gibel el Iman' ('The Mount of Faith') by the Arabs, after they witnessed a miracle by the Madonna there, now the site of an annual pilgrimage (8 September).

From Cefalù the SS286 heads south to **Castelbuono** in the Madonie Mountains. The castle here, built in 1289, was the seat of the powerful Ventimiglia princes of Geraci, the rivals of the Chiaramonte family. The main square, with a pretty fountain, has the 1350 **Matrice Vecchia** with frescoes and other artworks; the **Church of San Francesco** contains the Ventimiglia chapel and tombs. The Sagra delle Ciliege (the festival of cherries) takes place here in June.

Another earlier castle of the Ventimiglia family is in **Geraci Siculo** south of here, this one built in the 11th century. In the **Church of Santa Maria della Porta** the Madonna with Child was sculpted by Domenico **Gagini.** South of here the highway forks off, east to **Gangi** and west to **Petralia.** Gangi was the birthplace of the artist Zoppo Gancia, who painted the Michelangelo-inspired *Last Judgement* in **San Nicola Church.** The lovely campanile of San Nicola was built in the 14th century.

There are two Petralias: **Sottana** (lower) and **Soprana** (upper). Hardly low at 3280 ft, Sottana boasts many lovely churches in a variety of styles, in particular the **Chiesa Madre** with paintings by Zoppo Gancia and a fine belfry. In August the interesting festival of the Madonna dell' Alto takes place in the streets here, with a nocturnal procession on horseback and the *Ballo della Cordella*, an ancient dance. Some 500 ft above Sottana, **Petralia Soprana** has become a major summer and winter resort. The sculptor of crucifixes, Fra Umile Pintorno, was born here in the 15th century and the **Convento dei Minori Riformati** contains an example of his art. Also notable is the 18th-century **Santa Maria di Loreto,** with its two 14th-century campaniles adorned with colourful majolica tiles.

West along the main road from here **Castellana Sicula** sponsors a very traditional carnival with parades and masks. North, another picturesque old town, **Polizzi Generosa** (no, it does not mean 'Generous Policeman') has a disproportionate number of churches—the best of these, the **Chiesa Madre,** containing a Flemish triptych, a Venetian organ and sculptures salvaged from other churches. The Festival of Hazelnuts is held here in September. The 16th-century **Caltavuturo,** off the highway, perches beneath the Saracen castle which Roger I captured; it is very picturesque in an untidy way, and the streets consist of stairs.

The coast: Cefalù to Milazzo

A number of small resorts dot the Tyrrhenian coast from Cefalù eastwards. One of the smaller ones, **Castel di Tusa,** is near ancient Halesa, founded in the 5th century BC by Archonides of Herbita, a Sikel. The Romans granted Halesa special privileges in return for its loyalty in the First Punic War. Excavations of **Halesa** (open daily, 9am to sunset), still in progress, have unearthed its grid street plan, part of the *agora*, walls and the remains of two temples. There are a few interesting churches in Tusa itself, notably the **Chiesa Matrice** with its medieval campanile and Gothic door, and the 14th-century Church of San Nicola. **San Stefano di Camastra** to the east is a major ceramics town. **Sant' Agata Militello** is one of the most important resorts. From here you can visit pretty **San Marco d'Alunzio** (ancient Aleuntine), where Robert Guiscard built the first Norman castle in Sicily back in 1061—now in ruins. The roofless **Church of San Marco** was built on the site of a temple of Hercules (you can see the ancient *cella*).

Capo d'Orlando, Brolo, and **Gioiosa Marea** are popular Italian resorts with campsites near sandy beaches. Brolo is dominated by a distinctive medieval tower, and on Capo d'Orlando's sea-sweep and promontory is the 14th-century **castle** where Roger of Lauria, with the fleets of Catalonia and Anjou, defeated Frederick II: the church next to it dates from 1598. Capo d'Orlando has a unique beach at **San Gregorio,** the fine sand strewn with odd-shaped boulders.

Oddly named Naso ('nose'), a small village about a mile inland, has a beautiful 15th-century church, the **Minori Osservanti,** located just outside the town. Built partly in Gothic and Renaissance styles, it contains the tomb of Artale Cardona (died 1477) with allegories of the six virtues. The rosary chapel of Naso's parish church also has many works of art inside, belonging to the 14th and 15th centuries. Further east, in the town of **Patti,** in the Cathedral, is the tomb of Adelasia, the wife of Roger I, who died in 1118. There is a fine beach nearby at **Marina di Patti.**

Tindari

On the Capo Tindari, a sanctuary of the Madonna attracts many pilgrims on 8 September in honour of the Byzantine black-faced icon of the Virgin. This little church is built on the ancient acropolis of Tyndaris, the excavations of which can be seen nearby. Founded by Dionysius of Syracuse in 396 BC, Tyndaris acted as garrison to protect Sicily's northern coast from the Carthaginians. The town's name comes from the Tyndaridae (the Dioscuri, or twins), worshipped by the colonists, who were mainly refugees from the Peloponnesian War. Under Roman protection, the town prospered and had an archbishop in Christian times; however, the Arabs demolished Tyndaris in 836 BC.

The extensive excavations of Tindari (open daily 9–12 and 3–6) have revealed the large **theatre** of the late 4th century BC, adapted by the Romans for gladiatorial and circus use. Like the theatre of Taormina, this is in a magnificent situation, facing the Aeolian Islands, the sea and Mt Etna. Some of its stone was quarried to build the exceptionally well-preserved walls and towers. There are ruins of houses, some with mosaics, along the main street towards the 1st-century BC 'basilica' or *Propylaea* (entrance) to the *agora*, partly restored. Further walls, with the main gate and barbican, can be seen on the other side. Near the entrance is an **Antiquarium,** with models and finds from Tyndaris. In June there are Classical drama performances in the theatre.

Castroreale

Further east, at **San Biagio,** by the station, the remains of a 4th-century **Roman villa** have been excavated, including a section of the ancient baths and some mosaics, the best of which shows a fishing scene. **Rodi,** near Castroreale, was a flourishing Sikel town known as Longane. As yet it is unexcavated, but you can make out the walls and a temple foundation.

Castroreale gets its name from the ruined castle of Frederick II of Aragon, who spent a good deal of his time here. Among the fine works in the various churches in town are pieces by Antonello Gagini, in both the Chiesa Matrice and Sant' Agata. The churches **Immacolata, Santissimo Salvatore** and **Candeloro** all date from the 15th century. There is a youth hostel at Castroreale, on the Salita Federico II d'Aragona (open June–September). A scenic road leads to the coastal resort and thermal spa Castroreale Terme.

Milazzo

Milazzo, on its narrow promontory, is the main port for the Aeolian Islands, and one of the busiest in Sicily, with the island's largest single industry—a huge oil refinery. Colonised by Greeks from Messina in 716 BC, Mylai, as it was then called, was the scene of Duilius' victory at sea over the Carthaginians in 260 BC and Garibaldi's victory over the Bourbons in 1860, which all but cemented the 'Risorgimento' in Sicily. The **castle**, on Mylai's acropolis, is the main attraction in Milazzo, originally built by Frederick II in 1239, enlarged by Charles V, then restored in the 17th century. The Gothic door is very fine. Inside the castle walls, the domed **Duomo Vecchio** belongs to the 16th century but is being replaced by a new church. The old prison, **Palazzo dei Durati,** dates back to the 15th century.

The railway station in Milazzo is within easy walking distance of the port for the Aeolian Islands; the Giunta bus from Messina stops right in front of the hydrofoils. From Milazzo a good road leads to the tip of the cape, where there is a restaurant and a fine view of the islands and the Sicilian coast.

The Nebrodi Mountains

Some of the towns in the Nebrodi Mountains merit a visit, including **Mistretta** (ancient Amestratus), dominated by its castle. The parish church of **Santa Lucia,** though renovated in the 17th century, retains its medieval-fortress appearance, and contains some interesting works. A popular excursion from here is through the watershed **Portella del Contrasto** to Castel di Lucio. Another mountain town is **San Fratello,** originally colonised by Lombards who came to Sicily with Adelaide di Monferrato, the wife of Roger. The inhabitants still speak a Lombard dialect and retain various old customs, like the Feast of the Jews (Maundy Thursday/Good Friday). The simple Norman church of **Santi Alfio, Filadelfio e Cirino** of the 12th century is quite lovely. From San Fratello the road south to **Cesarò** (another mountain town) passes through the picturesque **Portella della Femmina Maorta**—though why it is named 'the Pass of the Dead Woman' is just one of those Sicilian mysteries.

At **Frazzanò,** south of Capo d'Orlando, one can visit the Basilian abbey of **San Filippo di Fragala,** built in the 11th century. South of here (highway 116 from Naso) is **Floresta,** at 4000 ft the highest town on the island, remote and grey, dominated by Mt Etna. **Montalbano Elicona,** known simply as Montalbano, has another example of Frederick II's 14th-century castle building, this one particularly monumental and well preserved. In its chapel, frescoes can be discerned, though faintly.

The South Coast and Interior

Marsala

HISTORY

Nowadays synonymous with wine, Marsala is situated near ancient Lilybaeum, founded by the Phoenicians after Dionysius of Syracuse destroyed their base at Motya (see the section on the Egadi Islands). Although the original settlement occupied only the westernmost point of Sicily at Capo Boeo, the name Lilybaeum eventually came to include most of the land occupied by present-day Marsala. Powerfully fortified by the Carthaginians, Lilybaeum was the only place Pyrrhus failed to take in his whirlwind conquest of the island. The Romans besieged it unsuccessfully for nine years and only took it in the peace following their victory at Erice. Cicero described it as a splendid city, and in 204 BC Scipio Africanus and his fleet sailed from Lilybaeum to conquer Carthage.

The Saracens renamed the town *Marsah-el-Allah* ('the port of God') and made it their main port in Sicily. In the 18th and 19th centuries the English set up various wine import establishments, first the Woodhouse and then the Ingham-Whitaker firms, still very visible today. Garibaldi landed at Marsala in May 1860, and the city was all but destroyed in the bombing during World War II.

WHAT TO SEE

Nevertheless, Marsala has retained much of its Saracen air, if not any of its physical structures. One survivor of the bombing is the **cathedral,** on the Piazza della Republica, dedicated to St Thomas of Canterbury. It contains the tomb of native son Antonio Lombardo (died 1595) who was Archbishop of Messina and Ambassador to Spain. The Spanish King Philip II gave him eight 16th-century **tapestries** illustrating the conquest of Jerusalem; these are on display in the church and are quite remarkable. Of the Gagini works here, Antonello's St Thomas is the best. Via Garibaldi passes through the **Porta Garibaldi.** Various Spanish bastions mark the perimeter of the old

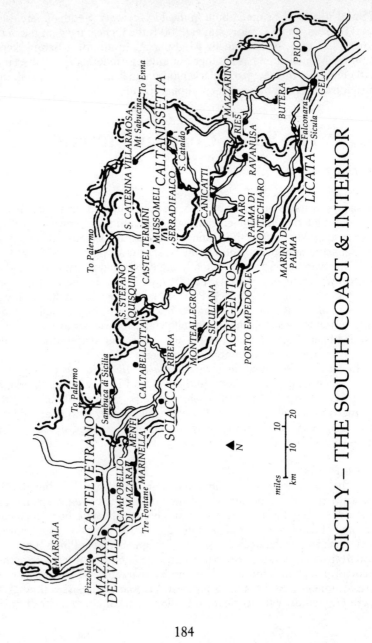

SICILY – THE SOUTH COAST & INTERIOR

city walls, and to the northeast, by the Scuola dei Cappucini, there is a large Punic–Roman necropolis.

Leaving the town through the western gate, going towards the flat, littered shore where the **Excavations of Lilybaeum** can be seen at Capo Boeo (open daily 9–12 and 2pm until dusk). The remains here are mainly Roman. Some vestiges of the city walls have been uncovered near Viale V. Veneto along with the baths and mosaics. At the **Baglio Anselmi,** at the tip of Capo Boeo, a new, mammoth structure houses the marvellous **Punic ship,** recovered by the archaeologist Honor Frost in the early 1970s. The ship, a liburnian, was found off Isola Lunga in the Stagnone group of islands, and may have been sunk in the Battle of the Egadi Islands. Measuring 114 ft and manned by 68 rowers, it is a unique example of Classical warships, and amazingly well preserved (open 9–1 and 4–6; closed Mondays). Here also stands a marble obelisk commemorating Scipio Africanus's departure, Garibaldi's arrival, and the Battle of Lepanto.

Marsala wine

Marsala, one of the most popular wines in England in the 18th and 19th centuries, was developed when a certain soap merchant in Liverpool named John Woodhouse noticed that Sicilian wine, when fortified with alcohol before the long trip to England, was much better than the plain wine. He moved to Marsala, reproduced the same effect in his winery, and shipped the first batch to England in 1773, where it soon became a roaring success. In 1806 Benjamin Ingham opened another winery; in 1833 Vicenzo Florio opened a third. For the next hundred years the three firms ruled the industry, until 1929 when Cinzano bought them up (though it continues to bottle the wine under their old labels).

The **Florio Winery,** south of the town on the Lungomare Mediterraneo, may be visited daily 10.30–1 and 3.30–6, with abundant tastings provided. The sweetest of the sweet wine brewed in those great wooden casks is **Marsala all'uovo**—with egg yolks. Others have various flavours added; **Marsala secco**—dry only by Marsala standards—may be your favourite as an aperitif.

Besides Florio, there are a number of other wineries along the roads to Selinunte and the airport.

FESTIVALS

Maundy Thursday procession, with participants dressed as characters from the Passion. In August, a competition of contemporary Italian art with the *Premio Città di Marsala* at stake.

Mazara del Vallo

South along the coast, past the resort of **Lido Ponticello,** is the important fishing town of Mazara del Vallo, at the mouth of the River Mazaro. Originally a colony of Selinunte, Mazara was destroyed at the same time as that city by the Carthaginians. In 827 the Saracens conquered Mazara, their first territory in Sicily, then Count Roger took it in 1075, and 20 years later the town saw the first Norman parliament. Over the door of the **cathedral** is a statue of Count Roger who founded the church, although nothing remains of the Norman structure. Inside are two Gagini works: a tomb by Domenico (1485) and a Transfiguration by Antonello. Antonello also sculpted the **Santa Caterina** in the church of that name. An old **Palace of the Knights of Malta,** now containing a small Roman museum (open 10–1), is on the Via Carmine, near the harbour. For the Knights, Mazara was the nearest Christian city and port, as well as the home of the Spanish viceroys, to whom the Knights paid homage.

Due east lies wine-making **Campobello di Mazara,** where the parish church contains a 15th-century crucifix by Fra Umile da Petralia. From here take the *Strada di Tre Fontane* to the Greek quarries at the caves of the **Rocche di Cusa** (from SS115, turn off at Principe–Torre Cusa). It was from here that Selinunte took the stone to build its temples, and some of the column drums, still waiting to be taken in ox carts to Selina, can be seen amidst the trees. The Carthaginian invasion in 409 BC interrupted the work on Temple G, and the quarries have not been dug since that time. In that respect they are particularly interesting—indeed, impressive.

Castelvetrano

The largest town in the area, Castelvetrano is a wine and furniture-making centre and a good base for visiting Selinunte. In the Municipio in Piazza Garibaldi you can see the city's beautiful jewel—the *Ephebe of Selinunte*, an excellently preserved bronze statue of an athlete dating from 460 BC. The **Chiesa Madre** contains an altarpiece by Orazio Ferraro and works by Serpotta. Those with time should not miss the Arabic-influenced Byzantine chapel of **Santissima Trinita di Delia,** built in the 12th century and restored to its original state. To see the interior, ask the caretaker. The chapel is a couple of miles west of town (look for the yellow signs).

Selinunte

Buses leave Castelvetrano for the beach and village of **Marinella Lido** and for Selinunte (you can also go by train). Ancient *Selinus*, lying between the rivers Selinus and Cotone, was the most westerly of all Greek colonies, founded by Megara Hyblaea around 650 BC. Its name derives from the Greek word for the wild celery (*selinon*), the symbol of the city, which still grows there on the fertile plain. This plain that attracted colonists so far westward was the cause of the city's prosperity, mainly in the 6th and 5th centuries BC, as well as its woes, for Segesta coveted the land and ceaselessly fought for it, using fair means and foul.

Finally, in 409 BC, Segesta's ally Carthage sent 100 000 men to attack Selinunte, and they took the city in only nine days, before Syracuse could send aid. Although Hermocrates of Syracuse later attempted to found a new settlement on the plain, he was later killed and the site returned to Carthaginian hands. In 250 BC they removed the inhabitants to Marsala and destroyed Selinunte for strategic reasons.

As Selinunte was in non-Greek territory, it absorbed many foreign influences which, combined with Hellenic ideals, contributed to the high artistic traditions of the city. The metopes and vases at Palermo are examples of this, as well as the bronze athlete at Castelvetrano. The grid plan of the streets is one of the oldest in the world, dating back to a century before Hippodamus supposedly invented it. This is not all that surprising: Sicily was the 'New World' for the Greeks, and on virgin turf the grid is the easiest way to divide property—witness all the grid cities in the USA.

The excavations

The excavations of Selinus (open daily, 9 until dusk) lie on rather desolate low hills facing the sea. Since most of the temples have fallen in earthquakes over the years, the ruins are more romantic than impressive. Identified by letters, as their dedications are uncertain, the temples stand on either side of the River Cotone, where the ancient harbour has long since filled with silt. Of the three temples on the eastern bank, near the station, the most prominent is **Temple E,** recently reconstructed (1958) as can be seen by the different degrees of weathering that the individual columns have suffered. This gives the magnificent 5th-century BC structure a piecemeal, fragile look. Measuring 220 ft by 83 ft, the four metopes removed from here to the Palermo museum suggest a dedication to Hera. **Temple F,** beside it, belongs to the mid 6th century BC, and is unusual in that the spaces between its columns were filled in with 10-ft walls, perhaps to prevent outsiders from watching the sacred rites inside. These may have inspired the architect of the huge Temple of Olympieon Zeus at Agrigento, as well as the grandeur of **Temple G** on the other side of the road. Begun in the 5th or 6th century

187

BC, this vast edifice measures 361 ft by 164 ft; like the Temple of Zeus, to which it is second in size, it was unfinished when the Carthaginian bully-boys came to town. Over the years of its construction, fashions changed, and the temple is partly Archaic, partly Classical. Only one column still stands, built of 100-ton drums.

The Acropolis

The Acropolis stands on a small plateau on the other bank of the Cotone, where there are more temples, the remains of the walls (begun 6th century BC) and the site of the city, located on another hill just to the north and connected to the Acropolis by a path. Dominating the Acropolis is the 1927 reconstructed colonnade of **Temple C,** a large temple (208 ft by 78 ft) thought to have been dedicated to Hercules. The Archaic metopes in Palermo came from this temple, which was built in the 6th century BC. Some of the columns were monoliths instead of divided drums, and when these collapsed in an 8th-century earthquake, they flattened a Byzantine village on the hill.

Across the ancient street are the vestiges of **Temple O** and **Temple A.** Of Temple O only the platform (stylobate) remains, while pieces of the 36 columns of Temple A, as well as its stylobate, can be seen. Both of these temples date from 480–490 BC, the last and most refined temples built in Selinunte. Only the base remains of little **Temple B,** constructed in the Hellenstic period. **Temple D** (183 ft by 77 ft), on the main street leading to the ancient city, was built in 535 BC. The nearby ramparts of the **North Gate** belong to 250 BC.

Sanctuary of Demeter

To the west, on the other side of the ancient River Selinus (modern Modione), a path leads to the Sanctuary of Demeter Malophoros ('the apple-bearer'). The walled sanctuary, or *megaron*, was built around 575 BC, replacing an older one. Outside the sanctuary worshippers set up carved *stellae*, and more than 12 000 votive figures of Demeter have been recovered, attesting to the importance of the cult, which appears to have had some connection with death, as a vast **necropolis** is spread around the sanctuary, and for several miles along the coast tombs and bones are still visible in places.

Menfi, to the east, once a picturesque feudal town, was destroyed by an earthquake in 1968. The new town has been constructed above the old, which remains in ruins. **Porto Palo,** 5 miles away on the coast, has a fine beach. Inland, north of Menfi, **Santa Margherita di Belice,** childhood home of Guiseppe di Lampedusa, has an elegant piazza worth visiting if you are passing through on the SS188. A late Bronze Age settlement, **Monte Adranone,** has been found north of Sambuca di Sicilia. The inhabitants of the simple round huts here were Hellenised by Selinunte; the Romans destroyed the settlement in the 1st century. **Lake Arancio,** by Sambuca, reputedly offers excellent fishing.

Sciacca

To the east, Sciacca has been a thermal spa since ancient times, when it was known as *Thermae Selinuntinae*. During the 15th and 16th centuries one of Sicily's greatest feuds, the *Caso di Sciacca*, divided the town's population into factions loyal to the Luna and Perolla families. The feud left the town devastated and decreased its population by half. Sciacca today is the prettiest town in Agrigento Province, especially in the upper quarters, which recall places in North Africa. The traditional way of entering this terraced town overlooking the sea is through the grandiose **Porta San Salvatore,** built in the 16th century within the older fortifications. The lower town contains many fine churches—among them **Santa Margherita,** built in 1342, with sculptures on the facade by Francesco Laurana, and the **Church of the Carmine** nearby, with its rose window. The Norman **Cathedral** has since been modified, decorated on the outside with five statues by Antonino and Gian Americo Gagini. The eastern part of the church is original and quite lovely. The interior is mainly Renaissance, with a statue of the Virgin by Laurana. Near here, in the central piazza, the **Palazzo Municipale** dates from 1615. On Via Incisa note the beautiful 15th-century palace of **Casa Arone,** and the **Steripinto** on Via Gerandi (also 15th century) is also worth a visit. Near the Steripinto is the derelict 12th-century **Church of San Nicola.** Among the pretty houses in the upper town stands the solemn **Luna Castle** and the **Church of Santa Maria della Giommare,** a fine Norman church with frescoes by Mariano Rossi (18th century).

Monte San Calogero

North of Sciacca, Monte San Calogero is another thermal spa, where people since antiquity have come for the natural steam baths (the *stufe vaporose di San Calogero*). The seats and water channels were hollowed out in ancient times; legend has it that Daedalus made the baths, while other sources claim that St Paul sent San Calogero to Sicily to put an end to a plague raging there, and during his stay he found the caverns in the mountain that bears his name, as well as the natural saunas which are reputed to cure rheumatism and are still in use today. Beneath the steam baths, where the sulphurous vapours are more concentrated, lie two underground caverns, open since very ancient times, where archaeologists and speleologists (cave specialists) have discovered huge Copper Age jars and the tiny arm bones of children sacrificed as an offering to the terrible gods inside. The sulphurous fountains near here are dedicated to the Madonna degli Ammalati.

Perhaps strangest of all the stories concerning San Calogero involves a small uncharted island offshore. In 1831, British seamen discovered and claimed it for Britain. Sicily, of course, disputed the claim, but before Britain could make a full reply, the island sank out of sight, disappearing as mysteriously as it had appeared.

Caltabellotta and Ribera

The **Castello** at nearby Caltabellotta saw the 1302 signing of the peace ending the War of the Vespers. Among the buildings of this medieval town is the Norman **Chiesa Madre** containing two works by the Gagini—the *Madonna della Catena* and a St Benedict.

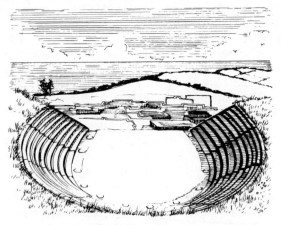

Eraclea Minoa, Agrigento

Ribera was founded in 1627 by Prince Luigi Paterno who named the town after his wife Maria di Ribera. Here the famous Prime Minister Francesco Crispi was born in 1818. Ribera is also famous for its strawberries, which make Sicilian mouths water at their mention.

Eraclea Minoa

Monteallegro, an 18th-century town built below the old hill town, is the base for visiting Eraclea Minoa (Heracleia Minoa) near the mouth of the River Platani. Although no public transport goes to the excavations, the beach and campsite near the ruins attract enough traffic to make hitchhiking a viable way to get there in the summer. The old place name, *Minoa*, suggests the legend of King Minos, who came to Sicily in search of Daedalus and was killed by the daughters of King Cocalos in his bath. Indeed, when Akragas captured the city, Theron supposedly discovered the tomb of Minos, considered by the inhabitants to be the founding father.

The town as it exists was founded in the 6th century by Selinunte; the name commemorating Hercules was added later, perhaps in the 4th century when the city belonged to Akragas. During the Carthaginian Wars, Eraclea Minoa was depopulated, as the River Platani (the ancient Halykos) formed the boundary between Greek and Punic territory. Timoleon repopulated the city with a mixed Greek–Carthaginian population; it changed hands a few times and suffered so much in the 1st-century Slave Wars that it was abandoned for good. The **excavations** (open 9 until dusk, shown by custodian) date mainly from the 4th century BC and include the powerful *walls*, built in four stages, though landslides have destroyed the southern part of the walls. The interesting **theatre,** built of soft marl and now covered over to protect it from further weathering, was designed after the main theatre in Athens. An **Antiquarium** on the site contains a few items from the digs and a plan of the ancient city, which is still being excavated.

Further east towards Agrigento, **Siculiana** has a large castle dating from 1356 and a beach at Marina Siculiana.

GETTING TO MARSALA
By train: Marsala is connected by train regularly with Trapani; the line continues to Mazara del Vallo and Castelvetrano, where it loops back up to the north. From Castelvetrano there is an erratic service along the coast to Selinunte, Menfi, Sciacca, Ribera and Montallegro on the way to Agrigento.
By bus: buses ply the same routes; Marsala, Mazara and Campobella di Mazara are all on the autostrada and quickly reached from either Trapani or Palermo. Services to other points originate in Marsala, Sciacca and Agrigento.

TOURIST INFORMATION
In Sciacca; Corso Vittorio Emanuele 84 (tel. (0925) 21182).

WHERE TO STAY
In Marsala there isn't a lot of choice, the best being the **Stella d'Italia***** in the town centre (Via M. Rapisardi 7; tel. (0923) 953003; single room 20–32 000 lire, double 37–50 000, depending on whether you want a bath). Near Selinunte you can stay on the beach at **Giani**** (Via Pigafetta 2 tel. (0924) 46222; single room 27 000 lire, double 46 000 with bath) or at the **Lido Azzurro,** with an excellent seafood restaurant on the terrace (Via Marco Polo 98; tel. (0924) 46057; single room with bath 16 000 lire, double 25 000 lire). Both of these are at Marinella, officially part of Castelvetrano.

In Sciacca, the big resort hotel is the **Torre Macauda***** on the SS115 (tel. (0925) 26800; single room 34 000 lire, double 57 000; garden, tennis courts, beach and pool). The **Piccolo Mondo**** in Siculiana is similar (tel. (0922) 815531; double rooms only 32 000 lire—with the dubious chance of watching Italian TV in your room.)

EATING OUT
Zio Ciccio, near the Florio winery on Lungomare Mediterreo 211, has couscous and seafood specialities for 30 000 lire. **Enzo e Nino,** a trattoria on Via Favorita 26, also has couscous and fish and—rare in an Italian restaurant—dessert specialities, for around 25 000 lire total. *Scaloppine al Marsala* is a speciality at **al Fanaletto** (20 000 lire; Via F. Crispi 53). Every restaurant in Marsala, not surprisingly, serves the local wine.

In Mazara local specialities are served at the inexpensive but good **La Bettola** on Corso A Diaz 20 (15 000 lire). In Castelvetrano, try the good ravioli at **Efebo,** Via Campobello 6 (25 000 lire); in Selinunte, after seeing the ruins, try the fish at **Lido Azzurro** on Via M. Polo (20 000 lire). Seafood again is the pride of Sciacca, at restaurants like **La Maniatoia,** Viale delle Vittoria 14 (25 000 lire; closed Mondays).

Agrigento

HISTORY
Colonists from Gela and Rhodes founded Agrigento, then known as *Akragas,* in 581 BC, on a landshelf between the rivers Akragas (San Biagio) and Hypsas (Sant' Anna), easily defensible and very fertile. The early colonists must have been very confident about Akragas' future, for unlike most ancient cities, it is thought the new colony was laid out with a large plan to

grow into, and its extensive walls were built at one time in the 6th century.

Akragas soon became one of the major cities in Sicily, owing to an early tyrant, Phalaris, who reigned until 549 BC. Credit is given to him for the city walls and grand building programme and for annexing Licata from the Sikans. Pindar, who lived as a guest in Akragas under the later tyrant Theron, wrote that Phalaris roasted his enemies alive in a large brazen bull, a recurring theme in Rhodian mythology but not very likely to have happened in reality.

Under Theron (who ascended to power in 488 BC) Akragas expanded its territories up to Himera (Imera) on the north coast of Sicily, provoking the mass attack of Carthage on that city. Theron and his ally, Gelon of Gela, won a sweeping victory here, and the captives and disbanded soldiers of this campaign were set to work erecting the temples and other public works. The city became fabulously wealthy—'the people built temples as if they would live forever, but lived as if they would die the next day', marvelled an ancient writer. The pre-Socratic philosopher Empedocles was born here; he theorised that all matter was made of Earth, Water, Fire and Air (he was the first to discover air as a substance) and that Love and Strife moved them. Believing hot air would make him rise like a god, Empedocles jumped into the fiery crater of Mount Etna. Akragas was also famous for its horses, which won the great Games of the Ancient Greeks and were depicted on contemporary coins that have been found.

Time was running out for Akragas, however. When the city's great enemy, Syracuse, defeated the Athenians, the Carthaginians saw their chance to extract revenge for Imera. They besieged Akragas for eight months before capturing it. Many of the citizens took refuge in the Temple of Athena and set fire to it and themselves as the Carthaginians looted the city. Later the Carthaginians allowed some inhabitants to return; it became independent, was rebuilt by Timoleon in 340 BC and eventually enjoyed a bit of its old prosperity under the Romans, when it became a centre of the coin market. By the 3rd century, however, *Agrigentum*, as the Romans called it, began a slow decline. The medieval town was built up around the ancient acropolis (Rupe Atenea) and was known as *Girgenti*. Mussolini, in his name campaign, changed it back to Agrigento in 1927.

Modern Sicily's most famous son, the playwright Luigi Pirandello (1867–1936), was born in Agrigento. In July and August performances of his plays are given in the *Settimana Pirandellana*.

WHAT TO SEE

Agrigento today is a slick town, or so it seems at first sight. The young people on the tree-lined Viale della Vittoria, with the splendid panorama of the temples below, wear the latest fashions, and in the main shopping street, Via Atenea, the shops compete for your attention with shiny glittering displays. Outside these centres, however, Agrigento is just another dusty, shabby provincial capital with its modern extensions of dull concrete apartment blocks. The surroundings are all: the sloping hills covered with almond orchards, dazzling the eye when they blossom in February, and the magnificent Valley of the Temples, one of the major Greek sites in the world that keeps visitors coming all the year.

Sloping **Piazza Roma,** just north of the station (Piazza Marconi) is the centre of the city and one of the few green spots in Agrigento. At the bottom of the square, the Via F. Crispi leads down to the Archaeological Museum and the temples; on the opposite side, the Via Atenea takes you to the old town. On this street, the 17th-century church known as the **Purgatorio,** with fine sculptures by the Palermitan Serpotta, stands over the entrance to a complex underground system of cisterns of the 5th century BC (stone removed from here was used to build the temples). The **Municipio,** also on Via Atenea, is in a pretty 11th-century convent on the same square as the **Teatro Pirandello** and the **Museo Civico** (open 9–12 and 3–5; closed Sundays), the latter containing a variety of paintings from many centuries. Up the stairs and alleyways from here you reach the old whitewashed Greek quarter of town, which indeed looks more Greek than Italian; signs will direct you to the old Orthodox cathedral, **Santa Maria dei Greci** (open 9.30–12 and 4–7; leave a tip). This little church with a lovely portal was constructed in the 13th century and incorporated a temple, perhaps of Athena. Six bases of Doric columns remain inside, as well as some frescoes and ceiling painting.

Via del Duomo

Further up you will find the Via del Duomo and the large 14th-century **Cathedral** at the very top of Agrigento. This and the Diocesan Museum next to it were damaged in a landslide in 1966 and the museum's collection has since been moved to the Archaeology Museum. Founded by San Gerlando, Roger I's bishop, the church was dedicated to him in 1365 and contains his relics in a silver casket. Partly painted, partly coffered, the ceiling offers the main interest in the interior, along with the grand arch in the nave. The phenomenon known as *Il porta voce* allows someone in the apse, beneath the cornice, to hear whispering in the main doorway, and so the priest could discreetly listen to comments on his sermon as the parishioners departed. Also on Via del Duomo is the **Biblioteca Lucchesiana,** founded in 1765 by the Bishop of Agrigento as a public library, now containing 40 000 volumes.

The finest church in Agrigento, however, lies towards the east side of the old town, at the top of dead-end Via Fodera, not far from the round *fascisti* Post Office. Known as La Badia Grande, the Cistercian convent and **Church of Santo Spirito** was founded by Marchisia Chiaramonte in 1290. The windows of the convent belong to that lovely style in Sicily known by the Chiaramontc name. The church preserves a beautiful doorway (on the west) and a white interior with stuccoes by Serpotta and a Madonna by the school of Domenico Gagini.

At the **Rupe Atenea** (Via San Vito on the east side of town), the old acropolis of Akragas, were temples of Zeus and Athena and the oldest part of the Greek colony. Some ruins of ancient structures remain, as well as the hypogeum.

The Valley of the Temples
The **Archaeological Zone** below Agrigento (Via F. Crispi) is always open, with the exception of the Temple of Zeus and the Temple of the Dioscuri (open 9 to dusk) and the Hellenistic quarter by the church of **San Nicola** (open 10–12 and 2–4 in summer; 9–2.30 in winter; closed Mondays). Every night the temples are illuminated from 9.30–10.30.

Archaeology Museum
Spread across 2 miles in the valley, the temples take a good part of the day to explore, and you may consider stopping first at the **National Archaeology Museum,** near the 15th-century cloisters of San Nicola—the first stop of the bus to the temples (open 9–3; Sunday and festivals 9–12; closed Mondays). This fabulous collection of vases, statues, coins, etc. found on the site, makes a fine introduction to the splendour of ancient Akragas and its unique temples. Particularly good are the Greek vases and the heads and one body of the giant telemons of the Temple of Zeus. By these a display of models offers various conceptions of what this monstrous temple—the Radio City Music Hall of its day—used to look like. Among the sculptures, there is a Praxitelian torso and the Phaedra sarcophagus of the 2nd century AD, moved here from the damaged cathedral. A small **Greek Theatre** was discovered next to the museum during its construction, and near the so-called **Oratory of Phalaris,** actually a shrine dedicated to an unknown woman of the 2nd century BC, converted to a chapel in the Middle Ages.

Across the Passegiata Archeologica (the main road to the temples) lies the **Hellenistic Roman Quarter,** where along the grid streets some of the houses have good mosaics with protective coverings, and reconstructed columns of their peristyle courts. From here you can continue south on the Passegiata to the main temples on either side of the Posto di Ristoro (a café-bar) or backtrack a bit to the north turning east (right) for the Strada Panoramica and the Via Demetra; this, along with some ancient wheel ruts, leads up to **San Biagio,** at the edge of the Rupe Atenea shelf.

San Biagio and Gate I

The Normans built the San Biagio chapel over a **Temple of Demeter and Persephone,** begun shortly after the Greek victory at Himera in 480 BC. Of the temple, part of the foundation can be seen by the chapel and two round altars remain to the north; in one of them, a hole called the *bothros* received the wine, etc. offered to the Chthonic (underworld) gods, to whom the cult of Demeter and Persephone was naturally closely attached. Even more interesting in this respect is the **Rock Sanctuary of Demeter,** below San Biagio (steps in the rock). Pre-dating the Temple of Demeter and the Greek colony of Akragas itself by 200 years, the sanctuary is of Sikan origin, although the walls they built demonstrate how Greek influences infiltrated Sicily very early on. The sacred area consists of three natural caves, once filled with votive statues of Demeter and Persephone of various periods, the oldest dating back to the early 8th century BC, when water deities apparently were worshipped (channels and drains for the water can still be seen in the caves). Timoleon added the Nymphaeum to the sanctuary. A short walk south of here, by the wall of the cemetery, is the first of eight city gates, **Gate I,** and the V-shaped **Bastion,** located at a particularly vulnerable point in the defences.

Gate II and Temple of Juno Lacinia

The Strada Panoramica heads south from here, taking you past Gate II (known as the Gela Gate) from where the ancient road to the mother city-state can still be seen. At this important gate, more votive offerings to Demeter and Persephone have been uncovered. The Temple of Juno Lacinia, the easternmost of the great temples, comes clearly into sight as you descend to the south. Its name derives from an 18th-century confusion with another temple, and its original dedication is unknown. Built around 460 BC, the temple still shows signs of when the Carthaginians set fire to it; the Romans later restored it, only to have their good work undone by an earthquake. Only 25 of the original 34 columns remain, windblasted on the southeast by the sirocco. The temple is currently undergoing restoration and cannot be entered.

Gate III and Temple of Concord

Between this temple and the Temple of Concord, Gate III has suffered the borings of Byzantine tombs. These continue throughout the natural rock wall up to the Temple of Concord, which along with the Theseion in Athens is one of the best-preserved Greek temples in the world, owing to its conversion into a church by the 6th-century bishop of Agrigento, San Gregorio delle Rape ('of the turnips'). Dismantled in the 18th century, the church left this Doric structure of the mid 5th century BC almost intact, with its 34 columns, *stylobate, cella,* etc. Originally coated with ground marble stucco and painted in bright colours that have long since worn away, the rough, dull-golden limestone beneath surprises people who expect all temples to look like the Parthenon or their local bank branch.

Temple of Hercules
Still heading west you cross an unusual deeply-cut street known as the **Street of Tombs,** which passes through an early Christian cemetery. The Roman **catacombs** north of here were adapted by the Christians in the 3rd century, and continue all the way to the garden of the Villa Aurea, the old Antiquarium (whose collections have been transferred to the main Archaeological Museum). The columns near here, rising above the Passegiata Archeologica, belong to the oldest temple in the valley, the Temple of Hercules. Built around 500 BC, on an artificial platform, it measures 220 ft by 83 ft—longer than most. The Carthaginians burned it and the Romans repaired it, although the predatory Praetor Verres did his best to make off with a famous statue of Hercules that once graced the temple. For once the outrage of the citizens deterred him. In 1923 eight of the temple's columns were re-erected by Sir Alexander Hardcastle.

Gate IV and the Temple of Aesculapius
The Passegiata leads south to the **Tomb of Theron,** which you can see from the Temple of Hercules. Like almost everything else it is erroneously named, for this two-storey monumental tomb belongs to the 1st century BC. It is located just outside the city walls, where the city's main gate Porta Aurea (Gate IV) once stood, through which a road ran to the port. A large Roman cemetery, partially destroyed by landslides, spreads out over the hill from the gate. South of the Tomb of Theron, on the other side of the SS115, lies the Temple of Aesculapius, built in the 5th century and different from the other temples in that it has solid walls instead of columns. Aesculapius was the god of healing, and this temple, along with all others dedicated to him, is built beside a spring with curative properties. The treatment offered by the priests, however, was more psychological than medicinal and consisted of dream interpretations, restful surroundings, and taking of the waters. The success of this simple cure is attested to by the great popularity of the cult throughout the Greek world.

Temple of Olympian Zeus

The next temple within the walls, across the Passegiata and next to the Posto di Ristoro, is the Temple of Olympian Zeus, the largest Greek temple in the world and one of the most remarkable. Although totally ruined by an earthquake and its stone quarried to build Porto Empedocle, what remains is still very impressive, measuring 369 ft by 184 ft (larger than a football field). The columns, thought to have been 55 ft tall, were made of small stones plastered over to look like whole marble pillars—the flutings in these were wide enough to hold a man. Walls and buttresses filled the spaces between the mock columns and on top of these stood the enormous telemons, or stone giants, supporting the architrave. A copy of one of these Atlas-like figures lies within the temple, to give you an idea of the vast scale the Carthaginian slaves were forced to work on: columns, telemons and architrave combined, the whole thing stood over 100 ft high. Begun in 780, after the victory at Himera, the temple was still unfinished in 705 BC when the Carthaginians invaded the city.

Gate V and the Sanctuary of the Chthonic Deities

West of here, the newly excavated Gate V once had a tall projecting tower, designed as many of these gates were to hamper the shield arms of opponents trying to enter. Here also are four temples dating from the foundation of Akragas, known collectively as the Sanctuary of the Chthonic Deities. The first two temples, begun in the 6th century BC, were never completed and the third, commonly known as the **Temple of Castor and Pollux** or **of the Dioscuri,** was finished at the end of the 5th century. In 1836 four columns and a piece of architrave were pieced together for picturesque effect but without any attempt at historical accuracy: it's a mishmash of items from the numerous ruins of altars and sanctuaries that litter the area, some of which date back to the Sikans (like the Sanctuary of Demeter), and one altar is prehistoric. The **fourth temple,** with its platform and fallen columns, is from the Hellenistic period. Below this sacred area the River Hypsas runs through some extraordinary countryside.

Gates VI–IX

A path from the sanctuary (look for signpost) leads to the **Temple of Vulcano,** beyond the railway. Difficult to reach, it is only recommended for enthusiasts. Two columns remain standing of this temple, thought never to have been completed, and certainly not dedicated to the smithy god. Gates VI–IX are also in this area if you are intent on making the complete circuit of the ancient walls.

Porto Empedocle

Just below Agrigento at Caos (on the road to Porto Empedocle), the **birth-place of Pirandello** has been turned into a museum (open 12.30–2.30), which is well worth a visit if you are a fan of *Six Characters in Search of an Author*. Pirandello's ashes are buried in a rock underneath a pine tree nearby. Connected by frequent buses is Porto Empedocle, Agrigento's port, named after the famous philosopher. On the harbour stands an 18th-century tower partly made from the stone of the Temple of Zeus, as was the mole. Porto Empedocle is one of Italy's main mineral ports and the port for the islands of Lampedusa and Linosa. Unless you have to go there, avoid this town: there isn't a good word to be said for it. The nearest beach to Agrigento is at **San Leone** (bus every half-hour from the station).

SPECIALITIES

Cuscusu (a sweet made of almonds and pistachios by the monks at the monastery of Spirito Santo); *coniglio in agrodolce* (sweet and sour rabbit).

FESTIVALS

These include the famous *Sagra del Mandorlo in Fiore* (Festival of Flowering Almonds) in February, with European folklore and marching bands; the winter concert season at San Nicola; the San Calogero Festival (first Sunday in July), with local folklore and exhibitions; and the Holy Week processions.

GETTING TO AND AROUND AGRIGENTO

Agrigento is connected by rail directly with Trapani, Caltanisetta and Ragusa; connections to the rest of Sicily are patchy—one or two trains a day, with a change to make. The station is on Piazza Marconi, in the exact centre of the city. Most of the buses leave from here as well—to Porto Empedocle (for Lampedusa) and other points in the province, though there are some (for Enna) that stop around the Piazza Vitt. Emanuele, three blocks away. Regular city buses make the circuit of the Valley of the Temples, starting from Piazzale Roma.

TOURIST INFORMATION

The city's AAST information booth is just around the corner from the station on the Piazzale Roma (tel. (0922) 20454). The EPT office is at Via C. Battisti (tel. (0922) 26922).

WHERE TO STAY

The only hotel actually located in the Valley of the Temples is the elegant and serene **Villa Athena******, built around an old villa and garden near the Temple of Concord (tel. (0922) 23803; 60 000 lire single room, 92 000 double). In the town, the **Bella Napoli**** is good and less expensive than the others (Piazza Lena 6; tel. (0922) 20435; 10–22 000 lire single room, 15–32 000 double).

EATING OUT
The **Aurora,** just off the Via Atnea, is one of the better cheap trattorias you'll find (15 000 lire). **Prinzinelli** is a popular, animated pizzeria on the Viale della Vittoria. For atmosphere, a view of the temples, and their own *scaloppine Pirandello,* the **Taverna Mosé** is at San Biagio.

In the interior: Sant' Angelo Muxaro

In the centre of the province, near the small village of Sant' Angelo Muxaro in the Platani Valley, *tholos* (domed tombs) have been excavated which seem to link the site to **Camicos,** the ancient capital of the legendary King Cocalos who lived around 2000 BC. Long famous in Greece before Sicily was even colonised, King Cocalos supposedly built Camicos for Daedalus, said to have made many wonderful things here. None of these things remain, although some of the ceramics and gold found in the tomb bear a remarkable resemblance to items in the eastern Mediterranean, suggesting a link between Greece and Sicily a few centuries before the first colonies. The rock-carved tombs in the walls around the modern town also show eastern influences, the lower ones dating back to the 10th century BC. The largest of these is known as the **Tomba del Principe,** or 'tomb of the Prince' (enquire in Sant' Angelo for directions). It is well worth the effort to see this; it is the finest such tomb in Sicily.

In **Aragona,** south of here, you can find a guide to visit the **Macalube**— funny little volcanoes only a few feet high, bubbling with mud. Nearby **Raffadali** has a Roman sarcophagus in the church, in an ancient necropolis on Busone Hill. Two villages in the north of the province, **Bivona** and **Santo Stefano Quisana,** have notable churches. **Cammarata** to the east is an increasingly popular mountain resort, although it has only one hotel. **Racalmuto** (from the Arabic *Rahal-maut*) was the birthplace of Pietro d'Asaro (1597–1647), whose works may be seen in some of the churches. Nondescript **Canicatti** to the east is an important wine centre, though nowadays the whole area is coated with plastic during the winter, as if all the farmers had been inspired by Chrysto.

Licata

The next town to the east along the coast, **Palma di Montechiaro,** with its fine mother church, was founded in 1637 by an ancestor of Giuseppe di Lampedusa, who inherited it. There is a beach at the Marina di Palma below.

Located at the mouth of the River Salso (known as the Himera in ancient times) Licata developed on the site of ancient Phintias, a colony of Agrigento named after its founder, who transferred the inhabitants of Gela here when that city was destroyed. Excavations have recently begun, the finds of which are in Agrigento's museum and in the **Palazzo del Municipio.** Besides the ancient reliefs, this building, designed in 1935 by Ernesto Basile, contains a small art gallery and a statue of the Madonna by Domenico Gagini (1470). The **Palazzo Canarelli** on the Corso is embellished with monstrous heads, while the **Cathedral** at the end of the street has a highly decorated chapel. Of the squares, **Piazza Sant' Angelo** is the finest, surrounded by baroque buildings. A wide sandy beach at **Mollarella Bay** attracts its share of sun- and fun-seekers in the summer. Along the coast from here to Agrigento you can see the ruins of medieval defences.

North of Licata on the bank of the River Salso are the ruins of a proto-historical settlement on **Monte Saraceno,** later Hellenised by Gela and Agrigento. Little of the town has been excavated; you can see the acropolis on top, vestiges of a temple and the town plan on the hillside. To visit the site, go to Ravanusa and ask for precise directions.

Gela

HISTORY
Gela, on the coast to the east, was once the most powerful city in Sicily, founded by colonists from Crete and Rhodes in 680 BC. Under the Rhodians the city prospered, producing mainly wine, oil and grain. By the 6th century BC the southern coast of Sicily belonged to Gela, and the Geloans founded Akragas in 582 BC (modern Agrigento). The city specialised in terracotta votive figurines, some of them prefabricated.

In 498 BC the grasping tyrant Hippocrates seized control of Gela, and he and his mercenaries proceeded to conquer half of Sicily, including Leontinoi and Naxos. Jealous of their harbour, Hippocrates defeated the Syracuseans but later returned their city to them in exchange for the colony of

Camarina. At this point Gela was the strongest city on the island. However, Hippocrates attempted to force the native Sikels into Greek ways; he started the one and only national uprising among the Sikels (led by Ducetius) and died in a Sikel battle. He was succeeded by his cavalry commander, Gelon. With his father-in-law, the tyrant of Akragas, Gelon defeated the Carthaginians at Himera in 480 BC. Subsequent political turmoil in Syracuse provided Gelon with a chance to muscle in, and he took control, moving half of Gela's population to Syracuse because of its fine harbour. A few years later, though, the Geloans were allowed to go home, and the city prospered once more, on terracotta and literature—Aeschylus wrote his *Oresteia* trilogy here, and died in Gela in 456 (when an eagle dropped a turtle on his head!). Another poet, the comic Apollodoros, was born and raised in Gela.

In 405 BC the Carthaginians destroyed Gela; when the inhabitants returned, their fine city was no more. Timoleon, the good tyrant of Syracuse, had Gela laid out anew in 338 and sent colonists to repopulate it. However, by the ascendancy of Agathocles, Gela had allied itself with Carthage, and Agathocles conquered the city, putting 7000 Geloans to death. The town was again destroyed by the Mamertines in 282, after which Phintias of Akragas removed the Geloans to what is now Licata. The site was repopulated in 1233 and known as 'Terranova' until 1928, when the city was renamed Gela.

During World War II Gela was the site of the American landings on 11 July 1943, and was the first town in Europe to be liberated.

WHAT TO SEE

Gela today (bus from Caltanissetta, Syracuse or Agrigento) is prosperous once more, with its large oil refinery; its long sandy beach (with a splendid view of the refinery) also attracts many tourists, mostly Italian, in the summer. However, between the Carthaginians, the Mamertines and the shifting sand dunes of the coast, little remains to tell of Gela's ancient glory. The town itself is not much to look at although the people are friendlier than most Sicilians.

The best treasures of ancient Gela are housed in the new **Archaeology Museum** at the eastern end of the long main street, Corso Vittorio Emanuele (open 9–1 and 4–5 in summer; 9.30–2 in winter). The museum contains some excellent examples of Gela's terracottas, coins and vases, and two magnificent horse heads. Next to the museum is the Mulino Vento Acropolis, mainly with Hellenistic houses from Timoleon's re-colonisation. One Doric column in a garden setting is all that remains of a temple of Athena.

Capo Soprano

At the other end of the town (Corso Vittorio Emanuele to Via A. Manzoni and Via Indipendenza) are the Capo Soprano fortifications (open daily, 9 am to dusk). These 5th-century BC Greek walls are the best preserved in the world, having been covered by 70-ft sand dunes until they were excavated in 1958 (in some places the walls are still 26 ft high). The fortifications have been covered in part by a plastic shield to protect them from the sea winds, especially the upper parts of the walls which are made of brick rather than stone.

Very near Capo Soprano, next to the hospital on Via Europa, are the sheltered **Greek public baths** (always open). Dating from Timoleon's time, they are the only ones found in Sicily and the only hot baths to have seats.

TOURIST INFORMATION
AAST: Via Palazzi 66 (tel. (0933) 932026).

EATING OUT
Da Giovannini, also known as 'The World Famous' (Via Cairola): Giovanni is an old sea salt who's been to many a port, and his jovial chatter adds as much to your enjoyment as his sauce does to the fish; his inexpensive restaurant is a sort of landmark in nondescript Gela and should not be missed.

Gela Riviera

The sandy beaches of the 'Gela Riviera' stretch all along the bay, and you have the choice of bathing with the crowd or on your own. West along the coast is the **Falconara Sicula** with its isolated 15th-century castle housing a fine ceramic collection. On either side of it are huge sandy beaches.

On a low hill by the road north to Caltanissetta stand the lonely ruins of the **Castelluccio**—very picturesque. This castle was built by Frederick II. North of here, by Lake Disveri, is a Pantalica-like oven-tomb necropolis of the late Bronze Age.

Butera

Inland Butera is the prettiest town in the undistinguished province of Caltanissetta, built on a hill which is dominated by an 11th-century castle. In the **Chiesa Madre** you can see a Renaissance triptych and a painting of the Madonna by Filippo Paladino. In the Middle Ages the princes of Butera, the Barresi, held sway over most of the region. They founded nearby **Mazzarino,** where their palace still exists. Another Barresi palace may be seen at Pietraperzia in Enna Province. Southeast of here is a site known as **Sofiana** or Castellazza where some 1st-century thermal baths have been discovered; they remained in use until the 4th century. A small basilica and necropolis have also been excavated, their contents now housed at Gela.

Central Sicily: Caltanissetta

HISTORY

Thought to be located on the site of ancient Nissa, whence its name 'Kalat' (Arabic for castle) Nissa is derived, Caltanissetta was captured by Count Roger in 1086 and presented to his son. In the 15th century it fell into the hands of the Moncada family. The city suffered various bombardments in World War II.

WHAT TO SEE

In Caltanissetta today the main source of income is the sulphur and potassium salt mines, which have made it modern and prosperous, but not very interesting for tourists. The old part of the town, however, has a few memories of its medieval and baroque heritage. Of these, the most striking is the **Castello di Pietrarossa,** who ruins are perched high on a crag. During the war between the Chiaramonte and Ventimiglia families, Frederick II found shelter here, and the castle became a favourite residence for his son, Frederick III. The 16th-century **Cathedral**, in the central Piazza del Duomo, was unfortunately hit in the war, the bombs damaging the masterpiece ceiling of the Flemish artist Borremans, painted in 1720. A prettier church is **Santa Maria degli Angeli,** built in the 14th century, with fine reliefs on the main door. The **Civic Museum,** on Via Napoleone Colajanni (open 9–1.30; Saturdays 9–12; closed Sundays and holidays), contains finds from the province, mainly from Sabucina; the early Bronze Age figures are the oldest found in Sicily.

Just east of the town, by the new museum, is the **Badia di Santo Spirito,** the basilica founded by King Roger and Queen Adelaide, and consecrated in 1153, which contains some good 15th-century frescoes.

FESTIVALS

Carnival (February). Spectacular Maundy Thursday procession of the *Misteri,* with musical bands from all over the province. Good Friday: procession of the Lords of the City. St Michael's Fair (September).

Caltanissetta Province is the least visited in Sicily. However, some of the hill towns are quite charming and certainly untainted by tourism, and there are a few minor archaeological sites scattered throughout the area. One of these is **Mount Sabucina,** 5 miles northeast of Caltanissetta, by the Salso river. Inhabited originally by Sikels in the first millennium BC, the site was later Hellenised and fortified. Excavations have uncovered the 6th-century BC town, huts and tombs from the Bronze Age and a small Sikel temple outside the town wall. To visit the digs, ask at the Museo Civico, Caltanissetta.

Near San Cataldo, **Vassallaggi** is another archaeological site, spread over five hills. This was a Greek settlement in the 5th century BC, under the wing of Agrigento; you can still see the sanctuary, the fortifications, part of the town, and a rich necropolis of fine painted vases and urns, now in the museums of Gela and Agrigento. At **Mussomeli,** northwest of San Cataldo, stands the castle of the same name high on a crag (Rocca di Mussomeli) which belonged to the Chiaramonte family. (The nearest railway station to Mussomeli is at Acquaviva, north of Agrigento.)

Enna

HISTORY

Ancient Sikan 'Henna', in one of the most strategic positions in Sicily—high in the Monti Erei, almost in the dead centre of the island—was also the centre of the cult of Demeter and her daughter Persephone, whom Pluto abducted into the underworld. According to Diodorus Siculus, the Sikans made a peace treaty with those other early Sicilians, the Sikels, after a brief conflict. This, if true, would make it one of the earliest peace treaties in the world (8th–7th century BC).

Enna was gradually Hellenised by Greek colonists who lived in peace with the natives (the Via dei Greci still runs through the ancient Greek quarter) and Gelon built a temple of Demeter here in 480 BC. The Romans called Enna 'Castrum Hennae' and their government of the town could hardly be termed happy. In 214 BC the Consul Pinarius had the leading citizens massacred, fearing they would side with Carthage, and later, in 135 BC, a slave from Enna named Euno led the First Slave War, giving the Romans no end of trouble until they recaptured the city two years later. In 859 the Saracens took Enna from the Byzantines, who had made it their headquarters, by climbing through the sewer—so impregnable was Enna's position. Under the Saracens, the town's name was corrupted to 'Kasr

Janna'. Count Roger manipulated his way into Enna in 1087 and called it 'Castrogiovanni', but in 1927 Mussolini returned its Classical name and made it a provincial capital.

WHAT TO SEE

At 3100 ft above sea level, Enna is the highest provincial capital in Italy. Favoured by both Frederick II of Hohenstaufen and Frederick II of Aragon for its unique position, Enna not only has marvellous panoramas in all directions, but some fine medieval and Aragonese towers and churches. If your itinerary allows time for only one town in the interior of Sicily, Enna would be the obvious choice, especially as Piazza Armerina, with the Villa Imperiale and its fabulous mosaics, is only a short distance away.

Via Roma, the main street of Enna, takes a sharp turn in the heart of town at Piazza Matteoti, and is strung with lovely piazze, like pearls on a necklace. In the first of these to the east, Piazza Vittorio Emanuele, is the **Church of San Francesco** which has a fine tower. In the adjacent **Piazza Crispi,** with its extraordinary belvedere, is a copy of Berninin's *Rape of Persephone.* Continuing east along the Via Roma, the **Piazza Umberto** stands out like a sore thumb with its *fascisti* public buildings. The next square, Piazza Coppola, is named for the Arabic cupola on the elegant tower of **San Giovanni.** Just around the corner the city has opened its new **Archaeological Museum** in an old palace. None of the finds is of special interest, but if you read Italian it will provide a good background to the regions ancient history.

The cathedral

Still heading east on the Via Roma you come without warning upon the cathedral. Founded in 1307 by Eleonora, wife of Frederick II of Aragon, it caught fire in 1446 and was restored the following century, which may account for its idiosyncratic facade and the few remaining Gothic elements on the south side, including the walled-in Holy Portal. Inside, the iron gate of the baptistry once guarded the Saracen harem. The two stout columns near the entrance, carved with puzzling allegorical monsters, are the work of one of the Gagini—a peculiar work to have come out of that normally tradition-bound clan of Sicilian masters. Another Gagini work, the font, rests on a pedestal of ancient origin, perhaps from the Temple of Demeter. Filippo Paladino painted the scenes in the choir and the nave ceiling in the 16th century, and Giovanni Gallina—a local artist—sculpted the marble pulpit.

Across the street from the cathedral, spread about the rooms of a house, is the **Museo Alessi.** It contains a good collection of coins and a few antiquities from Enna Province, along with some neglected paintings, but the extremely rich cathedral treasury, formerly housed here, has been removed and is in the custody of the priest.

Emperor Frederick's Castle

The eastern end of Via Roma opens out on the Castello di Lombardia (open 8.30–1 and 3–5 pm), constructed by the Swabians under Frederick II, and used as a residence by Frederick III of Aragon who proclaimed himself 'King of Trinacria' here and summoned the Sicilian parliament in 1324. 'Lombardia', an unusual name in Sicily, is thought to derive from the Lombard troops that Frederick quartered here to keep them out of trouble. Six towers remain of the original twenty, the tallest of which—the **Torre Pisano**—can be climbed for its commanding view of the surrounding countryside. Below, in the courtyard, where excavations are in progress, is an underground chapel with odd incisions on the wall resembling upside-down tridents, dating from ancient times and of unknown origin. Legend has it that King Sikanus and the goddess Demeter are buried together under the castle.

On the promontory east of the castle is the **Rocca di Cerere** (or **di Demeter**) where a temple once stood—perhaps the one built by Gelon. Only a few traces of it remain today.

Taking the Via Roma south of the Piazza Matteoti, you can visit the lower town, passing the church of **San Tommaso,** with a distinguished altar, and the **Carmine.** Both have 15th-century campaniles (the good people of Enna like their church bells and ring them often). Further down, on a knoll in the public garden, is the Swabian **Torre di Federico II** (entrance on Viale IV Novembre, open daily until dusk). Scholars believe that 'Stupor Mundi' built this 'tower of the winds' to mark the crossroads of ancient Sicily's three main thoroughfares, symbolised in the three legs of the Trinacria symbol. Considered to be in the absolute centre of the island, the tower (as well as the rest of Enna) acquired the name *Umbilicus Sicilae* ('Sicily's navel') and served to divide the island into three districts: the Val Demone, the Val di Noto, and the Val di Mazara—a partition borrowed by the Arabs during their domination. The tower itself is octagonal with three floors. It is rumoured that at the bottom there is an underground passage to the Castello di Lombardia. A spiral stairway leads you up inside the 10-foot-thick walls to the top unfinished floor. From here, on the clearest of days, the three corners of Sicily are visible.

The *Templum Caelesti*

Frederick's tower was not the first on this site, and it is an open question whether the subtle emperor was aware of the true significance of this spot. Thirty years ago a Sicilian historian, Umberto Massocco, propounded a theory that this was the centre of a giant geomantic construction, created perhaps by the Sikans, that covered the whole of Sicily. Like the *leys* in Britain (which Massocco appears not to have known about), there seems to be a network of alignments of holy places and landmarks, meeting at right-angles and running the length of the island. Massocco, with the aid of aerial photography and the writings of Diodorus Siculus, discovered that many of the oldest sites on the island—Mount Erice, Segesta, Selinunte, Ortygia Island and Eraclea Minoa among them—fall along these alignments. He calls the work the *Templum Caelesti*, an attempt to make the whole of Sicily into one great geometrical temple. In Enna, he notes that the two central alignments that cross at Frederick's tower pass through the churches of San Marco (Piazza VI Dicembre) and San Bartolomeo (Piazza San Bartolomeo) and that these three sites form a neat Pythagorean triangle of sides pro-portionately 3, 4, and 5.

FESTIVALS
Estate Ennese, operettas in the Castello di Lombardia (July–August). Fasci-nating Holy Week celebrations in Spanish costumes of the medieval frater-nities.

Enna Province, the only province in Sicily without a coast, compensates for this lack with its six large natural and man-made lakes and beautiful mountain scenery. Its inland position has also made it less vulnerable to out-side influences and change, and almost all the towns retain a medieval aspect, especially Calascibetta and Nicosia. Piazza Armerina is the second city of the province, famous for the mosaics at the Roman villa and thus on the itinerary of many package tours. The town itself should not be neglected however; it wears its Norman and Aragonese traditions proudly, and in the middle of August hosts one of the major festivals in Sicily, the Norman Joust.

South of the capital Enna, the town of **Pergusa** borders on the famous lake of the same name. But don't expect any Classical epiphanies here, where Pluto abducted the goddess of spring, Persephone, from her flowery fields. The lake is now encircled by a motor speedway, and motorboats and waterskiers skim the surface of the lake instead of demons patrolling its sullen depths. In May the 'Sagra del Lago' takes place here, with local folk-lore and fireworks; April to September are the months for auto racing.

The attractive hill town across the valley from Enna is **Calascibetta** (go by bus or train from Enna), its Arabic origins apparent in its old reddish buildings as well as in its name. It is a quiet, brooding place. The nearby **Necropolis of Realmesi,** its 'oven tombs' hollowed out of the rock, dates back to the 9th century BC. On the edge of **Leonforte,** northeast of Calascibetta, the lavish great fountain (La Gran Fonte), constructed in 1651, has 24 spouts along its unusual length. Leonforte was founded by Prince Nicolò Branciforte in the 17th century. His family's funeral chapel is in the **Capuchin Church** on Piazza Margherita; also in the chapel is *The Election of St Matthew* by the fine Sicilian artist Pietro Novelli.

Nearby **Assoro** is worth a visit for its 14th-century **Church of San Leone.** Outside note the late Gothic portal; inside are a fine wooden ceiling and floral reliefs decorating the pillars. Further north, in the mountains, beautiful **Nicosia** is as fine a medieval backwater as one could hope to find. As a free city, Nicosia prospered under the Arabs and then the Normans who settled the town with Lombard and Piedmontese colonists; the local argot is said to contain their northern influence. Upon a crag above the town stand the ruins of the **Norman castle.** In the **Church of Santa Maria Maggiore** (Via Francesco Salomone) is an early 15th-century marble polyptych of the Virgin's life, by Antonello Gagini, as well as the throne used by Emperor Charles V when he visited Nicosia in 1535. The **Cathedral of San Nicola** has a lovely 14th-century doorway and a campanile in a mixture of styles. The ceiling dates back to the early 13th century. Among the works of art inside are paintings by Velazquez, Pietro Novelli and Salvatore Rosa, sculptures by the Gagini, and a crucifix carved by Fra Umile da Petralia.

West of Nicosia rise the picturesque ruins of the **Castle of Sperlinga,**

Castello di Gresti, Valguarera, Enna

the only safe refuge the French found in the War of the Vespers. From Nicosia to **Troina** the road is very scenic. Troina itself qualifies as one of the highest towns in Sicily, 3380 ft above sea level. Captured by Roger I in 1062 from the Arabs, Troina retains many Norman souvenirs, including the **Church of San Basilio,** founded by Roger himself in 1082, making it the first Norman diocese in Sicily. The **Chiesa Madre's** tower is also Norman, and its treasury contains a famous 13th-century silver pastoral staff. Inhabited since the Sikel period, Troina still has a few parts of its **Greek walls.**

Agira, ancient Sikel 'Agyrion', is another picture-postcard hill town, south of Troina. In 339 BC Timoleon of Syracuse colonised and Hellenised Agyrion, the birthplace of Diodoros Siculus, the 1st-century historian who was the first to attempt a history of the world. In later days San Filippo Sirriaco (or of Agira) performed many miracles here—actually thought to be the deeds of ancient Agyrion's patron god Hercules in Christian clothing. The **Church of San Salvatore** contains a good treasury.

Regalbuto and Centuripe

Regalbuto to the east is only a few miles from the large artificial Lake Pozzillo, a favourite of anglers. In 1261 the inhabitants of Centuripe decimated Regalbuto, which had been populated largely by the hated Swabians. The present town was rebuilt by Manfred. To the east the old enemy **Centuripe** is magnificently situated in front of Mt Etna and the sea; Garibaldi nicknamed it the 'balcone della Sicilia'. Known in ancient times as 'Kentoripa', Centuripe was the site of an important Sikel town. The 1st-century physician Celsus was born here. Despite this antiquity, the present town dates back to 1545, as both Frederick II and Charles of Anjou razed Centuripe for its defiance of their authority. During World War II the Nazis made the town a key base, and its fall to the 38th Irish Brigade forced the Germans to abandon Sicily. Centuripe has a small but extremely interesting **Museo Civico** (open 9–1; closed Mondays) housing the distinctive locally-produced polychromatic pottery and ceramics renowned in Hellenistic times. On the outskirts of town a road leads to the so-called **Mausoleo Romano,** a 2nd-century ruin, perhaps of a tower.

Piazza Armerina

South of Enna (frequent bus) is Piazza Armerina, known in Sicily simply as

'Piazza'. Its excellent hill site was inhabited in antiquity, but only became more than passingly important in the Middle Ages. In 1161 King William 'the Bad' destroyed the old town in retaliation for a massacre of Saracens by its citizens, but three years later the Normans rebuilt what they had demolished and the new town prospered. In 1240 Frederick II elevated Piazza to one of the eleven imperial towns in the parliament of Foggia. Throughout the medieval and Spanish periods the town retained its importance, and it was often the centre of factional rivalries and feudal plots against the overlords of the day.

The rectangular **Piazza Garibaldi** is the heart of the old town, with the Municipio, the **Church Fundrò** (1613), various palazzi, and the ever helpful AAST information office (where you can get excellent detailed information about the Roman villa). Turn west up Via Vittorio Emanuele for the baroque **Church of Sant' Anna** and the 14th-century **Aragonese Castle** where King Martin I of Aragon once resided. At the summit of the city, in the Piazza del Duomo, is the **Cathedral,** built in 1627 with funds donated by Baron Marco Trigona, whose portly statue and palazzo also adorn the square. The Catalan campanile is a hundred years older than the cathedral, while the facade is some hundred years later. Inside is the Byzantine icon of the Madonna given to Count Roger by Pope Nicolas II, and a medieval crucifix painting on wood by an unknown artist. The treasury contains a statue of Roger among the more typical church vestments and reliquaries.

Of the many other churches in this elegant town, the best are the 13th-century **San Giovanni dei Rodi** (the chapel of the Knights of Rhodes before they moved to Malta), also called the Commendo; the **Collegium of St Ignatius;** and, north of the town, the **Church of Sant' Andrea,** built in 1096 by the Normans and containing some intriguing early Sicilian frescoes.

FESTIVALS
The major medieval fete in Sicily, *Il Palio dei Normanni* (the Norman Joust) takes place every year on 13–14 August. The ceremonies, in which hundreds participate in medieval costume, re-enact Count Roger's taking of Piazza Armerina and the tournament presented before him between four teams representing the four quarters of the town. The winning team in the various competitions receives a standard from 'Roger' which they keep in their parish church for the year. The locals take their pageant very seriously, and the competition between the teams is fierce. Another festival, known as 'The Third of May', takes place at the Sanctuario di Santa Maria delle Vittorie.

To reach the excavations of the **Roman villa** (open daily from 9 until sunset), generally called the Casale, 4 miles southwest of Piazza, you must either walk or take a taxi from the Piazza Gen. Cascino, as there is no bus. Unless there are many in your party, the taxi isn't much of a bargain, but the walk is very pleasant if it is not too hot. But whatever the means, the journey rewards the visitor with the magnificent, uniquely well-preserved mosaics. This is the best Roman site in Sicily and one of the most interesting in all Italy.

Scholars generally hold that the villa was built as a summer retreat near the end of the 3rd century AD for a member of the Imperial family, perhaps even for the Emperor Maximilian, Diocletian's co-emperor, who ruled from 286 to 305. Later, the Arabs made some use of it, as well as the Normans, until William the Bad ordered its destruction for its pagan artwork. A landslide covered it and only since 1950 have serious excavations revealed the treasures that were buried.

There are some 40 mosaic floors in all, now covered with a clear protective roof supposedly following the ancient design. After passing the aqueduct that supplied the villa, one comes to the monumental entrance and the **baths** where the mosaics represent various stages of the elaborate Roman bath ritual and some mythical sea creatures. The remains of the plumbing

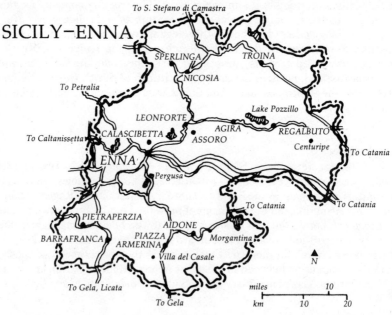

SICILY–ENNA

212

are visible in the **tepidarium** (warming room), where the floor was built on brick pillars, allowing heat to rise into the room through vents (the **hypocaust**). The central latrines are also nearby. The vestibule contains damaged mosaics of guests being welcomed into the house, and leads into the large rectangular court (the **peristyle**), with mosaic animal heads along the side floors and a fountain in the centre. Following the walkway to the left, the **Hall of the Circus** (*palaestra*) is named for its mosaics depicting a chariot race at the Circus Maximus in Rome, the four contestants bearing the colours of the four teams of Rome—red, green, blue and white.

Passing a series of bedchambers with intricate geometric designs you reach the **Room of the Small Hunt,** with realistic scenes of a local hunting expedition and the hunters' subsequent picnic. Whimsical mosaics of the **Fishing Cupids,** a very popular theme of the age, follow this, as well as the main hall, the 200-ft-long **Hall of the Great Hunt,** whose mosaic masterpiece depicts the hunt and capture of wild animals for use in Roman games. Remarkable for their lively and realistic details, the various scenes seem to move before your very eyes. At either end are allegorical figures of Africa and the Middle East. An adjacent room contains the bland but very famous **Bikini Girls** desporting on some Roman lido, and the next room has a mosaic floor that shows Orpheus enchanting the savage beasts.

The walkway leads out to the **Elliptical Courtyard** where the mosaics portray industrious *putti* harvesting grapes, pressing wine and fishing. Entering the villa once more, the walkway ascends into the **Banquet Hall** (*triclinium*) with powerful mosaics of the Labours of Hercules. The five giants, struck by Hercules' arrows and writhing in pain, are particularly impressive, reminiscent of Michelangelo. Another remarkable room follows, showing the Cyclops and Odysseus; the wily Greeks are offering Polythemus wine, hoping to intoxicate him and thus make their escape. Next is the so-called **Chamber of the Erotic Scene,** followed by the private apartments that compose the rest of the villa, including two charming nursery mosaics, one showing the **Children's Hunt** with youngsters chasing rabbits and ducks, the other showing the **Small Circus** with children racing carts pulled by birds in imitation of their elders. There is also a room with mosaics of Greek instruments and musical notation, and another representing the myth of Arion the musician.

Other important excavations northwest of Piazza Armerina are of **Morgantina,** a few miles from old Lombardian **Aidone.** Excavated by Princeton, this Greco-Sikel town of the 6th century BC rebelled against the Romans in the 3rd century and was given to their Spanish mercenaries. Located at the Serra d'Orlando, the excavations (signposted; open 9 until dusk, Sundays and holidays 9–2) include the large *agora* and trapezoidal stairway, a theatre, a gymnasium and Hellenistic houses, many with mosaics. Finds from Morgantina are housed in the Capuchin convent in Aidone.

GETTING TO AND AROUND ENNA

Enna's station lies along the Palermo–Catania railway line. When you arrive you may look at the surrounding fields and orchards in disbelief—no trace of a city can be seen. It's up above the clouds, and a bus timed to meet the train will soon arrive to take you up (this bus also connects Enna with Calascibetta). Rail connections along the main line are easy; travelling to or from Agrigento and the south will probably mean an exasperating stop at a junction called Caltanisetta-Xirbi, the black hole of Sicilian railways. Enna's new bus station, with connections for Piazza Armerina, villages in the province and the rest of Sicily, is in the newer part of the city, in the Viale Diaz.

TOURIST INFORMATION

In Enna the EPT is hard to miss, the three giant letters pointing the way to Piazza Garibaldi (tel. (0935) 1184), and the city AAST is nearby on the Piazza Cologianni (tel. (0935) 26119; very good maps of the entire island are available here). In Caltanisetta there's an EPT office in Corso V. Emanuele 109 (tel. (0934) 21731). In Piazza Armerina, the AAST is on the Piazza Garibaldi (tel. (0935) 81201).

WHERE TO STAY

The **Hotel Belvedere*****, facing the pretty Piazza F. Crispi on one side and half of Sicily on the other, truly lives up to its name. Its friendly staff and gracefully mouldering art deco furnishings will win a place in your heart; make sure you get a room with a balcony (tel. (0935) 21020; single room 21–26 000 lire, 32–42 000 double; open all year). A cheaper, unlisted place in town is the cosy little **Albergho Enna** on Via S. Agata (single room 8000 lire, double 12 000 lire). There are several hotels around Lake Pergusa and in Piazza Armerina; in the latter the fairly new **Park Hotel Paradiso***** is adequate (tel. (0934) 85700); single room with bath 26 000 lire, double 42 000).

EATING OUT

An old favourite (Mussolini dined here) is the **Centrale,** at 6 Via VI Dicembre, off Via Roma (30–35 000 lire). Less expensive is the good, lively pizzeria–trattoria that recently opened on the Viale Marconi, just off the Piazza Crispi, called Da-somebody-or-other (good pizzas for around 8000 lire). Least expensive of all (and with good *scaloppine*) is the **Grotta Azzurra,** a hole in the wall off the Piazza Matteotti. In Piazza Armerina, **Da Toto,** on Via Mazzini 29, is a good bet for 15 000 lire.

Part IV

ISLANDS OFF THE COAST OF SICILY

Il Faraglione, Lipari, Aeolian Islands

The Aeolian Islands

The Aeolian Islands, also known as the Lipari Islands, are the seven sisters of Lipari, Vulcano, Salina, Panarea, Filicudi, Alicudi and Stromboli. Along with numerous smaller islets, they form one of the most unusual little archipelagos in the world. All are volcanic—Vulcano and Stromboli actively so. They are also the islands of the wind, and the sea surrounding them is the most violent in the Tyrrhenian if not the entire Mediterranean. The islands' beauty is almost other-worldly. Volanic eruptions and wind erosion have left their coasts sharp and menacing, in strange formations and colours, and within a mile of the soft, rolling green hills there are inhuman regions of unmitigated white (the pumice slopes of Lipari) or black (the *Sciara del Fuoco* of Stromboli's volcano). On calm days each island has its own little cloud over its highest peak, like a genie or the ghost of some ancient volcanic eruption.

Homer first mentioned the Aeolian Islands in *The Odyssey*; Odysseus

215

landed here after passing through the Strait of Messina. Aeolus, the king of the islands and god of the wind, welcomed him and gave him a gift to speed his voyage home to Ithaca—a bag of wind. Overcome with curiosity, the Greek sailors opened the bag as soon as they left port, and the wind rushed out, pushing them right back to the island. Seeing his great gift so squandered, the king berated them and sent them on their way.

HISTORY

According to legend, the first people to settle the islands were from Asia Minor, having fled westwards at around the same time as the Elymnians of Segesta, at the time of the Trojan War. Diodorus Siculus, the ancient historian from Sicily, recounts the following tale, Liparo, son of King Auson of southern Italy, left home to found a colony on the islands, which he named after himself. One of his companions was Eolo, or Aeolus, who married a girl on one of the islands (Lipari or Stromboli) and stayed there as king when Liparo returned to Ausonia. It was he who entertained Odysseus and whose sons colonised parts of Calabria and Sicily.

Prehistory

A castle on Lipari has proved to be an archaeological goldmine, with each successive culture neatly layered one on top of the other, and so we know much more about the early inhabitants of the Aeolian Islands than did Diodoros. Lipari was first inhabited in 3000 BC by a people from the Near East, who also settled the east coast of Sicily: their first pottery bears the same Stentinello decorations of simple incisions or impressions.

Then, it appears, the islanders discovered obsidian, and began to mine and export it on a large scale. Obsidian, hard volcanic glass, was highly prized in the Neolithic Age as being superior to flint for making tools. Obsidian from Lipari found a wide market; examples have been discovered in France, Spain and Malta. The contact with different peoples introduced different styles of ceramic decorations—the *Capri* style, the *Serra d'Alto* style, and a rather charming style thought to have been developed locally, the *Diana* style, named for the fertile Diana plain around the castle, the first part of the island to be cultivated.

Around 2350 BC, this flourishing obsidian-exporting civilisation suddenly vanished, for reasons unknown, and was succeeded by what is known as the Aeolian Medieval Period, towards the end of the Neolithic and beginning of the Copper Age. The pottery found on Lipari, at Punta Conte, is primitive compared to the Diana style.

However, what importance the islands lost through the decline of the obsidian trade, they eventually made up as ports on the east–west trading route between the Aegean and the Tyrrhenian Seas. This, too, shows up in their

216

ceramic ware, similar to styles found in the eastern and northern Aegean. Settlements were found on the islands of Salina, Filicudi and Panarea, and later at Ginostra on Stromboli. They became thriving commercial centres, producing their own ceramic styles (Piano Quartara, Capo Graziano and Milazzese cultures). Particularly interesting is the Milazzese style of Panarea; the motives adorning the vases are distinctly of Cretan origin.

Sometime in the 13th century BC Bronze Age peoples frm Ausonia and Sicily invaded the islands, burned the settlements and killed or enslaved the inhabitants. They were resettled by the Ausonians, themselves an Appennian tribe, initiating the cultures known as Ausonia I and II, producing the typical bull's head vessels of the day. During this period lived Diodoros' Liparos and Aeolus, but their civilisation, like the one they destroyed, didn't last long. In 850 BC it suddenly declined, leaving a wretched population barely surviving at subsistence levels.

The Greeks

In 580 BC a group of Greek colonists from Cnidos and Rhodes attemped to colonise the west coast of Sicily, but were pushed out by the Segestans and Carthaginians. Discouraged and with their leader Pentathlus dead, the would-be colonists made for home, stopping at Lipari on the way. The 500 Liparesi then living on the island received the Greeks well and entreated them to stay—which they did, attracted by the rich volcanic soil of Lipari.

One of the first things the new colonists did was refortify the castle against the constant menace of the Phoenician and Etruscan pirates. It wasn't long before the islanders established their own fleet to fight the pirates on the high seas, and the Liparesi, intimate with the local coasts and conditions, were more than a match for the marauders. Pausanias, the 2nd-century tour-guide writer, relates how Apollo's oracle at Delphi told the Liparesi that if they wanted victory they should fight the pirates with the bare minimum of ships. As usual, this seemingly ill advice saved the day. When the Etruscan pirate captain saw only five Liparian ships defending the island against his squadron, he confidently sent only five of his ships against them. They were all captured. Again the captain sent five ships, with the same result, then another five, and another five—all captured by the Liparesi. In disbelief and awe, the Etruscan captain withdrew the remaining ships of his fleet and escaped from these 'sea devils' while he still could. In thanksgiving, the islanders built a treasury at Delphi and raised a statue of Apollo for every ship they had captured. But the Liparesi were not only thwarters of pirates; they themselves indulged in the occasional spot of piracy to augment their income.

In 427 BC, Lipari—as an ally of Syracuse—was attacked by the Athe-

217

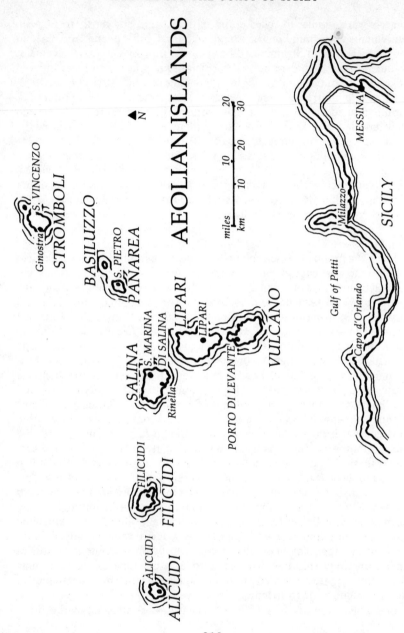

AEOLIAN ISLANDS

N

S. VINCENZO
Ginostra
STROMBOLI

BASILUZZO

S. PIETRO
PANAREA

LIPARI
LIPARI

SALINA
S. MARINA
DI SALINA
Rinella

VULCANO

PORTO DI LEVANTE

FILICUDI
FILICUDI

ALICUDI
ALICUDI

miles
km
10
10
20
20
20
30

SICILY

MESSINA

Milazzo

Gulf of Patti

Capo d'Orlando

218

nians, who wanted to establish a base there during their Great Expedition against Syracuse. They failed utterly, losing some 30 ships and more than 3000 men to the Aeolian defenders. In 396 BC, a ship bearing golden ex-votos to Apollo at Delphi for the Roman victory at Vei, was ambushed and taken in the Strait of Messina by the Liparesi pirates. When the commander at Lipari found out from the Romans what they had been carrying and to whom, he convinced the sailors that the sacred nature of the cargo demanded not only that they return the ship to Rome, but escort it to Delphi themselves. In gratitude the Roman senate made the commander Timasiteos an *ospitum publicum*—an honorary citizen of Rome.

Perhaps the most worthy accomplishment of these brave islanders was their communal system of self-government. All land, ships, houses and other goods were owned by the people and redistributed amid great festivities every 20 years. The inhabitants divided themselves into 'people of the earth', who farmed Lipari and the other Aeolian Islands and parts of the mainland as well; and 'people of the sea'—fishermen, pirates and defenders of Lipari. Whatever loot was captured was shared by all, and annual tributes were sent to Delphi.

The Liparesi remained faithful allies of Syracuse for many years in their battles against Carthage. The islanders were thus caught totally unawares when the cruel tyrant of Syracuse, Agathocles, landed in the guise of a friend, then proceeded to sack the rich temples of Aeoles and Hephestos, filling eleven ships with their gold. In rage at this sacrilege the god of the wind blew the sea into a terrible storm, and all eleven ships sank with their cargoes of stolen gold. Only Agathocles' ship escaped destruction, the tyrant to die a more lingering death from plague.

In the Punic Wars Lipari sided with Carthage, as did most of Sicily. Some of the most important naval engagements of the First Punic War were fought in Aeolian waters, but the Lipari luck finally ran out. In 251 BC the Romans sent 60 ships to take and destroy the island, leaving few survivors. Later there is mention of Romans coming to bathe in the volcanic hot springs.

Henceforth the history of the Aeolian Islands more or less follows that of Sicily. In 1340, however, the island passed into the hands of the King of Naples, Robert I, although the formation of the Kingdom of the Two Sicilies brought Lipari and Sicily together once more. In 1544 the pirate Barbarossa left the islands depopulated and in smoking ruins. Because of their strategic position the Emperor Charles V had them recolonised a few years later. In the 19th century the island-hopping Archduke Luis Salvator de Hapsbourg 'discovered' the Aeolians and wrote a book about them, published in 1896.

In the early 20th century a prison was established in Lipari's castle, much to the anger of the islanders, who stormed and destroyed it in 1926. However, a few years later, when the Fascists began to send political undesirables to the island, they were made welcome, and not only shared the islanders' toil but founded a lending library in the little town.

The Islands today

Until only 20 years ago, accounts of the Aeolian Islands told of extreme destitution, of the inhabitants' struggle for survival on their windswept rocks, scratching out a living in the pumice mines, or fishing or tending the vines. Many have migrated to the mainland and to Australia since then, so that while life is much the same, there is more to go around for the islanders who have remained.

Tourism continues to grow on the islands and forms an ever larger chunk of the local economy. Of all the islands off Sicily's coasts, these are the most popular, and with good reason. Few travelling experiences are as dreamlike as sailing out of Milazzo to the islands, watching them rise like an enchantment before you, green mountains in an indigo sea. The Aeolian islands have an intimacy which larger archipelagos lack, but enough variety, beauty, eccentricity and history to occupy an entire holiday.

GETTING TO AND AROUND THE AEOLIAN ISLANDS

The main port for the islands is Milazzo, and if you're flying into Catania, a Giunta bus in the summer can pick you up at the airport at 2pm and get you to Milazzo in time to take a steamer out to the islands. Giunta bus also provides a year-round service connecting Messina and Milazzo nearly every hour, taking you directly to the port (a far easier manouevre than taking the train, which requires a walk that seems particularly long if you have baggage). Giunta buses depart from the piazza of the Stazione Centrale in Messina; for information contact their office at Via Terranova 8, (tel. (090) 773782) in Messina.

By sea: steamers to the islands are few, and unreliable after October; they depart only from Milazzo. In the summer, however, there are connections from Messina, Naples and Reggio Calabria, mostly by hydrofoil. Siremar runs all the ferry services from Milazzo and Naples as follows:

From Naples to Stromboli, Panarea, Salina, Lipari, Vulcano, and Milazzo; 3 a week; 18 hours.
From Milazzo to Lipari, Panarea, Stromboli; 3 a week; 6 hours.

From Milazzo to Lipari, Filicudi and Alicudi; 4 a week; 6½ hours.
From Milazzo to Lipari and Vulcano; 2 a day; 2 hours.
From Milazzo to Vulcano, Lipari and Salina; daily all year round; 3½ hours.

Although the ferries do take cars, their main purpose is transporting goods to the islands. Only Lipari and Salina are large enough to justify the trouble and expense of bringing a car, but they also have efficient bus services, as does Vulcano on its one stretch of road. Panarea, Stromboli, Filicudi and Alicudi all have virtually no roads to speak of. The main advantage of the ferries is their lower prices and leisurely pace, which allows you to drink in your fill of some very special island scenery. The Naples ferries leave at night, so you 'save' a night in a hotel.

Most people, however, don't like to 'waste' time and want to get to the islands as quickly as possible; they choose the hydrofoils (*aliscafi*) from Messina or Milazzo and go thumpety-thump to their destination at top speed. Beware of the confusing acronyms of the hydrofoil companies— SNAV, SI.RE.MAR—and their equally confusing schedules. Always make sure that you buy the right ticket and get on the right boat. The hydrofoil schedules are as follows:

From Milazzo to Vulcano and Lipari; 3 a day (4 in summer); 1½ hours.
From Lipari to Salina; 2 a day; 40 minutes.
From Lipari to Salina, Panarea and Stromboli; daily; 1 hour 40 minutes.
From Lipari to Salina, Filicudi and Alicudi; daily; 1½ hours.

SNAV Aliscafi runs a daily hydrofoil service in the summer:
From Messina to Lipari, Salina and Stromboli; 5 hours 20 minutes.
From Reggio Calabria to Messina, Lipari and Vulcano; 2 hours.
From Naples to Stromboli, Panarea and Lipari; 5½ hours.

The hydrofoil from Reggio Calabria coincides with ATI flights to the airport there. There are other summer hydrofoil services out of Milazzo (COVEMAR), and a ship out of Patti Marina (also daily from July to September).
Note: Exchange your money before you go. Lipari has the only bank on the islands; Stromboli, Panarea and Vulcano have only summer branches, opening 2 June.

Sub-aqua enthusiasts will find a bottle service on all islands except Alicudi.

Lipari

The largest of the Aeolian Islands (13 square miles), Lipari was known in ancient times as *Meliguente,* and as *Lipara* in the Greek period. Geologically it was formed by a number of volcanic eruptions. The last eruption was around the 18th century BC, when Monte Pelato spewed out the lava that solidified into the Rocche Rosse and obsidian streams, as well as the snowy pumice slopes on the northeast of the island which occupy about a quarter of its entire surface area. The volcano today is in the dormant state.

Lipari town

The main centre on the island, the town of Lipari, serves as the capital of the Aeolian Islands—except for Salina, which is autonomous. The pretty **Marina Corta,** the town's hydrofoil port, lies between the castle walls on the north side and the natural rocky mole and church of **Anime del Purgatorio** on the south. Next to the church is the ticket office for the hydrofoils which dock nearby. A good many of Lipari's cafés line the waterfront.

The charming main street, the **Corso Vittorio Emanuele,** with most of the shops and the tourist office, divides the town rather neatly into new and old. The old part is dominated by the castle with a grand pebble stairway penetrating the walls, built in the 16th century by the Spanish after Barbarossa's rampage.

The Castello and Museum

The Castello (castle), the ancient acropolis, has been inhabited since at least 3000 BC. In places you can see the pits dug by archaeologists into the strata of various millenia. Such excellent time capsules are very rare, and the pottery finds of Lipari castle have been used to date many other prehistoric discoveries in the Mediterranean. The two buildings of the Archaeology Museum near the digs contain one of the best Neolithic collections in the world. The finds are well arranged chronologically, beginning with Stentinello potsherds and continuing through to the Roman era, with several items of outstanding interest. These include the faithfully reconstructed necropolises of the Middle Bronze Age and the Ausonia II cultures; the beautiful polychromatic vases made during the Greek era, attesting to the island's importance as an innovatory art centre in western Greece; and the recently discovered collection of small figurines representing characters from Greek tragedies and comedies. These figurines are quite amusing, and are sometimes displayed in models of scenes from the various plays. A group of carved stone masks completes the collection. The museum is open daily, 9–

1 and 3.30–6; 9–1 on holidays from May to October, and 9–1 from November to April.

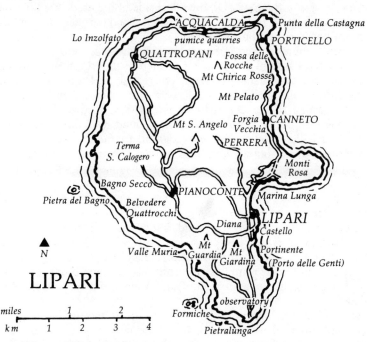

Cathedral of San Bartolomeo
Between the museum buildings is the Cathedral of San Bartolomeo, patron saint of the Aeolian Islands, after whom many of the islanders are named. San Bartolomeo's body in a marble coffin floated ashore at Porto di Genti on Lipari in 264, and as depicted on the doors of the Cathedral—he once saved the town from fire. The Cathedral was originally built by King Roger of Sicily in the 11th century, but reconstructed in 1654. Inside are 18th-century frescoes and a silver statue of San Bartolomeo (who, having suffered martyrdom by being skinned alive, traditionally carries his skin under his arm), as well as a fine *Addolorata* by Girolamo Alibrandi. The baroque church of the **Addolorata** nearby is built on an older, Byzantine plan.

Along the cobbled street of the castle are various excavations, with placards explaining what you see. Although nothing remains of the once famous temples of Aeolos and Hephestos (the smithy god, associated with volcanoes) there is still a Neolithic shrine. The **Archaeological Park** (open

223

9–1 and 4–6) contains a collection of Greco–Roman tombs found on the Diana plain. Above the little theatre the walls offer splendid views of the Marina Corta and the town. On the other side of the castle are the camp-sites, the youth hostel (open March to October) and the gate and road leading down towards the Marina Lunga.

Marina Lunga, where the ferries dock, is also the major beach on the island. It curves around the small bay formed by the Monti Rosa promontory, where a small pleasure port has been created, the **Pignataro,** crowded in the summer with yachts and other boats from many shores.

In the garden of the **Esposito house** on Via Garibaldi you can see the 1st-century BC sculpture of a woman found near there. Behind the town, towards Porto delle Genti in the south, are the excavations of a vast **necropolis,** whose some 1300 tombs produced many of the finds in the Archaeology Museum.

Around Lipari

A road completely encircles the island, but to see it all by bus you have to double back twice. The URSO company's buses leave Marina Lunga four times a day for Canneto, Porticello and Acquacalda; and for Quattrocchi, Pianoconte and Quattropani (also four times a day); and buses run twice a day to Perrara on the slopes of Monte Sant' Angelo, and twice a day to Leni, by Pianoconte.

Two roads leave Marina Lunga for **Canneto** to the north, the prettier one being further inland. Canneto, the second largest centre on the island, depends mainly on fishing. To the north rise the white slopes of **Monte Pelato** (1547 ft) and behind Canneto a road leads up to the old obsidian fields of **Forgia Vecchia** and the tiny hamlet of **Perrera** beneath Monte Sant' Angelo.

Monte Pelato's slopes are white because of the pumice. Pumice is the lightest rock in the world, so light that it floats on water, and is formed by obsidian filled with volcanic gas while being cooled. It has diverse uses, for example in the soap, toothpaste and glass industries. The pumice of Monte Pelato, mined in long galleries, is shipped off from the long docks beneath the mountain. At **Porticello** the beach is made of pumice and obsidian, the veins of which are red and black. These obsidian streams can be seen most spectacularly at the **Rocche Rosse,** where huge blocks of it remain in the old quarries. To visit the site, take the path from Porticello or Acquacalda to Monte Pelato; the Rocche Rosse are on the way. Other pumice quarries are behind Acquacalda on the slopes of Lipari's highest mountain, **Monte Chirica** (1956 ft).

Pianoconte

Quattropani, with its simple church, the Chiesa Vecchia, overlooks the distant island of Salina. Scattered white houses, gardens, vineyards and trees give this whole area a contented rural appearance. The road south winds past the Lipari hospital toward Pianoconte, where Bronze Age lava weapons have been discovered, and then the road branches off to the **Bagni Terma San Calogero,** the only exploited thermal establishment on the island (open July to September). According to legend, St Paul sent San Calogero to Lipari, where he found the spring—just as he did in Sicily, in the province of Agrigento at San Calogero. Famous for their curative powers in the Roman era, a few remains can still be seen of the ancient baths, near the modern establishment built in 1867. To take the baths you need a certificate from the doctor at Pianoconte (and also a reservation). The waters are recommended for gout, rheumatism and skin disorders.

From Pianoconte a path winds up to the crater of the extinct volcano, **Monte Sant' Angelo** (1949 ft). Although the path is steep, the climb rewards your effort with lovely views of the entire island and the unusual stratification inside the crater. Next to Pianoconte you may also visit the fumaroles, or little volcanic steam kettles, at **Bagno Secco.** On the south side of Pianoconte is the **Belvedere Quattrocchi,** with a magnificent, much photographed panorama of Vulcano and the four Faraglione in the sea between the islands. Another path descends from here to the **Valle Muria** and a lonely beach.

Monte Guardia

The large promontory to the south largely consists of Monte Giardina and Monte Guardia, volcanic cupolas formed in a relatively recent eruption of Monte Sant' Angelo. South of Monte Guardia (a 45-minute walk from Lipari town) is the **Geophysical Observatory,** run by the National Research Centre and funded by UNESCO. The scientists here make volcanic and seismic observations of the Aeolian Islands and the Tyrrhenian Sea, pinpoint the epicentre of Mediterranean earthquakes, and correlate volcanic and seismic phenomena, their data being sent to geological institutions throughout the world. Peripheral stations are located on Vulcano, Alicudi, Panarea, San Fuscaldo in Calabria and at Novara di Sicilia, all helping to determine the level on the Richter Scale of a particular earthquake. For the average visitor, however, the main interest at the observatory is the wonderful view of Vulcano.

Portinente (also known as Porto delle Gente), a short walk south of Lipari, has several hotels. The **Church of San Nicola** near here has an ancient architrave. If at all possible, a sea excursion around Lipari, or at least this southernmost part of it, is highly recommended. With the different coloured cliffs, the towering offshore rocks such as **Le Formiche** and **Pietralunga,** and the intense blue of the sea, the trip is truly enchanting.

FESTIVALS
San Bartolomeo (24 August), with a procession of the saint's statue.

TOURIST INFORMATION
AAST for the Aeolian Islands, Cia Vittorio Emanuele 239 (tel. (090) 911580). Information office (summer only): Via Marina Corta (tel. (090) 911108).

WHERE TO STAY
The most comfortable place to stay on Lipari is the villa hotel **Melingunis***, on Via Marte (tel. (090) 981 1004; double room 62–70 000 lire; open all year round, with TV, garden, a beach, etc.). Less costly is the **Odissea**** in Canneto, which has twelve rooms (single with bath 13–15 000 lire, double 24–29 000; tel. (090) 981 2337). For real peace and quiet, stay in Quattropani at the little **Nenzyna*** (tel. (090) 982 2265; single with bath 14 000 lire, double 27 000); there's a good little restaurant and garden as well. Other accommodation may be found in private houses and locandas.

EATING OUT
There are some very good restaurants on Lipari, which gets enough tourists to stimulate competition. Nearly all close by the end of October, however. Good choices are **Filippino** in the Piazza Municipio, noted for island specialities and fish (30 000 lire); also good for Aeolian specialities is **'e Pulera** on Via Stradale Diana 51 (30 000 lire). In Acquacalda, **La Lauro** is the best (25 000 lire); in Pianoconte **A Cannata** serves local cuisine and pizza (25 000).

Vulcano

Vulano, anciently *Iera* (the sacred island) or *Thermessa,* has at present much volcanic activity but no active volcanoes. This certainly wasn't true in the past: Aristotle, Diodoros Siculus, Strabo and Thucydides all record various eruptions, one so destructive as to cover the town of Lipari in ashes in the 4th century BC. Vulcanello, on the extreme north of the island, rose out of the sea only in 183 BC. The main crater, the Fossa (1230 ft), has been quite active for centuries, last erupting in 1890 when it obliterated the alum-extracting industry of a Scotsman named Stevens, who once owned the entire island.

Composed of five different volcanic structures, Vulcano is a bizarre island of strange colours and bitter odours. Legends breed here as naturally as wild flowers. The ancients believed that Hephestos, the god of fire and blacksmiths, had his headquarters on the island, and in the Middle Ages the island was thought to be the entrance to Hell. San Bartolomeo was accredited with separating Lipari from Vulcano to protect his island from eruptions.

The emergence of Vulcanello off the north coast, connected by a narrow isthmus, conveniently formed the island's two harbours: **Porto di Ponente** (for pleasure boats), lined with warm black sand, and **Porto di Levante,** where hydrofoils and ferries dock (at the moment only the vehicles of islanders are permitted, so don't try to bring your car). Your nose is immediately insulted by sulphurous fumes rising from the steaming fumaroles on the isthmus. To the immediate north of the Porto di Levante lies the great rock known as the **Faraglione della Fabbrica,** where alum was once extracted. (Alum, a whitish astringent mineral, is used in tanning, dyeing, medicine and fireproof materials.) The colours here are quite marvellous—ochres, yellows, reds and oranges—and they paint the earth around the two hot springs of **Acqua del Bagno** and **Acqua Bollente,** very near the port. In these hot shallow pools the protruding heads of people taking the baths are an odd sight to behold. If you join them, you'll have to bathe in the sea afterwards; otherwise you'll offend your dinner companions by smelling like a rotten egg. But even on the beach you can't escape volcanic manifestations; underwater fumaroles cause the sea to bubble, and the sulphur deposits on the sea bed give the coast a scabrous appearance. In another part of the port there are miniature geysers which sometimes shoot mud into the air.

There are hotels and restaurants at each of the ports, and most of the island's 400 people live here. But the little rustic houses and flower gardens cannot match the wonders—or abominations—of Mother Nature.

Around Vulcano
The only bus on Vulcano takes the one road up to **Vulcano Piano,** a very scenic drive across the middle of the island up to the earthquake-shattered ruins of the **Church of Sant' Angelo.** The entire route has been planted with pink flowers. Most of the houses at Vulcano Piano were built after the earthquake in the 1950s and are mainly used as summer residences. There are a few bars and small restaurants, and many opportunities for quiet walks in the woods or among the sheep grazing on the hillsides.

VULCANO

From Porto di Levante it is an hour's walk (in sturdy shoes!) up to the summit of the **Gran Cratere di Vulcano,** known simply as the **Fossa.** On the way up you'll pass the obsidian vein at Pietre Cotte and clouds of smoke rising from the side of the mountain, near the red rocks. Further up, a large number of 'bread crust' volcanic bombs lie scattered about from the last eruption; above them at 1230 ft is the hollow of the great crater, more than 500 yards in diameter. The floor is completely solid, but it is hardly recommended to descend into it; the acrid gases from the fumaroles makes it difficult to breathe, even on the crater's rim. Bereft of vegetation, the whole area of the crater is like a lunar landscape; from the highest point of the mountain you get a moon's eye view of the entire Aeolian archipelago.

Also from Porto di Levante you can visit the crater of **Vulcanello,** across the isthmus of lava with its toy-like volcanoes and stinking fumaroles. Passing the summer villas clinging to the slopes of Vulcanello, the path ascends to the top of the little volcano, notable for its brilliant colouring. Inside the crater visitors can enter a brightly hued cave where alum used to be mined.

The only way to see the rest of the island is by boat, unless you are a hiker. Made of old and more recent lava, the coasts of the island are rugged and often spectacular; sailing between Lipari and Vulcano in the narrow

Bocche di Vulcano—less than a mile wide and adorned with monoliths such as the 236-ft Pietralunga—is a unique experience. On the south side of the island, beneath the tallest mountain, **Monte Aria** (1625 ft), are two lighthouses, Faro Vecchio and Faro Nuovo, and the tiny village of **Gelso.** One of the truly forgotten places on the Aeolian Islands, Gelso is visited by only one boat a day. Although there are no hotels or rooms to be found at Gelso, there are two restaurants. On the west side of Vulcano there is a fine beach at **Spiaggia Lunga,** near the pretty Punta di Capo Secco and the boulder called Pietro Quaglietto.

FESTIVALS
Sant' Angelo (2 October). His church, however, at Vulcano Piano, fell down in a recent earthquake and has yet to be rebuilt.

SPECIALITIES
Home-made cheese.

TOURIST INFORMATION
In summer only, at Porto di Levante (tel. (090) 911108).

WHERE TO STAY
The islands oldest hotel, **Les Sables Noirs***,** at Porto Ponente, has, as its name suggests, a beach of black sand, as well as a garden (tel. (090) 985 2014; 34 000 lire single, 67 000 double; open April to October). For the totally up-to-date, the **Archipelago***** at Vulcanello is built beside the sea, with a garden and pool for those who'd rather not swim off the rocks (tel. (090) 985 2002; 37 000 lire single, 68 000 double). In Porto Levante there is the very simple but clean **Casa Fiorita*** (tel. (090) 985 2006; single room 13 000 lire, double 23 000, some rooms with bath).

WHERE TO EAT
The island's best restaurant, **Blue Moon** in Porto Ponente, features very good food which is served on a terrace with a very good view (30–35 000 lire). For something cheaper, try **Scaffidi** in Volcano Piano (25 000 lire) or the pizza at **Palrovita** in Porto Levante (15 000 lire).

Salina

The twin volcanoes that gave Salina its ancient name, *Didyme,* are long extinct—Monte Fossa delle Felci (3157 ft), the tallest peak of the Aeolian archipelago, and Monte dei Porri (3000 ft). From a distance the island looks like a child's drawing—simple, entirely green, with two rounded mountains and a smooth coastline. It is the second largest of the islands, but unlike the others Salina does not belong to the commune of Lipari; instead it supports three autonomous communes of its own: Santa Marina di Salina, Leni and Malfa.

Tourism has made few inroads here, and most of the people earn their living from the very fertile land, producing tons of capers for export and the sweet white wine *Malvasia*. Despite its name, Salina no longer has any salt-pans, although these used to be an important industry at Lingua. Ships and hydrofoils to the island call at Santa Marina di Salina, and occasionally at Malfa and Rinella as well. All villages are connected by reasonably good roads, and Salina's bus schedules coincide with the arrival of the ferries.

Santa Marina di Salina
The main port is a straggling little village at the foot of the Fossa. Like every other town on Salina, it has little to 'see', but offers much in the way of peace, quiet and friendliness (many of the inhabitants are returned Australian migrants and speak a variety of English). By the lighthouse to the north a Bronze Age town once flourished; among the finds here was a necklace of Egyptian beads, a popular style in Mycenean days (similar necklaces have been discovered in England).

On the southern side of Santa Marina, the road leads to **Lingua,** some 2 miles away. The small lake near here was once used as a saltpan, on one side of which stretches a pebble beach where the sea is renowned for its clearness. In the 18th century the ruins of a typical Imperial Roman villa were noted here, but they have since sunk into the ground. Behind Lingua and Santa Marina, on the slopes of the Fossa, several Roman tombs have been excavated. A path from Santa Marina leads to the summit of the mountain (about two hours' climbing), from where on a clear day you can see not only all of the Aeolian Islands, but also Reggio Calabria and Mount Etna.

Around Salina
The coastal road north of Santa Marina passes many curious offshore formations of lava and basalt, and lonely beaches of pebbles and rock. Much of the land is neatly cultivated, although for lack of labour large tracts have become overgrown. The first village on the route is **Malfa** in the north, located on a wide plain overlooking the sea. West of here lies **Pollara,** by the natural arch of **Punta del Perciato,** the only place on Salina where you can see the white pumice attesting to the volcanic origins of the island; the last eruption took place here in 10 000 BC, from the crater near the village.

Between Malfa and Leni, in the saddle known as **Valdichiesa,** between the twin volcanoes, is the **Sanctuary of the Madonna del Terzito,** built in

1630. The religious centre on the island, it attracts pilgrims on the main feast days of Mary, such as the Assumption (15 August).

Leni, another small community, is notable mainly for its location in Valdichiesa, overlooking the tiny fishing port of **Rinella** at the end of a steep winding road. The bus there stops by the overgrown public garden and a wide shady piazza with a café and fine views of the sea. The small beach down below has a series of grottoes behind it. Fishermen will often take you on brief excursions along the coast—westwards to the interesting **Grotto di Racina,** or eastwards to the **Grotto di Basalto** at Punta Grottazza, which easily wins the prize as the loveliest on the island (it can also be reached from Lingua).

TOURIST INFORMATION
AAST, Santa Marina Salina (tel. (090) 913003).

WHERE TO STAY
The nicest hotel on Salina is in Rinella: **L'Ariana**** (tel. (090) 984 2075) with a beach and good restaurant (23 000 lire single, 40 000 double). In Santa Marina there are five 1-star hotels, all about the same: **La Marinara***

at Lingua (tel. (090) 984 3022) has a nice garden and some rooms with a bath (13 000 lire single, 22 000 double). In Malfa the **Punta Scario**** (tel. (090) 984 4139) has a nice little restaurant and pleasant double rooms for 28 000 lire (33 000 with bath).

EATING OUT
The restaurants are inexpensive and simple on Salina. **Da Santa** in Santa Maria is one that stands out (15 000 lire). Others may found in all the major settlements in the summer.

Filicudi

The ancient name of Filicudi, *Phoinikodes*, either referred to its abundant ferns or (according to Strabo) its palms. Capo Graziano, the first settlement on the island, is thought to date back to the 18th century BC. Eventually abandoned and then extensively resettled all the way up to the slopes of Montagnola, Capo Graziano became an important trading centre. Potsherds from Mycenae and the Cyclades attest to links between Filicudi and the Aegean in 1500 BC. In 800 BC the village was invaded and destroyed.

Filicudi was inhabited off and on throughout history. The Greeks left an inscription near Pecorini, and later peoples left the numerous terraces cut like grand stairways in the mountains; although many of these have since been abandoned, from a distance they give the island a striped look. Many of Filicudi's 450 inhabitants make a living from the sea. Although the coral they once gathered is virtualy gone, men still harvest the sponges, as well as fish.

Filicudi Porto, where the ships and hydrofoils call, is one of the three main communities on the island. A long beach curves towards the promontory of Capo Graziano. To see the excavations there, apply in the port for the custodian, who will open the gate for you.

Capo Graziano, on a natural rock terrace some 300 ft above sea level, was actually the successor to an earlier village on the plains, which was entirely indefensible. Some 20 oval-shaped huts have been uncovered on the cape, and the ceramics found here, with simple undulating scratched designs, gave their name to the Capo Graziano culture in the southern Tyrrhenian Sea (1800–1400 BC). All the ceramics are now in the Archaeology Museum in Lipari, but in one of the huts you can still see the smooth rocks and what appears to be a prehistoric altar. The Necropolis of Capo Graziano extended up the steep sides of Montagnola, where people were

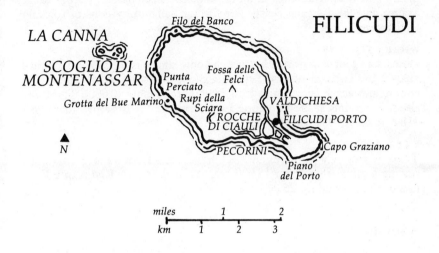

LA CANNA

SCOGLIO DI
MONTENASSAR

Grotta del Bue Marino

▲
N

Filo del Banco

FILICUDI

*Punta
Perciato*

*Fossa delle
Felci*
∧

*Rupi della
Sciara*

*ROCCHE
DI CIAULI*

PECORINI

VALDICHIESA

FILICUDI PORTO

Capo Graziano

*Piano
del Porto*

miles | 1 | 2
km | 1 | 2 | 3

buried in communal graves in the rock, much like those found in Sicily.

From the Porto you can also climb to the tallest of the island's three peaks, **Fossa delle Felci** (2384 ft), passing through **Rocche di Ciauli** (with post office and public telephone) and **Valdichiesa,** the main village of Filicudi, with the large **Church of San Stefano** (constructed 1650) perching on the rim of an ancient crater. From here the path continues up to the summit of Monte Fossa and its charming views of the island.

The only proper road on the island, built in the mid 1970s so that cars could replace the mules previously used, connects the Porto with the other seaside village of **Pecorini,** where the Ancient Greek inscription may be seen on the rocks. From here, or the Porto, you can hire a boatman to take you around the island, the highlight of a stay on peaceful Filicudi. The west coast of the island is particularly lovely, with the famous volcanic obelisk called **La Canna** (300 ft) towering out of the sea, popular with nesting seagulls. Next to it is another rock, the black **Scoglio di Montenassar.** Also along the wes⁺ coast, a pointed natural archway forms the entrance to the marvellous **Grotto del Bue Marino** ('of the sea bull', after the hooded Mediterranean monk seals that once lived there). You can enter this large

233

cavern in a small boat or swim around its ample perimeter; the intense silence and ever-changing light patterns are almost unreal. Other grottoes include the deep Maccatore and Perciato. The steep precipice **Rupi della Sciara** and the Fortuna coast offer further delightful visions of volcanic landscaping.

WHERE TO STAY

Other than rooms in private houses, the only choice is the modern **Phenicusa*****, open from June to September (tel. (090) 984 4185) with a restaurant and beach (single with bath 28 000 lire, double 40 000). There are also a few rooms at the **Pensione La Canna,** 43 Via Rosa (tel. (090) 984 4187; single 12 000 lire, double 16 000).

EATING OUT

There is more choice here: on Via Porta there's **Lopes** and **Paino,** both serving local hearty fare for 18 000 lire; at Canale there's **Ristorante Ferlazzo** with seafood for 25 000 lire.

Alicudi

The furthest west of the Aeolian Islands, and one of the most remote islands in the entire Mediterranean, Alicudi is a round green bump on the sea, some 2 square miles in size. Its ancient name, *Ericusa,* derived from the heather that still covers this fertile little island, which is formed by the cone of an ancient volcano. In 1904 some tombs of the 9th century BC were discovered at Fucile, made out of lava, but it is not known if Alicudi was ever settled in ancient times; lacking any natural defences it may have been only a burial ground.

The gently sloping eastern part of the island is corrugated with green terraces and has the only village on Alicudi, the **Porto** (pop. 130). Lacking electricity, it is a very peaceful place indeed. The one public telephone serves the bar as well as the hotel, and among the humble pink-and-white houses scattering the terraces there is only one prominent building, the **Church of San Bartolomeo,** splendidly situated at the top of a small stairway.

High above the Porto is the steep **Serra della Farcona,** where women used to hide from the pirates in a spot called the **Timpone delle Femmine.** Higher still is the depression of the very old crater, called the **Filo dell' Arpa** (2195 ft). The western side of Alicudi is too steep for houses or farming, but there are small scattered beaches and natural grottoes made by the wind, such as the **Grottazzo.** The few tourists who visit Alicudi come

ALICUDI

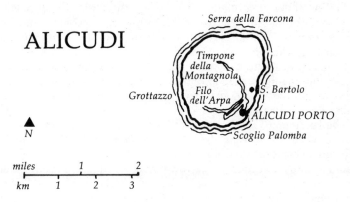

Serra della Farcona

Timpone della Montagnola

Grottazzo

Filo dell'Arpa

S. Bartolo

ALICUDI PORTO

Scoglio Palomba

▲
N

miles		1		2
km	1	2	3	

mainly for the crystal-clear waters and the excellent fishing, especially for the Mediterranean lobsters, the *aragosta.*

FESTIVAL
San Bartolomeo (2 August).

WHERE TO STAY
There's one hotel, the **Ericusa*** (tel. (090) 981 2370; 12 double rooms with showers, 24 500 lire). Otherwise, you'll have to seek accommodation in private homes.

EATING OUT
There's a trattoria at the hotel, **Ericusa,** and **De Salvatore** nearby, both simple and serving good seafood for around 20 000 lire.

Panarea

Panarea, the smallest of the Aeolian Islands (1.3 square miles), is nevertheless one of the most charming. Surrounded by numerous small islets and rocks like the Byzantine-named Basiluzzo, it is the queen of its own little archipelago. Known in ancient times as *Euonymos* ('of good omen'), it was the site of an early settlement at Piano Quartara (contemporaneous with the Capo Graziano culture on Filicudi), as well as a more famous settlement at Capo Milazzese (1400–1250 BC), a culture that produced the zigzag cera-

235

mic designs displaying symbols closely associated with the Minoan civilisation on Crete.

The inhabited area of the island is spread across three neighbouring shores—**Ditella, San Pietro** and **Drauto,** connected mainly by mule tracks. As there is no pier for the ferries or hydrofoils, you must clamber into small rowing boats to reach the shore; they will take you to whichever settlement you request. By the little quay at San Pietro there is a locally-utilised hot spring, said to have medicinal powers. Among the picturesque rocks off the coast of Panarea is **Bottaro,** where underwater fumaroles makes the sea seem to boil.

The landing at **Cala Junco,** south of Drauto, is surrounded by cliffs of bizarre volcanic prisms just below the **Punta Milazzese.** Here in 1948, 23 oval huts were excavated on the basalt-walled promontory, joined to the main island by an extremely narrow tongue of land. Between 100 and 200 people lived here and maintained religious cults at Calcara and Punta Cardosi. Some of the pottery found at Milazzese bears a Minoan-like script which the early inhabitants may have been able to read. In approximately 1250 BC, however, the settlement was gutted by fire and ruined by Bronze Age tough-guys, who used their new metal-working technology mainly to destroy—behaviour repeated over and over again in history.

North of the village of Ditella is the **Calcara Beach,** which is reached by following a hairpin path down the rocky cliffs that comprise much of Panarea's coast. At Calcara fumaroles have left the stone a variety of colours; in places steam still rises from the ground and patches of sea and land are quite hot. In Neolithic times the fumaroles were worshipped as infernal gods, and deep pits were dug on the beach to receive their votive offerings.

From Drauto another path leads towards the **Contrada Castello;** from here you must make your own way up the terraces to the highest point of Panarea, the **Timpone del Corvo** (1370 ft), with splendid vistas of Stromboli and its active volcano. Just below Punta Corvo archaeologists have found traces of the ancient cult at **Punta Cardosi.**

Around Panarea

Anyone who visits Panarea will not want to miss the short trip around the island and a visit to the offshore archipelago of rocks and islets. The mountainous west coast of the island has many unusual formations of hardened lava, like the **Pizzo Falcone** which can be seen above San Pietro.

Most fascinating of all is the trip to **Basiluzzo,** a more recent creation of the underwater volcano thought to have formed Panarea itself. Much of Basiluzzo consists of stratified lava in delicate shades shaped like giant columns. By the landing point you can see remains of the Roman dock under

PANAREA

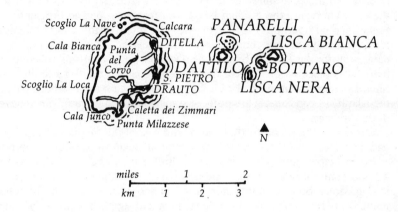

the water; indeed the whole islet is covered with traces of Roman habitation. One wonders whether the Romans were attracted by the weird beauty of the place, or merely used the islet as a cruel prison for political deportees; traces of mosaics found on Basiluzzo suggest the former. The capers that grow on the little plain of the islet are harvested by the people of Panarea. The other rocks and islets in the area are also interesting, in particular **Lisca Bianca** and **Lisca Nera** with their many colours.

WHERE TO STAY
The only hotel on the island with a pool is **La Piazza** at San Pietro (tel. (090) 981 1190), with a garden but no restaurant; (double rooms are 44 000 lire). At Costa Galletta there's the **Raya****, with a garden but no restaurant (single 29 000 lire, double 44 000).

There are also a number of locandas, like **Stella Maris** with one of Panarca's restaurants (rooms for 15 000 lirc).

EATING OUT
Like the accommodation, food tends to be simple on Panarea; a couple of the best establishments are **Trattoria La Sirena** on Via Drautti, and **G.**

237

Tesoriero on Via San Pietro. Both will charge around 18 000 lire for a full meal.

Stromboli

In the 1950s the island of Stromboli became a household word with the really awful movie of the same name starring Ingrid Bergman, and it is still the most famous of the Aeolian Islands for its active volcano. Ancient writers remarked upon this: 'On Strongyle "the round island",' wrote Pausanius, 'you may see fire coming up from the earth.' This may sound a bit dangerous for the 400 inhabitants of Stromboli, but it's not—all volcanic activity takes place on the **Sciara del Fuoco** ('the fiery trail'), naturally confined by the montain itself. From the two parishes on the northern part of the island, all you can see are puffs of smoke, and at night only the apogees of the fireworks.

Stromboli, the island furthest north and east of the Aeolian archipelago, had a special importance before the advent of steam ships as the main port between Naples and Sicily. It seems a little hard to believe today, as the black beaches of San Vincenzo and San Bartolo have no protection from the raging winds, but the sailing ships used to anchor here, and the islanders made it a hereditary profession to ferry men and supplies between the ships and the shore. The brand-new concrete mole at Scari will unfortunately eliminate the need for these brawny sailors and their romantic rowing-boats.

Visitors to **Scari** are met by little three-wheeled vehicles which take your luggage up the hill to your hotel, for only they can manoeuvre the narrow streets of the villages; the one main road that skirts the shore from Scari to Ficogrande is scarcely used. **San Vincenzo** is named after the large parish church of San Vincenzo Ferreri, which overlooks the village and the unusual islet of Strombolicchio. Here the houses, mostly whitewashed, are of a delightful simplicity and proportion known as the Aeolian style. There are particularly fine examples at **San Bartolo,** the other parish, with an equally fine church. Most of the tourist amenities on the island are to be found here or below on the beautiful black sand beach of **Ficogrande** ('the big fig'). These settlements have a melancholy air, however, thanks to the numerous abandoned houses and farms. No one seems to want to stay on this rarest of islands, and the delicious white wine of Stromboli—the finest in the Aeolian Islands—grows increasingly scarce for lack of labourers.

Around Stromboli
From San Bartolo it is about half-an-hour's walk to the **Osservatorio di**

Punta Labronzo, at the northernmost point of the island, offering a fine view of the volcano if you aren't up to climbing to the summit. Signs painted on the streets in the western part of San Bartolo direct you to the Observatory, best visited at night and with binoculars to see the volcanic sparks.

If you want to visit the **crater of the volano** itself, allow 3 or 4 hours for the ascent and perhaps another 2 hours for the descent. You would do well to take a powerful torch if you go in the evening, and you must wear good sturdy shoes and warm clothing—ideally a windcheater—for it is very gusty at the top, and much cooler than at sea level. Ideally the climb should be made at full moon, beginning around 4 or 5 pm. Of course, many people do go up during the day, but in summer it is too hot, and during the hours of daylight all you'll see is smoke. If you are wary of making the trip alone, trained guides may be hired in the villages.

The ascent begins from the Observatory, where the well-made path has lately become somewhat overgrown. Beaten and narrow, it passes through thick undergrowth and prickly bushes, which become gradually thinner until they peter out all together. Here the track becomes a bit difficult to

239

discern, paths wandering every which way over the rocks, but it doesn't matter which one you take as they all eventually meet. Little red and white stripes have been painted on the boulders to guide you, and you may have to do a little Alpine climbing to reach the peak.

The Volcano of Stromboli, Aeolian Islands

At 3040 ft, the **Pizzo** is the highest point of Stromboli; it is covered with sand which has a nasty tendency to blow into your eyes. However, from the Pizzo you have an excellent view of the crater some 200 yards below; the amount of volcanic activity, the wind and your own stamina will determine how much closer you get.

It is an extraordinary sight. Stromboli has given its name to the constant, explosive nature of some volcanoes, for almost every ten minutes exactly the red sparks flare up in an enormous fountain of fire, accompanied by appropriate deep rumblings inside the volcano. On busy nights the volcano hurls chunks of volcanic debris down the infernal Sciara del Fuoco; and when the fog gathers around the crater, as often happens, the effect is even more eerie. On good nights (little wind and no bitter volcanic gases), it is easy to stay up until dawn, always a magnificent sight from a mountain top, and particularly breathtaking on top of the world's most active volcano.

In summer there are boat excursions to the base of the **Sciara del Fuoco** in the evenings—another impressive experience. The contrast between the verdant hills of the rest of the island and the hellish black slag of the Sciara couldn't be greater, and while the volcano isn't as immediate or awe-inspiring as when you make the big climb, the red sparks spraying over the side of the Sciara provide a truly memorable sight.

240

Ginostra
Other possible boat excursions on Stromboli are to Ginostra and Strombol-icchio. Ginostra (pop. 30) lies very near the Sciara del Fuoco, on the far western side of Stromboli. This perfectly charming, remote village—much diminished through widespread emigration to Australia and America—has literally the smallest port in the world; no more than two tiny fishing boats can fit in it at a time. Lava rocks in the sea form a natural protective wall against the frequent violent storms. The inhabitants of Ginostra are mainly fishermen and their families, a people impressive in their dignity. There is a tiny church among the fine white houses, many built on ledges carved out of the lava. A mule path once connected Ginostra with San Vincenzo, but it has become impassable. The only contact that Ginostra has with the outside world is by boat, either from other parishes on the island, or the steamers from Milazzo, which call twice a week or so. **Mario Lo Schiavo** (tel. 981 1760) has five double rooms to let in the village, the sole accommodation. The three trattorias—Internazionale, Lo Schiavo and Merlino—serve mainly day-trippers in the summer.

One last excursion by sea is to **Strombolicchio,** about a mile off the north coast of Stromboli. From the distance this mass of volcanic rock looks like a cathedral; it is surrounded by strange currents, and its spires turn out to be petrified monsters. Between 1920 and 1927, some 200 concrete steps were hewn in Strombolicchio's side, leading up to the lighthouse, a vital installation in these frequently rough seas. The views from the summit of the islet sometimes extend to the peak of Mount Etna, although perhaps most interesting of all are the many queer shapes and the sheer sides of the rock carved by Aeolus, the old god of the wind, whose headquarters are on Stromboli.

TOURIST INFORMATION
At Ficogrande, in the summer only.

WHERE TO STAY
For resort facilities and a pool, **La Sciara***,** (tel. (090) 98604) has single rooms for 38 000 lire and double rooms for 71 000, open April to September. Also good, **La Sirenetta***** (tel. (090) 98625) has a pool and garden and beach (28 000 lire single, 48 000 double, with bath). There are a number of inexpensive locadas, the best of which is the **Villa Petrusa** (tel. (090) 98645) which has some rooms with a bath, and a restaurant. There are a few rooms to let in Ginostra.

WHERE TO EAT
Il Gabbiano is a long-standing favourite at 10 Via Vito Nunziante, with fish

and meat dishes for 25 000 lire. Less expensive choices are **Roma** on Via Roma, and nearby **Saccavino**.

Ustica

HISTORY

Ustica was inhabited about 2000 BC by a people with close cultural links with both Sicily and the Aeolian Islands. Located at Falconiera and near the present Saracen castle, their settlements have yielded many interesting finds, but have yet to be completely excavated. In the nearby Grotto dell' Uomo items from early tombs were discovered.

The first historical account we have of the island comes from the Greeks, who called Ustica *Osteodes* ('bony island') for the remains of 6000 mutinous Carthaginian soldiers who were abandoned here to die of hunger and thirst. The Romans, who named the island *Ustum* ('burnt'), referring to the charred-looking volcanic black rock of Ustica, probably used it as a base. As the power of Rome declined, pirates took over, and although the Benedictines briefly maintained a monastery on Ustica, the pirates successfully prevented any colonisation until the 18th century, when the Bourbons under Ferdinand IV, King of the Two Sicilies, sent a group of settlers from Trapani and Lipari to Ustica. Two years later, in 1762, the pirates massacred the unprotected colonists in a three-day rampage, with only two men escaping to tell the terrible tale in Palermo. The Bourbons then fortified the island, and ten years later sent a new group of colonists, who had better luck; they are the ancestors of the 1000 people who live on Ustica today. In September 1943, British and Italian commanders met secretly on the island to discuss Italy's switch to the Allies during the war.

WHAT TO SEE

The little island (3 square miles) lies a lonely 36 nautical miles north of Palermo. Ustica looks like a giant turtle swimming away from Sicily; it is just far enough away to escape the pollution of the larger island. For this reason Ustica is well known among sub-aqua enthusiasts, who gather here every July for the 'International Festival of Underwater Activities' to discuss new scientific discoveries and compete in numerous underwater sports.

But Ustica has many charms for landlubbers too. Its volcanic structure has created some marvellous scenery, easily accessible on foot or by donkey. Wild flowers cover the island except in the hottest months, and a well-maintained little wood offers possibilities of shady picnics and afternoon snoozes. Although the wild coastline, dotted with magnificent grottoes, has

242

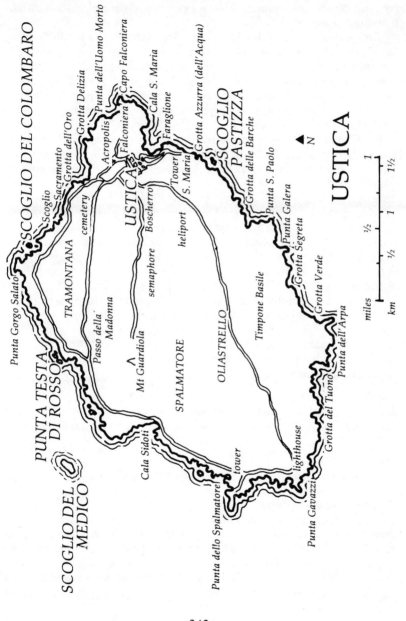

SCOGLIO DEL COLOMBARO

Punta Gorgo Salato

PUNTA TESTA
DI ROSSO

SCOGLIO DEL
MEDICO

Scoglio

Sacramento

Grotta dell'Oro

Grotta Delizia

Punta dell'Uomo Morto

Capo Falconiera

Cala S. Maria

Faraglione

Grotta Azzurra (dell'Acqua)

Acropolis

Falconiera

S. Maria

Tower

SCOGLIO
PASTIZZA

Grotta delle Barche

Punta S. Paolo

Punta Galera

Grotta Segreta

Grotta Verde

Punta dell'Arpa

N

USTICA

USTICA

Boscherro

cemetery

TRAMONTANA

Passo della
Madonna

Mt Guardiola

SPALMATORE

Cala Sidoti

Punta dello Spalmatore

semaphore

heliport

OLIASTRELLO

Timpone Basile

lighthouse

tower

Grotta del Tuono

Punta Gavazzi

miles

km

½

½

1

1

1½

1½

243

no sandy beaches, there are several rocky coves and the major hotels all have swimming pools.

This port and town of **Ustica** on the Baia Santa Maria has 90% of the island's population. Steps and one of Ustica's few paved roads lead up to **Piazza Umberto,** the centre of town (it is hardly worth while bringing your own car to the island, unless it's a jeep). Many of the houses are adorned with brightly-painted murals of every different style and theme, a legacy of the mural-painting contest sponsored on Ustica in even-numbered years. The effect is quite charming.

The **Church of San Bartolomeo** occupies a dominant position in the square. Don't be surprised to see the young gallants of Ustica playing baseball in the open space in front of it; Ustica has one of Italy's finest youth teams, and the boys wear their purple caps decorated with a U proudly. Although the church has little of interest architecturally, the parish priest is an avid supporter of archaeological explorations on the island, and will show you some of the beautiful finds and photographs of the excavations which he keeps at the back of the church. The **Museum** contains items from the off-shore wrecks found by undersea explorers, but it is closed except for July, during the Festival. Above the church, on the site of an 11th-century Bene-dictine monastery, is the **Palazzo del Commune,** built in 1763.

More steps and another path lead up from the town to the ruins of a Sara-cen castle on **Falconiera,** the highest point of the island, from which you can see Sicily. Here a number of ancient sites have been excavated. The modern inhabitants constructed the nearby **Calvario,** and further down on the **Guardia di Mezzo,** the ridge that divides Ustica in two, there is an abandoned **Semaphoro.**

FESTIVALS
San Bartolomeo (24 August); International Festival of Underwater Activi-ties (June–July); international mural-painting contest (even-numbered years only).

SPECIALITIES
Wine; quail in April/May and September/October; fish dishes.

Around Ustica: by boat
The principal port of Ustica, **Baia Santa Maria,** has been in use since ancient times, when the Phoenicians constructed a long mole of volcanic rock where the concrete mole stands today. In the season it is easy to hire a boat or a boatman to take you around the splendid little island. Some of the most impressive parts of Ustica's coastline lie just to the south of the port, with the steep ochre cliffs of stratified lava and the **Grotta Azzurra,** which,

like its namesake in Capri, derives its chief beauty from the reflections of light on the blue sea. While the entrance to the cavern its quite narrow, inside it is an ample 100 yards long. The walls of the grotto are caked with petrified shells, and in the centre a steep greyish rock with stalactites drips water reputed to cure skin diseases.

The next grotto, **Pastizza,** just to the south, is almost as lovely as the Grotta Azzurra. Near it, just under the water, are a large bank of petrified shells and the half-submerged entrance to another fair-sized grotto, **Naiada.** Further south still is the majestic **Baia San Paolo,** one of the prettiest bays on Ustica, with a giant lava arch and yet another grotto, known as the **Barche** ('of the boats'), where fishermen beach their boats during storms, and where 18th-century 'ladies of scarce virtue' who accompanied the Bourbon soldiers to the island used to frolic in the evenings. Off the **Punta San Paola** a Roman ship went down, and scuba divers still find amphorae here.

The entrance to the **Grotta Segreta** ('the secret cave'), next to Punta Segreta, has been blocked by a chunk of lava, so you cannot enter this cave, but the exquisite turquoise colour of the water inside the nearby **Grotta Verde** is particularly impressive. Next are the rich fishing grounds of Cala Sciabica and Punta dell' Arpa, and a long stretch of rugged coast towards the **Punta Gavazzi** with one of the island's two lighthouses. Beneath the lighthouse is the **Piscina Naturale,** a natural sea pool that attracts swimmers and sunbathers. Another local feature is the **Torre Spalmatore,** an 18th-century defensive tower at the southern end of the Spalmatore coast, with numerous inlets and pebbly beaches. The **Baia Sidoti** is the most striking cove, with the **Scoglio del Medico** ('the doctor's rock') a little way out to sea, a popular nesting place for sea gulls. The bay is surrounded by orange cliffs of tufa, and has a reputation for its remarkable quantity of fish.

The steep cliffs north of Sidoti bear the hilly tract known as the **Passo della Madonna,** one of the highlights of a walking tour of Ustica (see below). Here the rocks are coloured a deep red at the Testa di Rosso, a mighty precipice; at the bottom is a small pebbly beach.

Following this you pass a series of fantastic volcanic rocks—the Colombaro or **Faraglione,** made of black and green crystals, the **Sacramento** rock with its unusual stratification, and two grottoes with curious mineral formations in their walls. The lighthouse on **Punta dell' Uomo Morto** (Dead Man's Point) stands on a cliff, where a deep cave contained vestiges of ancient tombs.

Around Ustica: on land
If you prefer to explore the island, rather than merely admire it from a boat,

you can easily see it all on foot (or hire a donkey) within 3 or 4 hours, circling around the Guardia di Mezzo. You can see many of the same things mentioned above along the coast from new and sometimes better angles, as well as the **Torre Santa Maria,** a watchtower (built 1766) with pleasant views over the sea. You can also see where there were once prehistoric villages at Spalmatore and in the Tramontana region. The **Passo della Madonna,** with its sheer precipices, forms the most dramatic part of the journey—that is if you don't encounter the red bees of Spalmatore. These pesky little blossom-suckers like to buzz around your head and legs when you cross their turf, but they rarely sting.

GETTING TO USTICA
The daily 2-hour Siremar ferry from Palermo (not on Sundays in the winter) is joined by two hydrofoils daily in the summer, one in the winter when weather permits, also operated by Siremar. The boats are conveniently scheduled to make a day excursion from Palermo.

WHERE TO STAY
There are a number of places in the town, which include the **Locanda Castelli*** (9000 lire single, 15 000 double without bath) and the **Clelia*,** Via Maggazzini (tel. (091) 999034) are the least expensive. Resorts have appeared at a few of the most choice spots along the coast: at Spalmatore, the **Punta Spalmatore**** is a large and well-equipped tourist village (tel. (091) 999048; 28 000 lire single, 51 000 double).

EATING OUT
La Campanile, in an old house just outside town, has excellent fish and pasta dishes in the 20 000 lire range. The **Clelia Hotel** also has a good and inexpensive restaurant, where *lenticchie all'usticese* is a speciality (18 000 lire).

The Egadi Islands

The three Egadi (sometimes spelt *Aegadi* in English) Islands—Favignana, Levanzo and Marettimo—are just off the west coast of Trapani in western Sicily. Between them and the coast lie the Formiche ('ant') islets, one of which has an abandoned tuna cannery. As islands go, they are all relative newcomers. Marettimo, the island furthest from Sicily, separated from that land mass 600 000 years ago during the Quarternary Period, while Favignana and Levanzo, inhabited by Paleolithic Man in 10 000 BC, were parted from Sicily only by about 5000 BC, owing not only to earthquakes but also to

EGADI AND STAGNONE ISLANDS

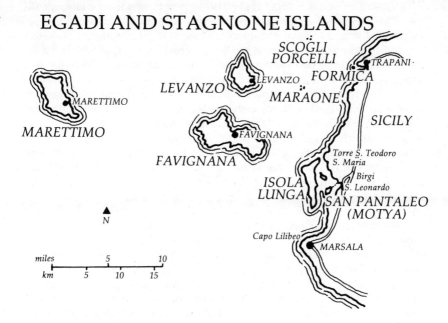

the glacial periods and the rising sea level.

Because of the currents, the sea around the Egadi Islands is extremely rich with fish, especially tuna, which pass through the channel dividing Favignana from the Formiche islets between April and July, the period of the famous *Mattanza* or tuna slaughter. Among the Neolithic paintings in the Grotta del Genovese on the island of Levanzo are several of tuna fish, perhaps a mainstay in the diet even then. A sacred ritual developed around the *Mattanza* which still exists today, although modern techniques of catching the tuna have made inroads on the tradition.

Each of the Egadi Islands has a unique beauty and personality of its own. Favignana, the largest and by far the most populated, is the island of tufa and tuna, and nowadays of tourism too; Levanzo, the smallest island, is quaint and rocky; mountainous Marettimo has fascinating rock formations and grottoes and a charming fishing village scarcely touched by the passing of time. In his book *The Authoress of the Odyssey*, Samuel Butler claimed that Marettimo was the Ithaca of Odysseus, and that Homer was actually the princess Naussica of ancient Trapani. Later writers have supported his theory, including Robert Graves.

247

What traces we have today of the various people who lived on the islands for 12 millenia are concentrated in the caves of Favignana and Levanzo, many of which were inhabited up to the 17th and 18th centuries AD. Most beautiful and moving, however, are the very first signs left in the Grotta del Genovese some 12 000 years ago, where the people of the Old Stone Age carved pictures of bulls, dancing figures, an ass and a marvellous deer, with incredibly natural and fluid lines. The much later inhabitants of the cave in Neolithic times further adorned the walls with simple black and red paintings, crude beside the art of their Paleolithic ancestors.

Early on, the Egadi Islands found themselves sitting on an important Phoenician trade route and were settled by these Semitic people, although their main centre was Motya, just to the south (see the section on the Stagnone Islands). During the First Punic War, the islands saw many of the sea battles between Rome and Carthage, including the final one in 241 BC. After 20 years of war, both Rome and Carthage decided to end it once and for all, sending their fleets to Lilybaeum (Marsala), the last Punic stronghold on Sicily. The two armadas met just northeast of Favignana, the Romans with 200 new warships, the Carthaginians with 400 ships crammed full of soldiers coming to the rescue of besieged Lilybaeum. Before they could land however, the Romans demolished them, sinking 120 and capturing some 10 000 prisoners. So many Phoenicians died and were washed ashore on a small inlet of Favignana that their blood supposedly gave it the name of Cala Rossa ('red cove').

Although the inhabitants of the islands eventually adopted Roman ways—as witnessed by several buildings, mosaics and the development of the tufa quarries of Favignana—their hearts perhaps were still Phoenician, for several inscriptions from the 1st century BC found in the grottoes are in Punic characters. These same grottoes also bear the later symbols of Paleo-Christianity (4th and 5th centuries). An interesting inscription found in the Grotta della Stele on Favignana is linguistically important for determining the evolution of languages in the Mediterranean, as well as offering an insight into the life of the island's troglodytes: translated it means 'House, tomb, stable.'

After the Fall of Rome little is known about what happened to the Egadi Islands. The Saracens used them as a base for their conquest of Sicily, and afterwards, under the Normans, Favignana and Marettimo were fortified. Under the Aragonese the islands became a port of call for Genoese merchant vessels; some of the sailors from Levanto near Genoa gave Levanzo its modern name. When the Spanish established a base at Marsala, the Egadi Islands saw many of their comings and goings and encounters with the Turks. The Spanish were the first to develop on a large scale the great banks of coral around the islands, although most of the profits of this went to the Trapanese.

Spain's never-ending wars caused ever-increasing debts, and to help pay them off she sold the Egadi Islands to the Marquis Pallavicino of Genoa in 1637. The Pallavicino family did much to develop the islands economically, and the islanders were finally able to leave their caves to found a town around the Castello San Giacomo (the modern penitentiary), as well as to develop their farms, excavate the tufa of Favignana, plant vineyards on Levanzo, and cut down the forests of Marettimo. The cave houses of Favignana became stalls for sheep and donkeys.

The Bourbons, always looking for somewhere to send their political prisoners, turned Favignana into a penal colony. However, the islanders welcomed the extra income they made selling supplies to the prison and even became known throughout Italy for their kindness and tact as prison guards, so that even today a large proportion of prison guards in Italy are Favignanese.

Since the Egadi Islands lie so close to Marsala, they were liberated from the Bourbons early by Garibaldi, and soon achieved a new prosperity, fishing, farming and digging the tufa to build homes not only on the island but also in Trapani and Tunis. After World War II, however, their economy nosedived, and many emigrated to other parts of Italy and the New World. Only the advent of tourism in the late 1960s and '70s has begun to turn the tide and keep the young people at home.

Favignana

The Phoenician *Katria,* the Greek *Aegusa,* and the medieval *Faugnana* (from *Favonio,* the name of a wind), Favignana today is the capital of the Egadi Islands. Tourist brochures tend to emphasise the island's butterfly shape, although the 'wings' hardly match—the eastern wing is a level plain, pitted with tufa excavations, while the western wing is mountainous. Beyond the Montagna Grossa, the **Boschetto** ('little wood') consists mainly of abandoned farmland but has several very fine examples of Siculo–Arab architecture.

On an island where fishing is such an important industry, it hardly comes as a surprise that the main town is also the port. Known simply as **Favignana,** its dock has two impressive structures on either side of it: the large abandoned **tuna canneries** by a rocky beach, and the house of their founder, the **Palazzo Florio.** This palace, built in 1876 and surrounded by an unkempt garden with only two palm trees and a pine for company, is impressive and melancholy. Built for Ignazio Florio and his family to use during the tuna season, it is today Favignana's Municipio (town hall).

Ignazio Florio, son of a successful tuna entrepreneur in Palermo, bought the Egadi Islands from the last of the Pallavicino family in 1874, and applied his father's new techniques to the industry on Favignana. He built two processing plants (one on Favignana, the other on the islet of Formica) which are outstanding examples of 19th-century industrial architecture, the Alhambras of fish canneries with their arches and ogival doors. His son Vincenzo, through high living and personal tragedy, managed to ruin the business, and a Genoese company took over in 1937, then the S.p.A. da Florio. Today, however, the canneries are just empty galleries; the tuna caught in the *Mattanza* is either served fresh in Sicily or taken to Japan and canned there.

Giving onto the port, the Piazza Europa has a statue of the portly Ignazio Florio, benefactor of Favignana. Behind him stands the **Old Municipio,** in typical 19th-century Italian provincial style with a clock on top. A busy street of shops leads from here to the main Piazza Madrice, named for the **Chiese Madrice** at the end of the long square. Built in 1704, the Marquis Pallavi-

250

cino insisted that it should be out of range of the Forte San Giacomo, directly in front, which is why the church was constructed in its unprepossessing location.

The **Forte San Giacomo,** today a maximum-security prison, served an important role in Favignana's defence from the time of its foundation in 1120 by King Roger. Rebuilt in 1498 under orders of Ferdinand II the Catholic, it was converted into a prison in 1837 by the Bourbons, who had many uprisings to deal with that year. Unfortunately, the Forte cannot be visited. But near here is the **studio** of local artist Zu Sarina, whose smiling, childlike tufa heads add a charming note to many homes.

To the right of the church lies the old part of town, the **Rione Sant' Anna,** with its narrow streets and typical houses made of native tufa. Just behind this are several examples of abandoned tufa quarries, unremoved bricks carved in the walls and a luxuriant garden invariably at the bottom, protected from the wind. There are tufa dovecots and tufa well covers and tufa roadside shrines. Some of the newer buildings on the outskirts of town have been unhappily whitewashed, as modern architecture in the Mediterranean seems to dictate. As can be seen in Sant' Anna, however, the natural colour of the volcanic tufa is quite pretty, as well as versatile.

The **public telephone** is at Piazza Europa 45, the **post office** near the Piazza Madrice. The Arte Sport Sub (Via Roma) will care for the needs of underwater sportsmen, and boats may be hired at Leonardo, the fishermen's port (north of the commercial dock). Unfortunately Favignana has no regular public transport. Although you can see a great deal on foot, people with only a short time to spend on the island will probably wish they had a car or bicycle since most of the roads here have been asphalted. Hotel minibuses collect guests as they arrive on the hydrofoils or ships.

Eastern Favignana

Heading east from the town along the coast, it is a short walk to the **Punta San Nicola.** Ancient and more recent tufa excavations are very much in evidence, and many of the caves have been inhabited for thousands of years. At San Nicola the island's cemetery has been used since ancient times; indeed, the whole area is full of signs of the generations who lived and died here from the Paleolithic era onwards. Everything looks unorganised, uncared for, since the State hasn't the funds to excavate and explore the area properly. Nearby you can visit the **Grotta del Pazzo,** with late Punic inscriptions and early Christian symbols, and the **Grotta degli Archi,** with several tombs of a Paleo–Christian necropolis dating from the 4th and 5th centuries. To the right of the Cala San Nicola lies the entrance to the so-called **Bagno delle Donne** ('the women's bath') of Roman date, where water was pumped in from the sea. Traces of mosaics found here were put in the Antiquarium, but this too has closed for lack of funds.

A cross on the road to Cala San Nicola marks the crossroads to Cala Rossa at the eastern end of Favignana. Among the abandoned fields are two enormous abandoned tufa quarries. An overgrown path from the electric plant nearby leads to a prehistoric tomb cut in the rock, and further up there is a ledge with an excellent view of Favignana's coast. At **Cala Rossa,** ancient tufa quarries in the rock have left wonderfully unnatural towers of clean-cut angles and long underground galleries, like a ruined, imaginary city. If you can get to Cala Rossa before dawn, the chances are very good of seeing the *Fata Morgana,* a meteorological phenomenon that causes mirages over **Punta San Vituzzo,** similar to the one in Messina. According to the islanders, the mirage once saved the island from Turkish pirates, when it formed the illusion of a great fleet approaching on the horizon. At other times they say it looks like a vast army marching over the sea, or an invasion of Japanese monsters.

Those determined to walk around the eastern wing of Favignana can take the path from Cala Rossa south to **Punta Marsala** and the distant lighthouse facing the port of the same name. The dirt road west of here passes the **Cala Canaleddi,** also known as Cala Azzurra for the intense blue of the sea next to the almost snowy whiteness of the rocks around it. At the far end of the bay stands the modern white hotel complex of Villagio Punta Fanfalo, which has little to recommend it aesthetically.

The road continues up the wild coast to the picturesque **Grotta Perciata** ('pierced cave'), on the other side of which a tiny harbour can hold a total of three small fishing boats. Then comes Punta and **Lido Burrone,** a 15-minute walk from the port. This long stretch of sand facing a shallow sea is the best beach on Favignana, and although there are several villas nearby it could hardly be said to be spoiled. To the west the rocky coast towards the promontory of **Punta Longa** constitutes the 'head' of the Favignana butterfly. A seldom-used road covers the short distance from here to the town.

Western Favignana

From Favignana town a mule path zigzags up the mountain to **Forte Santa Caterina** but, sad to say, this is a military zone and it cannot be visited without special permission. Originally built by the Saracens, Roger II of Sicily renovated it in the 12th century and used it as a watchtower. Further additions were made in 1498 and 1655, and during the reign of the Bourbons it held some of the most notable figures of the Risorgimento, the Italian national renaissance leading up to the unification of Italy.

The Montagna Grossa (highest peak: Monte Santa Caterina, 1010 ft) makes a fairly effective barrier to the west side of the island; the one paved road skirts the extreme southern edge of the mountains at the **Scindo Passo.** Numerous islets and rocks adorn the coast here, offering safe havens for the much pursued fish of Favignana. The largest islet, **Preveto,** once supported a colony of wild rabbits, but eager hunters have since eliminated them all.

This part of the island, euphemistically called **Il Bosco** ('the wood') is nothing more than several hectares of abandoned farmland. Near the Case Casino the paved road forks, one branch leading to the south side of **Cala Grande** and the Villagio Approdo di Ulisse, the hotel for underwater enthusiasts, for this part of the island is richest in fishy prey. Near the village you can see an **ancient well** with a pendulum mechanism, still used by the few farmers who live in the area.

The northern fork of the paved road leads to **Punta Sottile** on the northern point of Cala Grande, where there is a lighthouse. An unpaved track to the right, halfway to the lighthouse, leads past the coast at Calazza to **Faraglione,** a strange rocky landscape more typical of Utah than the Mediterranean. The Faraglione itself, a steep-edged peninsula, offers a fine view of Levanzo a short distance away. Just below the Faraglione lies the entrance to a wonderful cave, the **Grotta delle Uccerie** (take an electric torch) with beautiful coloured stalactites which join the roof to the floor of the cave like columns. There are actually two chambers, the second less desecrated by souvenir-hunting shepherds.

FESTIVALS

In May and June it is possible to witness the *Mattanza* (the tuna massacre), a wild and bloody spectacle. The tuna return from the Atlantic through the Straits of Gibraltar to breed in the warmer waters of the Mediterranean, the currents pushing them towards their destiny off the island of Favignana. Here, beside the upside-down cross of St Peter suspended over the water, they swim into the tuna coral (the *tonnara*) where they are trapped. Under the command of the *Rais*, the *Mattanza* chief, the fishermen chant their traditional songs about the saints while slowly raising the great net. The fish struggle and squirm in their frenzy as the net is hoisted higher and higher in the water. Then, one by one, the fishermen impale and drag their silvery victims into the boats, and when the last 300–400 lb fish is lugged aboard, then the fishermen gather their great net and take the catch home. Usually the fishermen make enough money from the two or three months of the *Mattanza* to tide them over until the next year.

Port of Levanzo, The Egadi Islands

Levanzo

At 2.2 square miles, Levanzo is the smallest of the Egadi Islands. In ancient times it was known as *Phorbanzia* or *Bucinna*; the Saracens called it 'dry' (*Gazirat al ya bisah*), and in the Renaissance it became *Levanto*. Unlike Favignana and Marettimo, Levanzo has no fresh water, which keeps its population down to a minimum (about 2000), concentrated around the Cala Dogana. The entire coastline is rocky and inaccessible except for a few inlets. Inland, a charming valley used mainly as pastureland is surrounded by hills, the highest being the Pizzo del Monaco (910 ft). Although there is but one small hotel on the island, Levanzo has a major attraction in its prehistoric artwork at the Grotta del Genovese.

The town and port of **Levanzo,** its houses gazing over the sea towards Favignana, exemplifies Schumacher's theory that 'small is beautiful'. Even the dogs have nothing better to do all day but sleep in the middle of the street, letting cats and even tourists walk by unmolested. Fishing and dairy cattle provide a decent, simple living for the islanders, although some of them commute to work in Trapani. They are an extraordinarily friendly folk, and seem to spend a good deal of their free time collectively spoiling the three or four little children who live on Levanzo.

A 20-minute walk along the dirt road west of the port takes you to the **Faraglione,** an odd-shaped rock off the rugged coast. This same track leads up the coast and through the hills to the Grotta del Genovese, although the route through the centre of the island is shorter and more

scenic. To see the Grotta you must contact its custodian, Giuseppe Castiglione, who lives directly above the hydrofoil dock (Via Calvario 11; tel.
921704). The ideal way to get there is by mule; you may get a ride in a jeep
or else you can walk—a pleasant enough proposition if it's not too hot.
Ideally you can go out in the morning with Signore Castiglione.

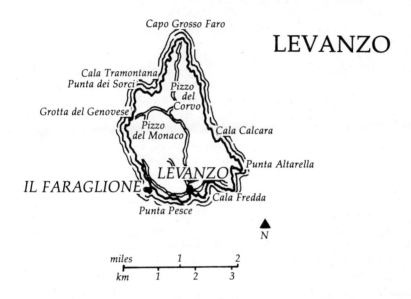

The main road branches off to the left after about an hour's walk,
descending towards Punta del Genovese (named for the 16th-century
Genoese who used Levanzo as a port for their sailing ships). About 100 ft
above the sea opens the dark entrance of the **Grotta del Genovese,** discovered in 1949 by an artist, Francesca Minellono, who was on holiday on
Levanzo. The incisions on the walls were made by Paleolithic Man while
Levanzo was still part of Sicily, 6000 years ago, and are as fragile as they are
magnificent. The beautiful deer beside the entrance is under a protective
glass because the slightest touch causes the stone to crumble. The stylised
paintings of men and women, tuna fish and unfinished animals by Neolithic
artists, 2000 years later, are not as skilful; their magic was apparantly of a
different variety. In all there are 29 animals and 4 human figures by the earliest artists, and several confused rows of painted figures by the later ones,

255

all in the second, closed-off chamber of the cave to which Signore Castiglione has the key.

The **public telephone** is at Vita Azzaro's. For **bottle service** contact Nitto Mineo, Via Calvario 39. Besides the port, there are isolated rocky 'beaches' at Cala Fredda, Cala Minnola, Cala Tramontana and Cala Calcara (easier to reach by boat).

Marettimo

Marettimo, the first island to break away from Sicily, is also the furthest away—and not only in distance. The men of Marettimo, invariably fishermen, have little to do with Favignana or Sicily; proud, soft-spoken and independent, they stick to their magnificent rocky island, their simple houses, their families and their brightly painted boats. The glamour and money of the tourist industry hold no attraction for them, and even though the big names of tourism have plans for the construction of x number of hotels with x number of beds, the islanders haven't made any moves towards that goal. Visitors are kindly received into their own homes, and several Italians from the mainland have built summer villas on Marettimo. That is the extent of tourism on Marettimo.

The sheer dramatic beauty of its coastline and numerous grottoes puts Marettimo into the same class as Capri, yet you can only know it by sea. The mountainous hinterland of the island is almost inaccessible. One bumpy track follows the southern coast to the lighthouse, another winds up to the Semaforo on Punta Lisandro. The highest point, Monte Falcone (2235 ft), is by far the highest peak in the Egadi Islands. These mountains, apart from the *macchia*, are barren rocks, although pine trees have been planted with some success. The ancient names of the island, *Iera* (sacred) in Greek, and *Malitimah* in Arabic (whence comes Marettimo), are of uncertain derivation.

The village of **Marettimo,** on the eastern side, is the only inhabited place on the island, its growth limited by the dominating mountain directly behind it. There are two piers protruding on either side of town: the **Scala Nuovo,** recently constructed for the delicate hydrofoils, and the **Scala Vecchia,** the fishermen's port, with the fine red, white and blue fishing boats—some purchased with money raised in Anchorage, Alaska, expressly for the purpose of buying boats for Marettimo. The main street has the few shops needed to supply the 800 residents, as well as Marettimo's one church which is built over an old warehouse, and takes care of their religious needs. The silent side streets, many quite narrow, have several pretty corners, although dec-

Punta due Frati
Punta Mugnone — *Scalo Maestro* *Grotto dell Tuone*
Castello di Punta Troia
Capo Bianco
Cala Bianca *Cala Manione*
BARRANCO
Grotta Perciata ∧ *Grotta Cammello*
Mt Falcone
GIRODIFALCO
Punta Pegna *Scala Vecchio*
Grotta Presepio *Roman houses* **MARETTIMO**
Grotta della Bombarda *Scalo Nuovo*
SPALMATORE
MARETTIMO *Punta Libeccio* *lighthouse semaphore*
∧
Punta Lisandro
Punta Cretazzo *Cala Marino*
Punta Galera
▲
N *Punta Martino*

miles 1 2
km 1 2 3

oration is certainly minimal. There are beaches on either side of the town's promontory, the only ones on Marettimo.

All excursions from the town on foot are a bit on the arduous side, and shouldn't be attempted in the noonday sun of August. The path leading up to the abandoned Semaforo also leads to a spring, and to the **Case Romane,** about a 45-minute climb from the port. The Case is a late Roman defensive work and quite well preserved. Next to it lies a tiny anonymous **church,** built in the 12th century and showing very obvious Arabic influences, with barrel vaulting and central rounded drum, a design unique in Italy. Thought to have been built by the Byzantine monks allowed to pursue their religion in Sicily by the two Rogers, this lovely little piece of ecclesiastical architecture has become dilapidated over the past few decades and needs some major restoration work.

The one road south of the village leads to the lighthouse on the western coast. Pine trees have been planted along the sides of the road, making the walk shady and pleasant, although the way is often tortuous. The scenery is splendid, especially on the western coast, where the sight of the steep vertical cliffs plunging into the sea is awesome. Just beyond the lighthouse, a path leads down to the Cala Nera, where you can swim off the rocks.

A path north of the town (or take a boat) leads to the **Castello di Punta Troia,** built on a precipice over the sea, and connected to Marettimo by an isthmus. There is a spring of fresh water by the isthmus to refresh the weary traveller before making the winding climb up the 380 feet to the castle. The original tower on this site was built by the Saracens in the 9th century; Roger II enlarged it, and the Spanish completed the existing building in the 17th century. They also constructed cisterns here, and a small church (the only one on Marettimo until 1844), and a prison so inhuman and cruel that when Ferdinand II, the Bourbon King of the Two Sicilies, visited it in 1844 he ordered it closed—he who founded so many other prisons all over the Italian islands. Some marvellous views of Marettimo and the sea can be had from the castle terrace.

GETTING TO AND AROUND THE EGADI ISLANDS
The Siremar line operates all the ferries to the islands, and all depart from the port of Trapani.

Three days a week (Tuesday, Friday and Sunday) the ferry makes the grand tour of all three islands, leaving early in the morning for the 3-hour cruise, returning immediately. On the other days (Monday, Wednesday, Thursday, and Saturday) there is no service to Marettimo, but 2 daily runs (3 in the summer) to Levanzo and Favignana only.

You needn't inconvenience yourself, though, unless you have a car, for there are always hydrofoils—the 'school buses' for the Egadi children. Even in winter there are 6 a day to Favignana, 4 continuing to Levanzo, and 2 reach Marretimo, with a few extra in the high season. It's always easy to hop from one island to another—providing you can decipher the complicated schedules.

TOURIST INFORMATION
On Favignana there's a Pro Loco information office in the town at Piazza Madrice 7 (tel. (0923) 21647).

WHERE TO STAY
Favignana is the only island equipped to handle a large number of visitors, with hotels and campsites. On Levanzo and Marettimo the accommodation is rustic and simple. All islands have rooms available in private houses; spending a few days among a family is usually a very rewarding experience if you are friendly and speak a little Italian.

In Favignana, the two resort hotels with pretentions are the **L'Approdo di Ulisse***** (at Cala Grande, tel. (0923) 921287, 34 000 lire single, 53 500 double) and the **Punta Fanfalo***** (Punta Fanfalo, tel. (0923) 921777, 23–

34 000 single, 42–54 000 double). Both have pools and a stretch of sea-shore. There are no pretensions at all at the **Tourist Village 4 Rose**—named by the owner, a retired migrant from Trenton, New Jersey, after his favorite whisky. He also runs a campsite, restaurant, and disco, with the aid of his several cats and one monkey (tel. (0923) 921223, 15 000 for a single, 26 000 double).

Levanzo's only hotel is the **Paradiso*** (tel. (0923) 921580, 13–17 000 single, 21–27 000 double).

WHERE TO EAT
An inexpensive restaurant on Favignana, where you can try several different seafood and pasta concoctions, is **Angelo e Peppe**, Piazza Madrice 63 (15 000 lire). **La Tavernetta**, a few doors away at no. 59, is a little dearer but the seafood is a little better. Couscous, the speciality of Trapani province is also the speciality at **Trattoria del Matteo**, Via V. Emmanuele 19, for 20 000 lire. There are simple, but good fish restaurants as well on Levanzo and Marettimo, but they're open only in the summer.

The Stagnone Islands

Just off the coast north of Marsala in western Sicily are the three Stagnone Islands: Isola Lunga, Isola San Pantaleo and Isola Santa Maria. Isola Lunga (or Grande) runs along the coast, protecting the two smaller islands from the high seas. This neat arrangement wasn't always the case. In the 4th century BC Isola Lunga was connected to Sicily at Capo San Teodoro; by the 3rd century BC the Carthaginians had dug two canals (*fretum*) through Isola Lunga, dividing it in two and separating it from the mainland, although not at Punta di Tramontana but across the present saltpans. Today Punta di Tramontana and San Teodoro are separated by a strait less than a quarter of a mile wide. Even stranger is the road 3 ft under the sea, built by the Phoenicians, connecting San Pantaleo (ancient *Motya*) to the mainland necropolis at Birgi, near where the airport is today. Of all the islands in this book, San Pantaleo is the only one you can walk to if you don't mind getting your trousers wet.

These islands, belonging to the commune of Marsala, are uninhabited except for the caretaker and his family on San Pantaleo. Isola Lunga, strangely beautiful with its saltflats (exploited since the 15th century), lagoons and numerous windmills, has been declared a Regional Park. The few men who still work the saltpans live on the mainland. What the park authorities are really interested in, however, is fish farming on or near the island. Archaeologists, for their part, have a treasure trove off the coast of Isola Lunga; here Honor Frost and her team discovered the Punic ship dating from the wars with Rome that is now in Marsala.

To visit Isola Lunga, see the tourist office in Trapani or Marsala for information on obtaining permisson from the park authorities. Isola Santa Maria is off limits, being owned by a private family who spend their summers in a villa here, while visitors to San Pantaleo and the extremely interesting ruins of the Phoenician city of Motya need written permission either from the Superintendent of Antiquities in the Archaeology Museum in Palermo, or from the Fondazione Giuseppe Whitaker in Marsala (Via Garraffa 74). The telephone number of the caretaker is (0923) 959598; call him to make an appointment and he'll pick you up in his boat from the quay near San Leonardo. Allow at least half a day to see the ruins properly.

San Pantaleo

HISTORY

The Phoenicians founded Motya in the 8th century BC, and it soon became one of their most important trading posts in Sicily, mainly doing business with the mother city Carthage. Some of the ceramics excavated from this earliest period have distinct Cypriot and Palestinian influences, examples of the extensive cultures the Phoenicians came in contact with through trade.

Motya soon became a force to be reckoned with in western Sicily, and the rapid colonisation of the eastern part of the large island by the Greeks gave them much concern. For the Phoenicians, control of the trade route was of vital importance, and the Greeks were muscling in on their business. To protect themselves, other colonies were founded on Sardinia at Nora, Sulcis and Tharros. When a company of Greeks attempted to colonise Lilybaeum (Marsala), Motya and Segesta, the Punic ally in the northwest of Sicily joined forces to kick them out. The few Greeks who survived the battle ended up on Lipari in the Aeolian Islands.

To keep the Greeks on their own side of Sicily, Carthage and Motya mounted a successful campaign between 560 and 550 BC. Motya was heavily fortified, and the city became so large that the necropolis had to be transferred to the mainland at Birgi—hence the famous submerged road, which oxcarts carrying goods could use as well as funeral processions.

In 510 BC, Motya and Segesta again united to drive out a hopeful Greek colony on the west coast. This was the beginning of the long drawn-out war between Greeks and Carthaginians for the rule of Sicily, a war that never really ended until the Romans defeated Hannibal in the Second Punic War.

The Greeks and Romans regarded the Phoenicians not only as a powerful enemy but also as heathens who believed in the ritual sacrifice of infants— not people they wanted living next door to them. When the united Greek forces defeated the Great Carthaginian army in the Battle of Himera (480 BC), the Greeks took the usual prisoners and demanded ransoms and fines, and also ordered the Carthaginians–Phoenicians to stop sacrificing babies. Motya survived the war and continued trading with the Greek cities—one of the reasons, perhaps, why the Greeks didn't rout the Phoenicians once and for all from Sicily when they had the chance. They probably wished they had when in 409 Motya assisted Segesta and Carthage in destroying Selinunte and, three years later, Akragas, one of the most splendid Greek cities that ever existed. Only the outbreak of plague in the Punic army prevented the destruction of mighty Syracuse and the rest of Hellenised Sicily.

At that time the tyrant Dionysius was holding the reins in Syracuse. Dionysius was one of history's great politicians; he faked a peace treaty with Carthage, then began to amass his forces. He summoned engineers from all corners to invent new weapons, and sent out propaganda to unite the independent Greek cities against the Barbarian threat. After nine years all was ready and in 397 BC the Greeks set sail with a powerful fleet to destroy Motya, the heart of Phoenician power in Sicily.

The ensuing battle was one of the most curious in ancient history. The Motyans boxed themselves in on their tiny island, walled up their gates and cut their marvellous road to Birgi, then sent to Carthage for help. At this time Isola Lunga was a huge peninsula surrounding Motya, and the only outlet to the sea was to the south, near Marsala. It was so narrow that only one ship could pass through at a time.

Dionysius landed 80 000 soldiers, who camped at Birgi. They destroyed the Carthaginian–Elymnian strongholds of Segesta, Eryx and Soluntum and repaired the underwater road to Motya to transport their secret weapons. Carthage meanwhile sent a fleet to attack Syracuse, to lure Dionysius from Motya. But Syracuse was well defended, and Dionysius couldn't be distracted from his prey. Himilco, the Carthaginian general, then decided to make a sneak attack on the Greek ships, breached at Punta Palermo.

At dawn the Carthaginians struck. Dionysius quickly brought his army from Birgi to Punta Palermo, along with his secret weapons—the catapult, huge spiked flaming projectiles and other war machines never seen or used before. These caused such destruction and panic among the Punic fleet that Himilco could do nothing but withdraw, but he withdrew in such a way that the Greek fleet was left trapped in Motya's unusual harbour: only one ship could leave at a time, and it would be a sitting duck for the Carthaginians.

Quickly assessing the situation, Dionysius had a brilliant idea. While leaving part of his army to hold off the Punic fleet with their horrible weapons, he ordered the others to chop down hundreds of trees and lay the trunks along the 1½-mile peninsula of Isola Lunga to the open sea. As Himilco and the Carthaginians watched in disbelief, the Greeks then pushed their entire fleet across land and in turn began to surround them.

Himilco couldn't take any more. He ordered a quick retreat and sailed for Africa to escape the Greeks' monstrous weapons and ships that 'sailed' across the land. Without even giving battle, he left Motya to its fate.

Dionysius destroyed the city and its inhabitants with a vengeance. The Greek residents of the city who took refuge in Motya's Greek temple were either spared to become slaves, or, according to another account, crucified. The island city was never rebuilt; when Himilco returned to the scene of battle he chose Lilybaeum (Marsala) for his new base.

At the beginning of the 20th century, one of the great English wine merchants of Marsala, Joseph (Pip) Whitaker, took an interest in the island of Motya, by now known as San Pantaleo. Strange rocks had been found under the roots of the vineyards planted there, and Whitaker, fascinated by the excavations of Troy and Crete, bought the island in order to do some archaeological research of his own. He spent so much time digging on the island that he built a villa, and planted the trees that beautify the island today.

WHAT TO SEE
The fascinating **ruins of ancient Motya** occupy most of the island, many of them still unexcavated. Near the port are the **city walls** that proved so useless without the power of the Punic fleet to support them, and a **cemetery,** dating from the 8th–6th centuries BC, before the necropolis was established at Birgi. There is also a **temple,** dedicated to the goddess Tanit who protected the Phoenicians in return for the lives of their first-born, and you can still see the **Cothon,** the artificial harbour surrounded by walls. Near here begins the **submerged highway** to Birgi. In the residential area of Motya are the ruins of numerous houses, some with mosaics, one a particularly fine carpet of black and white pebbles with lions. The foundations of a 6th-century **Greek-style temple** demonstrate how the Phoenicians learned to imitate techniques from the countries they traded with; while the **Tophet,** where the babies were sacrificed, betrays their true barbaric sentiments. More than 1000 small burial urns (some still containing the tiny bones of the victims) and grave-marking steles carved with the various fashionable symbols of cruel Tanit have been uncovered and may be seen in the **Whitaker Museum** on the site. Other interesting items in the museum

include a beautiful enamelled vase in the Egyptian style of the time, and a carved group of lions attacking a bull, found at Motya's north port and believed to be of Mycenean origin.

Pantelleria

The island of Pantelleria lies 70 miles southwest of Sicily and 50 miles west of Cape Bon, Tunisia. Its 32 square miles merit a dot on most maps, but its distant location attracts few foreigners apart from archaeologists and anthropologists, the latter considering it to be one of the last truly agricultural communities in Europe. Students of architecture come to examine the *dammuso* style of homes built by the natives, and ecology students come to observe their admirable management of natural resources.

In short, Pantelleria is one of the most unusual islands in the Mediterranean. Despite determined efforts to develop it as a holiday paradise, with the same bright white hotels you see everywhere else along the coasts of the *Mare Nostrum*, there is an equally determined group of people who want Pantelleria to retain its ethnological identity, encouraging visitors to stay in the traditional *dammuso* houses, to understand the way of life that once existed throughout Europe. It isn't easy, however, to compete with the easy money that tourists will pay to lie in the sun. At the moment, 60% of Pantelleria's income still comes from agriculture (*zibibbo* grapes and capers), while 40% derives from tourism. Perhaps both sides can claim victory from these figures.

HISTORY

The elusiveness that characterises Pantelleria begins with its history. The product of innumerable volcanic eruptions, the island may once have been landlocked between Sicily and North Africa before the continents drifted apart. Volcanic eruptions occurred well into the period of human habitation. One clue, a fragment of handworked stone found under the basalt of a late eruption in the Quaternary Period, suggests some kind of aboriginal people.

A little more is known of the people who settled Pantelleria in the 18th century BC. These Neolithic immigrants were probably a tribe of Pelagians, a name which confusingly includes many different people in different places, in this instance from Tunisia. At Mursia, on the Cimillia shore of Pantelleria, they built a village and the strange stone *sesi* unique to the island. Although they bear a resemblance to the Sardinian *nuraghes* and the Neolithic monuments on the Iberian peninsula, Paolo Orsi, the great Sicil-

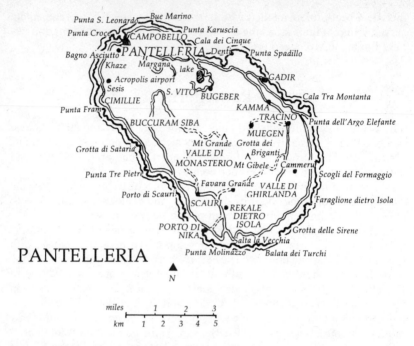

PANTELLERIA

▲
N

miles | 1 | 2 | 3
km | 1 2 3 4 5

ian archaeologist, believes they were built by a different people; the *sesi*, more primitive in construction and technique, may have been the ancestor of more refined structures found elsewhere.

The *sesi* is a circular domed structure made of natural volcanic rock, somewhat resembling the modern *dammuso* of the island. Within the thick walls are various entrances into tomb-like cells, still in the wall itself, while the actual interior of the *sesi*, with a floor of beaten earth and pebbles, has no entrance at all. The purpose of the *sesi* is a mystery, but defence has been almost ruled out, for the Neolithic village is protected by strong walls which have given it its name *Alta Mura* ('high wall').

An upsurge in volcanic activity is thought to have caused the village's abandonment. A poor place, it must have only been a base for those sailing on to bigger and better things.

In the 7th century BC, the Phoenicians founded a colony on Pantelleria and named it *Hiranin* ('isle of birds') or *Cossyra* ('the smaller'), referring to the larger size of Malta not far away. The wealth of Cossyra was earned by trade, and the island's settlements were invariably clustered around small harbours providing refuge in bad weather. The main town stood at the site

264

of the modern *centro urbano*, with an acropolis on the northeast side of San Marco hill.

Because of its location, Pantelleria became a bone of contention in the Punic Wars. Rome took it during the First Punic War in 255 BC, but lost it a year later. In the Second Punic War Rome regained and kept it, an event celebrated by the minting of coins and a holiday in Rome. The Romans administered the island from Lilybaeum (Marsala) and used it as a place of exile for over-demanding soldiers during times of peace.

The Romans were succeeded by the Vandals, the Byzantines and most importantly the Arabs, who perhaps more than anyone shaped modern Pantelleria. They called it *Ghusiras* at first, and then *Bent el rion* ('daughter of the wind'). Many place-names on the island—such as Zighidi, Khagiar and Bugeber—recall the Arabs' domination, like the names of towns in modern Malta. Unlike all the previous inhabitants of Pantelleria, the Arabs were farmers, and they were the first to cultivate the rich red soil of the island. They introduced vineyards, cotton, vegetables, citrus and palm trees, as well as barley, with which they made a long-lasting hard bread, common until recently. They also built irrigation systems and *dammuso* houses all over the island to be near their fields.

When the Normans conquered Sicily they took Pantelleria as well, and it has been ruled from Sicily ever since. Politically its history is the same, but the constant flow of events made little difference to the good islanders, who lived mainly around the port. The island was owned by various noble families who had done the king of Sicily a good turn; one family, the Requesens, proudly attached the title of 'Prince of Pantelleria' to their leading male. Their presence was noticeable only at tax time. Their ownership of the land, however, prevented all but 12% of it from being cultivated.

The 19th century brought winds of change. An odd portent of this occurred in 1831, when volcanic activity around Pantelleria caused the appearance of an islet off the southern coast of Sicily. The islet stayed around long enough to cause an international incident, then blithely disappeared (see Sciacca, in Agrigento Province; p. 190).

In 1845, feudal rights were abolished in Sicily and the land was redistributed among the people, so that by the turn of the century 50% of the island was under cultivation. Because both male and female children were now equally entitled to inherit their parents' land, the farms of Pantelleria were gradually divided into smallholdings—and the people now have fewer children.

During World War II the Fascists made Pantelleria their main base in the central Mediterranean, fortifying it and building an airport. When North Africa fell to the Allies, the base became crucial to both sides; the Allies had to take it before beginning the invasion of Sicily, to protect their rear. On 8 May 1943, the bombs began to fall, day and night. Pantelleria held out until 11 June; then, flattened and blockaded, the 11 000 soldiers stationed on the island surrendered and were taken prisoner.

Pantelleria today has one souvenir of the war that won't go away: the brutal concrete reconstruction of its main town, after the pleasant original was bombed beyond repair (see photos in lobby of Hotel Agadir). At best it's ugly and functional, at worst it's as spooky as any post-war town in Italy. If you come to Pantelleria by ship, it's a wretched introduction to an otherwise exceptionally charming island. The one old building still standing, the black reconstructed Spanish castle, isn't even very interesting. Next to it stands a hideous church; from here buses depart for Scauri and Tracino 5 times a day.

FESTIVALS
SS Pietro and Paolo (29 June). The Feast of the Three Maries (10–13 July). A Pantellerian handicraft exhibition (end of June through the first week of August). Horse race around the lake on the Assumption (15 August).

SPECIALITIES
Most famous is the raisin wine known as *Tanit,* made from *zibibbo* grapes, although other good wines come from Scauri, both reds and whites. Other favourites are *tumma* cheese, made from curdled milk; fish and vegetable couscous; *pesto pantesco,* a sauce made from tomatoes, garlic, pepper and basil; and *ravioli amari,* made with ricotta and mint.

GETTING AROUND PANTELLERIA
The Alitalia office by the AGIP station has a bus which connects with all flights to and from the island—get there an hour before your plane leaves. In summer the agency Santoro (Via Borgo Italia) runs chartered day excursions by air to Tunis. Santoro and Nautica Cossyra (Via Punta Croce) have boats to hire for excursions around the island, as well as for skindivers.

Those interested in the cultural aspects of Pantelleria should contact the Gruppo Etnologico Pantesco, Corso Umberto 66 (tel. (0923) 911029), which among other things can arrange for you to spend a night in a *dammuso.* In July you can talk to the professors at the Centre for Advanced Studies in Environmental Design at Cala Tramontana.

WHAT TO SEE
The ideal way of seeing the rest of Pantelleria is to take one of the two buses to some point in the countryside, and then walk. You have to take your time in order to absorb what is special about the island, the subtle beauty of the domed *dammuso* houses surrounded by drystone walls and the neat

266

vineyards that form beautiful designs all over the landscape. On one side stands the Monte Grande, a spent volcano (2743 ft) and a major landmark in this part of the Mediterranean; on the other is the crystal blue of the clean sea, with a wealth of lobsters, sponges and coral, which is exported to the coral-working industries of Torre del Greco in the Bay of Naples. In places you can see the old Arab irrigation system and the cisterns, some of which were originally catacombs—on Pantelleria nothing is wasted.

Along the road behind the town towards the airport, a branch to the right leads to Cossyra's **acropolis,** directly above the ancient town. Although only a few walls and foundations remain, there are some nice views. Another old road before the airport leads to the church of the **Madonna della Margana,** dedicated to the patroness of the island, which contains a picture of the Virgin and Child (15th or 16th century) salvaged from a ship-wreck. When the oxen pulling the cart with the image refused to budge when they arrived at Margana, it was interpreted as God's will, and a church was built on the spot. In the winter months the image is kept in the Chiesa Matrice in town.

Past the airport, the road across the centre of Pantelleria passes the pretty old town of **Siba,** where you can see some of the oldest *dammusos* on the island, with barrel roofs; the weight of the dome rests on the two longer walls of the houses. A rough track from here, suitable only for jeeps or mules, leads to the summit of **Monte Grande** with a panorma of the entire island. The nearby **Grotta dei Briganti** is associated with legends of bri-gands and other undesirables who made it their secret headquarters. Below Monte Grande lie two of the finest valleys on Pantelleria: the **Valle di Mon-asterio,** named after a derelict Benedictine abbey, and the **Valle di Ghir-landa** to the east, with the most fertile soil on the island, where the grapes are reputed to grow as large as plums.

The north coast (bus terminus at Tracino)

At **Campobello,** just east of Pantelleria town, the coast is level enough to permit bathing—but don't expect any wide stretches of sand; the coast, for the most part, is a picturesque tumble of volcanic rock. The famous lake near Campobello known as the **Specchio di Venere** ('Venus' mirror') is actually an old crater, a third of a mile in diameter. Supplied by the sea, a volcanic phenomenon called the *Mofette* makes the shores of the lake white, warm and highly alkaline. In summer, the fastest horses on Pantelleria take part in the festive races around the lake. A paved road along the shore leads up to the ancient town of **Bugeber,** with the best view over the constantly changing colours of the lake.

The main road (and the bus) continues further east to the wild, lovely

Cala dei Cinque Denti ('inlet of five teeth'), where the craggy blocks of lava under the cliffs do indeed look like a set of monster teeth. Just past the lighthouse to the east is **Gadir,** with its little bay, the prettiest fishing village on Pantelleria. The mildly radioactive black sand and hot spring on the shore make for a remarkable rustic spa; when you swim off Gadir you can feel the heat in the sea. Still further east is **Kamma,** a large sprawling village just above the **Punta dell' Arco Elefante** ('the elephant's head rock') beside the sea. The innovative *dammusos* built by the people of Kamma have been studied by the students of the Environmental Design Centre near Tracino, but even people who know nothing about 'environmental design' can appreciate the skill and imagination of the native builders. Above Kamma a path leads up to **Muegen,** an abandoned village of very old *dammusos* on the slope of Monte Grande. Enthusiastic hikers can follow the trail down to the Ghirlanda valley (road also from Kamma) where among the richest vineyards are **Neolithic tombs** and grottoes. Off the coast are some rocks with an unusual name: Cheese Reef (Scogli del Formaggio).

The extreme southeast coast of Pantelleria is known as **Dietro Isola** ('back of the island'), only accessible by private transport, for there are no villages in this harsh dry area. One of the inlets, the **Balata dei Turchi,** was supposedly the place where Turkish pirates landed and were thwarted by the islanders. Nearby, to the west, a 600-ft precipice towering over the sea has been curiously dubbed the **Salta la Vecchia** ('old lady's leap').

The southwest coast (bus terminus at Scauri)
Only a few miles from Pantelleria town there are a number of hotels at **Mursia,** near the ruins of the **Neolithic village** of the Pelagians, and the *sesis* themselves, mysterious and exotic and massive. At Khazen, a natural sauna called **Bagno Asciutto** was carved here in ancient times and may still be used; at Punta Fram to the south you can see the obsidian mines of the Pelagians.

The **Grotta di Sataria** further down the coast contains a notable hot spring, known for curing rheumatism and skin diseases. The water flows into a Roman basin. Here the lava forms canals of volcanic glass known as 'liparite' after the same material on the island of Lipari. Another cave, the **Grotta dello Storto,** may be entered by boat; it is the nesting place for numerous birds.

Scauri has been the second port on the island since Phoenician times, although the town itself stands on a shelf some 300 ft above the sea. The pretty white church forms the focus of the typically pretty cluster of white *dammusos.* There are paths from here leading to the **Valle di Monastero** with Phoenician tombs, and to the fumaroles and hot springs at **Favara**

Grande on the other side of the Torrente Nika, which runs from Monte Grande only in winter and when Pantelleria gets a lot of rain. By the beached fishing boats at Scauri another hot spring is collected in two basins, where it is possible to bathe.

Yet another hot spring rises in the **Grotta di Nika,** near the tiny village of the same name. Best reached by boat, Nika acts as a good base for a tour of the splendid sea grottoes on this part of the coast; also nearby are the awesome cliffs of Dietro Isola. Above Porta di Nika you can walk up to the scarcely-visited village of **Rekale,** another of those places on Pantelleria that does not seem to be a part of the 20th century.

GETTING TO PANTELLERIA
The Siremar ferry from Trapani makes the 4½-hour trip daily in the summer, and 6 days a week (Sunday excepted) from September to June. In addition, there are daily flights from Palermo and Trapani all year round, with some additional services in the summer.

TOURIST INFORMATION
There's a Pro Loco office in the town, at the Palazzo Ufficio on Via San Nicola (tel. (0923) 941838).

WHERE TO STAY
Among several hotels in Pantelleria town, the **Agadir**** (Via Catania; tel. (0923) 911651; 22 000 lire single, 39 000 double) and the **Miryam**** (18–24 000 single, 31–41 500 double) are comfortable. Several holiday hotels have opened, all quite near town, all in the area of Punta Fram–Mursia to the south, except the secluded **Turistico Residenziale**** at Bue Marino north of the town, which has a garden and park (23 000 lire single, 38 000 double).

To stay in a *dammuso* house, contact one of several firms offering short holiday lets like **Dammuso** on the Contrado San Vito (tel. (0923) 911827).

WHERE TO EAT
One speciality of Pantelleria is a variation of the south Sicilian couscous—*cuscus ai pesce,* which you may try at the **Ristorante Miramare** in the town on the Via Borgo Nuovo, or the **Trattoria Castiglione** on Via Napoli, with a good selection of Pantelleria's famous wines (both about 16 000 lire).

The Pelagie Islands

The Pelagie archipelago (from the Greek *Pelagia,* or 'sea islands') consists of three islands: Lampedusa, Linosa and the uninhabited Lampione. Flat, pistol-shaped and wind-whipped, Lampedusa is the largest of the Pelagie group and the southernmost point of the Italian Republic, just a mile closer to Monastir in Tunisia than to Porto Empedocle in Argrigento Province. Even Malta is further north. Geologically Lampedusa belongs to North Africa, while Linosa, a volcanic island, is the last tiny cone to the south of the great volcanic chain stretching from Etna to Vesuvius and the Pontine Islands. Remote, arid and sparsely populated, only recently have the Pelagie Islands attracted many visitors, who come almost exclusively for 'the cleanest sea in Italy' and for the miles and miles which lie between these islands and the industrial regions of the rest of Europe.

HISTORY

Although finds prove that Lampedusa and Linosa were inhabited in ancient times, and the former perhaps used as a Roman base in the Punic Wars, the islands have merited scarce mention in the annals of history, and for the most part were uninhabited and undefended. In 813 they were captured by Saracens who established small colonies on them. A few centuries later, in 1430, King Alfonso V of Aragon ceded the islands to the barons of Caro di Montechiaro. In 1553 the pirate governor of Tunis, Dragut, paid a visit to Lampedusa and carried off 1000 people—the whole population—as slaves, and a few years later the Montechiari built a fortress to defend Lampedusa from further such outrages.

In 1630, Carlos II of Spain gave the title 'Prince of Lampedusa' to Giulio Tomasi di Lampedusa, ancestor of the famous modern novelist Giuseppe Tomasi who wrote *The Leopard*. In 1800, the princes allowed some Maltese colonists, the Gatt family, to farm Lampedusa. Ten years later the Gatts subdivided the island with an Englishman named Alexander Fernandez, who brought 300 colonists of his own.

The modern visitor will find it hard to believe that in those days Lampedusa had trees, fertile soil, deer and wild boars—so totally has all this been destroyed by unwise deforestation and farming (all the topsoil blew away). But Lampedusa appears to have prospered in these early years.

In 1839 the princes of Lampedusa changed their minds about the island, and told the Gatt family and Fernandez they had revoked their rights. The Bourbons were helping neither to maintain nor to defend Lampedusa, so the Tomasi family tried to sell the island to England, who already had nearby Malta. This the Bourbon King Ferdinand II refused to permit, and instead purchased the islands himself for 12 000 ducats.

The first Bourbon colonists arrived on Lampedusa and Linosa in 1848. Thirty years later, the Italian Republic established penal colonies on the islands, much to the colonists' resentment. At the end of the 19th century a

A Fishing Harbour, Pelagie Islands

vast bank of sponges was discovered off the coasts of Lampedusa and Lampione, but the Italian government failed to establish either a sponge industry or telegraph wires to Lampedusa, so the hundreds of sponge fishermen from all over the Mediterranean made Sfax, Tunisia, their port instead.

During World War II the people of Lampedusa were evacuated and the island was turned into a fortress during the North African campaign. On 12 June 1943, the Allied fleet surrounded and bombarded it non-stop until the troops surrendered the next day. The peace treaty of 1947 stipulated that all fortifications on the island be destroyed.

Lampedusa

Lampedusa today is an extreme example of neglect and misuse of resources, its 8 square miles an ecological disaster area. Only a few of the oldest inhabitants can recall the days when the neat drystone walls enclosed rich farmland instead of piles of rock. One of the biggest jokes on the island is the 'national park'—two scrubby trees forever dwarfed by the wind and lack of rainfall. However, the lush greenery and flowers around the Sanctuary of the Madonna di Porto Salvo and a few vineyards recently planted demonstrate that the children of Lampedusa needn't grow up on such a lunar landscape. A lot of hard work could improve the islanders' surroundings, but at present their attitude seems to be 'the Italians cut down all the trees—what can we do? The Italians only think of Lampedusa when they need her ...'

271

Over 4000 people live on Lampedusa; 70% earn a living from the very rich fishing grounds surrounding the island, catching more fish than the small ice-packing plant can freeze. Fish is certainly one of the staple items of the islanders' diet, since the island lacks proper refrigeration for large imports of meat. The tourist industry employs another 15% of the work force—the lack of greenery apparently does not deter visitors in search of perfectly clean beaches and sea, and fresh fish dinners. A major boost to the local economy was the establishment of a US coastguard station at the far western tip of the island, which sends out a signal, in conjunction with stations elsewhere in the Mediterranean, to aid navigation. The games room, swimming pool, bar and stereo system supplied by the American government to keep the coastguard from going 'stir crazy' has earned the station the nickname 'the Lampedusa Hilton' and in summer it's quite over-run by Italian tourists looking for something to do. To get an invite (particu-larly if you are a woman), hang around the airport when the plane from Palermo arrives; the big event in the Americans' day is to see if any good-looking women arrive.

The town of **Lampedusa** is only one minute's walk from the airport and the wharf where the SI.RE.MAR ferry calls. Whether you arrive by ferry or plane, you are bound to meet Lampedusa's one-man welcoming com-mittee, Oreste, who will, among other things, take your baggage to your hotel in his van for a slight fee. Oreste is a good person to know if you plan to do some skin-diving during your holiday—he is the self-acclaimed 'Oreste la Peste, Il Terrore del Pesce' (Oreste the Plague, the Terror of Fish). He'll even give you a bumper sticker and read you his poetry.

After Oreste, the town seems colourless and dusty. The width of the main street in particular is overly optimistic; it lacks only the weeds to give it that special ghost-town air. The houses on the side streets are plain and un-adorned, each with a padlocked little cistern resembling an oven, rarely used, as most of the island's water comes from a desalination plant.

It is a 15-minute walk from here to the fine sandy beach at **Guitgia,** on the other side of the fishermen's port. Most of the hotels are here as well. On the way there you'll pass one of the landmarks of the island, the old prison, converted into a car repair shop (the rocks of Lampedusa destroy the average car in less than three years).

FESTIVALS
La Madonna di Porto Salvo (22 September), with a pilgrimage to the Sanctu-ary, and a procession as well as other events in town.

SPECIALITIES
Pagghiata di pisci (a sort of paella with rice and several different kinds of

LAMPEDUSA

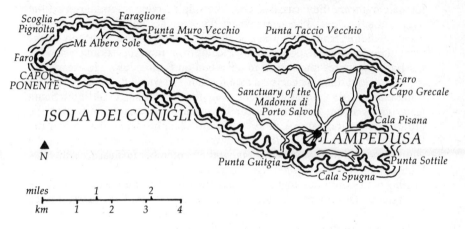

fish), spaghetti with sardines, grilled tuna fish.

The **post office** is by the main square, and the **public telephone** for long-distance calls is at the Cartoleria Brignone (Via Vittorio Emanuele 15). For information, guides, bottle refills, etc., see Salvatore Lo Verde at the Centro di Pesca e Assistenza Subacquea on Via Roma, or go to Boutique Lo Verde Sport on Via Mazzini.

Around Lampedusa

The rest of Lampedusa is shared by a few Italians, some wild rabbits, the 20 or so Americans, and rocks and boulders that jump out and trip the unwary. North of the town lies an abandoned, brand-new hospital built by the government, and the even more abandoned construction work of a *dammuso*-style tourist village begun by Giuseppe Sindona, the Sicilian who caused the Republic National Bank of New York to go under when millions of dollars were unaccountably lost. After being on the run for a long time, Sindona was captured in Italy in 1981, and the work on Lampedusa's tourist village has been at a standstill ever since.

273

Towards the centre of the island, the **Sanctuary of the Madonna di Porto Salvo** is the garden spot of Lampedusa, with real flowers and bushes. The legend behind the much venerated statue of the Madonna claims that it was sculpted in Cyprus in the 8th century, and was being transferred from Jerusalem during the Crusades when the ship carrying it foundered off the coast of Lampedusa. The grotto where the statue was taken had long been a place of hiding from the Saracens and slave traders and was then transformed into a small chapel. In 1619, a sailor from Imperia was taken slave by the Barbary pirates and forced to cut wood on Lampedusa. He escaped to the grotto, and there he carved a canoe of sorts in which he managed to flee Lampedusa, using a painted banner of the Madonna, Child and Santa Caterina as a sail. In gratitude for his miraculous escape, he turned the grotto into a sanctuary. A more mundane account claims that, when the Bourbon colonists arrived, the statue was found broken on the floor of the church and had to be restored, and that the September festival actually celebrates the anniversary of the day the first colonists arrived.

The road continues to the far western end of Lampedusa, where the coastguard station and a lighthouse may be found. Halfway there, a track branches off to the left, leading down to a lovely sandy beach facing the **Isola dei Conigli** ('island of rabbits'), easiest to reach by sea.

Going around Lampedusa by boat is rather more picturesque than making the trip by land. Among the excursion's highlights are the steep cliffs of **Albero Sole**, at 450 ft the highest point on the island, with its *faraglione* just a few feet out in the crystal-clear sea. Just to the west are the stratified cliffs of **Punta Parise**, full of grottoes and boasting a curious rock formation resembling a Madonna with Child. The north coast of Lampedusa has jagged bare precipices dotted with fish-filled grottoes, and an exploratory oil drilling platform that has yet to turn Lampedusa's waters into the new North Sea.

Linosa

About 30 miles north of Lampedusa lies its little sister Linosa (almost 2 square miles). The two islands have little in common, though, mainly owing to Linosa's volcanic origins. Linosa consists of three extinct craters: Monte Vulcano, the tallest (610 ft), Monte Rosso and Monte Nero, also known as Monte di Ponente. These volcanoes have not only enriched the soil but have also prevented the wind from blowing it away, as happened on Lampedusa. The disadvantages to this becomes obvious in summer, when the lack of wind and the black soil and rock combine to make the inhabitants toast—

it is one of the hottest places in Italy. Unlike Lampedusa, where the sea bed slopes gradually, the waters surrounding Linosa drop down quickly to great depths, as the island is only the peak of a much greater submerged volcano.

Several ancient cisterns and other scanty traces reveal that Linosa was inhabited by a few people in the Roman era, then by the Arabs, and again in the 16th century, when it is believed Linosa was a port of refuge for pirates and slave ships. In 1845 the first real settlers arrived, the Bourbon colonists, mostly hailing from Agrigento. They cultivated the good earth and fished and built their brightly coloured little village (pop. 400) between two craters and the sea. In the 1940s the government built a prison on the island, which has since been closed. Rome still has a bad habit of dumping its *personae non grata* on this charming little island, as in 1978 when the terrorist Roberto Mander was sent to live here, despite the understandable protests of the islanders.

As Italian islands go, Linosa today is as far out of the way as you can get. Here is civilisation in miniature: 2 miles of road, a tiny church, a few cars, 40 telephones, one tobacconist and a few descendants of the rats that were once such a menace on Linosa. There are several 'beaches' of lava, the cliffs of **Scogli di Tramontana** and the three **craters** to explore, adorned in spring with several species of wild flowers. At **Scala Vecchia** where the fishing boats are moored, there is a rather impromptu campsite.

Linosa is the idyllic isle of peace and quiet, and visitors looking for more should probably avoid it. Agriculture still occupies most of the people; their lives are extremely simple and natural. Unless the new barbarism of our society breeds another generation of pirates, life on Linosa will remain the same long after we've begun to sift through the rubble of our car factories and nuclear power plants.

Lampione

The uninhabited islet of Lampione lies to the west of Lampedusa and Linosa. Like Lampedusa it is geologically part of North Africa, and has almost no vegetation at all. At one time the ruins of a possible hermitage could be seen there, but no longer. The islet (about half a square mile in area) is very popular with sub-aqua fishermen, for the fish are exceptionally large in these protective, unfrequented waters. It can be reached in two hours in a small boat from Lampedusa.

GETTING TO THE PELAGIE ISLANDS
There are two ways to do it; on the daily flight from Palermo's Punta Raisi airport to Lampedusa, and by the Siremar ferry from Porto Empedocle, the unattractive port town of Agrigento. The ferry service runs daily (not Mondays in the winter), a 9-hour overnight trip that calls at both Linosa and Lampedusa.

WHERE TO STAY
A resort hotel has recently opened up on Linosa, the **Alqusa***** (tel. (0922) 972052; 33–35 500 lire single, 49–57 500 double). On Lampedusa there are a surprising number of modest establishments around the town—more than twice as many as a few years ago. Most have restaurants, including the pleasant, family-run **Lido Azzurro**** (tel. (0922) 970225; 22–28 000 lire double).

Part V

SARDINIA

Cala Gonone in Nuorno, Sardinia

History

The fact that Sardinia is the island in the Mediterranean furthest from the mainland prevented its settlement at an early date. The first inhabitants seem to have arrived about 3000 BC, perhaps by way of Corsica. About 2000 BC a second migration of peoples occurred, culturally in transition from what we would call 'Neolithic' to 'Megalithic'. Their origins are mysterious to an extreme; they may have come from Iberia, or from Africa—Africa is more likely.

We have the name 'Shardanas', one of the troublesome sea peoples that combined with Libyan tribes to invade and almost conquer the mighty Egyptian empire in the 15th century BC, and we have the legend of a Libyan Hercules (the use of that name reflects their religious practices more than

277

any mythological connection), whose sons Sardus and Kyrnos settled Sardinia and Corsica respectively. The story is probably the echo of a migration of a people called 'Shardana' or perhaps Iolai from Libya.

About 1500 BC, a division of some sort occurred in their society, and some of the moved north to found the Torréenne culture in Corsica. Whoever the Shardana were, they brought with them a new religion and built dolmens, menhirs and large, often decorated, rock-cut tombs called *domus de janas*. This Sard word is usually translated as 'witch's house', but *jana*, in fact, means something closer to 'fairy'. The associations that Neolithic monuments acquire in the popular imagination are often interesting; in Corsica, similar tombs are called 'devil's forges'. Most of these remains are found in the northern part of the island, and archaeologists distinguish two distinct but closely related cultures: the *Ozieri* or San Michele culture in the northwest, and the *Arzachena* in the northeast.

THE NURAGHES

About the time of their expansion into Corsica, this society began to change, though whether it was subject to some foreign influence or did it on its own is an open question. The most obvious sign of its evolution is the construction of the first *nuraghi*. A *nuraghe*, a word of ancient and unknown origin, is a tower-like structure of mortared large stones which stands one to three storeys in height. They clearly served a defensive purpose and may also have been the homes of chiefs. The Corsican *torres* are derivative of these, and the *talayots* of Minorca and Mallorca are very similar.

By this time, the Sards were developing into a large, powerful and culturally advanced nation, one of the greatest in the Mediterranean world. Expanding from the north, they occupied the entire island and made their presence felt far from home, as we see from their part in the alliance against Egypt. They created expressive works of art, bronze statuettes of kings and warriors and ritual ships. Their *nuraghi* evolved into true castles, as at Torralba or Barumini, with huge central towers surrounded by a wall containing four or five more. Picture reconstructions of these can be seen in the museum at Sassari—they are certainly imposing, even in the ruined forms that remain today. Archaeologists have counted the incredible number of 30 000 *nuraghi*. Of these, only 7000 remain, the rest picked clean for building stone over the centuries.

The largest *nuraghi* often have the remains of large villages of round stone huts adjacent to them, reflecting the increasing wealth and complexity of the culture. Metal-working appears to have been their chief trade. The great number of *nuraghi* and the absence of foreign enemies until the arrival of the Phoenicians suggests an island of contentious and competitive city-states, an atmosphere that is always a hothouse for cultural advancement.

Modern Sards cannot look at these works of their ancestors with detachment, as mere cultural relics. They reflect, after all, the greatest period of their people's history and are both a source of pride and a symbol. Their ubiquity ensures the visitor an opportunity to explore at least one of them. The towers have walls sloping inwards, giving them the appearance of the lower half of a cone. There is a low entrance with a lintel over it and perhaps windows in the upper storeys. The classic *nuraghi*—and the vast majority of them are simple defensive outposts or strongholds—have a single central chamber with storage areas dug out of the corners of the floor. Often, the structure has a double wall with a staircase spiralling around the central chamber to the roof or second floor, where some of the earlier *nuraghi* have recesses in the wall that perhaps served as beds for the warriors. In the later *nuraghic* complexes, which must have looked for all the world like medieval European castles, only the conical shape of the towers being different, there were originally corbelled roofs with platforms above them for the defenders to shoot down at their enemies. Almost always, a *nuraghe* was within sight of several others. In a few places where many still remain standing, we can have some sense of how impressive a picture they must have made, pulling together the entire landscape in a single piece of architecture.

A great incentive to *nuraghe*-building was provided in the 9th century BC by the arrival of the first Phoenician traders, who set up trading posts in the relatively unpopulated south at Nura, Tharros, Cagliari and elsewhere. The Phoenicians were tolerably peaceful trading partners but were soon succeeded by their western cousins, the Carthaginians. In the 6th century BC, Sardinia became involved in Mediterranean power politics, as Carthage sought to add the island to its growing empire. They occupied the western coasts and warred continuously with the Sards, gradually pushing them back into the interior. Olbia was founded as a foothold on the east coast and Karalis (Cagliari) and Nura grew into important towns. To secure the south, Carthage settled large numbers of their Iberian and Balearic allies there. The Sards defended their island with tenacity; some of the large *nuraghi* that they built at the time, such as the one at Barumini, were important fortresses marking the borders of the Carthaginian conquest.

The Carthaginians brought new methods and ideas to the island. They introduced their militaristic and oppressive state, slaves to grow grain for their army, and their thoroughly unpleasant religion. One of the major features of their archaeological remains is the *tophet;* a particularly interesting example can be seen at Sant' Antioco (ancient Sulcis). At these combination temple–barbecues, the nobles would sacrifice their first-born children to the glory of Tanit and Baal. Being culturally closer to the natives than other

279

people, they were the first to call the island by its true name, Sardinia. The Greeks, who had touched the coasts but never settled there, called it *Ichnoussa*, meaning 'footstep', either because of its shape (according to Pausanias) or because it was used as a stepping-stone for Greek traders on their way to Corsica and Provence.

THE ROMAN ERA

During the First Punic War, the Roman general Sulpicius invaded the island and won a victory at Sulcis. It was only after the conclusion of hostilities, however, that Rome was able to gain control, aided by a rebellion of Carthage's mercenaries in 238 BC. The Sards made the Romans feel as unwelcome as they had the Carthaginians, putting up a fierce resistance that wasn't even quelled by the tremendous Roman victory of 177 BC in which contemporary historians claimed that 12 000 Sards were killed. The remnants of the free Sards fled to the eastern mountains, a land the Romans called *Barbaria* for the barbarous valour of the people (the women, they said, were especially fierce and untamable).

The great age of *nuraghe*-building, and the civilisation of their builders, was drawing to its close. The last *nuraghi* to be built were complex maze-like structures—by then the Sards assumed that the dogged Romans would get in eventually and designed their last fortresses to enable them to split up and ambush their enemies inside. It was a futile gesture, but the difficult terrain of the east was to defend them as well as the *nuraghi* had. Despite all Rome's efforts, Barbaria was never fully brought under control.

Apart from constructing their usual public works, the Romans treated Sardinia as a simple agricultural reserve and largely neglected it. The island became one of the major sources of the Republic's grain, but received as few favours from Rome as it does today. By a stroke of luck most of the island sided with Caesar in the civil wars, and he and his successors rewarded it. Karalis (Cagliari), by then emerging as the leading city, received the status of a Roman municipality.

Under the emperors Sardinia did well. Karalis, Nura, Olbia, Tharros and the other towns became prosperous and up-to-date cities. Latin became the dominant language; the modern Sard language is closer to Latin than even Italian. The island received more than its share of exiles; Tiberius sent 4000 Jews there and later emperors used it to be rid of Christian soldiers spreading dissension in the legions. As a result of this, the early Church was particularly strong there. Sardinia produced two 5th-century Popes, Hilarius and Symmachus, and was a refuge from persecution for several others. The Christians had a rougher time among the more independent mountaineers. By AD 600, Pope Gregory was complaining that the Barbarians still worshipped 'stones and wood' (in fact, the ancient Sard religion was a cult of springs).

MIDDLE AGES

Records on Sardinia are scarce after AD 500, but the Dark Ages brought the Sards as much trouble as any of the other Mediterranean islands. The Vandals under Thrasamund came in 535 and, after a short stay, were expelled by Justinian's resurgent Byzantines. Ostrogoths and various bands of Saracens came and went. Through it all, the Sards of the interior were relatively safe but most of the coastal cities shrivelled and disappeared. As late as the 11th century, Muslims from Africa were attempting to settle the coasts. By this time, Sardinia had once again achieved, by default, a *de facto* independence.

Under the Byzantines, the administrator of the island was called the *judex*, or judge. This position gradually evolved into four *giudicati*, democratically elected and responsible to a popular assembly, each serving one of the four *giudicati* into which the island had been informally divided: Torres, Olbia (Gallura), Cagliari and Arborea. The emerging powers of medieval Europe, however, refused to leave them in peace. Early in the 11th century, the Papacy invited Pisa and Genoa to help it grab the island. The Pisans helped expel the last Saracens and insinuated themselves in the south of Sardinia while the Genoese sought a foothold in the north. The two city republics fought over the island for almost 300 years with the Hohenstaufen emperors keeping their hand in by proclaiming the *Giudicato* of Arborea King of Sardinia. During most of this period the Pisans had the greatest influence on the inhabitants—not political but artistic. The Sardinians called architects and artists from Pisa to build and embellish their churches. As in Corsica, these Pisan churches comprise most of the important architecture of the island. Some are severe, almost naive country chapels, some are large and ornate, but all have the seemingly effortless grace that marks all Pisan religious buildings.

The Pisans were soundly defeated by Genoa at Meloria in 1284, effectively putting an end to their dreams of dominating the region. By now, the Genoese had become bitter enemies of the Popes, who turned to the Kings of Aragon to advance their interests. The attempts of King Jaime II to conquer Sardinia were met with strong opposition, particularly in the north. The Aragonese responded with strict repression, going so far as to expel the entire population of Alghero, replacing them with Catalan settlers. In the south, they took a year to prise the Pisans from their last stronghold, Cagliari.

THE GIUDICATI

The greatest problem of all for the Aragonese came from the Arborean Kings of Sardinia. No longer imperial pawns, they gathered Sardinian opposition around them to become the island's leaders against the invaders. By the 1360s they had established themselves squarely across the path of conquest, beating off repeated Aragonese attacks on their capital of Oristano and even managing to capture a few towns themselves. King Mariano IV is one of the Sardinian heroes; upon his death, however, and that of his son seven years later in 1383, prospects for the Sardinian cause looked dim.

Here the hopes of the Sards were placed in the hands of the first and only *Giudichessa*, Eleanora of Arborea, daughter of Mariano. This Eleanora became a national heroine like Elizabeth I or Joan of Arc; from the first she proved herself a political and military leader equal to her father. The Aragonese were kept at bay in spite of treachery from within; even Eleanora's husband deserted to the scheming Spaniards. Perhaps her greatest contribution to Sardinia was her codification of the law, the *Carta de Logu*, which remained in effect for 466 years.

After her death in 1403, however, the Sardinian resistance crumbled. Oristano fell to the Aragonese in 1409, and Sassari, an independent city-state and the last hope for Sard liberty, in 1417. As if the Aragonese weren't bad enough, after the marriage of Ferdinand and Isabella in 1479, Sardinia passed under the rule of a united Spain. To be a Spanish possession in those times was perhaps the worst fate that could befall any people. The Spaniards were greedy and cruel; they introduced feudalism to an island where it had been largely unknown all through the Middle Ages. Free thought was stamped out by the terror of the Inquisition, and city and countryside alike suffered and grew poor from Spanish avarice and mismanagement. A crushing burden of taxes was imposed to pay for Spanish imperialism abroad. Armed opposition on the part of the Sards was not completely quelled until the end of the 15th century, and even after that it continued in the mountains as 'banditry'. Like all previous rulers, the Spaniards were for the most part confined to the coasts; their hold over the mountainous east was always tenuous at best.

THE KINGDOM OF SARDINIA

The Spanish were not deposed until the 18th century. During the War of the Spanish Succession the Austrian Hapsburgs temporarily occupied the island, and in the Treaty of London that followed the war (1718) Sardinia was given to the Dukes of Savoy on condition that they dropped their claim to Sicily. Sardinia's first Savoian kings ruled from the mainland—their Kingdom of Sardinia included much of northwest Italy—but after the Spanish they were a welcome change. One of them, King Carlo Emanuele, was a reformer who sought to rehabilitate the island's economy. His efforts to repopulate Sardinia (the number of inhabitants had dropped steadily under the Spanish) can be seen on the island of San Pietro, where Genoese colonists—actually refugees from their original colony on a Tunisian island—were introduced and named their town Carloforte after the King.

The tumult of the revolutionary era came to Sardinia in 1793 with a French attack from Corsica, which was unsuccessful. One of the leaders of the revolutionary troops was the young Napoleon Bonaparte. Shortly after this Sardinia had its own revolution against the king and the nobles, led by Giommaria Angioy. The revolutionaries controlled much of the island by 1796 and captured Sassari, but after a defeat near Oristano, Angioy was compelled to flee the island. During the Napoleonic Wars, the Savoian kings for the first and only time held their court in Sardinia, at Cagliari, as the Piedmont was occupied by France. After 1815, two more able kings of Sardinia, though now back in Turin, proved themselves reformers with an interest in the island's welfare. Carlo Felice continued economic development—he built the main road from Cagliari to Sassari that still bears his name—and Carlo Alberto finally abolished feudalism in 1847.

The Kingdom of Sardinia was becoming an important force in European affairs; it even played a role in the Crimean War against Russia. It was also to play a major role in the unification of Italy. Garibaldi began his campaigns on the peninsula and in Sicily from Sardinia, encouraged by King Vittorio Emanuele and his clever minister, Cavour. Through force and diplomacy, the Kingdom grew until, in 1861, Vittorio Emanuele became the first King of a united Italy.

This did not mean any particular benefits for the island itself. In spite of the efforts of Carlo Felice and Carlo Alberto, Sardinia was a poor and isolated place and continued as such into the 20th century. Many Sards were forced to emigrate, though not as many as those who abandoned Corsica, Sicily or other Mediterranean islands. Just the same, Sardinia proved its attachment to the new Italy by fighting enthusiastically for it in World War I. The famous Sassari Brigade was among the most effective and most decorated in the Italian army.

Mussolini probably did more for Sardinia than any of his royal predecessors. Roads, dams and irrigation systems were built, land was reclaimed from swamps and the cities of Arborea (originally Mussolinia), Fertilia and Carbonia were founded. Many Sards still think kindly of the dictator, not so much for his politics as for what he did for them. In the old town of Cagliari and elsewhere you can still see Mussolini slogans and pronouncements which were painted on the sides of buildings in the 1920s.

SINCE WORLD WAR II

Sardinia did not suffer battles and campaigns in the last war, but parts of it were heavily bombed, Cagliari worst of all. After the war the new Italian Republic made a creditable effort to improve the island's economy. Most importantly, the Sards were granted autonomy with their own assembly and executive to decide internal affairs, just as the Sicilians were. The developed activities of the *Cassa per il Mezzogiorno* include Sardinia, and a further impetus came with the *Rinascita* plan of 1962. Unfortunately, most of the public and private efforts have been unhelpful; all too often, 'development' efforts mean big factories in Cagliari or Porto Torres that foul the air but employ few workers. Lack of opportunities still force many younger Sards to emigrate to the mainland or beyond.

As in Corsica, one of the most encouraging events was the elimination of malaria by the US Army, with money from the Rockefeller Foundation directly after the war, making the settlement of many fertile coastal areas possible and allowing a burgeoning tourist industry to develop on the island's many beaches.

For many Sards, autonomy and industrialisation are not enough; they would like an even greater control over their homeland. A recurring complaint is the fact that there are no less than 24 NATO bases in Sardinia, unpleasant to live near and probably ensuring that the island would be quickly reduced to its component molecules in the event of war in Europe. Many Sards also see the process of modernisation and industrialisation turning their land into a colony of big business and the central government. They take a new look at their old way of life and compare it to what they can expect from the present. It is not surprising, then, to see the graffiti appearing on the walls of cities and villages over the last decade—proclaiming older, truer values, a less mechanised and regimented existence and Sard independence and self-sufficiency. These ideas are very much in the air in Sardinia and the visitor curious enough to ask will find them proposed by people in remote Sardinian villages with more sophistication and down-to-earth pragmatism than the intellectuals of Europe's big cities can ever manage. Politics seems to be one of the Sards' greatest talents. The famous socialist philosopher Antonio Gramsci came from a village near Oristano, and many of Italy's leading politicians today—President Pertini among them—are Sards.

Sardinia today

Geography
Sardinia is the second island in the Mediterranean in size, only a little smal-

miles 10   40
km 10   60

Palau

GALLURA

Olbia

Porto Torres

NURRA

SASSARI

Alghero

LUGODORO   Chilivani

Bosa

MACOMER

NUORO

Mt del
Gennargentu

SINIS

Tirso River

ORISTANO

BARBAGIA

Arbatax

ARBOREA

Mannu River

Flumendosa River

CAMPIDANO

SARRABUS

IGLESIENTE

Iglesias

Carbonia

CAGLIARI

Coghinas River

SARDINIA – PROVINCES, REGIONS
AND MAIN TOWNS

285

ler than Sicily. Its topography could best be described, perhaps, as confusing—it has certainly done a good job of bewildering various invaders over the centuries. Mountains, valleys, plains and plateaux are scattered across the map without any pretence of order or reason on the part of the Creator. Mountains come in patches instead of ranges, the greatest of them the Gennargentu, in the east-central part of the island.

This is a landscape where the native has a great advantage; the Gennargentu, particularly, has been equally effective in protecting the Sards from Romans and Spaniards and protecting sheep thieves from the *carabinieri*. Nowhere are the mountains as high as in the central range of Corsica, but like Corsica most of the island is volcanic in origin. Not a few of Sardinia's peaks are long-extinct volcanoes; another feature of the volcanic heritage are the *giaras*, large, steep basalt plateaux, several marking the border of Nuoro and Cagliari provinces.

Sardinia's coasts are a different matter altogether. There is a tremendous variety of coastal landscape: high cliffs, mountains diving straight into the sea, numerous marshes and lagoons (*stagnos* in Italian) that made it possible for Sardinia to supply almost all of Italy's salt, and everywhere there are caves. From the great marine grottoes full of tourists to the million little potholes around Nuoro, Sardinia probably has more caves than anywhere.

In the last hundred years, man has brought great changes to the Sardinian scene. The 19th century saw the virtual deforestation of the island; the big forests of holm oaks, cork oaks and pines you see now are only a small fraction of what was here before. More recently, dams have been built all along the four great rivers, the Tirso, the Flumendosa, the Coghinas and the Mannu, creating over a score of artificial lakes.

There is a great variety of fauna on the island, including some comparatively rare species. There is the usual Mediterranean array of rabbits, weasels and game birds such as the partridge, woodcock and duck, and tuna, shellfish and lobsters off the shores, and eels and trout in the rivers and streams. Wild boar are numerous, and they are hunted in the spring. Among the more exotic inhabitants of the island are the cranes of Sinis, small deer, eagles, wild sheep called *muflone* in the mountains, the Queen's hawk (which gets its name from Eleanora of Arborea, who reserved to herself the right to hunt them), and the Mediterranean seals of the caves near Dorgali. Not to be left out are the unique miniature wild horses that inhabit the Giara of Gesturi, and the world's only albino donkeys, on the island of Asinara.

People and customs

There is a cliché about Sardinia that one visits not for the sights but for the

atmosphere. This isn't entirely true; Sardinia will prove more than suf-
ficiently entertaining for the visitor interested in nature, in history and archaeology, in art, or in just sitting on a beach. However, what makes the
island special and compelling is something more than these; it is the Sardinian way of life in its uncompromised integrity. This is truly 'the uncon-
quered island' as the title of a recent book described it. Not the various hosts
of invaders, not even the conformist pressures of modern society have succeeded in changing it much.

The Sards maintain their costumes and festivals not to impress tourists
but to remind themselves of who they are. A nation as old as their *nuraghi*,
they have seen Phoenicians, Romans, Spaniards and the others come and
go without really altering the stock—this is especially true in the mountains
of the east. Today, they think of themselves as Sards first and Italians
second. Part of this feeling is expressed in the jealous maintenance of their
language, which betrays its non-Romance origins in strange words like
nuraghe and the use of the *u* and *x* (which is pronounced, incidentally, as *sh*).

Much of the vocabulary and grammar, however, is straight from Latin.
The word for 'house', for example, is *domus*, not *casa*. It is enough of a living
language to have many dialects; Lugodoro, Nuoro and the Campidano have
the most important. Besides this, accidents of history have placed other
tongues on the island. San Pietro still speaks a version of 16th-century
Genoese dialect, and Catalan is still common in Alghero. Surprisingly, this
makes life easy for the visitor with only an imperfect knowledge of Italian.
Almost all Sards speak Italian, and they do it with clarity and without collo-
quialisms.

Many of the ancient customs survive in country districts. The Sards have
their own calendar, with the new year starting on 1 September, and special
names for each of the months. Old traditions persist in marking life's
milestones—birth, marriage and death. Magic is used to guess the sex of an
unborn child, and christenings and weddings are elaborate occasions.
There is a courtship ritual called the *precunta*, where the successful suitor
and a friend visit the bride's father pretending to look for a 'lost lamb';
together they search the house until they find her—and the couple is
betrothed on the spot. At the wedding they are showered with grain, salt and
sweets, and at the wedding banquet they eat from the same plate, which is
then broken at their feet and the pieces are counted to see how many children they will have.

Poetry, music and dance are an important part of the old traditions. The
shepherds in particular are masters of extemporaneous versifying (in Sardo,
of course) and often compete before a jury of their peers at weddings and
festivals. Sard music is ancient and fascinating. The styles of Gallura, Lugo-

doro and Campidano show some Italian influence, but the music of the mountain people isn't diluted by anything foreign—indeed, it is probably unlike anything you have ever heard. The classic form, in Nuoro Province, is a *coro* (chorus) of four male voices, one singing the verses and the other three responding in a weird droning chorus. There are traditional instruments, such as the *launedda,* a difficult contraption of three pipes, which the *nuraghic*-era bronzes in the Cagliari museum prove to be a survival of the remotest past. Of course, you are more likely to see such modern additions as the accordion or concertina accompanying the folk dances. For an introduction to Sard music, vendors in Cagliari's Piazza Matteotti sell an infinite variety of tapes of *coro* music and other specialities from all over the island.

One of the most important features of Sardinian folk life is costume. In the villages the older women still favour traditional dress, but the real costumes, the beautiful and expensive outfits handed down from father to son and mother to daughter, are brought out only for the festivals. Every town and village has its own style; the best, predictably, are from the mountain villages of the Barbagia. For both men and women, black and red are the predominant colours. The men's costumes, with their loose white trousers and high boots, look more like eastern European than other Italian styles. At the new museum outside Nuoro you can see examples from all over the island, but you are sure to see them being worn if you are fortunate enough to attend any of the Sardinian festivals.

There's one subject we shouldn't neglect to mention, not because it is important, but because it is the average newspaper-reader's first impression of Sardinia—banditry. Stealing sheep is an old custom in the Barbagia and Nuorese regions, done more often than not out of need. The institutionalised banditry and vendetta that grew out of this way of life, never as common as in Corsica or Sicily, have largely dissipated, though the Gennargentu and Sopramonte still shelter outlaws today. Lately they have made the world's headlines by kidnapping wealthy tourists or their children. Those of us not falling within this category have little to fear (much less than, say, in Palermo or New York) and should take it in good humour when the Sards explain that, after all, the bandits at least conduct themselves as gentlemen.

Festivals

Here is where the visitor will really get to know Sardinia. In truth, they're hard to miss; most villages have at least one *festa* each year, and in the spring

288

and summer there can be as many as a dozen at the same time across the island. They range from simple festivals honouring a patron saint to the great events in the big towns that attract people from every province. Among the most interesting are those celebrated in the sanctuary villages in the countryside. These villages, a huddle of small structures encircling a church, often with the back walls joined together to turn a blank face to the outside as if they were walled towns, are empty all year. For the festival, families from the nearby villages move in for a week of singing, dancing and carrying on. The best known of these festivals are at San Cosimo, near Mamoiada (27 September), San Salvatore, Sinis, and San Francesco, near Lula (4 October). Some of the biggest festivals are listed below.

Sant' Efisio at Cagliari (1 May) with costumes and performers from all over Sardinia. The highlight of the festival is a pilgrimage to the saint's shrine at Nora, with the saint's image on an elaborate float and decorated ox-carts called *traccas*.

Cavalcata Sarda, the 'Sardinian Cavalcade' (Ascension Day) at Sassari. This is only 30 years old, but it has become one of the most popular festivals, a showcase for the costumes, songs and poetry of all Sardinia's villages.

Festa del Redentore (29 August) at Nuoro, with a pilgrimage to Monte Ortobene, processions through the streets of the city, and folklore exhibitions and performances.

Sa Sartiglia (at carnival time) at Oristano. The main event of this folk festival is a kind of medieval joust, introduced by the Spaniards but given a curious Sardinian flavour. Among the displays of equestrian prowess is this very strange piece of dream-imagery: a rider called Su Compoidori, wearing a costume with red ribbons tied on his arms and legs, a feminine mask and a top hat, gallops at full speed towards a silver star suspended from a ribbon, and tries to impale it with a short spear. They've been doing it since the days of the Giudicato of Arborea.

Carnival (in Mamoiada, Ottana, Bosa, Tempio). Carnival in the mountain villages of Mamoiada and Ottana, more than anywhere else, betrays its pre-Christian religious origins. A common practice in many cultures was the driving out of a 'scapegoat' at the beginning of the agricultural year to take the community's bad luck with it, and this is just what happens in Mamoiada. The *Mamuthones*, a group of men dressed in animal skins with wooden masks and thirty pounds of bells, are chased out of town by the *Socadores*, onlookers sometimes getting lassoed in the process. The similar festival at Ottana is called the *Boes*.

The word 'Mamuthones' is of an ancient and unknown origin, as is the festival itself. It may be a clue that, according to Frazer's *Golden Bough*, the ancient Romans had a similar ritual, driving out of the city each March a man dressed in skins called the 'old Mamurino' or old Mars. Mars before he became a god of war, was an agricultural deity, a 'god of the year'.

Li Candelieri (14 August), at Sassari, is something altogether different: not of religious origin at all, but a ritual of a medieval *civitas* unusual in southern Europe. The main event is the procession of the *gremios*, the medieval guilds, each group carrying a giant 'candlestick' decorated with emblems of the guild and its patron saint, and includes an act of symbolic submission of the city officials to the leader (*obriere*) of the Farmers' Guild, the *gremio* on whom the life of the city depends, and the 'judgement' of the mayor and council by the people during the *Faradda*, the 'descent' of the candlesticks.

In all of these Sardinian celebrations, visitors are more than welcome. Particularly in the village festivals, you are likely to leave overfed and inebriated. The local tourist office or Pro Loco can probably get someone to introduce you around.

Food and wine

The Sardinian table is a rich one, with many dishes derived from the Italian and many entirely Sardinian. *Antipasti* include many things similar to Corsican charcuterie: the sausages (*salsiccia*) and ham, either from pigs or from wild boar. There are also such delicacies as *bottarga* (roe of the mullet) and minced boiled octopus.

Most restaurant menus on Sardinia will feature some variety of Sardinian pasta, such as the *malloreddus*, little dumplings, or *sa fregula*, something like couscous. There is also *culingionis*, a Sardinian type of ravioli, and many kinds of *minestra* (vegetable soups with or without pasta).

Fish is of course popular and widely available around the coasts; the Sards make several different varieties of fish soup. Mutton and kid are also popular. You're less likely to encounter the more exotic traditional dishes, in which thrushes and blackbirds and the entrails of various animals figure prominently, such as *accarraxiau* or *sa frixioredda*.

Sardinia is famous for its wonderful artichokes, and a few kinds of strong cheese; one, called *casu beccio*, is eaten with the cheese mites still in it (an acquired taste, to be sure). Bread is as much an art form as a staple, and some special kinds are baked for special occasions: in the shape of towers, or castles for weddings, or something that looks almost like lace, and also the *carta da musica* (music paper), made for festivals. It is very thin and keeps for a long time; the shepherds carry it on their long trips into the mountains.

Sards, particularly those around Cagliari, are very fond of sweets, and an almost infinite variety is produced.

Wine is cheap and very good (much better than in Corsica). The island is best known for dessert wines of a formidable alcoholic content, such as the *Vernaccia* of Oristano and Sulcis. Every province has its wine-making regions, and some of the best wine, such as *Anghelu Ruiu* (red) and *Torbato* (white), comes from Alghero. Other varieties include *Muscatel, Aleatico* and the strong *Cannonau*.

Handicrafts

Unlike many places in the world, any souvenirs you buy in Sardinia are almost certain to have been made there. The most popular with the tourists are baskets, decorated with geometric designs that have probably changed little since the *nuraghi* were built. Sardinian carpets are beautiful, and often exported overseas, where they fetch high prices. Isili, Uras and Mogoro are centres of carpet-weaving. Other crafts include leather goods, carved wooden objects such as the bridal chests of the Barbagia, and moulds for cheese and bread. As in Corsica, there is a new 'artisan' movement, a reaction against cheap tourist trinkets (though you'll still find plenty of those) in favour of genuinely traditional quality goods. There are over 50 craft centres around the island.

Agriturismo

One of the most interesting possibilities for getting to know Sardinia and the Sards is this organisation, operated by a co-operative of stock breeders in Oristano province. They can arrange for you to stay quite inexpensively in the home of one of their members in a number of villages around Oristano. For details, write to the Cooperative Allevatrici Sarde, Casella Postale 107, Oristano 09170 (tel. (0783) 418006).

Getting to Sardinia

By air
Frequent domestic flights (as well as scheduled and charter flights from London in the summer) to Sardinia's three airports: Cagliari–Elmas, Alghero and Sassari–Fertilia, and Olbia. The only internal flights are be-tween Alghero and Cagliari on ATI Airlines (4 daily, a trip of about 35 min-

291

utes), and between Cagliari and Olbia on Alisarda Airlines (1 daily, a trip of 30 minutes).

By sea

There are many daily connections between Sardinia and the mainland, and they increase by half in the summer. Nearly all are overnight services. If you plan to go in July or August advance bookings are *essential*.

Tirrenia offers the following connections:

Genoa to Porto Torres: daily, depart 8pm, arrive 8.30am.

Genoa to Olbia: 3 a week, depart 8.30pm, arrive 9am.

Genoa to Cagliari: 3 a week, depart 6pm, arrive 2pm.

Civitavecchia to Cagliari: daily, depart 8.30pm, arrive 9.30am.

Civitavecchia to Olbia: daily, depart 11pm, arrive 6am.

Genoa to Arbatax: 2 a week, depart 6.30pm, arrive 12.30pm.

Tunis–Trapani to Cagliari: 1 a week, depart Tunis 11.30am, depart Trapani 10pm, arrive 8am.

Livorno (Leghorn) to Porto Torres: 3 a week, depart 8.30pm, arrive 8.15am.

Naples to Cagliari: 2 a week, depart 6.30pm, arrive 9.30am.

Livorno to Cagliari: 2 a week, depart 5pm, arrive 10am.

Palermo to Cagliari: 1 a week, depart 7pm, arrive 7.30am.

Nuova Tran-Tirreno Express

From Livorno to Olbia daily from mid July to September, and several times a week at other times between 6 April and 2 November.

Italian Railways has several daily crossings from Civitavecchia to Golfo Aranci.

Grandi Traghetti has a service once or twice a week between Genoa and Porto Torres.

NAVARMA links Sardinia and Corsica (Bonifacio), as do Tirrenia and others.

There are also frequent ferry services by Tirrenia and others to the offshore islets of Carloforte (from Portovesme or Calasetta, reached from Cagliari by frequent FMS buses) and La Maddalena (from Palau).

Getting around in Sardinia

Like Sicily, and unlike Corsica, getting around is relatively easy. Rail and bus systems are cheap, surprisingly efficient and extensive. Unfortunately most of Sardinia's attractions, natural wonders, *nuraghes* and Pisan churches are out in the country, and if you intend to see more than a few of them you'll need a car.

By rail

The service of the Ferrovie dello Stato on Sardinia consists of a Cagliari–Oristano–Macomer–Sassari–Porto Torres line, with a branch off at Chilivari for Olbia and Golfo Aranci. There are usually several trains a day at weekdays. The trip running the length of the island takes about five hours.

In addition, there are several subsidiary lines: one from Bosa to Nuoro, intersecting the main line at Macomer, and one to Carbonia–Iglesias–Decimomannu–Cagliari. Two old narrow-gauge lines are still in service: a scenic trip through the Barbagia from Cagliari to Mandas–Sevi–Lanusei–Arbatax, and the Alghero–Sassari–Tempio Pausania–Palau route operated by the Strade Ferrate Sarde (SFS).

By bus

As in Sicily, and for that matter almost everywhere else in Italy, riding the bus is almost a pleasure. The lines are subsidised by the state, so the fares are very cheap, and the coaches themselves new and clean.

From each of the four provincial capitals, regular services run to all the towns and villages in the province. In Cagliari and Oristano, the company is SATAS; in Nuoro and Sassari it is ARST. Both companies' buses are painted blue. Services between the provincial capitals are provided by the PANI line, with buses painted red.

It is possible to reach nearly every village from its provincial capital, but it's tricky. Buses are of course arranged for the convenience of the villagers, and schedules can be a problem; if you're making a day trip out to a village, check in advance if there's a bus coming *back* when you need it. Tourist information offices in Sardinia are very helpful (they often know more than the bus line employees) and villagers will usually know all the local routes.

Have faith: with a little foresight, you'll find even the most unlikely connections will materialise—including long, scenic trips on the back roads from one province to another.

The best map of Sardinia is that published by the ACI (Italian Automobile Club) and available throughout the island. It's indispensable for exploring Sardinia's out of the way places, and it shows all of the major natural attractions, country churches and *nuraghi*.

Cagliari Province

Cagliari

HISTORY

Cagliari (pronounced KY-li-ar-ee) has been the leading city since the time

The Old City, Cagliari

of the Phoenicians, who founded it as *Karalis*. Under them, and later under the Romans, the city prospered as a trade outlet for the island's grain and timber. Sant'Efisio, one of the numerous Sardinian martyrs in the reign of Diocletian, met his end here.

Cagliari's fine harbour, one of the best in the Mediterranean, kept the city from disappearing entirely during the Dark Ages. The steep hill overlooking the port made an admirable defensive position; when the Pisans seized the town in the 11th century as a base for expanding their influence in Sardinia, they built the walls of the Citadel that exist today. In spite of Pisa's string of military defeats at the hands of the Genoese, it managed to hold Cagliari until the Aragonese conquest in 1397. The Aragonese and later the Spanish and Savoian kings made Cagliari the island capital, ruling through a viceroy. In the 17th century the Spanish founded Cagliari's University.

The city reached its greatest period of prosperity, perhaps, only in this century. During the last war it suffered heavier bombing than any other Italian city; one-third of its buildings were destroyed, and the town was decorated for its bravery under fire. Since 1945, Cagliari's reconstruction has been dramatic. Most of Sardinia's new industries are located here, and one in six Sards call Cagliari home. The city has an impressive collection of tall buildings around its harbour; without the old Citadel to give it away it would look more like an American city than an Italian one.

WHAT TO SEE
Cagliari today, you might infer, is a very busy place. The city continues to expand in all directions, though parts of the centre have become somewhat neglected, which is a pity, as the old town is quite an attractive place. As for the industrial and residential sprawl surrounding the two great swampy lagoons, Stagno di Molentarguis and Stagno di Cagliari, the less said the better. The latter has saltpans that meet much of Italy's need for that product.

Cagliari's front door is its port, where the ferries to the Continent can dock almost in the centre of town. Along the port runs the wide **Via Roma,** the arcaded main thoroughfare with its many cafés. Where Via Roma meets the Largo Carlo Felice is the **Piazza Matteotti,** with the rail and bus stations, the tourist information booth, and the 19th-century neo-Gothic **Town Hall.** Giacomo Matteotti, by the way, for whom streets and squares are named everywhere in Italy, was a Socialist deputy of the 1920s who led the opposition to Mussolini until his murder by blackshirt thugs. A block north is the shady Piazza del Carmine with the port office and the offices of the provincial government.

Behind the Via Roma is a district of old, narrow streets on a grid plan that has changed little since Roman times. Here, especially in and around Via Sardegna, are many of Cagliari's restaurants and hotels. The northern boundary of the district, the Via Mannu, a lovely street with many old Spanish buildings, connects the Piazza Yenne, where there is a statue of King Carlo Felice, with the Piazza Constituzione. A network of narrow alleyways and stairs lead up to the **Citadello,** the old Pisan fortress, and one fancy marble stairway ascends from the Piazza Constituzione to the San Remy Bastion; at the top is the Terrazza Umberto I with a view over all Cagliari. Cagliari's unusually decadent teenagers, a social phenomenon of this fast-changing city, have made it their meeting-place.

In the Citadello
Around the Terrazza is the old **University,** with its fine 18th-century buildings on the Via Universita, where a 19th-century Cagliarese professor of physics, Antonio Pacinotti, invented the dynamo. The buildings are in a sad state of semi-abandonment (and there are few sights as sad as an abandoned library) while the University is gradually being moved to new quarters in the north of town. The move, like most of Cagliari's public improvements, has already been in progress several decades. Next to the

University is the **Torre dell' Elefante,** one of the remains of the Pisan fortifications. It still has its portcullis, and takes its name from the marble elephant over the gate. This tower and its twin, the Torre San Pancrazio on the
northern end of the Citadello, have the aspect of being stage props; the
tight-fisted Pisans built only three sides, leaving open the side facing
inwards.

On the Piazza Palazzo, besides the Archbishop's Palace and the Governor's Palace, is the **Cathedral.** There is little left of the original 13th-
century structure, and only the interior remains from the 17th-century
rebuilding. The present awkward facade was added in 1933—a clumsy copy
of the Cathedral of Pisa. Inside, however, are two beautiful pulpits carved by
the Pisan Maestro Guglielmo in the 12th century (he also did the four big
stone lions). Other works of art and religious artefacts can be seen in the
Cathedral's treasury, the **Museo Capitolare.** The crypt is also worth a visit
for its ornate vaulted ceiling.

From the Piazza Palazzo, the Via Martiri leads to the Piazza Indipendenza and the **Archaeological Museum** (may be closed through 1986 for
re-modelling). This collection was given by Carlo Felice, and has become,
along with the museum at Sassori, the major exhibition of Sardinia's distant
past. There are Neolithic finds, the 'little Venus of Macomer', and a fertility
goddess from Decimo Lutzo that bears no small resemblance to the Maltese 'fat ladies', but the stars of the collection are definitely the *nuraghic*
bronzes. At once elegant and homely, these little bronze figurines have a lot
to say about the people who built the *nuraghi.* There are archers and warriors, scenes of combat, men playing the *launedda* just as Sard shepherds do
today, animals, and the goddess with her child. The most artistic, perhaps,
are the ritual boats, with bull or deer heads, and sometimes dogs or other
symbols of the underworld. The Carthaginians are also represented, with
artefacts from Tharros, Nora and Karalis, including some grotesque masks
and idols of the god Bes. Bes, always a kind of smiling Buddah, looks out of
place in the gruesome Phoenician pantheon. Roman and Greek art, gems,
and grave steles, a collection of coins, and a Pinacoteca containing Sard and
Italian paintings complete the list.

Around the city
From the Torre San Pancrazio, the Viale San Vincenzo leads down from
the Citadel to the **Municipal Art Gallery.** Nearby are the ruins of the
Roman amphitheatre, which in its day seated 20 000 and the Botanical
Gardens. On Via Tigellio are the remains of a **Roman house,** believed to be
that of the poet Tigellius. To the west, between the quarters of Stampace
and Sant' Avendrace, rises the Tuvumannu hill, with the Punic–Roman

necropolis where some of the objects in the museum were found. The necropolis contains the tomb of Attilia Pompilia, also known as the Grotta della Vipera from the snakes decorating it, on Viale Sant' Avendrace.

On the east side of Cagliari, just off the Via Dante, the **Basilica di San Saturnino** stands in a small piazza. This is the oldest church on the island, dating from the 5th century, named after a Sardinian martyr under Diocletian. Part of the structure was actually added in the 11th century and the whole was severely damaged in the bombing, as were most of Cagliari's churches. The church has been lovingly restored—it looks as if they're still working on it, but what you see are excavations for the ancient cemetery that was discovered during the process of restoration. On the slope of Montixeddu hill is the **Santuario di Bonaria,** a large 19th-century basilica and adjacent 17th-century church with a statue of the Madonna that attracts many pilgrims.

The wide beaches of *Poetto* on Capo Sant' Elia, at the extreme eastern end of town, have become a popular and perhaps overdeveloped lido, frequented mostly by Cagliarese.

FESTIVALS
The feast of Sant' Efisio, is one of the most important *manifestazione folkloristiche* (first four days of May). It is primarily a religious event, with a pilgrimage to the saint's shrine at ancient Nora, though there are also processions, displays of traditional costumes, and a *cavalcata.* There is also a big trade fair in March, and the feast of Our Lady of Bonaria, with processions there (first week of July).

GETTING AROUND CAGLIARI
Cagliari is conveniently centralised for most of your needs. Hotels, restaurants, and cafés can be found mostly around the arcaded Via Roma. Piazza Matteotti is the transportation hub, with both the rail (FS) and bus (ARST) stations. For the FCS rail line to Arbatax, the station is in Piazza Repubblica; some buses to the villages leave from the FMS station on the Viale Colombo. Both of these are in the eastern part of the city.

TOURIST INFORMATION
The AAST information booth is in the Piazza Matteotti, near the train and bus stations (tel. (070) 651604). The EPT is in Piazza Deffenu 9 (tel. (070) 654811).

WHERE TO STAY
There's nothing special in either the high or low categories. The **Italia*****,

via Sardegna 31 (tel. (070) 656832; 40–48 000 lire single, 60–66 000 double) and the **Quattro Mori****, Via Angioz 27, just off the Largo Carlo Felice (tel. (070) 668535; 22–27 000 lire single, 36–41 000 double) are both good bargains and centrally located. Cagliari has an infinity of very inexpensive hotels. Most are small and often full, and you may need to look around a bit—on side streets off the Via Roma or the Corso Vittorio Emanuele. The **Firenze***, Corso Vittorio Emanuele 50 (tel. (070) 653678; 9000 lire single, 15 000 double) may be the nicest, but the **Londra***, Viale Regina Margherita 16 (tel. (070) 669083; 11–12 000 lire single, 19–24 000 double) has some rooms with baths.

WHERE TO EAT
In and around the Via Sardegna, just behind the Via Roma, are any number of very good restaurants, mostly inexpensive; Cagliari is altogether a wonderful town for dining. On the inexpensive side, try the **Due Archi**, Via Napoli 38, for grilled trout (12 000 lire for dinner), or the **Su Furriadorgiu**, Via Angioy, for ethnic surroundings and cuisine. At the opposite end of the scale, **Dal Corsaro**, Viale Regina Margherita 28, in an old nobleman's palace, will serve a good Sardinian feast for 30 000 lire and up.

Around Cagliari Province

East of Cagliari
This is an empty but ruggedly beautiful region called the Sarrabus, dominated by the peaks of the Setti Fratelli ('seven brothers'). The road hugs the coast, leading towards the recently developed resorts on the southeast corner of the island: **Solanas, Capo Boi** (a romantic setting with its old watchtower) and **Villasimius,** near the small peninsula called Capo Carbonara. Despite the number of new hotels and villas that have grown up around this corner of the island, at Capo Carbonara, Capo Boi, and other spots as far north as Muravera, the lovely coast is still pure primeval Mediterranean, with quiet coves and broad beaches everywhere, ideal if you're touring the area by car. The road through the mountains is just as scenic, passing through the lonely gorge of **Sa Picocca** with its grotesquely-eroded rock forms. North of the junction of these two roads are the market towns of **Villaputzu** and **Muravera,** at the end of the rich Flumendosa valley where almonds and figs grow. The beaches near Muravera are a popular vacation spot. The coast to the north features two ruined castles, Castello Gibas and Castello Quirra, and the 12th-century Pisan **Church of San Niccolo.**

SARDINIA– CAGLIARI PROVINCE

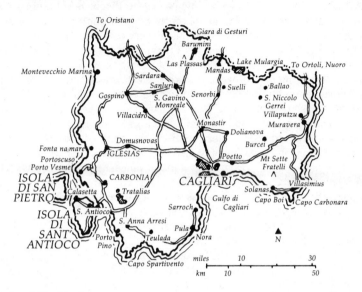

To Oristano

Giara di Gesturi

Barumini

Las Plassas

Lake Mulargia

To Ortoli, Nuoro

Montevecchio Marina

Sardara

Mandas

Sanluri

S. Gavino Monreale

Senorbi

Suelli

Ballao

S. Niccolo Gerrei

Gospino

Villacidro

Villaputzu

Muravera

Monastir

Dolianova

Domusnovas

IGLESIAS

Burcei

Fonta na mare

Portoscuso

Porto Vesme

ISOLA DI SAN PIETRO

CARBONIA

Calasetta

Tratalias

Poetto

Mt Sette Fratelli

CAGLIARI

Solanas

Villasimius

ISOLA DI SANT' ANTIOCO

S. Antioco

Sarroch

Gulfo di Cagliari

Capo Boi

Capo Carbonara

S. Anna Arresi

Pula

Porto Pino

Teulada

Nora

N

Capo Spartivento

miles   10   30
km   10   50

North of Cagliari

To the northwest the Carlo Felice (SS131), the island's main highway, traverses the **Campidano,** the broad plain stretching towards Oristano. Here, **Sanluri** saw the battle in 1709 that marked the end of Sardinian independence, when the forces of Arborea were finally defeated. Sanluri's castle (14th century) was a stronghold of the Giudicati of Arborea. There is a small historical museum inside. Another castle of the same era, the **Castello of Monreale,** can be seen near **Sardara,** a centre of the carpet-weaving craft with a large co-operative enterprise.

Directly north of the city, secondary highways and the old narrow-gauge FCS railway lead to Arbatax and the mountains of the Gennargentu, passing through a region of rolling hills and grey, quiet, resolutely Sardinian villages. In the little town of **Dolianova** the medieval church of San Pantaleo is built on the site of an early Christian structure; in the crypt are the original baptismal fonts cut from the rock. Farther to the north the small plain of the Trexenta, a recently reclaimed agricultural area, lies between the mountains and the artificial **Lake Mulargia** created by the damming of the Flumendosa. **Senorbi** has two interesting churches, the parish church with its carved wooden altars and the 13th-century **Santa Mulargia** in the hills

299

overlooking the town. **Suelli** has another restored Romanesque church, which served as a cathedral in the Middle Ages when the town was an episcopal see. South of the town lies the **Nuraghe Piscu. San Gavino Monreale** is a lead-smelting town, in the centre of the Campidano. The scenery, both here and in the surrounding hills, is very reminiscent of parts of the American West: Utah, Arizona or Texas. It isn't surprising that Italian directors often choose to film their 'spaghetti westerns' here.

The northernmost part of the province, the **Marmilla,** with its dozens of small villages, is dominated by a huge basalt plateau called the **Giara di Gesturi.** This natural wonder, covered with dense vegetation and some *nuraghi,* and home to a band of small, wild horses, has no roads; it's a steep climb if you wish to visit it. **Barumini** boasts the most important *nuraghic* complex of the south, **Su Nuraxi,** also one of the most visited. The central fortress is one of those resembling a medieval castle, and provided a bulwark in the defence against the Carthaginians. Remains of a *nuraghic* village surround the towers. Su Nuraxi was unknown until 1899, when a mudslide uncovered it. Most likely the *nuraghe* builders used wood for their domestic buildings. For that reason, and also because complexes like this are so rare, it is believed that these ruins are no mere village, but a palace or capital, or perhaps a trading centre for the Sards and their erstwhile Greek, Punic and Roman enemies. The collection of smaller towers and odd-shaped chambers, built of the same huge stones as the castle and connected by narrow, winding alleys, evokes the *nuraghic* civilisation more clearly, perhaps, than any other site on the island. Especially interesting are the two well-carved circular fountains. In the castle itself there's a small central courtyard and a maze-like network of stairways and passages hardly large enough to walk in—more like an anthill than a castle, and obviously meant for defence. Altogether, the complex resembles quite clearly one of the larger *talayot* complexes of Minorca

From the top of the castle, the view takes in an incredible sight, the ruined 12th-century **Castle of Las Plassas** at the summit of a bare, steep, perfectly conical hill, visible for many miles in any direction. There are a number of these hills in Sardinia; with ruins of a castle on top they are like something seen in a dream, and it is impossible to convince oneself these are natural formations and not the work of men.

One other village in this region, **Villamar,** is well known for its murals, literally dozens of them, covering its houses and walls, depicting aspects of Sard life, old and new, as well as contemporary political issues.

West of Cagliari
Beyond the Stagno di Cagliari, the coastal road plunges southwards towards

Capo Spartivento, the southern tip of the island. On the way, it passes through the villages of **Sarroch** with a large *nuraghe* nearby, and **Pula.** It also passes what seems to be the biggest oil refinery this side of Dubai, blighting the coast for almost a mile. On the coast near Pula are the ruins, recently excavated, of the great Punic–Roman city of **Nora** (open 8–1 and 3 pm to sunset). Here better than anywhere else in Sardinia one can get an idea of what Roman provincial cities were like. On Nora's narrow streets—often with the sewers underneath—can be seen the theatre, a temple to Tanit, and the mosaic floors in the homes of the wealthy. Part of the city, including the port, is today under the sea. Near the ruins a Pisan watchtower stands guard.

Also in the vicinity of Pula are the 11th-century church of Sant' Efisio, goal of pilgrims during the saint's festival in Cagliari in May, and the beach resort of **Santa Margherita,** near a small pine wood. More excavations, these of the ancient city of Bithia, are farther down the coast near Capo Spartivento, as well as another watchtower, the Torre di Chia (16th century), and another resort **Porto Pino,** on Capo Teulada. Near **San Giovanni Suergiu** with the turn-off for Sant' Antioco (see below) is a 13th-century church in the hamlet of **Tratalias** dedicated to Santa Maria. It was once a cathedral.

Another road west from Cagliari (route 130) passes through industrial sprawl north of the Stagno di Cagliari, past **Elmas Airport** and the road and railway junction of **Decimomannu.** Nearby are two towns, **Uta** and **Villaspeciosa,** both with interesting 12th-century churches built by French monks. With **Siliqua** we leave the Campidano and enter the mountainous mining country of the southwest. Near the town is the old feudal castle of **Acquafredda.** Farther west are two big mining towns, one very old and one very new: Iglesias and Carbonia, respectively the fourth and third largest cities on the island.

Iglesias and Carbonia

Iglesias dates from the early Middle Ages; some of its original fortifications can still be seen, and the Aragonese **Castello Salvatore** (begun by the Pisans) still looms above. Mariano IV besieged and captured this fortress in 1365. Two medieval churches are of interest: the 13th-century **Cathedral,** in Piazza Municipio, and the **Nostra Signora di Valverde** on Via Valverde. The centre of town is the **Piazza Quintino Sella,** named after the famous vintner, whose respected label *Sella & Mosca* is bottled in Alghero. **Via Matteotti,** leading from the piazza, is the main shopping street. The Technical Institute has a small mineralogical museum.

Iglesias has always been a mining town, though a more pleasant one would be hard to find. Today the mines are becoming uneconomical to operate—at least according to the government monopoly that runs them. The community is being forced to reconsider its future, and this is reflected in the murals that are appearing around the town. Some are celebrations of the old Sard ways, and some have political messages, but none is without artistic value (there's a good one on an elementary school a block from the railway station). Lead and zinc *aficionados* can visit the mines at Monteponi on a hillside 2 miles to the southeast.

East of Iglesias is another mining town, **Domusnovas,** to the north of which is the famous **Grotta di San Giovanni,** really a natural tunnel in the rock. It's the only cave in Sardinia you can drive your car through. Taking the road north from Iglesias towards Guspini will take you to one of the most unusual and little known archaeological sites in Sardinia, the **Tempio di Antas** (signposted on route 176, 9 miles north of the city). This *nuraghic* temple was taken over by the Phoenicians; later, under Roman rule, the mixed population constructed their own version of a Classical temple with odd Ionic-style columns. Many of these, along with a sculpted frieze above, still stand.

Carbonia is a new town, founded by Mussolini in 1938. When he invaded Ethiopia in 1936 the League of Nations imposed economic sanctions, and Italy had to mine its own coal. The town centre reeks of Mussolinian pomposity, with wide dusty streets and squares. Like Iglesias, though, it is pleasant enough for a mining town, not at all the horrible place most writers accuse it of being.

The port for these mines is the growing industrial town of **Porto Vesme,** with more oil refineries. This is the embarkation point for San Pietro and Sant' Antioco (see below). Almost adjacent to Porto Vesme is **Portoscuso,** an older port with an Aragonese tower and a beach. Just to the northeast is the *nuraghic* village of **Serrucci,** where some of the buildings are entirely intact. Perhaps because of the vicinity of the mines, the coast north of here has not been developed. The scenery is spectacular even by Sardinian standards, with the tall *scoglio* called **Pan di Zucchero** (sugar loaf) in the bay, with purple and green mountains and cliffs for a backdrop. There are fine beaches at Fontanamare and Porto Flavia. North of Iglesias, there are holiday villas on the coast, the 'Costa Verde', while a few miles inland are the old mining centres of Arbus, Guspini and the surreally-named Gonnosfanadiga, all on the slopes of Monte Linas. Guspini has a fine 15th-century Aragonese church. Near **Villacidro** to the south is a lovely waterfall.

Islands off the coast

Sant' Antioco

This isn't really an island now, though it once was. The Carthaginians began, and the Romans completed, a causeway over the shallow straits that still survives. Some arches of the Roman work are still visible. On the middle of the causeway are two standing stones, or *faraglioni,* that were an object of worship by the *nuraghic* people. The legend has grown since that they are a monk and a nun turned to stone by God when they attempted to flee the island together.

The aboriginal Sards had a sizeable colony on Sant' Antioco; there were over a score of *nuraghi,* though there isn't much left of most of them. The island was one of the first footholds of the Phoenicians. For them, and for Carthage, *Sulcis* (now Sant' Antioco) was the largest city in Sardinia. This city has been continuously occupied for 2600 years; ancient remains are found everywhere. This is not readily apparent to the visitor, who sees first the new town by the sea, with its tree-lined main street that sleeps all day but comes noisily alive for the evening *passegiata.* The old town is up on a height, surrounding the 11th-century **Church of Sant' Antioco.** Island, town and church are named for this saint, who took refuge here from Africa. Behind the simple baroque facade the old church seems almost like a cavern, lit with candles. Besides the relics of the saint, and some interesting early medieval reliefs, this church boasts two catacombs underneath, entered from the transept; also underneath are parts of a Punic hypogeum, which the Christians expanded in the 4th century to create the catacombs. Above the old town is the **Castello,** rebuilt in the 16th century by the Aragonese.

Just outside the old town are the Punic–Roman necropolis and one of the most interesting small museums on the island. The collection is presently housed in a farmhouse, but a new structure is being built next to the necropolis, a 5-minute walk away. Among the Punic artefacts are a number of gems decorated with mythical scenes, many toys of the children who perished on the *tophet,* grave steles and pottery. There is a tablet inscribed in Hebrew, testifying to the large number of Jewish settlers brought by the Romans, and some columns from the acropolis (where the Castello is now).

The necropolis and *tophet* are predictably grim. The *tophet* is one of the best preserved anywhere; you can see the stone slab where the sacrifices were performed, and the urns in which the ashes of Baal's little victims were deposited.

The remainder of the island is devoted to agriculture; some very good strong wine is made there. Off the southern tip are three islets—the 'Bull', the 'Cow' and the 'Calf'. There are a number of beaches all around the coast, but the only other town is **Calasetta,** founded in the 12th century, the point of departure for San Pietro.

FESTIVAL
Sant' Antioco (first Sunday after Easter).

San Pietro
This island was originally settled by the Carthaginians, though in the Dark Ages its population drifted away (or were carried away). San Pietro takes its name from a spurious legend that St Peter was shipwrecked here and taught the inhabitants how to catch tuna. King Carlos Emanuele, in his efforts to repopulate Sardinia, brought the Tabarchini, Ligurians from the town of Pegli who had started a colony on Tabarca Island near Tunisia, to San Pietro in 1737. More emigrants from Pegli arrived in the decades that followed. One of the last great pirate raids, in 1798, saw most of them abducted to Tunisia again, but piracy had become fairly civilised and the Sardinian government was able to buy them back five years later.

As a result of this colonisation, San Pietro is a very atypical corner of Sardinia. The inhabitants still speak their Genoese dialect, and most of them are fair-haired. The most obvious difference is in the town of **Carloforte,** named after the king. Carloforte is a tidy and very pretty town, of pastel-coloured houses, looking not surprisingly like any similar town on the Ligurian coast. It lies on the coast between a hill, with remains of an old fortress, and the extensive saltpans to the south. Life in Carloforte centres on the **Via Roma,** the shady esplanade with most of the restaurants. The town, indeed all of San Pietro, is fast becoming popular with the tourists.

One of the island's major attractions is the *Mattanza,* the ritual bludgeoning of tuna that is the island's chief source of income. A circle of boats, led by the *rais,* or chief (the word is Arabic and means admiral) surrounds a group of tuna and draws closer together, finally pulling up the nets and catching the tuna all at once. It's done the same way off Trapani and the Egadi Islands, and the spectacle takes place here by the islet of Piana just off San Pietro's northern tip, between April and July.

From Carloforte, a winding road crosses the centre of the island, past **Guardia dei Mori,** the highest point, where the Saracens are said to have had a fortress, through pine woods to Cala Fico. There are beaches along the western coast, near Carloforte, and on the western coast, where another road connects the town with La Caletta. Two grottoes on the coast, at Mezzaluna and Punta delle Oche, can only be reached by sea; excursions are arranged from the harbour at Carloforte.

At the southern tip of the island is the San Vittorio tower. Exactly on the

39th parallel, it houses an important astronomical observatory. Offshore here are twin *faraglioni*, called the 'columns'.

GETTING AROUND CAGLIARI PROVINCE
The services of the FS can take you to San Gavino Monreale (*en route* to Oristano) or else to Iglesias and Carbonia on the western spur, but to get anywhere else in the province without a car you'll have to rely on the buses. Another possibility is the antique FCS narrow-gauge railway that passes through Dolianova, Senorbi and Suelli on its way to Mandas, where it branches off for either Arbatax or Sorgono in Nuoro Province. Service is erratic but the scenery is some of the best in southern Sardinia.

TOURIST INFORMATION
Besides the information booth in Cagliari's Piazza Matteotti, where the staff are well versed in what's going on throughout the province, these towns can offer assistance: Muravera (for the southeast coast), Piazza Europa 5 (tel. (070) 993760); Villasumius, in the Piazza Incani (tel. (070) 791393); Iglesias, in the Piazza Municipio; Calasetta, at Piazza Municipio 10 (tel. (0781) 88534); and Sant' Antioco, in the Piazza de Gasperi.

WHERE TO STAY
Consult the provincial hotel listing for which villages in the interior are likely to provide accommodation. Most of them will be quite simple, like the **Hotel Italia***, in San Gavino Monreale (tel. (070) 933 9053; 11 000 lire single, 21 000 double; no rooms with bath). You may be lucky, though, and find another piquant institution like the **Su Nuraxi*** in Barumini (tel. (070) 936 8006; 9000 lire single, 17 000 double) which is exactly like staying at your grandmother's, except that this grandmother (known locally as Zia Annetta) is a very good cook.

Beach hotels here are mostly expensive, self-contained complexes built in the last decade. Santa Margherita, near Pula, has the fanciest, with swimming pools and private beaches, such as the **Flamingo***** (tel. (070) 920 8361; 50–60 000 lire single, 70–87 000 double).

Capo Boi and Capo Carbonara, near Villasimius, have similar complexes which are popular with groups. Less expensive holidays can be spent on the coasts near Muravera in the east or Portoscuso in the west, or on the islands of Sant' Antioco and San Pietro. In Calasetta (Sant' Antioco) there is the **Stella del Sud**** (tel. (0781) 88488; 29 000 lire single, 39 000 double), and there are similar hotels around Sant' Antioco town and at Carloforte. Finally, you can take your golf clubs along and stay at the **Is Molos Golf Hotel***** (4 miles outside Pula; tel. (070) 920 9440; 74–101 000 lire, double rooms only).

WHERE TO EAT
On the islands, you can wash down fish dinners and unusual specialities with *Vernaccia* wine (an honest 15° alcohol, the highest we've found yet) at the excellent **Da Nicola,** on the Lungomare Vespucci in Sant' Antioco (20,000 lire) or the **Tre Archi di Augusto** on Via Colombo in Carloforte. The **Rocca 'Ia** in Carloforte, Via Sedini, offers pizza and specialities *alle brace* (on the grill) for around 25 000 lire for a full meal. In general it will be fish along the coasts and modest Sard dishes like *mallorreddus* inland; the inexpensive **El Trocodero** in Pula, Via Sant' Efisio, is worth a stop on your way to the ruins at Nora.

Oristano Province

The old Giudicato of Arborea has been reborn since 1975 in the province of Oristano. Cut from parts of Cagliari and Nuoro, it is the smallest of the four Sardinian provinces. Even so, few parts of the island have so much natural and historical interest. The beautiful city of Oristano, and the Sinis peninsula, are two destinations that no traveller in Sardinia should miss, while the province's interior offers *nuraghic,* Classical, or medieval monuments in nearly every village.

Oristano

HISTORY
When ancient Tharros, on the Sinis peninsula, became too unsafe in the early Middle Ages, the population retreated to this defensible island site. The city was founded in 1070, and soon became the seat of the bishop and of the Giudicato. For 400 years the Giudicati maintained this independence by a continually shifting foreign policy, at times allied with the Pisans, the Genoese, and for a time even with Aragon. Imperialist Aragon, in the end, was to prove their greatest enemy.

In the 14th century—the great age of Mariano IV and his daughter, the Giudichessa Eleonora—Oristano attained its greatest prosperity and influence; Arborea's leaders spoke for all Sardinia in the struggle against the invaders. After 1410, when the city was finally taken, a period of decline set in that lasted until the present century. The irrigation and reclamation schemes of the Kings of Sardinia, Mussolini, and the post-war Republic have re-established Oristano, both as a capital and as the centre of a flourishing agricultural region.

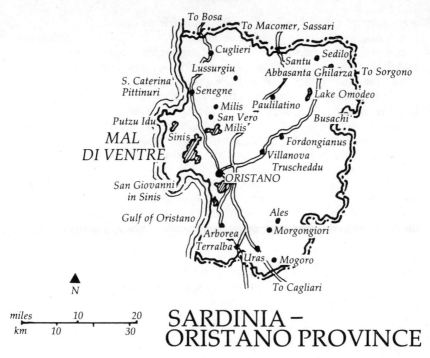

To Bosa
To Macomer, Sassari
Cuglieri
Sedilo
Santu
Lussurgiu
Abbasanta Ghilarza
To Sorgono
S. Caterina
Pittinuri
Senegne
Lake Omodeo
Milis Paulilatino
Putzu Idu
San Vero
Busachi
Milis
MAL
Sinis
DI VENTRE
Fordongianus
Villanova
Truscheddu
San Giovanni
ORISTANO
in Sinis
Gulf of Oristano
Ales
Arborea
Morgongiori
Terralba
Uras
Mogoro
To Cagliari

N

| miles | 10 | 20 |
| km | 10 | 30 |

SARDINIA –
ORISTANO PROVINCE

WHAT TO SEE

Oristano today is a city of many qualities, and much subtlety. Its quiet and dignified air, and the orderliness and simplicity of its streets and buildings, make it seem an almost otherworldly place. Of the four provincial capitals, Oristano is perhaps the most Sardinian in character, even more so than Nuoro. Like many of the small cities of the Mediterranean islands, it is a lesson to all of us accustomed to life in the metropolis in how much urbanity can be concentrated in a town of 20 000 or less.

Oristano's walls were torn down long ago, and a circle of broad avenues surrounding the old town has replaced them: Via Mazzini, Via Solferini, Via Cagliari. In the Piazza Mariano part of the fortifications remain, the **Portix-eddu** ('little tower'). Another tower, the **Porta Mannu,** or St Christopher's Tower, stands on the edge of **Piazza Roma,** the modern centre of Oristano. Behind the tower the **Corso Umberto,** a pedestrian-only shopping street, extends towards the **Piazza Eleonora,** with a statue of the great Giudichessa. Oristano is still very much Eleonora's city; her house can be seen

307

at 4 Via Parpaglia and her tomb at the Santa Chiara church.

Just behind this square, set in a small garden, is the **Cathedral**. Though begun in the 11th century, most of what exists today, including the lovely, slightly leaning, octagonal campanile with its leering faces near the top, dates from the 1700s. Across from the cathedral is the 18th-century **Seminary**; also here is the **Church of San Francesco**. The building itself is 19th-century neo-Classical, but inside is a striking medieval crucifix called 'Di Nicodemo', and a statue of San Basilio by Nino Pisaro. There is a small museum in Oristano, the **Antiquarium Arborense** on Via Vittorio Emanuele (open 9–12 and 3–5; closed Sundays), with a collection of Punic and Roman objects from Tharros and elsewhere.

Following Via Cagliari, 2 miles south of Oristano is the suburb of **Santa Giusta** with the 12th-century church of the same name; built by the Pisans this is one of the outstanding medieval monuments on the island. Some of the columns in the nave were taken from Roman ruins at Tharros.

FESTIVALS

Oristano has one of Sardinia's most famous folk festivals, *Sa Sartiglia*, in the last week before Lent (see Festivals, p. 289). Also, the festival of San Croce (12–14 September).

Around Oristano province

Sinis

This is a true wonderland, one of the best kept secrets in Sardinia. (There are no buses to Sinis; as with so many other of the island's sights, you'll need your own transport.) Sinis is a low, flat peninsula northwest of Oristano, covered mainly with heather. Just the same it is indeed a poetic landscape, as the Sards claim, and there is a wealth of interesting things to see. Sinis is separated from the rest of the island by the **Stagno di Cabras,** a lagoon full of fish and eels, near the town of Cabras. The road from Oristano passes over a narrow strip of land between the lagoon and the sea, passing the popular lido at **Torregrande.**

Where the road splits there is a *nuraghe,* and to the right is the **Sanctuary of San Salvatore,** surrounded by a festival village; deserted for most of the year, it springs to life in September for the festival. The church is built on an ancient religious site; a trapdoor in the floor leads to a 4th-century sanctuary dedicated to Hercules Soter, with Roman frescoes portraying Venus and Cupid, and Hercules slaying a serpent.

At the southern tip of the peninsula is the fishing village of **San Giovanni** in Sinis, a place where the 20th century is only a dim rumour. The village consists of a long row of huts made of rushes along the shore, built according to an age-old highly aesthetic design. The fishermen also use the rushes to build their boats. The parish church of San Giovanni is, after San Saturnino in Cagliari, the oldest in Sardinia, dating from the 5th century. Like San Saturnino and all the early Christian monuments in Sardinia, it is in the form of a Greek cross with a dome over the centre. There is an original baptismal font, carved with a fish at the bottom.

Close to the village are the excavations of **Tharros.** As in Nora, part of the city is under water. On the hill overlooking the town are the Punic necropolis and *tophet,* a Spanish tower of the 15th century and the remains of a synagogue. There are several beaches in the vicinity.

On the western coast of Sinis is another large beach of multicoloured pebbles, with a view of the uninhabited island mysteriously known as **Mal di Ventre** (stomachache) and the peculiar rock formations further up the coast. At Capo Mannu, on the northern end, is the small resort of **Putzu Idu.** A small lagoon nearby, the **Stagno di Sale Porcus,** is one of the last summer homes of the European crane (*fenicotteri* in Italian). They are a wonderful sight, but try not to disturb them.

FESTIVAL
San Salvatore (first Sunday in September).

South of Oristano

The swampy plain south of the city facing the Gulf of Oristano was good farmland in ancient times, but almost entirely deserted when its reconstruction was begun in 1919. A system of dams was built all along the Tirso, Sardinia's longest river, irrigation canals were dug and swamps drained. The centre of this new land is tidy, prosperous **Arborea,** founded by Mussolini in 1928. The Municipio houses a small archaeological collection.

Further inland, route 642 branches off the main Sardinian highway at **Uras,** where the last Arborean resistance was stamped out in 1470 by the Spaniards, to a string of mountain villages on its way to the Barbagia. **Morgongiori** has what is reputed to be one of the only working obsidian mines in the Mediterranean; it seems to have been worked since the Neolithic era. Today Morgongiori, and nearby **Mogoro,** are important centres of traditional Sardinian carpet weaving and other crafts. **Ales** is an ancient bishopric with a 16th-century cathedral.

West and North of Oristano

On route 388, running up the Tirso valley, **Villanova Truscheddu** has an important *nuraghe* nearby. **Fordongianus** is an ancient Roman settlement—*Forum Traianus*. Roman piers still carry the bridge over the Tirso, and there are ruins of an ancient spa, the *Acquae Hypoitanae,* with a modern establishment just across the river. The 13th-century **Church of San Lussorio,** site of that saint's martyrdom, is a mile west of Fordongianus. There are catacombs underneath. Many *domus de janas* can be seen at **Busachi.**

Directly north of Oristano is **San Vero Milis,** with the **Nuraghe Surachi** to the west of it, near Sinis. **Milis** and **Bonarcado** have 13th-century churches; the area around **Seneghe** is renowned for its many natural springs.

Near **Paulilatino** are many *nuraghi* and some giants' tombs. Nearby, a major *nuraghic* site has recently been discovered at **Santa Cristina,** with a temple, a sacred well and many tombs. These sacred wells are a fascinating relic of the *nuraghe* culture. Many, like this one, are triangular holes in the ground with steps leading down under a corbelled roof. Archaeologists are fond of reading them as symbols of the female principle. The builders saved their best work for them; their perfectly squared stonework is better than anything in the *nuraghes.* **Abbasanta,** on its plateau, is a large agricultural town; just south of it is the great defensive complex of **Nuraghe Losa,** with a three-storey central tower (only the first and second storeys remain). The Carthaginians did not succeed in capturing Losa until the 6th century BC. West of Abbasanta a cluster of villages on the heights surrounds **Lake Omodeo,** where a huge dam holds back the Tirso. The lake is named after the engineer who designed the dam, and is well-stocked for the enjoyment of fishermen. One of the villages is **Ghilarza,** where you can visit the home of the famous socialist and philosopher Antonio Gramsci. At the far end of the lake is the old and very traditional village of **Sedilo,** with still more prehistoric remains nearby.

Along the coast north of Sinis, a beach resort is developing around **Santa Caterina di Pittinuri.** Nearby is a natural formation on the shore called the 'Archetto' (little arch) and the ruins of another ancient city, **Cornus.** Further north, around the slopes of Monte Ferru, a not-quite-extinct volcano, is **Cuglieri,** in a pretty wooded setting, with the 15th-century church of **Santa Maria della Neve.** The Pro Loco has a small archaeological collection of objects from Cornus. South of the town is an interesting decorated Neolithic hypogeum. In the hills just to the north, near **Scano di Montiferro,** are a number of *nuraghi.*

To the east of Cuglieri is **San Leonardo** with a 13th-century church and some radioactive springs. Near Santa Lussurgiu is the beautiful waterfall known as **Sos Molinos.**

FESTIVALS

Abbasanta: Santa Caterina (25 November). Sedilo: Sant' Antine, folk festival with horse race (5–7 July); the race, called the *Ardilo*, commemorates the battle of the Milvian Bridge, where the Emperor Constantine (Sant' Antine) defeated the pretender Maxentius in AD 312. Constantine is only one of many saints recognised by the Sards but not by the Pope.

GETTING AROUND ORISTANO PROVINCE

In the city of Oristano, small as it is, both the railway station (Piazza Ungheria) and the bus station (Via Cagliari) are a good walk from the centre. If you take a train through the province, keep an eye out for *nuraghes*; the tracks follow a natural route of communication, and on the stretch from Oristano north to Chilivani at least a dozen of the most important sites in Sardinia, including *nuraghes* Losa and Sant' Antine, can be seen from the train.

Unfortunately there is no public transport into Sinis—though that probably helps keep it unspoiled and beautiful. The buses can take you to almost anywhere else mentioned in the text, though as always plan the trip out well in advance.

TOURIST INFORMATION

In Oristano, the EPT office is at Via Cagliari 276, near the bus station (tel. (0783) 74191).

WHERE TO STAY

Oristano city has five middle-range hotels which are all about the same, but for panache at bargain rates, stay at **Cocco and Dessy's***, Via Tirso, near the Porta Mannu (tel. (0783) 78372; 13–15 000 lire single, 22–25 000 double) where the years come and go but nothing ever changes. An inexpensive time can be spent on the beach at **Su Pallosu**** (at Su Pallosu; tel. (0783) 52021; 17 000 lire single, 29–30 000 double) or **Da Cesare***, at Putza Ida (tel. (0783) 52015; 18 000 lire single, 29 000 double), or else at the Torregrande Marina near Oristano: the **Del Sole***** (tel. (0783) 22000; 31–41 000 lire single, 51–69 000 double). There is one small hotel in southern Sinis, the **Casas***, at San Giovanni (tel. (0783) 290871; 13 500 lire single, 22 000 double). Modest accommodation can be found in the villages of Abbasanta, Cuglieri, Terralba, Ghilarza, Ales, Arborea, Bauladu and Santa Caterina.

WHERE TO EAT

Oristano is famous for a speciality called *bottarga* (the roe of a fish called the *muggine* that lives in the Stagno di Cabras), smoked and served as antipasto or with spaghetti. You can try it at **Il Faro,** on Via Bellini 25 in Oristano, or in the restaurant of the Su Palloṣu hotel (20–25 000 lire). Oristano, like Cagliari, is a good city for restaurants. **La Forchetta d'Oro,** on Via Giovanni XXIII, and **Stella Marina** on Via Tirso both specialise in seafood (25 000 lire for fish). In Ghilarza, **Da Zia Rita,** Corso Umberto 185, offers an innovative approach to local dishes (25 000 lire).

Nuoro Province

When the Romans were attempting, frequently and unsuccessfully, to extend their control here, they dubbed this part of Sardinia *Barbaria.* The name lives on as Barbagia for the areas below the Gennargentu, the mountainous roof of the island, and it's still wild, a land of shepherds and bandits. The province is also the repository of Sardinia's ancient customs and folk life; this, with the new resorts along the coast, is beginning to attract some tourists.

Nuoro

HISTORY
When the Barbagia became a province of Italy, it didn't have a city to use as a provincial capital, so it was necessary to invent one. Nuoro, or Nugoro, is really an overgrown village. In existence only since the Middle Ages, it began to achieve some importance in the 18th century when it became a bishopric. In 1926 Nuoro became the capital of the province, and it has grown steadily since.

WHAT TO SEE
Today Nuoro is a peaceful, relatively modern town of 20 000. Though its citizens are among the most ardent students and practitioners of the old Sard ways and arts, the town has a reputation in the mountain villages as a place where people stamp papers for a living.

Nuoro, as you will soon learn if you visit there, gave Italy two of its greatest writers of this century, Grazia Deledda, who won the Nobel Prize for literature in 1926 and whose novels are evocations of Sardinian life, and the poet Sebastiano Satta.

There aren't many sights; the old town is at the eastern end, on a height with occasional wonderful views over the countryside below. The **Cathedral,** on the Piazza Santa Maria della Neve, dates from the 19th century. Via Chironi 28 is the house where Grazia Deledda was born and spent most of her life; it is in the process of being transformed into a museum. The main street is the **Corso Garibaldi,** which terminates in the **Piazza Vittorio Emanuele,** a pretty park where it seems to be the hour of the *passegiata* all day.

One of Nuoro's two museums, the **Museo Regionale del Costume** (open 9–1 and 3.30–7, closed Mondays) is in a modern building recreating the traditional architecture, just south of the town on the Viale San Francesco; the building also houses an institute dedicated to Sard folklore. In the museum's collection are costumes of the various villages with explanatory notes, jewellery, handicrafts and photographs. At Via Leonardo da Vinci 5 is the often overlooked **Museo Civico Speleo** (open 8.30–12.30, holidays 9.30–1, closed Mondays). Though small, it is one of the best organised and most informative museums on the island. Besides exhibits of objects from the local *nuraghi,* and from Punic and Roman sites, it is the best introduction to the many caves around Nuoro and on the coast.

East of Nuoro is Monte Ortobene, with a giant statue of Christ the Redeemer at its summit. The mountain, with its fine views, has become a small summer resort with two hotels. Nearby is the church of **Nostra Signora della Solitudine,** where Grazia Deledda is buried.

FESTIVALS
29 August is the *Festa del Redentore,* one of the largest folk festivals on Sardinia, including a pilgrimage to Monte Ortobene. Also Santa Maria delle Grazie (29 November).

Around the province

North of Nuoro
This is a remote, mountainous district. There is a *nuraghic* village with a sacred well, just north of the town at **Noddule. Bitti** is a large village, and **Lula** a small one, both with popular festivals. The valley of the River Posada, not traversed by any road, and Monte Albo to the south, really a chain of rugged peaks, are haunts of shepherds, wild boar and *muflone.*

FESTIVALS
At Bitti: the *Madonna del Miraculo* (29 September); at Lula: San Francesco (1–10 May).

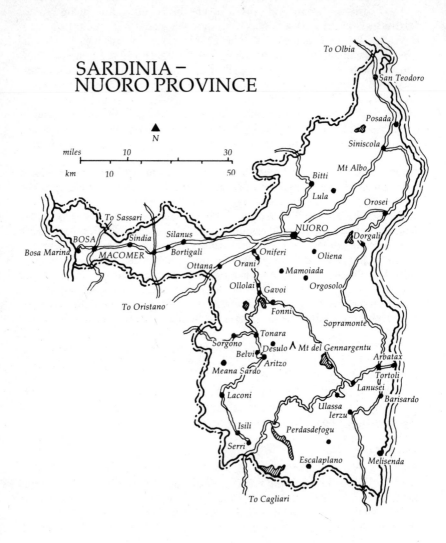

SARDINIA – NUORO PROVINCE

N

miles 10 30

km 10 50

To Olbia

San Teodoro

Posada

Siniscola

Mt Albo

Bitti

Lula

Orosei

NUORO

Dorgali

Oliena

Oniferi

To Sassari

BOSA Sindia Silanus

Bosa Marina Bortigali

MACOMER

Ottana Orani

Mamoiada

Ollolai Orgosolo

Gavoi

To Oristano

Fonni

Sopramonte

Tonara

Sorgono Desulo ∧ Mt del Gennargentu

Belvi

Meana Sardo Aritzo

Arbatax

Tortoli

Lanusei

Laconi

Barisardo

Ulassa
Ierzu

Isili

Perdasdefogu

Serri

Escalaplano

Melisenda

To Cagliari

314

Nuorese coast

The northern limits of the province border on the Costa Smeralda; the Nuorese coast is in many ways just as attractive, but less developed. **San Teodoro,** along with nearby Budoni, has in recent years become a popular resort area, considerably less expensive than the Costa Smeralda, just to the north. At Posada, on the mouth of the river of the same name, is the ruined medieval **Castello della Fava. Siniscola** is an old agricultural town, famous for its women's costumes, but it is becoming the centre of a big vacation area, with a broad sandy beach at **La Caletta,** and another by the old fishing village of **Santa Lucia.** Further to the south is a headland, **Capo Comino,** with the Nuraghe Artora, and further south another resort, **Cala Liberotto,** with another *nuraghe* in the hills above it.

Orosei is a Roman foundation, *Fanum Carisii,* that was important in the Middle Ages; it has a ruined castle. This is in the middle of another agricultural reclamation area, on a narrow plain under the mountains. There is a beach at **Marina di Orosei.** To the south, the road (route 125) curves inland to **Dorgali,** an important handicraft centre that produces leather, ceramics and jewellery. There are many *nuraghi* and a *nuraghic* village in the neighbourhood and another growing resort on the coast at **Cala Gonone.** From here, excursions by sea are available to the **Grotte del Bue Marino,** the largest of the many caves on this part of the coast. The 'Bue Marino' (sea-ox) is the Mediterranean monk seal; this cave is one of the last hiding places of these large animals, though you would be lucky to see one. Just inland from Dorgali the River Cedrino is dammed to create a large lake; on its shores is the important *nuraghic* village of **Serra Orrios.**

A long empty stretch of highway runs south of Dorgali, under the peaks of the **Sopramonte.** The coast is mountainous and inaccessible as far as **Arbatax,** on Capo Bellavista, the centre of a resort area that stretches from **Santa Maria Navarrese** to **Lido Orri.** The coastline is dramatic, including the rock of **Ogliastro** in the sea just off Santa Maria. **Tortoli** is an agricultural centre; this reclaimed area is largely devoted to subtropical fruits: oranges, persimmons and even bananas grow here.

Barisardo is in the middle of an area full of *nuraghi,* with some *domus de janas* on the hillsides. There is a beach by a medieval watchtower on the coast at **Torre di Bari.** South of here the landscape once again becomes rather empty, as the road follows a valley between two mountains. There are embryonic resorts, hard to reach, at **Sa Foxi Marina** and **Melisenda** on the coast.

315

FESTIVAL
At Dorgali: the 'Festival of the Grotto' (30 August).

South of Nuoro
This is the Barbagia, a land of intricate geography, with hills, mountains and valleys thrown down on the map seemingly at random. At its centre is **Gennargentu** ('silver gate')—a collection of the highest peaks on the island. Mountain villages surround it on three sides: in the Barbagia Ollolai to the north, the Barbagia Mandrolisai to the west, the Barbagia di Belvi to the southwest, and Barbagia Seulo to the south.

Just a few miles south of Nuoro is **Oliena,** one of the most typical of Nuorese villages, with its 15th-century church of Santa Maria. The village is famous for its costumes and its wine. Outside the town are two sanctuaries, those of **Nostra Signora di Monserrato** and **San Giovanni;** near the latter is a natural spring with a waterfall at **Su Gologone.** Above Oliena, to the south, are the **Sopramonte,** of which the tallest is Punta Corrasi (4754 ft). This is one of the most mysterious parts of the island, a stretch of mountains and valleys with hardly any roads and hundreds of caves, great and small. It is the perfect hideout for bandits. Deep inside it is a *nuraghic* complex at **Tiscali.**

Orgosolo, like Oliena, is a shepherd village, renowned as the centre of Sardinia's sheep-rustling activity, as it has been for many centuries. **Mamoiada,** in a lovely wooded setting, is famous as the home of the *Mamuthones* (see Festivals, p.289), stars of the pagan pre-Lenten festival. The highest town in Sardinia is **Fonni,** with its distinctive women's costume. Fonni is on the slopes of **Monte Spada** (5190 ft) and has Sardinia's only ski-resort. Route 389 from here passes west of Gennargentu, past the sources of the Flumendosa (one of which is a big artificial lake), and on over a stretch of 30 miles to Lanusei without passing a single village; it is a very scenic road.

North of Fonni is another artificial lake, Lago Gusanno; **Gavoi,** a mountain resort; **Ollolai,** the big shepherd town that gives the region its name; and **Orani,** a mining town near which is the mountain sanctuary of **Nostra Signora di Gonari.** Near Oruferi are some *domus de janas.* **Ottana**—it's hard not to get confused by the fifteen villages in this region that begin with O—is the site of a modest effort to industrialise the Barbagia. Nevertheless, it is still a traditional village, with ancient pagan rites at the Carnival which are similar to those of Mamoiada, though not as well known. The church of **San Nicola** is a beautiful 12th-century work. This is Pisan architecture at its best, with all the familiar motifs of false arches, diamonds and stripes of different coloured stone.

South of Fonni, in the Mandrolisai, are many forests of holm-oak, ilex and walnut. The centre of the region is **Sorgono,** a mountain resort and a very pretty one. Sorgono is the terminus of the secondary railway from Cagliari. Nearby at **San Mauro** is a fine 16th-century church with a big rose window. **Aritzo,** on the western slopes of the Gennargentu, has become one of the most popular centres for mountain vacations. A place of great natural beauty, if you are willing to take the trouble to get there, is **Desulo,** almost in the centre of Gennargentu, and close to the island's two highest mountains, **Punta la Marmora** (5960 ft) and **Brancu Spina** (5945 ft).

South of Sorgono, in a heavily forested area, are **Meana Sardo** with a 16th-century church and many nearby *nuraghi,* and **Laconi,** home of St Ignatius of Laconi (18th century), where you'll find the ruins of the **Aymerich Castle** (11th–17th centuries), a fortress of the Giudicati of Arborea. **Isili** is a famous centre for handicrafts.

South of here, on the borders of Cagliari Province, are the two striking plateaux, the **Giara di Gesturi** with its wild horses (see Cagliari Province) and the **Giara di Serri.** Near Serri are several *nuraghi,* including the well-preserved **Is Paras,** with the remains of a village around it.

The upper valley of the Flumendosa lies to the west, with two of Sardinia's largest artificial lakes, **Lago di Flumendosa** and **Lago Mulargia.** North of these, route 189 passes the southern borders of the Gennargentu through a number of tiny villages to **Lanusei,** a mountain resort very near the beach resorts at Arbatax on the coast. Lanusei is the largest town of a small region called the Ogliastro; to the south, near the towns of Ulassai and Ierzu, are odd limestone formations called *toneri,* and a large number of caves, some of which have yet to be explored. The land south of Ierzu is an almost barren plateau, a perfect site for the Italian rocket-launching station near **Perdasdefogu.** South of Escalaplano, near the border of Cagliari Province, is a sacred well of the *nuraghic* Sards called **Fontana Coperta.**

FESTIVALS

This is the great area for festivals in Sardinia; there are over 100 of them each year. The EPT in Nuoro keeps a complete list, and the chances are they can direct you to one whenever you visit, though most are in the spring or summer. These are the most important: Sant' Antonio (17 January) at Sorgono and Mamoiada; Carnival (Monday, Tuesday before Lent) at Mamoiada and Ottana; Easter processions at Oliena; Sant' Antioco (15 days after Easter) at Gavoi and Ulassai; Madonna delle Grazie (8 May) at Ierzu; San Nicola (3rd Sunday in May) at Ottana; the same day is Santa Barbara at Ulassai; San Mauro (first week in June) at San Mauro, near Sorgono; Madonna dei Martiri (first Sunday in June) at Fonni; the same day is Sant' Anania at Orgosolo; San Giovanni (24 June) at Escalaplano, Fonni and Oliena; San Giovanni Battista (last Sunday in June) at Isili; Santa Maria Maddalena (21–22 July) at Nuragus, near Isili; San Giacomo (25–27 July) at Ierzu; Sant' Anna (26 June) at Oruferi; Madonna di 'Sa Itria' (last Sunday in July) at Gavoi; Madonna della Neve (first Sunday in August) at Desulo; Ferragosto Fonnese (15 August) at Fonni; same day is 'Ferragosto' (Assumption) at Orgosolo and Ottana; San Lussorio (20–23 August) at Oliena; San Bartolomeo (24 August) at Ollolai; San Bartolomeo (26–28 August) at Isili; Sant' Ignazio (28–31 August) at Laconi; Nostra Signora di Monserrato (1–8 September) at Oliena; San Basilio (first Sunday in September) at Aritzo; San Basilio (13–14 September) at Desulo; Sant' Antonio (3rd Sunday in September) at Austis, near Sorgono; SS Cosimo e Damiano (25–28 September) at Mamoiada, *Sagra delle Nocciole e delle Castagne*, 'the feast of hazelnuts and chestnuts' (last Sunday in October) at Aritzo.

Chiesetta di Santa Sabina, Silanus

West of Nuoro

A narrow strip of land, along both sides of route 129, connects Nuoro Province with the west coast at Bosa. About 25 miles west of Nuoro is **Silanus** in the foothills south of Monte Lameddari. Here, visible from the road, a large *nuraghe* and the 11th-century church of **Santa Sabina**, resembling an early Christian or Byzantine work with its Greek-cross plan, stand facing each other in an open field. This area, from here to Macomer, is lined with *nuraghi*; then as now, this was the principal route across the island, and the *nuraghe*-builders took great pains to defend it.

Macomer is an agricultural market town, and the most important road and rail junction on the island. Travelling in Sardinia, sooner or later you'll end up in Macomer. The numerous *nuraghi* in the neighbourhood include **Nuraghe Santa Barbara,** northeast of the town. South of Macomer, at **Borore,** is one of the best of the 'giant's tombs'.

The little River Temo has the distinction of being the only navigable river in Sardinia—for all of 4 miles. It stops being navigable at the ancient town of **Bosa,** founded by the Carthaginians. This town, which shows must of the Spanish influence in its buildings, is famous for its handmade lace and its *Malvasia* wine. From the riverfront promenade, Bosa climbs upwards to the half-ruined **Serravalle Castle,** built by the Pisans in the 12th century. In between is the peculiar **Cathedral,** and the **Piazza Umberto** with its fountain. Outside the town is one of the earliest and best Romanesque churches, the 11th-century **San Pietro Extramuros.** To the north of the town are the ruins of another medieval castle, the **Malaspina.**

Bosa Marina, on the coast, is an old port with a 17th-century watchtower; it has a good beach, and is developing into a resort. A small island called Isola Rossa is joined to the port by a causeway.

FESTIVALS
San Pantaleo (27 July) at Macomer. At Bosa there is Carnival (on and before Ash Wednesday), SS Emiliano e Priamo (27–29 May), San Pietro (29 June) and Santa Maria del Mare (first Sunday in August). San Lorenzo, in Silanus (10 August).

GETTING AROUND NUORO
A spur of the main railway line of Sardinia connects Nuoro city with Bosa on the west coast; it crosses the main line at Macomer. Bus connections may be difficult, not from any deficiency in the service, but simply because the system is so complex, connecting the innumerable villages with the capital and with each other. Nuoro's bus station is on the Piazza Vittorio Emanuele. It's a madhouse; consult the enormous schedule board and then start asking everyone for further information. Try to reach a consensus, but meanwhile keep an eye on the buses.

If you're driving, expect some treacherous but wildly scenic mountain roads—particularly in the southern Barbagia. Remember that snow and ice can be a problem any time during the winter or spring. The villages are close together though, and there should be little problem with services.

TOURIST INFORMATION
In Nuoro the EPT is in Piazza Italia 19 (tel. (079) 230129 or 275395). The

Pro Loco organisations may be helpful in Oliena (Piazza Paloch), San Teodoro (Via Sardegna), Bosa (Via Ciusa), Macomer (Corso Umberto 180),
and Belvi (Viale Kennedy 26), but don't count on finding anyone about.

WHERE TO STAY

Nuoro city's hotels range from four stars to one, but the only one worthy of
note is the **Fratelli Sacchi****, high above the city on Monte Ortobene (tel.
(079) 31200; 22–26 000 lire single, 30–35 000 double). Along the east
coast, beach hotels are almost all recent additions, modern and up-to-date
if somewhat simple. In many of the resorts, as at San Teodoro, they are
spread out all along the coast—peaceful, but not convenient unless you have
a car. Cala Gonone, on the shore near Dorgali, has the largest selection, and
the **Villagio Palmasera***** is the biggest, offering tennis and a pool (tel.
(0784) 93191; singles 32–64 000 lire, double 52–105 000 lire). All the rest
are in the range 29–31 000 lire single, 35–42 000 double. Another such establishment, the **Villagio Saracena***** at Arbatax (tel. (0782) 667318; 33–
40 000 lire single, 55–66 000 double) is even more sports-oriented, with
everything from water skiing to *bocce*.

In the mountains, several towns and villages are now making a living by
entertaining tourists. Fonni, Aritzo, Oliena, and Gavoi are perhaps best
equipped.

The **Sporting Club*****, 5 miles from Fonni on Monte Spada, keeps its
visitors busy with skiing and Land Rover excursions into the wilds (tel.
(0784) 57124; 39–41 000 lire single, 54–85 000 double) while at Oliena, the
Su Gologone***, 5 miles from Oliena (tel. (0784) 287512; 34 000 lire
single, 48 000 double), has a fine restaurant and riding tours (lessons also
offered). More modest accommodation is available in most of the larger villages, such as the pleasant **Hotel Moderno**** in Aritzo, 6 Via Kennedy (tel.
(0784) 62229; 18–22 000 lire single, 31–42 000 double). Far from being the
forbidding mountain wilderness it often seems to outsiders, the Barbagia
can be explored quite comfortably. Just don't expect to find a room without
advance notice during any of the village festivals.

WHERE TO EAT

In a traditional region like this, it isn't surprising that most of the restaurants
are in hotels. Some—like the **Fratelli Sacchi** in Nuoro, mentioned above,
and the **Su Gologone** outside Oliena—are quite good (17–25 000 lire for
each). **Ai Monte del Gennargentu** in Orgosolo, is another. All these, and
most of the rest throughout the province, of course specialise in Sard cuisine. In fact, you should probably avoid anything which is not Sard; you can

find sorry pizzas along the eastern coast, and very peculiar hamburgers in
Nuoro. Try the **Ristorante Sa Talleri**, 224 Corso Umberto, if you are
stranded in Macomer (15–20 000 lire).

Sassari Province

This is the largest province in Italy (Nuoro, incidentally, is second, and
Cagliari fourth). It attracts most of the tourists in Sardinia to its many
beaches, and it's the best place to see the beautiful Pisan country churches.

Sassari

The first recorded mention of the village of Sassari (pronounced Tha-thari)
is in a register of 1131. At this time the ancient town of Torres, capital of the
region since the Carthaginians founded it, was beginning its long decline.
Pirates and disease ravaged the coasts, and the population was gradually
moving inland. Sassari grew rapidly; though originally under the protection
of Pisa, and later of Genoa, the town developed as a free city—the only one
on all the Italian islands—with its own code of laws administered by the
Council of Anziani (elders).

Under the Spaniards Sassari's privileges were taken away, but the town
continued to prosper. The archepiscopal see was moved from Torres in
1438, and the University, founded in 1558, was the first on the island.
During the War of the Spanish Succession, Sassari was occupied for a short
time by the Austrians.

One thing has been constant throughout Sassari's history—a contentious
passion for liberty that stands behind the city's frequent revolts. Already in
the 13th century Michele Zanche (whom Dante placed in the fifth circle of
the Inferno) was leading a democratic rebellion; Sassari fought the Spanish,
Austrians and Savoy kings with equal stubbornness. Always more attuned to
the currents of European thought than to the rest of the island, the Sassarese warmly embraced the ideals of the Enlightenment and played a role in
the various Sardinian insurrections of the Napoleonic era. In 1848 they
finally succeeded in booting the Jesuits out of town, and afterwards destroyed the old Aragonese Castello as a 'symbol of oppression'.

WHAT TO SEE
Sassari today has over 100 000 people, and is the second largest city on the
island. Its rivalry with Cagliari holds perhaps a modicum of disdain, for the

Sassarese take a great deal of pride in their town. Sassari somehow manages the clever trick of being a place very Sardinian in character, yet different from anywhere else on the island. There is still very much the air of a medieval free city here: the civic spirit is reflected for example in the 'Festival of the Candlesticks' (organised each year by the ancient guilds) as well as in the buildings themselves, and in the jewel of a medieval town that is the historical centre. The newer parts of the city fit harmoniously with the old, and the whole is beautiful and alive and one of the finest cities to be found anywhere on these islands.

Three almost contiguous squares connect the old town with the new. **Piazza Italia** is a 19th-century creation, with the obligatory statue of Vittorio Emanuele. The stately sandstone building houses the offices of the provincial government; its assembly hall is more worthy of a great nation than a mere province. Across the square is the **Giordano Palace.** Not a palace at all, or very old either, it is a splendid work of what must be the Mediterranean version of Victorian Gothic. A bank and the **tourist information office** share the ornate interior.

Next, to the north, comes the **Piazza Cavallino de Honestis,** often referred to by its old name, Piazza Castello. Here was the grim fortress that offended the 19th-century Sassarese; for 300 years it had been the local headquarters of the Spanish Inquisition. Today the square holds Sassari's two skycrapers and many cafés. Before the walls were demolished, this had been the main gate. We continue northwards into the old town through the pretty triangular **Piazza Azuni,** a busy shopping area, and down the **Corso Vittorio Emanuele,** main thoroughfare of the medieval town, with the **Civic Theatre** and two fine buildings from the 15th century at nos. 42 and 47.

North of the Corso is another fine square, the **Piazza Tola,** named after two brothers, Sardinian patriots of the 19th century. At its southern end is the 16th-century **Palazzetto Usini.** On Corso Trinita can be seen parts of the old wall and a tower.

Sassari now is quite a sophisticated place (would you expect, for example, a Sardinian town to name a street after Martin Luther King?) but it hasn't lost touch with the countryside. Two bridges off the Corso Trinita carry the city over to its northern extension, but beneath them, in a narrow valley, farmers still plant their crops. Down here, accessible by steps from the Rosello Bridge, is the **Rosello Fountain,** symbol of Sassari. This is one of those Renaissance fantasies that looks more like a stage-set than a fountain, decorated with figures representing the four seasons, dolphins and gargoyles.

South of the Corso, in a puzzle of narrow winding streets, is the **Cathedral.** Originally a 13th-century structure, of which only the campanile

322

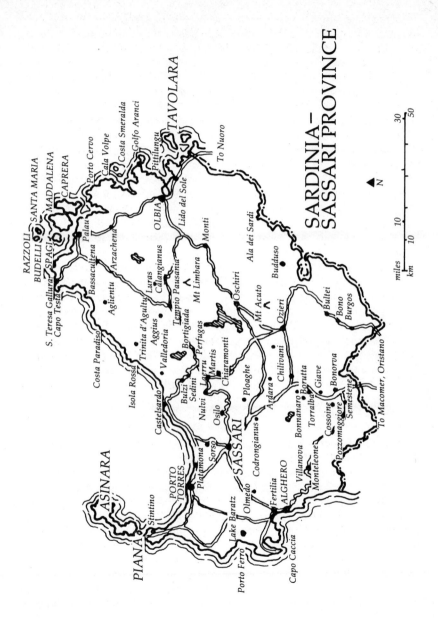

SARDINIA–
SASSARI PROVINCE

N

miles
km

323

remains, the church was completely rebuilt in the 15th century. Then, in the 1700s, the famous baroque facade was added. This facade is a work of rare beauty, a confection in stone unique in Sardinia; unlike so many other baroque works, the underlying simplicity and sense of proportion of this one makes the profuse decoration become part of the building; it is not just tacked on for decoration's sake. Inside there is a **Cathedral Museum,** with liturgical bric-à-brac and some paintings.

Around the corner, on Via Santa Caterina, is another fine building, the 18th-century **Ducal Palace,** now the Municipio. The reception rooms are an informal museum with works of art and Sard costume dolls. The **University** (17th century, though rebuilt), with a large library, is on the Piazza Universita. The western limit of the old town is the Corso Vico, with the **railway station**—a copy of the one in Trapani and several others; the Ferrovie dello Stato planted these all over Italy in the 19th century. At the end of Corso Vico is the 13th-century church of **Santa Maria de Betlem,** with carved wooden altars. The giant 'candlesticks' are kept here between festivals.

Just behind the University is the pleasant **Giardino Pubblico;** in the centre of the park is the modern **Handicrafts Pavilion,** with exhibits of Sard handicrafts, most of which are for sale. On **Via Roma,** main street of the modern part of town (a block from the squat, unlovely **Palazzo Giustizia**—Mussolini's contribution to Sassari), is the **Museo Archeologico Sanna.** The archaeological collection here is not quite as rich as that of Cagliari, but this is a 'progressive' museum, with a wealth of explanatory pictures and notes, extremely helpful and informative—but only in Italian. The art and artefacts of all the periods of early Sardinian history are represented; especially interesting are the exhibits on the shadowy Neolithic people who preceded the *nuraghic* builders, with finds from their important religious site at Anghelu Ruiu near Sassari. There are some *nuraghic* bronzes and ceramics, and a trepanned skull, testifying to Bronze Age surgical skill, as well as Punic and Roman relics.

Part of the museum is a separate collection, the **Museo Gavino Clemente,** a wonderful exhibition of Sardinian costumes, crafts and folk art. The attendant will probably play some Sard music on a phonograph to entertain you during your visit.

On the southern edge of Sassari, on Viale San Pietro, is a 13th-century church, **San Pietro in Silki.**

FESTIVALS

Ascension Day (May) sees the *Cavalcata Sarda,* one of the three big Sardinian folk festivals. They've only been doing it since 1950, but it has become tremendously popular and attracts people from all over the island. The day before the Assumption (14 August) is the festival of *Li Candelieri,* the candlesticks (see Festivals, p. 290).

Around the province

South of Sassari
This is a region called the Logudoro, the greater part of the old Giudicato of Torres. Route 597 runs southwest out of Sassari towards Olbia. This road is sometimes called the 'way of the churches'. Before it passes Chilivani the route passes near three of Sardinia's greatest medieval monuments. Of these, the best known is the 12th-century **SS Trinita di Saccargia,** in open country near Ploaghe and gloriously decorated with green-and-white stone stripes. The facade and a campanile are a Sard masterpiece in stone. **Ploaghe's** parish church, not impressive outside, has a big surprise inside: a fine collection of about 40 paintings, including one by Filippino Lippi, given to the church by a Sardinian historian named Spano who was born in the village.

In the Middle Ages, **Ardara** was an important centre, a rival to Sassari. Before the Spanish occupation it was the capital of the Giudicato. Still a pleasant town, it is worth visiting for the 12th-century **Santa Maria del Regno.** Inside this church is a beautiful wooden altarpiece of the 15th century, containing a number of paintings by Martin Torner and Giovanni Ruiu, a Sardinian. The third of these 12th-century churches is **Sant' Antioco di Biscarcio,** which, like SS Trinita, stands in open country.

Route 131, south from Sassari, is the main highway of Sardinia. It is still sometimes called the 'Carlo Felice' after the King who built it, connecting Sassari with Cagliari. Near the turn-off from Ardara is another 12th-century church called Mesumundo, built over the remains of a Roman thermal spa. Further south the road passes **Bonnanaro,** where some of the most ancient Neolithic remains on the island have been found, and **Borutta.** Here yet another Pisan Romanesque church testifies to the prosperity of the Logudoro in the Middle Ages; this one, **San Pietro de Sorres,** is perhaps the most beautiful of them all, isolated on a plateau overlooking the town, and with a fine view.

South of Borutta, on the plain around **Torralba,** is the **Sant' Antine nuraghe,** with Barumini one of the two largest and best preserved in Sardinia. It seems to have been an important religious site as well as a fortress. Inside the walls are a sacred well, two small towers and the great three-storey central tower. All over this plain are scattered other *nuraghi;* this site may possibly have served as a kind of capital for the *nuraghe*-builders, situated square in the centre of the region most densely populated by them—the northwest corner of Sardinia from the River Tirso to the northern coast.

From Torralba a second road (route 131 bis) travels to Alghero past the artificial Lake Bidighinza and the villages of Thiesi and Ittiri. The latter has another 12th century church, hidden behind a very peculiar modern facade; of the original work, a fine, tall campanile remains. On the 'Carlo Felice' south of Torralba are **Giave,** with a panoramic view from the ruins of its medieval castle, and **Bonorva** with the **Tres Nuraghes** nearby and some *domus de janas.* Further south is a vast barren plateau, the Altopiano Campeda, which forms the southern boundary of the province. West of Bonorva is a circle of small villages including **Semestene** (with another 12th-century church) and **Pozzomaggiore,** known for its embroideries.

East of Bonorva is a picturesque region of hills and forests called the **Goceano. Bono,** a pretty town, is the main centre; to the north, near Bultei, is the thermal spa of San Saturnino. **Burgos,** south of Bono, was settled first by Spaniards, as its name implies. Its well-preserved **castle** was the scene of many a conflict in the days of the Giudicati.

FESTIVALS
At Bono, San Raimundo (31 August) and Santa Restituta (7 May).

Alghero and the west coast
Alghero is a beautiful city in a beautiful setting, one of the prime tourist centres of the island. The British, in particular, favour it; they have been coming here for decades.

In a sense, Alghero isn't a Sardinian town at all. Founded by the Arabs, and controlled by Genoa in the early Middle Ages, the Aragonese found it a valuable and strategic site, and began their Sardinian conquest with Alghero's annexation in 1355. The Algherese did not prove to be very docile subjects; after two fierce rebellions the Aragonese solved their problem by deporting the entire population to the interior and replacing them with Catalans. Thus did Alghero become a kind of foreign concession on the island, as Bastia was under the rule of the Genoese in Corsica. Sards were forbidden to remain within its walls after dark, under severe penalty, and no more than ten at a time were allowed in during the day.

In Alghero today, the town's past is readily visible. It has all the appearances of a town built for noblemen ('You are all knights', Emperor Charles V said on his visit in 1542—the Algherese still recall this with pride), and this of course suits Alghero perfectly for its modern role—as a town built for tourists. The old town has most of its fortifications still intact. On the seaward side, the top of the walls makes a promenade with views of the town and its gulf. Five towers remain on the landward side; the **Torre dello Sperone,** the southernmost, is also called the Torre di Sulis after the Sardinian revolutionary who was imprisoned there following Angioy's rebellion, and the **Torre di Porta Terra** marks the old main gate. Across from it is the **tourist information office** (AAST). Through the Bastione della Maddalena is the small **harbour,** with excursions by sea to the Grotto di Nettuno on Capo Caccia.

Alghero still has a marked Catalan flavour; until recently, everyone spoke Catalan. The older ones still do. The city's landmark is the 16th-century **Cathedral** on Via Manno. Unlike most churches in Sardinia, the interior is more interesting than the plain facade. The real attraction, however, is the lovely, typically Catalan campanile that dominates Alghero's skyline. You'll need to go around the back to appreciate it best (on Via Roma); there is a finely sculptured portal at its base.

Across the street from the Cathedral is the **Palazzo d'Albis,** where Emperor Charles stayed during his visit. Two blocks east is the **Via Carlo Alberto,** with most of the shops. Also in the old town are the **Casa Doria,** a fine 16th-century palace on the Via Principe Umberto; the **Municipio,** with Alghero's historical archive, on the Piazza Municipio; and two churches on Via Carlo Alberto: San Michele (17th century) with its multicoloured tile dome, and San Francesco (14th century). Both have beautiful interiors.

Just outside the old town, across from the Torre di Porta Terra, is the **Giardino Pubblico,** a pretty park patrolled throughout the summer by a horde of pretty but audacious caterpillars.

Alghero is the centre of a big resort area, now being promoted as the *'Riviera del Corallo'*—since the success of the Costa Smerelda every strip of Sardinian coast has acquired a similar name. This one, however, may be the most attractive of all. North of Alghero there is a huge sandy beach that runs for several miles, all the way to **Fertilia,** a town founded by Mussolini as the centre of a big agricultural reclamation area, the Nurra. On the stream just before Fertilia are the remains of a **Roman bridge.** Beyond the town is another beach, **Le Bombarde,** and the **Palmavera Nuraghe,** then a bay, Porto Conte, with some small undeveloped beaches.

The western side of this bay is another of Sardinia's natural wonders, **Capo Caccia,** with its dramatic cliffs and views of Alghero and the two great rocks in the sea, **Isola Piano** and **Isola Forada.** Near the cape the cliffs are several hundred feet high, forcing the visitor to walk down 650 steps to visit the **Grotta di Nettuno.** It's more than worth while, however; this is one of the most beautiful caves in the world. Only a few hundred yards of it have been fully explored, but what has been opened out is now a big tourist attraction, with guided tours and electric lighting. The sea surges against the narrow entrance, but inside calm reigns. Neptune's Grotto is special not only for the subterranean lagoons and delicate stalactites—they look like a forest drawn by Antonio Gaudi—but for the colours. There's another cave, reached by another set of stairs, just to the north, the **Grotta Verde,** but it is not nearly as interesting.

North of Capo Caccia are numerous other small resorts, at **Porto Ferro, Argentiera** and **Nurra,** near Capo Mannu. Just inland from Porto Ferro is tiny Lake Baratz, which has the distinction of being the only natural lake on the island.

North of Alghero, off the road for Porto Torres, is the great Neolithic necropolis of **Angelu Ruiu,** the largest in Sardinia. The 36 *domus de janas* contain interesting decorations, mostly of bulls' heads; the statuettes and ornaments found here are housed in the Sanna Museum in Sassari. Near the necropolis is **Fertilia Airport,** which serves Sassari, Alghero and Porto Torres.

FESTIVAL
Festa dell'Immacolata (8 December).

The northern coast

The northwestern corner of Sardinia is a narrow peninsula dotted with lagoons. Near the tip is **Stintino,** a fishing village that is in the process of becoming an important resort. Off **Punta del Falcone** is the uninhabited islet of Piana, and beyond it the island of Asinara.

Asinara is a big island, and looks very picturesque from across the strait, but you can't visit it; it suffers from the curse of so many Italian islands, being the home of a penal colony. Its natural inhabitants were evicted in the last century, and now make up the population of Stintino. (They catch tuna in the spring and summer, performing the *Mattanzas* as in San Pietro.) Asinara's claim to fame is that it's the only place in the world where albino donkeys are bred.

East of the peninsula is **Porto Torres,** which flourished under the Carthaginians and Romans as *Turris Libyssonis,* and again in the Middle Ages as capital of the Giudicato of Torres. The city's long decline began in the 14th century, and only recently has Porto Torres come back to life as a port and industrial centre.

The effects of the decline can still be seen in the old town, half-abandoned and decrepit; modern Porto Torres has gravitated back down to the port area, with its main street **Corso Vittorio Emanuele** connecting the old and new. In the old town is the largest medieval church in Sardinia, the **Basilica di San Gavino.** It is a simple and beautiful work, but somewhat idiosyncratic—there's no facade at all, but apses at both ends. There may have been an ancient temple on the site; the basilica incorporates 28 Roman columns in its interior.

West of the Corso, next to the railway station, excavations continue in the remains of old Turris. This is the romantically but deceptively named **Palazzo di Re Barbaro** (Palace of the Barbarian King—really a Roman governor named Barbarus), with ruins of various structures, a temple and baths. A new museum, the **Antiquariun Turritano,** has recently been opened to show off the finds. Nearby, a **Roman bridge** still in use crosses the River Turritano. Where the Corso meets the waterfront is the **Piazza Cristoforo Colombo,** with a Roman column marking the end of the road from Karalis (Cagliari). The old Roman road followed the course of the modern 'Carlo Felice'.

There are beaches near the town at **Marinella** and **Platamona,** a lido popular with the Sassarese. On the road to Sassari are many *nuraghi,* and a Neolithic sanctuary at **Monte Accodi,** with tombs, remains of temples, two menhirs and a great altar.

East of Porto Torres, near **Sorso,** is the 11th-century church of **San Michele di Plaiano.** Further east, along route 200, is **Castelsardo.** Originally called *Castelgenovese,* this great fortress defended the coast of the Giudicato of Logudoro. The castle is on the height of a narrow promontory, with the village on the slopes around it; on a clear day, Corsica and much of northern Sardinia is visible from here. The **Cathedral** houses a wonderful painting, *The Madonna with the Angels,* by an unknown artist called the Master of Castelsardo. Other examples of his work can be seen in the small picture collections around Sardinia (as in the Cagliari Museum); they have considerable artistic merit. Castelsardo today is famous for its basketwork, made from palm branches.

The coast around Castelsardo has many unexploited beaches. South of the town is the 12th-century church of **Nostra Signora di Tergu,** and on the side of the road east to Tempio is a peculiar rock formation, typical of the weird eroded forms on the northern coast, called the **Elephant Rock.** The early Sards chiselled two small *domus de janas* into it. **Valledoria** is an agricultural village near the mouth of the largest river of the north, the Coghinas. Just south of it is the thermal spa of **Casteldoria,** with ruins of a medieval castle.

The coast to the north has been named **Costa Paradiso** between **Isola Rossa,** the name of both an islet and a village on the coast near it, and **Porto di Li Francesi.** In between are a few beaches, but not many hotels. Most of the coast is dotted with villas managed by private associations, as on the Costa Smeralda.

329

FESTIVAL
Procession of San Gavino (first week of June) in Porto Torres. Holy Week processions in Castelsardo.

Traditional costume for the Ascension Day Procession, Sassari

East of Sassari
There are remains of several castles in Sardinia built by the noble Malaspina family; one of them is at Osilo in the mountains just east of Sassari. This has a fine view over the northern coast and Corsica. Between Osilo and the River Coghinas are a number of villages: **Nulvi** is known for its devotion to the old customs. Just west of **Martis** there is a **petrified forest**. **Perfugas** and **Sedini** have Aragonese Gothic churches: near the latter is a big *domus de janas* and many limestone caves, the largest of which is the **Grotta della Conca Bulia.**

To the south in the centre of the province is **Chilivani,** the rail junction where the track divides for Sassari and Olbia. The town, it seems, is named after the Indian wife of Benjamin Pierce, the English engineer who built the railway. East of Chilivani is **Ozieri,** a distinguished-looking town occupying a natural amphitheatre on a hillside. The **Cathedral,** rebuilt in the 19th century, contains works by the 'Master of Ozieri' along with some by the 'Master of Castelsardo', one of the two great anonymous Sardinian artists of the 11th century. The town has many fine small palaces with loggias, and there is a beautiful fountain in the Piazza Grixoni. This corner of Sardinia, known best for the breeding of horses (there are occasional races near Chilivani) has recently begun to take a very active interest in its ancient patrimony. Ozieri has a new **Archaeology Museum,** with *nuraghic* finds from the many sites in the neighbourhood as well as Punic and Roman items. Another new museum is just to the southwest in the hamlet of **Ittireddu;** here the star exhibit is a famous ancient bronze work—a model of a *nuraghic* castle.

Some of these artefacts were found at the *nuraghic* castle at **Burghidu,** north of Ozieri just off the Sassari–Nuoro road, with a sacred well and remains of a town.

East of Ozieri **Monte Acuto** rises, a 'patch' of mountains like Gennargentu only smaller. Between Ozieri and Olbia is one of the most sparsely populated and lonely regions of Sardinia, the bare mountains and dry valleys of southern Gallura. In all of it there are only a handful of villages: **Budduso,** a mountain resort; **Monti,** with a famous festival; and **Oschiri.** Budduso is known for the skill of its craftsmen in woodcarving. Another village nearby, **Pattada,** is equally famous for handmade knives. Three miles west of this village, near the big dam and lake on the Coghinas, is a site with ruins of a medieval church and castle, a Roman fort, and a *nuraghe,* all very near each other.

To the north, on the opposite slopes of **Monte Limbara,** highest mountain in the province, is a greener and pleasanter side of Gallura, around **Tempio Pausania.** This is of Roman foundation, but like Sassari it became an important place when the coasts became unhealthy and unsafe in the early Middle Ages. Today it is a mountain resort, with a famous medicinal spring called **Fonte Renaggiu,** south of the town, and the surrounding countryside produces, conveniently enough, both wine and cork. The use of grey granite in the buildings makes Tempio, like many towns in the Gallura, reminiscent of Corsica. Indeed, many Corsicans have migrated to this corner of the island over the centuries; their influence is felt in many of the region's villages, some of which are almost entirely Corsican.

Piazza Gallura is the centre; the **Cathedral** (15th century, rebuilt 19th century) is on the nearby Piazza San Pietro. An **Oratorio,** also on Piazza San Pietro, was built by the Aragonese, rebuilt in the 18th century, and incorporates some Roman remains—combining all into a pretty facade. West of Tempio is **Bortigiada** with many *nuraghi,* and **Aggius;** to the east is **Calangianus,** centre of the cork industry and renowned for its boar-meat salami.

FESTIVALS
Sant' Antonio (middle of August) at Osilo; San Paolo (29 June) at Monti; *Ferragosto* (15 August) at Nulvi; *Madonna del Remedio* (29 September) at Ozieri.

331

The east coast

This is the Sardinian playground, the greatest concentration of resorts on the island. Santa Teresa and Olbia are the major centres, with the famous Costa Smeralda and the archipelago of the Maddalena in between.

Olbia is an ancient city; it was the first Carthaginian settlement on the east coast and, with its harbour, the best on the island, Olvia knew prosperity through the periods of Punic and Roman rule. Like Porto Torres, it declined greatly after Rome's fall. Until 1939, when Mussolini restored the old name in the 'Imperial Revival', Olbia was known as *Terranova Pausania*. Now, thanks to DDT and tourism, Olbia is prosperous again, an unpleasant and very un-Sardinian town of overpriced restaurants and overdressed youths. The only 'sights' are the plain 11th-century church of San Simplicio, ruins of the **Roman baths,** and a necropolis.

The coast around the Gulf of Olbia is especially scenic, and has many big resorts. **Lido del Sole** to the south and **Lido Pittilungu** to the north are the most popular. Everywhere the view is dominated by the fantastic bulk of the **Isola Tavolara,** one of a few uninhabited islands in the bay. North of Olbia, off route 125, is a *nuraghic* sanctuary with a view at **Cabu Abbas,** and on a long promontory at Capo Figari, the fishing village of **Golfo Aranci—** the name comes from *granchi* (crabs), not *aranci* (oranges)—which is becoming a popular resort.

The Costa Smeralda

Twenty years ago, were you to ask the average citizen about Sardinia, you would get a blank stare in reply. Today, the chances are that he would say 'Ah yes, the Costa Smeralda!' In the early '60s, when this strip of coastline between Golfo Aranci and Arzachena was one of the emptiest corners of the island, the Aga Khan, Muslim nabob and international playboy, and some friends started buying up the land.

What they had in mind was a little principality devoted entirely to vacations, and it has become just that, one of the great successes of the modern tourist industry. In a way, the Costa Smeralda is the suburban dream applied to tourism. The consortium begun by the founders exercises strict planning controls and regulations over architecture and land use; the effect is tidy, tasteful, and all of a piece. Unfortunately, however, it has almost nothing to do with Sardinia. The hotels and villas, in a phony 'traditional' style, are the epitome of contemporary tourist architecture, closer in spirit to Disneyland than to Gallura.

A frequent complaint from the Sards is that all the land and hotels are owned by foreigners; very little, if any, of the money that tourists bring in ever stays in Sardinia. Nevertheless, the place is extremely popular, both with the rich and with status-seekers on package tours. The coast itself is pleasant, but there is little to see. The only centre (everything is spread out in suburban style) is **Porto Cervo,** whose recently built **Stella Maris** church has a painting by El Greco, the *Mater Dolorosa.*

North of the Costa Smeralda are more resorts: **Baja Sardinia, Palau** and **Porto Pozzo.** Palau is the terminus of the narrow-gauge railway from Sassari, and the point of departure for the island of La Maddalena. The coast in this area, even more than the rest of Gallura, is marked by bizarre forms in granite eroded by the strong winds. One, near Palau, is unmistakably 'The Bear', and the rest, like Les Calanches in Corsica, will put your imagination to the test.

Arzachena, the old town inland from the Costa Smeralda, has been changed as much as Olbia by the tourist tide. In the vicinity are some unique *nuraghic* sites. An unusual necropolis at **Li Muri,** just to the south where the road turns east for Luogosarto, consists of a long, paved trench-like grave, closed at one end by a row of enormous dolmens. At **Li Macciunitta** there's a circle of standing stones with a tomb at its centre, and other curiosities at the sites of **Malchettu, Caddi Vecchiu,** and **Li Lolghi,** all little-known and recently excavated.

At the northern tip of Sardinia is **Santa Teresa di Gallura.** In the Middle Ages this town was known as *Porto Longone,* but it dwindled, and was refounded in 1808 by King Victor Emanuele, who resettled it with Piedmontese and named it after his wife Teresa. The port, with connections of Corsica and La Maddalena, is an inlet half a mile east of the town centre; this was the site of the medieval town. Santa Teresa is a big resort in its own right. There is an excellent beach at **Rena Bianca,** guarded by a Spanish watchtower, and impressive views of Corsica from the heights at Punto Falcone and Capo Testa. The latter has been a quarry since ancient times; you can still see some Roman columns lying about, and stone from here was used in the famous baptistry in Pisa.

FESTIVALS
Sant' Antonio (early June) and Santa Teresa (14–16 October), both at Santa Teresa di Gallura. San Simplicio (15 May) at Olbia.

La Maddalena and Caprera
Off the coast between Santa Teresa and the Costa Smeralda is a small archipelago. Two of the islands are part of Corsica, the remainder are Italian. La Maddalena is the largest, and the only inhabited island; it would be fair to speak of La Maddalena and Caprera as a single island, since they are

joined by a causeway. Of the others, and there are about 60 of them, the vast majority are tiny chunks that serve only to decorate the coastline. Razzoli, Spagi, Budelli, Santa Maria and San Stefano are each about one square mile in size, but there is nothing to see (San Stefano and Budelli have beaches, and San Stefano has a campsite). During the season excursions run from La Maddalena around the archipelago.

The islands' only brushes with history came in the 19th century. During the Napoleonic Wars, Nelson and his fleet spent a few months cruising the area while waiting for the French to come out and be sunk at Trafalgar. The King of Sardinia's official neutrality prevented Nelson from ever actually landing, but the admiral sent regular reports to London explaining what a lovely base Sardinia would make and how he thought it could be had, at the time, for a song. London was not impressed, and chose Malta instead.

Caprera, as every Italian schoolboy knows, is the burial place of Garibaldi, who spent the later years of his life there.

La Maddalena, the town, is a prosperous and charming place. Some of that prosperity comes from tourism, but the Americans you'll see everywhere in town aren't tourists at all; they are sailors from the huge NATO base on the island. (American servicemen never wear their uniforms while on leave, but you'll recognise them by the bulky portable radios they carry.) La Maddalena is renowned as the easiest station in the Mediterranean, and most of them never want to leave.

There are two small harbours, with the ferry dock in between. That on the left is the **Cala Gavetta,** where excursions to the other islands depart, also the buses for Caprera and the rest of La Maddalena. Two blocks north of the port is the **Piazza Garibaldi,** from which runs the Via Garibaldi, the main shopping street. La Maddalena's church of **Santa Maria** still has a pair of silver candlesticks, a gift from Nelson.

From this town a 'Via Panoramica' circumnavigates the island's coast. Beaches are everywhere, notably at **Spalmatore** and **Cala Maiore** on the northern side. West of town the road passes over the long causeway and onto Caprera, most of which is beautifully planted with pines. The road leads directly to Garibaldi's house, the **Casa Bianca,** now a national museum. The 'hero of two worlds' arrived here after his sojourn in America, and the house is built in South American style. Living in this rustic idyll, pottering around the house and garden, Garibaldi spent the last 33 years of his life—that is, when he wasn't campaigning through Sicily and the peninsula and scaring the daylights out of Italy's ruling classes. His tomb, the pine tree he planted for his daughter Clelia, his bed (in a big glass case), and the other memorabilia are explained on the guided tour.

GETTING AROUND SASSARI

Sassari's station (at Piazza Stazione on the western edge of the old town) is the centre for rail connections in the province. FS trains for Porto Torres, Olbia, Oristano and the south leave from here, as well as the SFS (Strade Ferrate Sarde) narrow-gauge trains for the Alghero–Tempio Pausanio–Palau route. This line, whose trains are more like trams than real trains, passes through some wonderful scenery, and provides a delightful excursion through the Gallura region.

Sassari city does not have a bus station as such; buses depart from a piazza, the Emiciclo Garibaldi, next to the Giardino Pubblico. Olbia and Alghero are other centres for bus transport, with connections to most of their neighbouring villages.

Four different companies handle the Palau-La Maddalena ferry service, and between them there are several runs a day. Some call at Santa Teresa. For another fascinating excursion, consider a quick trip to Corsica. The Tirrenia Line (Via Porto, in Santa Teresa; tel. (0789) 754156) runs a regular ferry service to Bonifacio, surely one of the most unusual and distinctive cities in the Mediterranean, with its medieval granite houses perched on the edge of lofty cliffs over the sea.

TOURIST INFORMATION

In Sassari, the EPT is at Piazza Italia 19 (tel. (079) 275395) and there are local AAST organisations at these towns:

Sassari, Via Brigatta Sassari 19 (tel. (079) 233534).
La Maddalena: Via XX Settembre 24 (tel. (0789) 736321).
Palau: Via Nazionale 94 (tel. (0789) 709570).
Santa Teresa: Piazza Vittorio Emanuele (tel. (0789) 754127).
Olbia: Via Catello Piro 1 (tel. (0789) 21453).
Arzachena: Via Risorgimento (tel. (0789) 82624).
Alghero: Piazza Porterra 9 (tel. (079) 979054).
This last is one of the best run and most helpful on the island. In addition, there are Pro Loco organisations in:

Bonorva: Corso Umberto 9.
Calangianus: Via Garibaldi 11.
Castelsardo: Via Bastione 2.
Porto Torres: Piazza Colombo.
Tempio Pausanio: Piazza Gallura 2.

WHERE TO STAY

The phenomenon of tourism, not only on the Costa Smeralda and Alghero but all around the province's long coastline, has certainly transformed this end of Sardinia. It's all happened relatively recently, though, and resort hotels are almost all modern. Some resort areas are considerably more expensive than others (anything around the Costa Smeralda, of course, and recently, Stintino). Note that you can spend a much more economical holiday in Alghero or La Maddalena, where there's much more to see and do, or in a quiet, unspoilt resort area like Castelsardo.

In Alghero, there's a tremendously wide choice of hotels, from the elegant **Villa Las Trovas******, Lungomare Valencia (tel. (079) 975390; 58–71 000 lire single, 105–129 000 double) in an old palace with a private beach, to modest places like the **Eleonora****, also on Lungomare Valencia (tel. (079) 970236; 26–30 000 lire single, 30–38 000 double), and even cheaper hotels a block or two from the beaches. In the quieter area of Porto Conte and Fertilia north of the town, there are others like the **Porto Conte***** (tel. (079) 942036; 35–52 000 lire single, 53–75 000 double) on the lovely peninsula around Capo Caccia.

At Castelsardo there are hotels on the shore in town, but the beaches are about 2 miles away at Cala Ostiva and Lu Bagnu; at the latter is the **S'Istuffa**** (tel. (079) 474010; 20–22 000 lire single, 31–38 000 double). Similarly, at La Maddalena you'll have a choice between places in town or on the beaches like the quiet **Cala Lunga*****, at Porto Massimo (tel. (0789) 737540; 45–78 000 lire single, 66–118 000 double, with private beach and pool). Santa Teresa and its environs also have a wide range, with many at pretty Capo Testa, and the **Villaggio Santa Teresa***** (tel. (0789) 751520; 31–39 000 lire single, 62–76 000 double) at La Marmorata.

On the Costa Smeralda, the best (and most expensive) is the **Pitrizza*******, cottages in a secluded forest setting (tel. (0789) 92000; 146–275 000 lire single, 295–520 000 double). The **Cala di Volpe******* (tel. (0789) 96083) and **Romazzino** (tel. (0789) 96020) are similarly exclusive and exhorbitant, though you can get by on the cheap at the **Residenza Capriccioli**** (tel. (0789) 96016; 20–31 000 lire single, 38–58 000 double—but no rooms with baths!) Resorts at Baja Sardinia, Cammigione and Porto Rotondo take advantage of their proximity to the Costa Smeralda to charge a third or half as much again as similar hotels elsewhere; those in Golfo Aranci and Olbia are cheaper—and the scenery and beaches on average are more pleasant.

In the cities and villages accommodation seems a little harder to find than in other provinces—perhaps because everyone's building on the coasts. The **Sardegna**** is a very comfortable and inexpensive hotel in the centre of old Sassari (Corso Vitorio Emanuele 100; tel. (079) 234636; 15–17 000 lire single, 23–27 000 double) and the same could be said for the **Cen-**

trale** in Olbia, although prices on the east coast are always higher (Corso Umberto; tel. (0789) 23017; 29 000 single, 44 000 double).

WHERE TO EAT
In Sassari **La Forchetta Sarda** on Via Cagliari is well known for specialities like *spaghetti alla bottarga,* and relatively inexpensive (20 000 lire). **Ziromira,** Largo Sisini, makes memorable pizza (8–10 000 lire). Along the coasts it's mostly seafood—and why not? Alghero has many very good places for it: **DaTore,** 4 Via Gioberti, is exceptional (25–30 000 lire for fish). At **Il Pavone,** Piazza Sulis, there's an open-air terrace overlooking the sea. Catalan cuisine still survives in Alghero at the **Corsaro,** Via Columbano, where you can eat good paella for 25 000 lire.

Some other places for seafood: in Stintino, the **Marina Piccola,** Via Cala d'Oliva; at Castelsardo (on the beach at Lu Bagnu) the **Su Ferula** for *zuppa di pesce;* at Porto Torres, the **Ristorante Cristallo,** Via XX Settembre. All are fairly expensive; expect to pay at least 25 000 lire for a fish dinner. In La Maddalena there are several places along the seafront: **L'Araosta** and **Trattoria Marina** are cheap and very good (around 15 000 for a full meal with wine).

CONVERSION CHARTS

Weights and measures

1 kilogramme (1000 g)—2.2 lb   1 lb—0.45 kg
1 etto (100 g)—¼ lb approx
1 litre—1.76 pints

1 pint—0.568 litres
1 quart—1.136 litres
1 Imperial gallon—4.546 litres
1 US gallon—3.785 litres

1 metre—39.37 inches   1 foot—0.3048 metres
1 kilometre—0.621 miles   1 mile—0.609 kilometres

Temperature

To convert Fahrenheit to Centigrade: subtract 32, multiply by 5, then divide by 9.
To convert Centigrade to Fahrenheit: multiply by 9, divide by 5, then add 32.

Tyre pressures

lb per sq in	kg per sq cm	lb per sq in	kg per sq cm
10	0.7	26	1.8
12	0.8	28	2.0
15	1.1	30	2.1
18	1.3	33	2.3
20	1.4	36	2.5
23	1.6	40	2.8

Sizes

Men's suits and overcoats

British/US	35	36	37	38	39	40	42
Continental	36	38	40	42	44	46	48

Men's shirts

British/US	15	16	17	18
Continental	38	41	43	45

Women's Dresses

British/US	10	12	14	16	18	20
Continental	40	42	44	46	48	50

Shoes

British/US	2	3	4	5	6	7	8	9	10	11	12	13
Continental	34	36	37	38	39	40	41	42	43	44	45	46

FURTHER READING

Tuscan Islands

Racheli, Gin, *Le Isole del Ferro*, Mursia, Milan, 1978.

Elba

Hoare, Sir Richard Cole, *A Tour through the Island of Elba*, W. Bulmen, London, 1814.

Pickthall, Rudolf, *The Comic Kingdom: Napoleon, The last phase but two*, John Lane, London & New York, 1914.

Ischia

Bret Harte, Geoffrey and Kit, *The Island in the Sun*, Little, Brown & Co., Boston, 1937.

Douglas, Norman, *Summer Islands*, Colophon Press, New York, 1931.

Lowrie, Walter, *Enchanted Island*, Philosophical Library, New York, 1953.

Procida

Lamatine, Alphonse de, *Graziella* (trans. James B. Runnion), A. C. McClurg, Chicago, 1911.

Capri

Cerio, Edwin, *That Capri Air*, Thomas Nelson, London, 1957;
——, *The Masque of Capri*, Harper & Bros, New York, 1929.
Douglas, Norman, *Siren Island*, M. Secker, New York, 1929.

Tremiti Islands

Mancini, Enzo, *Isole Tremiti Sassi Diomede*, Mursia, Milan, 1979.

Sicily

Aziz, Ahmed, *A History of Islamic Sicily*, Edinburgh University Press, 1953.
Brea, Luigi Bernabo, *Sicily Before the Greeks*, Thames & Hudson, London, 1957.
Brydone, Patrick, *A Tour through Sicily and Malta*, London, 1776.
Campbell, Rodney, *The Luciano Project: The Secret Wartime Collaboration of the Mafia and the US Navy*, McGraw Hill, New York, 1977.
Cronin, Vincent, *The Golden Honeycomb*, Hart-Davis, London; Dutton, New York; 1954.
Dolci, Danilo, *Outlaws* (trans. R. Munroe), Orion Press, New York, 1961.
Durrell, Lawrence, *Sicilian Carousel*, Viking Press, New York, 1977.
Fineley, Moses, *A History of Sicily: Ancient Sicily to the Arab Conquest*, published in a 3-vol. set with D. Mack Smith's *Medieval Sicily, 800–1713* and *Modern Sicily, after 1713*, Viking Press, New York, 1968.
Guido, Margaret, *Sicily: An Archaeological Guide*, Faber, London, 1977.
Norwich, John Julius Cooper, *The Kingdom in the Sun, 1130–1194*, Harper & Row, New York, 1970; Faber, London, 1976.
Pirandello, Luigi, *The Old and the Young* (trans. C. K. Scott-Moncrieff), Dutton, New York, 1928.
Quennell, Peter, *Spring in Sicily*, Weidenfeld & Nicolson, London, 1952.
Randall-MacIver, David, *Greek Cities in Italy and Sicily*, Clarendon Press, Oxford, 1931.
Runciman, Steven, *The Sicilian Vespers*, Cambridge University and Penguin Paperbacks.
Sciascia, Leonardo, *Salt in the Wound* (trans. Judith Green), Orion Press, New York, 1969.
Tomasi di Lampedusa, Giuseppe, *The Leopard*, Harville, USA; Fontana, London; 1972.

Verga, Giovanni, *The House by the Medlar Tree* (trans. Eric Mosbacher), Dutton, New York, 1928.
——, *Mastro-Don Gesualdo* (trans. D. H. Lawrence), Jonathan Cape, London, 1925.

Aeolian Islands

Racheli, Gin, *Eolie di Vento e di Fuoco*, Mursia, Milan, 1977.

Egadi Islands

Maxwell, Gavin, *The Ten Pains of Death*, Dutton, New York, 1959.
Racheli, Gin, *Egadi, Mare e Vita*, Mursia, Milan, 1979.

Pelagie Islands

Mancini, Enzo, *Le Isole del Sole*, Mursia, Milan, 1978

Sardinia

Balducci, Carolyn Feleppa, *A Selfmade Woman: Biography of Nobel Prize Winner Grazia Deledda*, Houghton Mifflin, Boston, 1975.
Boucher, Edmund Spenser, *Sardinia in Ancient Times*, Blackwell, Oxford; Longmans, Green & Co., New York; 1917.
Delane, M., *Sardinia: The Undefeated Island*, London, 1968.
Deledda, Grazia, *The Mother, The Woman and the Priest* (trans. Mary G. Steegman), Jonathan Cape, London, 1923.
Ferracuti, F., R. Lazzari and M. Wolfgang, *Violence in Sardinia*, Rome, 1971.
King, Russell, *Sardinia*, Stackpole Books, Newton Abbot, 1975.
Lawrence, D. H., *Sea and Sardinia*, Viking Press, New York, 1972.
Waite, Virginia, *Sardinia*, Batsford, London, 1977.

INDEX

Note. Islands are indexed both individually and within each group of islands. Alternative spellings or names are shown in brackets.